Economics Confronts the Economy

For Clarence E. Ayres
who taught me how to study the economy lyrically
and
Geoffrey H. Moore
who taught me how to study the economy empirically.
They never met, but they should have.

And for my grandchildren,
Maya, Justine, and David
who will have to live in and with the economy we leave them.

Economics Confronts the Economy

Philip A. Klein
Professor Emeritus of Economics, Pennsylvania State University and Senior Research Scholar, Economic Cycle Research Institute, New York, US.

Edward Elgar
Cheltenham, UK • Northampton, MA, USA

Published by
Edward Elgar Publishing Limited
Glensanda House
Montpellier Parade
Cheltenham
Glos GL50 1UA
UK

Edward Elgar Publishing, Inc.
136 West Street
Suite 202
Northampton
Massachusetts 01060
USA

A catalogue record for this book
is available from the British Library

Library of Congress Cataloguing in Publication Data

Klein, Philip A.
Economics confronts the economy / Philip A. Klein.
p. cm.
Includes bibliographical references.
1. Economics–Study and teaching. 2. Economic history. I. Title.

HB74.5.K554 2005
330'.071'1–dc22

2005044042

ISBN-13: 978 1 84064 650 4
ISBN-10: 1 84064 650 0

Printed and bound in Great Britain by MPG Books Ltd, Bodmin, Cornwall

Contents

List of Figures

List of Tables

Acknowledgments

In the process of putting this book together I had much help from a wide variety of people. My biggest obligation is to Marc Tool, who supported the project from the beginning, and who read and commented on several versions as well as contributing much valuable editorial advice. I am deeply indebted to John Kenneth Galbraith, who was instrumental in talking me into starting this book and who encouraged me throughout.

I owe a profound thank you to Monroe Newman, who similarly encouraged me from the start to attempt this book and commented insightfully on various chapters.

At Penn State it's a pleasure to thank my colleague Norman Clifford, not only for much valuable advice along the way, but for undertaking to check all references. I thank other colleagues Susan Esteban, Irwin Feller, Paul Graf, Nezih Guner, Barry W. Ickes, James Jordan, Dirk Mateer, Jon P. Nelson, Bee Yan Roberts, Mark J. Roberts, David Schlow, and Neil Wallace.

Among my colleagues outside Penn State I got help from William Baumol, James Galbraith, William H. Greene, Lawrence R. Klein, Owen Nankivell, Michael Niemira, Deborah Redman, Geoffrey Schneider, Johan Snyman and Randall Wray.

I also want to thank Robert S. Friedman, who read and commented on the whole manuscript, and Paul Cutler, for some valuable advice.

I am grateful to Dan Newlon, in charge of the economics program at the National Science Foundation, for providing much data and help in sorting it out. My secretary, Nancy Cole, was in charge of all the manuscript preparation, as well as much of the correspondence and has my deepest thanks for her efficiency and skill.

I am grateful for the suggestions of Mark Blaug, as well as two anonymous referees. Edward Elgar, Dymphna Evans, Alexandra Minton and Kate Emmins at Elgar Publishers were a pleasure to work with.

I thank my late wife, Peggy Klein, for putting up with my absences while I worked on this book, and for very much more that I can't really express in words here.

Finally, I need to add that none of these people are responsible for what I have done with their assistance. I have to take full responsibility for the book.

Introduction

The themes of this book are large and, I think, important. Whatever others' criticism of the modern discipline of economics, no one has ever charged that it did not deal with a critically important area of human life. I shall try to deal critically with the way in which we teach economics to graduate students, the basic theory which undergirds that teaching, and the relationship of that theory to economic policy. The charges I shall make are not made lightly and are major. The challenge will be to substantiate them, for in unsubstantiated form they would be gravely irresponsible.

I shall make no apology for writing occasionally in the first person, for this is my view up front and is based on a lifetime of study of economics, many years of trying to teach economics to young people, and lots of listening to what economists say and write about the state of the economy, and what should or should not be done about it.

I should probably be apologetic about the origins of my interest in economics but really I am not. If I tell the world that in my 17-year-old naivete in Texas I went into economics as a means of fighting poverty in the world, I surely distinguish myself from many of my students who will tell you that they go into economics to have an affluent career. If I add that my youthful world was a world in which economists worried explicitly about unemployment, instability, price fixing, widespread monopolistic behavior and antitrust alternatives, income inequality, inadequate job training, and a host of similar problems, the reader will begin to appreciate the distance we have come in the intervening years. Today economists contemplate 'the full employment unemployment rate,' the 'folly of antitrust,' equilibrium business cycles, two sector models, markets which clear instantaneously, overlapping generations models, chaos theory, models which explain 'stylized facts,' and sundry similar ideas which would have undoubtedly bemused economists from the Physiocrats to Keynes. As for all of the materials written before 1980 – they are by definition of little importance and less influence on the ruling elite among economists today. Our graduate students are not burdened with having to study the views of fossil economists. Instead they concentrate on what appeared last year in the *Journal of Economic Theory*. I will no doubt be labeled at the outset a hopeless idealist and do-gooder, not to mention being a mushy-headed economist. Still, that perspective, hopelessly old-fashioned as it may be, will suggest why I cling so relentlessly to these antique moorings and why I have from the outset regarded the connection between economic theory and economic policy as pivotal.

In most fields of human endeavor the link between theory and ameliorative policy is clear, implicitly or explicitly. Doctors want to improve health (prevent or cure diseases). Engineers want to build new structures (or shore up old structures) to improve the quality of life for the people. Closer to home many political scientists eschew following the lead of trend-setting economists and have an interest in making democracy both more sensitive to the people's freely expressed wishes and more efficient. Why, then, is it so extraordinary to take an equally pragmatic view toward economics? Whatever the attractions of doing research on 'basic theory' sooner or later the discipline cries out to be connected to policy so that economies can function better. Almost alone, economists go to great lengths – they make numerous simplifying assumptions, deal with 'stylized facts' instead of real facts, endlessly contemplate the implications of perfectly functioning systems, convert malfunctionings of the economy into 'normal adjustment paths,' cast their explanations either in jargon or (more and more commonly) into complex advanced mathematical form so that few, if any, normally intelligent non-economists can see what has been done – all so that they rarely need to worry about flaws in the system we actually have or what can be done about them. While this trait in economics has arguably gotten more and more pronounced, it is not new. As long ago as 20 years Robert Heilbroner coauthored a book, *Is Economics Relevant*? suggesting that there was a disjunction between the discipline and the economy to which it presumably pertained.

The pages to follow will attempt to deal with these trends more or less systematically. The anomalies mentioned above by no means exhaust the list. Perhaps the most fundamental one of all involves the core of the people who constitute the trend setters and standard bearers in economics today. Their position is both widely acknowledged and self-acknowledged. Moreover, they are among the most vociferous in insisting that economics is a 'positive science' while at the same time amply demonstrating that there are no voices more loudly raised in debates about right and wrong in economics than their own. These voices which proclaim their devotion to positivism and their eschewing of all things normative insofar as economics is concerned nonetheless manage to pick and choose what market interventions are consonant with their view of a market-oriented economy and which are not. (As we shall see, it is OK to bail out Lockhead – it is 'big.' Trade unions are mostly bad – they distort market outcomes.) One often gets the impression that an economy in which all things are 'left to the market' is what our positive discipline truly encompasses. Core members allow themselves to select the exceptions. Most interventions – they insist – represent mostly unnecessary and always controversial intrusions of the normative into the positive world of the pure discipline.

The origin of this *weltanschauung* is no doubt the all too human tendency to be comfortable not making value judgements about states of which one approves.

The problem, of course, is that 'the market' is a human institution and, like most things human, is not necessarily and certainly not definitionally flawless. So the customary assumption that the market constitutes 'what is' and intrusions represent diverse 'ought to bes' is excessively simplistic. The market does many things marvelously well, but a core theme in the pages to follow is that what the market does has in virtually all places and all times been subject of necessity to societal monitoring. It is also true in our economy. But our theorists mostly prefer to look the other way.

In the pages to follow I shall try and go beyond delineating the disputes between Neo-Keynesians and New Classical economists or between orthodox and heterodox economists, important as those conflicts continue to be (at least to some of us). In this book 'orthodox economists' are also referred to as 'mainstream economists.' We use the term as it is commonly used, most particularly in the United States, but also in Europe and elsewhere in the market-oriented world. Characterizing the mainstream is the particular task of Chapter 7. Suffice it here to say that mainstream economics has various manifestations – in the basic perspective taken in what are regarded as the best graduate programs in economics, the most widely accepted basic text books, the publication criteria of the 'most prestigious journals,' etc. They all show the influence of the 'formalist revolution.' (See below.) A related theme is that the virtually total 'mathematicization' of economic theory has, among other things, made it almost impossible even to discuss the older disputes. Instead of marshaling more persuasive counter arguments, a far better means of ending a dispute is to change the parameters of discourse so that the dispute cannot even be meaningfully verbalized. (Economists, of course, demonstrate my point by suggesting that there is no need to verbalize the quantitative approach!)

The 'quantitative revolution,' today often called 'the formalist revolution,'[1] has done more than make the older disputes even harder to raise. It has, I shall argue, totally infected the teaching of economics, certainly in the United States, and particularly at the graduate level. Alternative approaches, diverse methodologies, have all been virtually eliminated. The history of thought before 1950 for all practical purposes does not exist; there is little attention to economic history, and policy considerations have been pretty well dismissed in favor of attention to 'basic theory.' Very little attention is paid in theory courses

1. See for example, Ben Ward, who asserts that what 'might be called the formalist revolution' is 'more profound than the Keynesian' (Ward 1972, p. 40). Similarly Mark Blaug has written several times of the 'Formalist Revolution' (Blaug 1999, pp. 257–80 and Blaug 2003, pp. 395–410).

to the actual world, and so the relationship between the theory being taught and conditions in the real economies (which at least in terms of the limited criteria of success permitted in the world of modern micro- and macroeconomics have in many countries, especially the US, performed quite well in recent years) need not ever be contemplated. I shall argue that the help applied economists get in the modern world from economic theorists is remarkably small, but that situation is not a very prominent concern among the major current participants in the quantitative revolution. A major reason for that, we reiterate, is that the dominant perspective of these major players is that they emerge from their positive economics, quantitative style, with a profound, almost Panglossian, perspective leading to non-interventionist conclusions.

This virtually brings us full circle. The quantification revolution not only makes 'normal' conversation more difficult but it renders it easier for its practitioners to come to the conclusions that their initial *weltanschauung* suggested to them. Laissez faire remains as attractive as it was to those who originally held to it. So economic theory in its quantitative state, especially, and the teaching of economics – especially graduate economics – reinforce each other's implicit value system. The flaws, if such they be, in the actual economy escape the attention of both because they remain trapped inside the *ceteris paribus* assumptions (where they have languished for all my adult lifetime!). All this plays into the hands of the assumption promulgators as has always been the case. The self-proclaimed 'theory elite' who set the tone for the discipline, provide a back door for their values to creep into the elegant, precise, sophisticated mathematical expression of received theory. That theory is, of course, so brilliantly expressed that it requires no one to budge from their oft repeated conviction that economic theory generally is part of a positive discipline – indeed the most elegant discipline in the social sciences. So we have values (status quo values) in our positive theory!

It is possible to conclude that thinking, writing about, and teaching, economics have all been caught up in the process just described in a sort of sick symbiosis. Arguably, the result has left economics as a useful science offering guidance to policy makers in something of a shambles.

At its core, which is to say in its basic theory, economics today is a tiny life raft cast adrift in increasingly alien waters. It has cut itself off from its own past; it has turned its back on the prior history of the major economies; it has burned its bridges to the world of policy; and it has 'purified' itself through ritual fires, in which all methodologies save the highly mathematical ones have been cleansed from the scene, leaving it with the one approach it likes to sanction nowadays. Say it in equations or don't try to say it at all. Precision *über alles*.

The raft that is modern economics (most particularly modern economic theory) is therefore cast adrift far from shore. It finds it difficult to connect with other social sciences, with changing technology, and with the aspirations of flesh and blood human beings. It can no longer see the shore and so cannot relate easily to anything much outside itself. Far from worrying about its parlous condition, it revels in it, proud of its distinctiveness and particularly impressed with what it sees as its own rigor, its precision, its objectivity, and its mathematical elegance. It worries scarcely at all that it has cut itself off from most of the other social sciences and from much of the real world, arguing explicitly that the world it contemplates is a 'stylized' world in any case, and not terribly concerned with whether or not what emerges from its contemplation of that stylized world is helpful or not to those charged with formulating public policy for the actual world. (After all, if the end result of most theory is that we should eschew intervention in the operation of the market, public policy becomes relatively insignificant.) This is the situation in the modern positive science of economics – it pronounces most interventionist policy as bad (an unfortunately normative term, but no matter). Public policy is, at the end of the day, no longer the ultimate justification for economic theory. It is not that a sound economy is denigrated, it is only that a sound economy derives from the unfettered market (rather like good health some may feel derives from other sources than the ministrations of the medical profession).

Heterodox economists have often been charged by mainstream economists with being overly general in their criticisms of conventional economics and with being fuzzy thinkers at best. All authors hope to be taken seriously by their readers and this one pleads guilty to that hope as well. I have tried to present with considerable detail one view of the state of modern economics and why it may be open to the charges to which heterodox economists have long drawn attention. It is my hope that by the time the reader has perused this book, including the final chapter which sketches in an alternative view of the discipline, that at least some of what has been said might lead to some rethinking.

Finally I should add a word about the audience to whom the book is addressed. It is my hope that my colleagues in the economics profession will find the book of interest. I hope some adventurous graduate students will find this book thought provoking. Even students who disagree with the perspective taken may find it useful to learn that there are other approaches to the discipline than the perspective so entrenched in mainstream economics programs.

In addition to my colleagues in the profession there are non-economists who take the world seriously and interest themselves in the manner in which the study of current resource deployment is proffered, particularly in light of the actual consequences of that deployment for humankind. I would like to think that some of these people will also find these pages of interest.

This has meant that a fine line needs to be drawn between repeating 'what everyone already knows' and being clear about what we presumably agree on and how some of what is disseminated as political economy can be criticized.

If I have erred in the direction of too much explanation of 'what we all know' it is because that seemed a smaller error than taking for granted that there is common understanding where in fact it is lacking.

And finally, all this spills over into how we teach the discipline to the young. A few years ago I summarized the implications of this approach by noting,

> I tell an old and by now familiar story. Young economists in our 'top' universities who – God forbid – might wish to concentrate on studying the Corn Law Controversy or the Abstinence Theory of Interest, or who wish to question the underlying value system of conventional price theory, or the formation of consumer tastes, or the interrelationship between an economy and the larger society in which it operates, or to take any truly idiosyncratic, not to say original, approach will soon learn the folly of their ways. They will have difficulty as students finding professors to work with and if they manage to negotiate the student hurdles, unlikely in my judgment, they will find as fledgling professors that they cannot get research grants or released time (all of the above possibilities would be characterized as not having a clearly thought out research agenda). They will likely not have colleagues with whom to discuss their work; they will not easily be able to get their work published by publishers considered adequately prestigious, and ultimately they will most likely not be found tenurable, let alone promotable, in major American economics programs. This fate, I submit, is probable in any American university where the economics program aspires to what we now label 'excellence'. (Klein 1986, p. 127)

It is to this state of affairs that the chapters to come are devoted.

REFERENCES

Blaug, Mark (1999), 'The Formalist Revolution or What Happened to Orthodox Economics after World War II?', in Roger E. Backhouse and John Creedy (eds), *From Classical Economics to the Theory of the Firm: Essays in Honor of D. P. O'Brien*, Cheltenham, UK and Northampton, MA, USA: Edward Elgar, pp. 257–80.

Blaug, Mark (2003), 'The Formalist Revolution of the 1950s', in Warren J. Samuels, Jeff Biddle and John B. Davis (eds), *A Companion to the History of Economic Thought*, Malden, MA and Oxford, UK: Blackwell, pp. 395–410.

Klein, Philip A. (1986), 'How Should Economists do Economics? A Pragmatic Perspective', in Steven G. Medema and Warren Samuels (eds), *Foundations of Research in Economics: How do Economists Do Economics*?, Aldershot, UK and Brookfield, US: Edward Elgar, p. 127.

Ward, Benjamin (1972), *What's Wrong With Economics?* New York: Basic Books, Inc.

1. The unchanging focus of modern economics

RECENT BULLETINS FROM THE QUEEN OF THE SOCIAL SCIENCES

The conclusion that Walrasian allocations yield Pareto optimal allocations is an expression of the *first fundamental theorem of welfare economics*, a result that . . . holds with great generality. Note, moreover, that since each consumer must be at least as well off in a Walrasian equilibrium as by simply consuming his endowment, any Walrasian equilibrium lies in the contract curve portion of the Pareto set.

The first fundamental welfare theorem provides, for competitive market economies, a formal expression of Adam Smith's 'invisible hand.' Under competitive conditions, any equilibrium allocation is a Pareto optimum, and the only possible welfare justification for intervention in the economy is the fulfillment of distributional objectives. (Mas-Colell, Whinston and Green 1995, p. 524)

. . . an equilibrium price makes marginal utility equal to marginal cost and simultaneously makes demand equal to supply. Hence, the market equilibrium necessarily maximizes welfare, at least as measured by the sum of utilities. (Varian 1992)

Adam Smith's invisible hand guides demanders and suppliers to a point on the contract curve although each participant has only a tiny piece of private information about the market – what quantity the individual will demand or supply at each price ratio. Neither *A* nor *B* knows anything about the utility of the other market participants or the quantities of *X* and *Y* held by them. Each takes the price ratio as given and trades with the sole objective of maximizing his or her own utility. Yet, a competitive market guides all inhabitants on the contract curve so that the marginal rates of substitution of all consumers in the economy are equal to each other and to the relative price ratio, and the economy achieves Pareto efficiency in exchange. (Pashigian 1998)

Modern economists no longer can speak of the welfare of 'society,' because the utilities of different individuals cannot be compared. The advantage of the concept of Pareto optimality is that we need not compare the utilities of different individuals.

> The concept of a welfare optimum means only that the economy achieves a point on the utility-possibilities curve. (Ruffin 1992)

From the acorn that was Smith's invisible hand we see has grown a mighty tree – quantitative, precise, logical, elegant, rigorous, and beautiful. Would Smith be proud to see what he has wrought? The opening quotations offer some possible reactions.

VALUE AND PRICE IN SMITH'S WORLD: THE BIRTH OF THE INVISIBLE HAND

Arguably the most famous notion introduced in Adam Smith's *The Wealth of Nations* (1776/1985) is the invisible hand. It is the lynchpin of his view that selfishness and indeed personal greed can somehow be transmogrified into that which is socially most beneficial. That is, individuals pursuing their own best interests are contributing optimally to societal welfare. Much flows from this position. Arguably it is the treatment of the invisible hand that undergirds the entire structure of modern economics. For one thing, because it all works automatically, there is no need for government regulation. In this chapter we explore the origins of the invisible hand in the views of Adam Smith, the impact of subsequent economic history on Smith's views, and the implications of these changes for, among other things, the difference between price and value, the characterization of economics as positive not normative, and the role of the public sector.

The full title of Smith's volume is *An Inquiry into the Nature and Causes of the Wealth of Nations*. It is in the context of accounting for the wealth of a nation, which for Smith depends on labor productivity (a product of technological progress) and capital (which depends ultimately on resources) that the 'wealth of a nation' arises as an interesting question. For Smith this is roughly like national income or output and so he begins from a national income and product perspective:

> But the annual revenue of every society is always precisely equal to the exchangeable value of the whole annual produce of its industry, or rather is precisely the same thing with that exchangeable value. As every individual, therefore, endeavours as much as he can both to employ his capital in the support of domestic industry, and so to direct that industry that its produce may be of the greatest value, every individual necessarily labours to render the annual revenue of the society as great as he can. He generally, indeed, neither intends to promote the public interest, nor knows how much he is promoting it. By preferring the support of domestic to that of foreign industry, he intends only his own security; and by directing that industry in such a manner as its produce may be of the greatest value,

> he intends only his own gain, and he is in this, as in so many other cases, led by an invisible hand to promote an end which was no part of his intention. Nor is it always worse for the society that it was no part of it. By pursuing his own interest he frequently promotes that of the society more effectually than when he really intends to promote it. I have never known much good done by those who affected to trade for the public good. It is an affectation, indeed, not very common among merchants, and very few words need be employed in dissuading them from it. (Smith 1985, p. 225)

We present this to make several points:

1. Smith does indeed say that the agent, in pursuit of his own gain and not that of society, nevertheless ends up also furthering the public interest as much as possible. But it does not read as though Smith thought he was making a major pronouncement, on the order for economics of what the law of gravity is for physics.
2. Smith himself did not regard this bit of magic (a device converting personal greed into socially ideal behavior) as guaranteeing that there would be anything ideal or 'perfect' about how the market system carried out its functions.[1] He merely mentions the term in passing, and without a great deal of emphasis. To put it in neoclassical terminology, he used it to suggest that competitive markets might produce ideal economic performance. He does not quite say that cleared markets and equilibrium prices could routinely be assumed to reflect societally ideal performance. This is a way of asking, if assuming we had competitive markets, could we also assume that the emergent prices effectively removed the distinction between price and value that looms so large for heterodox economists? If one can, this would mean that Gordon Gekko, in the motion picture *Wall Street* – the one whose personal mantra was that 'Greed is Good' – was a modern day anthropomorphized reincarnation of the Invisible Hand!
3. There is some evidence to suggest that Smith from the beginning recognized limitations to the invisible hand. Thus Spencer Pack has called attention to the significant qualification in the sentence following the introduction of the term 'invisible hand:'

' Note . . . that Smith says, by pursuing their own interests the capitalists frequently

1. As Ahmad has pointed out, the 'second' invisible hand 'takes the form of the residual selfishness of the landlord . . . acting upon his . . . frivolous wants, . . . and thus advances the interests of the society . . .' This can be directly related to the subtitle of Mandeville's famous *Fable of the Bees* , . . . (Private Vices, Public Benefits , Ahmad 1990, p. 139).

> promote the interests of society more effectually than when they really intend to promote it – not that the capitalists will always or necessarily do this. This is an important point. For example, capitalists will not promote the interests of society when they engage in monopolies or cartels which restrain trade, thus increasing both prices and their own private profits.' (Pack 1991, p. 35)

Thus presumably the invisible hand would not operate in a world of oligopoly, a point to which we shall return in Chapter 4.

We argue that there is evidence in the *Wealth of Nations* to suggest, therefore, that Smith would not have carried the implications of the invisible hand as far as is suggested in point 2, and he would surely have insisted that Gordon Gekko's mantra be qualified. For one thing, there is much evidence in the book that suggests that Smith himself clearly made a distinction between what emerged from the market and what would emerge from his own value system presumably derived from the wider society. He does not explicitly distinguish 'what is' from 'what ought to be' but simply comments on all aspects of the functioning economy as he sees it.

Consider, for example, his views on poverty in China:

> The poverty of the lower ranks of people in China far surpasses that of the most beggarly nations in Europe. In the neighborhood of Canton many hundred, it is commonly said, many thousand families have no habitation on the land, but live constantly in little fishing boats upon the rivers and canals. The subsistence which they find there is so scanty that they are eager to fish up the nastiest garbage thrown overboard from a European ship. Any carrion, the carcase of a dead dog or cat, for example, though half putrid and stinking, is as welcome to them as the most wholesome food to the people of other counties. Marriage is encouraged in China, not by the profitableness of children, but by the liberty of destroying them. In all great towns several are every night exposed in the street, or drowned like puppies in the water. The performance of this horrid office is even said to be the avowed business by which some people earn their subsistence. (Smith 1985, pp. 73–4)

Reading this passage, can there be any doubt that this is not Smith merely being descriptive, but Smith in a state of profound repugnance at what he was reporting? Would not Smith have been appalled if he knew that one hundred years later neoclassical economists would have taken his child drowners and their 'business' and presumably put them into Smith's invisible hand by arguing that their pursuit of their own gain in this way somehow added to the general welfare? I think he would, indeed, be appalled. I am reasonably confident, therefore, that what was subsequently done with the invisible hand was a good deal more than Smith would have claimed for the pervasiveness with which it converted personal greed into acts which could be regarded as socially ideal.

If the reader wishes to argue that I exaggerate – that, of course, Smith found much that was repugnant in far off places – well, the invisible hand's ability to convert self-interested pursuits into ideal social acts was designed to apply as well – perhaps especially well – to the market of England. We ask, does the disparity raised above really disappear when we focus on civilized countries like England?

Poverty and the Invisible Hand

Smith was well aware of widespread poverty and high infant mortality in his own England. He wrote,

> In some places one half the children born die before they are four years of age; in many places before they are seven; and in almost all places before they are nine or ten. This great mortality, however, will everywhere be found chiefly among the children of the common people, who cannot afford to tend them with the same care as those of better station. (1776/1985, p. 81)

The fate of these 'common people' was of course, very much tied up with the Industrial Revolution which is customarily dated as beginning in the second half of the 18th century and continuing for perhaps the next hundred years.[2] The initial impact of industrialization was, therefore, beginning to be very much in evidence at the time Adam Smith was writing, and indeed for the next 75 years, at least. Any reader of Charles Dickens would recognize what that impact produced for many impoverished English people. A vivid description of the impact of this process on the most impoverished of the employed workers appears in the testimony which one father gave before the Committee on Factory Children's Labour in 1832. Though a bit lengthy, this testimony by one Samuel Coulson concerning the mill working conditions of his two daughters, merits our attention:

> Court: At what time in the morning, in the brisk time, did those girls go to the mills?

---

2. Cf., for example, Pauline Gregg (1969), Chapter II. One who would not have been surprised by this testimony was Karl Marx. He wrote:

> The value of labour-power is determined . . . by the labour-time necessary for the production . . . of this special article . . . Labour-power exists only as a capacity, or power of the living individual . . . For his maintenance he requires a given quantity of the means of subsistence. Therefore, the labour-time requisite for the production of labour-power reduces itself to that necessary for the production of those means of subsistence . . . . (Marx 1906, pp. 189–90)

Coulson: *In the brisk time, for about six weeks, they have gone at 3 o'clock in the morning, and ended at 10, or nearly half-past at night.*

Court: What intervals were allowed for rest or refreshment during those nineteen hours of labour?

Coulson: *Breakfast, a quarter of an hour, and dinner half an hour, and drinking a quarter of an hour.*

Court: Was any of that time taken up in cleaning the machinery?

Coulson: *They generally had to do what they call dry down; sometimes this took the whole of the time at breakfast or drinking, and they were to get their dinner or breakfast as they could; if not, it was brought home.*

Court: Had you not great difficulty in awakening your children to this excessive labour?

Coulson: *Yes, in the early time we had them to take up asleep and shake them, when we got them on the floor to dress them, before we could get them off to their work.*

Court: What was the length of time they could be in bed during those long hours?

Coulson: *It was near 11 o'clock before we could get them into bed after getting a little victuals, and then . . . my mistress used to stay up all night, for fear that we could not get them ready for the time.*

Court: What time did you get them up in the morning?

Coulson: *In general me or my mistress got up at 2 o'clock to dress them.*

Court: So that they had not above four hours' sleep at this time?

Coulson: *No, they had not.*

Court: For how long together was it?

Coulson: *About six weeks.*

Court: The common hours of labour were from 6 in the morning till half-past eight at night?

Coulson: *Yes.*

Court: Were the children excessively fatigued by this labour?

Coulson: *Many times; we have cried often when we have given them the little victualling we had to give them; we had to shake them, and they have fallen asleep with the victuals in their mouths many a time.*

Court: Had any of them any accident in consequence of this labour?

Coulson: *Yes, my eldest daughter when she went first there; . . . the cog caught her forefinger nail and screwed it off below the knuckle, and she was five weeks in Leeds Infirmary.*

Court: Were her wages paid during that time?

Coulson: *As soon as the accident happened the wages were totally stopped.*

Court: Did this excessive term of labour occasion much cruelty also?

Coulson: *Yes, with being so very much fatigued, the strap was very frequently used.*

Court: Have any of your children been strapped?

Coulson: *Yes, every one.*

Court: What was the wages in the short hours?

Coulson: *Three shillings a week each.*

Court: When they wrought those very long hours what did they get?

Coulson: *Three shillings and sevenpence-halfpenny.*

Court: For all that additional labour they had only 7½ d. a week additional?

Coulson: *No more.*

Court: Could you dispose of their wages, when they received them, as you wished?

Coulson: *The children have said, 'If we do not bring some little from the shop, I am afraid we shall lose our work.' And sometimes they used to bring a bit of sugar or some little oddment, generally out of their own head.*

Court: That is, they were expected to lay out part of their wages under the truck system?

Coulson: *Yes.*

Court: Had your children any opportunity of sitting during those long days of labor?

Coulson: *No.*

Court: At the time they worked those long hours, would it have been in their power to work a shorter number of hours, taking the threes?

Coulson: *They must either go on at the long hours, or else be turned off.* (Gregg 1969, p. 192)

We present this vivid portrait of how the market system was operating in England in 1830 because while it is true that the Industrial Revolution was getting underway, conditions generally in English factories and the conditions of child labor in particular, were not that much better when Smith was writing than they were in 1830. It was, therefore, presumably the system in which Smith's invisible hand was operating from its very 1776 introduction. Bearing in mind that we are not yet talking about the 'have-nots' (beggars, charity, etc.) but of the people employed in the market system, can one presume that the three shillings a week these children were earning represented their pursuit of their own self-interest, thereby enabling them to achieve 'a goal that was no part of their original purpose' – namely making an optimal contribution to social welfare? I think not. We argue that Smith never believed that the invisible hand was as powerful as his latter day interpreters have asserted.

More broadly we suggest that even in Smith's world, and taking his view of the economy on his own terms, despite the invisible hand there was a clear distinction to be made between price and value, between what the market system produced and what society thought of it.

The venality of the factory owners was no doubt very real. Smith did not underrate self-interest, far from it. Recall his comment, 'It is not from the benevolence of the butcher, the brewer, or the baker that we expect our dinner, but from their regard for their own interest' (1776/1985, p. 16). But in view of Smith's clear attitude toward conditions in the market economy of China, can one argue that he would not have found intolerable the report just given of how that system was operating in England? The fact that a select committee was probing into the condition of factory children suggests that even if the market system of England were determining the level of employment, including child labor, and the wages of each worker, including the three shillings paid the children, Smith clearly would not have argued that the invisible hand was operating the way subsequent generations of economists have interpreted it to be. Clearly in the case at hand, the relentless pursuit of profits by the employers, no doubt in their own interests, could not be judged to be invariably in society's interests. Even in that relatively simple world, where competitive pin factories could be used as illustrative of the industrial scene, there was a distinction to be made which suggests ultimate limits to the area covered by the invisible hand.

For one thing, in Adam Smith one does not get the impression that he made a distinction between his normative views (not just in *The Theory of Moral Sentiments*, but as we have seen also in *The Wealth of Nations*) and Smith the positive economist. For Smith 'what is' included what the invisible hand produced, what the government produced, and indeed what the churches via charity produced. Smith did not write as though the invisible hand was the sole pristine allocative thermostat of the economy. Smith's attitude toward the three shilling wages would have been a part of his attitude toward how the economy was working and so was at least partially ascribable to the invisible hand. Later generations would not see this so clearly, as we shall observe below. Robbins distinguished rigidly between 'what is' and what 'ought to be' and was followed, in his time by Milton Friedman, Robert Lucas and all the 'new classical' economists. For them the 'what is' is what the invisible hand produces in the market and the rest was a product of interventionism, normative in motivation. They would underscore the limited role that Smith gave to the state, but would fail to note that the discussion of the public sector constitutes a third of the pages in the *Wealth of Nations*.

Smith, in short, gives evidence of espousing the approach of modern heterodox economists – namely that there is a chasm between the allocation that occurs via prices in the markets, and how the larger society regards that allocation. This is the monitoring process which heterodox economists have always insisted exists and that always and everywhere accompanies that market process. (See Chapter 8.)

In short Smith regarded the invisible hand as a valuable aid in furthering useful insights. But I think he would have been shocked to learn that his results would be converted, as later economists seem to have done, into a device of incredible power to place at the center of complicated mathematical models (on a par with the alchemist's ability to turn coal into gold), which could all by themselves convert the most venal self-interest into the most valuable imaginable contributor to optimal community welfare. No magician's sleight of hand could hold a candle to such a feat.

Smith's role for his invisible hand was more modest. He also wrote, 'No society can surely be flourishing and happy, of which the far greater part of the members are poor and miserable' (1776/1985, p. 80). Judging whether society is flourishing and happy is clearly, therefore, more than adding up the marginal utilities of the households and the marginal returns of the business firms. The latter, we are told today, as illustrated at the beginning of the chapter, is the quantitative standard reflected by the invisible hand. Parenthetically, we may add that Smith's standard – the degree to which society is 'flourishing and happy' – is remarkably like that of Thorstein Veblen (of all people!) who wrote that expenditures had to be judged on their ability to 'enhance the life process.' The exact quote: 'The test to which all expenditure must be brought in an attempt to decide that point [whether or not it is wasted] is whether it serves directly to enhance human life on the whole – whether it furthers the life process taken impersonally' (Veblen 1994, p. 99).

In the final analysis, of course, we need – even in Smith's world – to go beyond the market in judging how flourishing and happy a society can be. There was a whole layer of resource deployment beyond the market in Smith's time. Not only, as we have seen, did Smith have a role for government, but he included contributions of church-driven charities. The only way to get help was for the whole family to enter the poorhouse. The latter were made as unpleasant as possible – families were separated, no drinking or smoking was allowed, etc. The Poor Laws were governed by the principle of 'Less Eligibility.' By this was meant 'the condition of any workhouse inmate was to be "less eligible" – that is, more miserable – than that of the lowest-paid worker' (Gregg 1969, p. 162).

The only point in mentioning all this here is to reiterate that Smith's ultimate standard was whether society was 'flourishing and happy,' not whether the invisible hand was leading to cleared markets. The impact of the workhouses and the two principles which guided them was clearly to get the fewest possible people on public relief.

Smith's Conclusions

In sum, for Smith, contrary to his many interpreters, the invisible hand never guaranteed the Panglossian best of all possible worlds. If it had he would not have felt obliged to devote so much attention to conditions in China, to the impact of the Poor Laws in England, etc.[3]

Our investigation of Smith's attitude toward the economy in his own time leads to several conclusions:

1. There can be no question that Smith thought the invisible hand was a device which made self-motivated pursuits coterminous with optimal contributions to the public welfare.
2. The invisible hand, however, does not dominate *The Wealth of Nations* (it is mentioned only once).[4] It is not viewed in the way in which it dominates

3. For a different view of Smith consult Pauline Gregg:

> The economists, as represented by Adam Smith, had a slightly different version of the theme. Each man had to work, not in the position to which God and birth had called him, but in the place into which his own exertions had brought him. Supervising his efforts and ensuring that the sum total of all such activity in the community would result in the greatest possible good was an 'invisible hand.' So, in place of God and birth, the economists substituted the invisible hand and competition, which in the long run, came to the same thing. For all were agreed that the poor should work for the rich and that lavish poor relief was a mistake. (Gregg 1969, p. 185)

4. In the *New Palgrave Dictionary of Economics*, edited by John Eatwell, Murray Milgate and Peter Newman (1987), the editors assert that it is mentioned twice, once in the *Wealth of Nations* and once in *The Theory of Moral Sentiments*. There is some indication that the other mention of the hand is in *The Theory of Moral Sentiments*, cf. Dome (1994, p. 11). Karen I. Vaughn (1987) asserts that Smith mentioned the invisible hand twice – once in *The Theory of Moral Sentiments* and once in the *Wealth of Nations*. She added, however, that 'the idea the metaphor connotes permeates all of his social and moral theories.' In the text we argue that Smith would have qualified the impact of this metaphor on his social and moral theories rather more than Vaughn is here suggesting.

Finally we mention that Syed Ahmad argues that Smith used the expression three times: once in *The Theory of Moral Sentiments* (published in 1759 but it came out in a last edition in 1790), once in *The Wealth of Nations* (published in 1776) and once in the *History of Astronomy*, published in 1795. He is doubtless correct that the mention in the *Wealth of Nations* has received the most attention.

Ahmad insists that Smith's use of the term in these different locations is not the same: to begin with the mention in the *Theory of Moral Sentiments* suggests two uses for the hand. The first arises because the capacity of the human stomach is limited and is unrelated to the enormity of a person's desires. This invisible hand (though not yet explicitly mentioned) prevents the death of the many who otherwise would be killed off by human greed and selfishness. But, as noted above, Ahmad insists that Smith uses the invisible hand in a second sense later in the same paragraph when he writes, 'They are led by an invisible hand to make nearly the same distribution of the necessaries of life,' (quoted p. 138) as would have been made had distribution been equal to all. The first use prevents selfishness from consuming all there is and the second distributes the residual among the needy. Ahmad says both these uses are different from the use in the *Wealth of Nations*. In the former the invisible hand causes selfishness to generate demand; the use in the latter suggests that the invisible hand 'causes selfishness to optimize production' (p. 140), 'a matter of supply' (p. 140). This is the best known statement. Finally, in the *History of Astronomy* the fourth view of the invisible hand according to Ahmad is 'a preserver and enforcer' of (the natural) 'order' (p. 142).

This may all be reading far more into the invisible hand than Smith ever intended, but it shows that even while one can speculate about precisely what these fleeting mentions of the hand may

modern day discussions, particularly of welfare economics, as a device removing most concerns about the adequacy of the price system to enable peacetime economies to carry out their basic function successfully.

3. While most discussion of Adam Smith suggests that he saved very few functions for the public sector (defense, administration of justice, education) the fact remains that he devoted a third of the book to these and related areas. This is far more space than modern microeconomic theory books devote to the public sector.
4. Smith ranges far in his discussion of a flourishing society. The ills he contemplates are often beyond the implicit ability of the invisible hand, however generously interpreted, to cope with successfully.
5. Smith seems always to be commenting on the economy in his capacity as a person writing on economics. In spite of his theological background, including his previous book, Smith nowhere seems to suggest the distinction between the normative and the positive so dear to the hearts of modern economic theorists. If his book is 'descriptive,' he has no compunction about using prose which includes adjectives conveying strong emotion (as in his discussion of Chinese poverty). In short, Smith does not give himself the ceteris-paribus-assumption-plus-economics-is-a positive-science out as a means to escape commenting on the real world the economy confronts.
6. In the end, therefore, even in the relatively simple world of Adam Smith it is difficult to argue that the invisible hand disposes of all the obstacles in the way of achieving an ideal economy in welfare terms, solely by the use of the price system.
7. It seems evident that, even if Smith seemingly focused on the impact of the invisible hand on what happened in markets, in the end he was anchored in a discussion of value and progress rather than price and goods.

The Invisible Hand Today: Elegance and Precision Fight with Realism

We have argued thus far that even if we assumed that the world was unchanged from the time of Adam Smith, the modern interpretation of the invisible hand would be difficult for him to accept. Modern price theorists have the benefit of the marginal revolution of neoclassical economics and the precision which the more recent mathematical revolution gives to the entities on which marginal analysis concentrates. The ability to argue that an equilibrium price in every market equates marginal cost and marginal revenue through the price which

---

mean, it is also difficult to argue that he ever viewed the hand to be the major organizing principle in his scheme of things, which is the view of the invisible hand today so often attributed to him.

emerges is the springboard for concluding that the invisible hand leads to optimal welfare. As all beginning students learn to recite, marginal cost reflects the self-interest of the firm, marginal utility reflects the self-interest of the household. All firms are forced to search for technological improvements leading to cost reductions. Optimal productive improvement is guaranteed! Neophyte students understand why, therefore, it is the market itself which ensures that both efficiency (minimal cost) and the only equity that counts is being miraculously achieved. Being able to get the maximum satisfaction from goods and services which expenditure of your income can produce, and at the same time giving the firms maximum achievable profits, is guaranteed by the invisible hand. As miracles go this must be right up there with what any saint can produce. This then is the world that economists love and admire to this day!

We showed that even for Smith that framework was too narrow to encompass all that would be required for an economy in which people can be productive, happy, and flourishing. That can be attained only by granting that any economy consists of the arena in which markets can determine some economic outcomes and the public arena in which collective decisions must determine other economic outcomes. From the beginning of Smith's famous work he dealt with the fact that all who consume do not necessarily produce. To exist, let alone flourish, all must consume. Thus, from the outset not just Smith, but Smithian economics confronted those who have and those who have not.

In the years since Smith wrote, the economics profession has moved on two fronts to keep the invisible hand *au courant*. At the level of graphic and mathematical presentation the implications of the invisible hand can now be presented with an elegance and precision which Smith with his single reference could scarcely have dreamed of. Recall that all he said was an individual 'intends only his own gain, and . . . is . . . led by an invisible hand to promote an end which was no part of his intention' (1776/1985, p. 225). The end he promotes is in the best interests of society![5]

A consensus presentation today of the central thrust of microeconomic theory, all derived from a vast elaboration of Smith's invisible hand, might run as follows. If we assume pure competition (that is, we consider many buyers and sellers, each too small to affect the market price) of homogeneous products and assume as well that competition is perfect (resources are mobile, all agents have perfect knowledge of all alternatives available to them) then we can consider fairly completely the normative implications of market adjustments.

The story of how self-interested competitive units are forced by the market to pursue that self-interest constrained by the invisible hand is the quintessential

---

5. The specific words Smith uses: 'By pursuing his own interest he frequently promotes that of the society more effectually than when he really intends to promote it' (Smith 1776/1985, p. 225).

success story told in the beginning of every microeconomic theory course. The long run equilibrium adjustment is shown in Figure 1.1 (long run being the time period long enough for all resources to be variable).[6]

In our long run the number of firms has presumably been adjusted to the number just required to meet the market demand at price *P*.

Along the way to this long run adjustment are any number of possible short run adjustments, depending on the market price. Whatever that price the competitive firm responds by being forced (because of its size relative to the market) to assume it faces a horizontal demand curve at that price. Thus at any temporary market price greater than *OP* the competitive firm would produce to the point where its marginal cost equaled that price and it would be at a price greater than *OP*. Hence the competitive firm would make short run excess profits because *OP* would be greater than *atc*. This excess profits situation would lure new profit seeking firms into the industry (from some other industry where there were no excess profits). Hence so long as conditions did not change the situation shown in Figure 1.1 would continue to be the long run equilibrium conditions for both the firm and the industry involved.

What are the implications of the adjustment shown? These, after all, constitute the heart of the wondrous story economists tell.

1. Those self-interested households get the goods at the lowest possible market price and pay exactly as much for each product as the last unit they purchase adds to their 'utility' (the economist's all-purpose designation for how much satisfaction the last unit of the product acquired gives the buyer). Eventually we would need to elaborate the equilibrium just described to allow for technological progress, the discovery of new and/or different resources, etc. These factors could alter the cost structure of firms and hence the profit possibilities in the industry. Hence the altered possibilities could enable (and require) the exit or entry of firms from the industry. So, for example, we can elaborate the complications of technological change as follows.
2. The self-interested seller gets a price exactly equal to the costs of producing the last unit sold. (Marginal cost equals price, which in competition equals marginal revenue.)
3. 1 and 2 ensure, therefore, that the firm is getting maximum profit (competitive profits are included in the cost curves and this really means that the firms get no excess profits, customarily considered as 'bad,' even by our positive economists! and the households are getting maximum utility.

6. We assume here that we are dealing with a 'constant cost industry' (the number of firms each producing OQ_e) is just enough to satisfy the market demand without the cost – hence the price per unit – of the equilibrium output varying.

If one remembers that the diagram shown can be replicated for every other good or service in the economy it means that the households are maximizing their total utility and the firms are maximizing their total profits. (Clever economist–draftsmen can show this as 'maximum consumer and producer surplus.' This is impressive – take my word for it!)

4. The above outcomes flow partly from the fact that each firm is forced to produce at the minimum point on the average cost curve (the invisible hand makes them!). This means that the number of firms required to satisfy the market demand is 'ideal.' That is to say, the individual unit's output is some fraction of the total market output – OQ_e – and this means that the market can absorb exactly the number of firms necessary to meet the market demand if all the firms are producing at their ideal (lowest cost) point.

Eventually we would need to elaborate the equilibrium just described to allow for technological progress, the discovery of new and/or different resources, etc. These factors could alter the cost structure of firms and hence the profit possibilities in the industry. Hence the altered possibilities could enable (and require) the exit or entry of firms from the industry. So, for example, we can elaborate the complications of technological change as follows:

1. If technology improves, the average total costs will be lower, and the firms will be forced to pass the cost savings on to the consumers as lower prices (competition, remember!). Moreover, all the firms have access to the new technology, as in this world there are no patents! And at lower prices the market demand will increase. That means that the market supply curve will shift to the right (really 'with it' teachers can show all this diagrammatically with computerized pictures that move!). The market price will reflect these changes so the price to the consumers will stay the same (if both are of equal size) but more firms will enter the industry. Technological changes get reflected in how households and firms rearrange the use of resources!
2. If for any reason market demand were to increase (households decide they like this product more, and wish to substitute more of this product for less of another) the increased demand would make the market price rise, which would lure new firms in (drawn by the prospect of higher profits) so that in the end the larger supply produced would force the price back to the old lower price. Moral? Once again we see that the market, thanks to that wonderful invisible hand, changes in conformity with household attitudinal

Figure 1.1 Pure competition: long run equilibrium adjustment

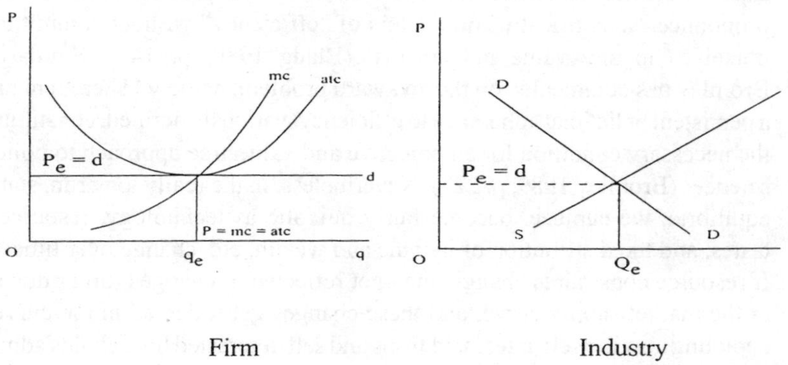

changes just as it did with technological changes. Nobel Prize winning economist Herbert Simon tried some years ago to inject greater realism into this model by suggesting that firms are often characterized by 'bounded rationality:' '*The central concern of administrative theory is with the boundary between the rational and nonrational aspects of human social behavior*' (Simon 1997, p. 118, italics in original).

The prevalence of bounded rationality leads to the behavior of human beings who satisfice . . . 'because they have not the wits to maximize.' . . . 'Whereas economic man supposedly maximizes . . . his cousin, the administrator, satisfices – looks for a course of action that is satisfactory or "good enough" (Simon 1997, pp. 118–19).

While this may seem a reasonable if minor emendation to conventional price theory it is not often mentioned by contemporary price theorists. (It is not, for example, included in the text, referred to earlier, by Mas-Colell, Whinston and Green.)

Household demand decreases would, of course work in the opposite direction.

3. Just how wonderful is the world of competitive equilibrium? The resultant nirvana is called Pareto Optimality. A Pareto optimal state is one in which no one can be made any better off without making someone else worse off. There is a little catch – not stressed as much as it should be – Pareto-optimal resource allocation 'leaves out the justice of the underlying

distribution of resources in competitive equilibrium[7], (Blaug 1980, p. 153). So it measures welfare exclusively in terms of 'efficiency.' As Blaug has said, 'immense confusion has been sown by the pretense that we can pronounce "scientifically" on matters of "efficiency" without committing ourselves to any value judgements' (Blaug 1980, p. 148). Similarly, Bromley has commented on the awkward problem, namely 'There remains a persistent belief that adherence to efficiency, variously defined, constitutes the necessary condition for an objective and value-free approach to policy science' (Bromley 1989, p. 223). Nevertheless, in the really long run, static equilibria, we can see, become fairly quixotic as technology, resources, tastes, and the distribution of income and wealth, etc. change over time!

4. If resource constraints change, they get reflected in changes (up or down) in the market supply curve, and these changes get reflected in the curves depicting how the self-interested firms and self-interested households adjust to the changes in resource availability. These changes are designed to keep intact the conclusions summarized in the earlier points.

What we have tried to show is that the detailed logical implications of Smith's casual throwaway line can and have been elaborated to a fare-thee-well. With logic, modern economists can display all these insights graphically – we gave here but a modest example of how changes in aspects of firm or household behavior can be displayed to illustrate the invisible hand in dynamic action. No self-respecting microeconomic theory text would be presented without dozens of graphs showing various equilibria reflecting firms and households making various self-motivated changes in their possible adjustments for diverse time periods. In a later chapter we shall certainly see that all the adjustments that can be imagined in reaction to the changes in real demand and supply have by now been described in mathematical models of varying degrees of complexity. It is the appeal of all the adjustment processes just illustrated constantly reestablishing new equilibria, all in optimal fashion, and doing so through the self-serving behavior of economic agents and without any involvement by any level of government, which has held so much appeal for economists all these years. The depiction is elegant, precise, logical, and so fraught with reassuring implications, and so complete and self-contained, that economists cannot and will not give any part of it up. The children of the world would sooner give up their security blankets than would the economists give up their competitive market economy.

---

7. The reader will not be surprised to learn that we shall have to return to all this.

On rare occasions some dangerously insightful young economist might be tempted to say, 'Wait a minute – how realistic is all this?' There are various ways to surmount such a crisis and arrive back on terra cognita with faith in the model intact. If all else fails one can always fall back on statements like this: 'The conclusions derived from the model of perfect competition have proved very useful in explaining and predicting behavior in the real world. They have permitted a reasonably accurate view of resource allocation in important segments of our economy' (Mansfield 1970, p. 225).

The statement may arguably apply in parts of the economy but there are many parts it cannot apply to, and many significant problems including most particularly the consequence of concentrated market power that it can't begin to confront. Another approach to this question, fairly typical of how price theorists think, is the following:

> No economist insists that pure competition characterizes any economy, nor does anyone claim that it ever has. The question arises, then, as to why study the principles of pure competition at all. Three important answers may be given. First, the principles of pure competition furnish a simple and logical starting point for economic analysis. Second, a large measure of competition does exist in the United States today, although perhaps not in pure form. Third, the theory of pure competition provides a sort of 'norm' against which the actual performance of the economy can be checked or evaluated. (Leftwich 1979, p. 31)

One might comment that simplicity and logic are acceptable 'for starting points' provided the simplicity does not do excessive violence to relevance. One might add that logically one should ultimately move well beyond 'logical starting points.' In the case at hand, price theory has remained more or less mired in its overpowering fascination with the competitive model. As to whether a large part of the US economy is price competitive, there are surely many economists who will grant that, except for possibly agriculture in the days before the government intervened heavily, there are few sectors where the structural requirements for pure competition ever held and a good many, as we shall see, particularly in manufacturing, where the customary assertion is that 'oligopoly is ubiquitous.' The third, sometimes called the 'theory as benchmark' argument is the most convincing but we shall have to ask: how convincing in the end is it?

But we get ahead of our story. That the modern theoretical presentation of the full implications of the invisible hand is a work of genius no one can deny.

The Invisible Hand and the Real World

However, a funny thing happened to the invisible hand. The more elegant its presentations got, the less relevant the whole approach was to the real economy, thanks to the changes to which the real economy was subject. Thus began the developments which mainly characterize economic theory today. The road down which the economy traveled and the road down which the theorists traveled diverged. Were Robert Frost still with us he would no doubt be able to set in poetry the way in which the economic theorists chose 'the road less traveled' while the economy went down the well traveled road.

It is largely because the world where prices emerge is so rarely coterminous with the world in which resources are combined with the latest technology (to contribute to the flourishing of members of society) that we concluded that even in Adam Smith's world price and value were vastly different.

Here we carry the implications of this dichotomy further. The major point to add is that the technological changes which have occurred as a consequence of the industrial revolution have robbed Adam Smith's world of one of its most attractive features. As we have just seen, in a time of simple technology, firms pursuing their own interest are forced by their pursuit of profit (i.e., minimizing costs) to produce each unit of output at the most efficient point on the average total cost curve.

Today modern price theory has adumbrated that condition to a very high art. The efficient plant (the technological unit) can be viewed as a part of the efficient firm (multi plants) which take advantage of 'managerial economies.' The efficient firms can be viewed in the short run (some costs are fixed, some variable). But in the long run the intricacies and limitations produced by the law of diminishing returns will be spun out to whatever extent the skill, mathematical prowess, and love of detail the theorist permits and provides.

This is, of course, not the end. While we indicated that technological change had to be factored in as part of some version of the long run, the considerations enumerated in the previous section lead primarily to 'short run equilibria' – every firm producing at the minimum point on its (short run) average total cost curve. One of the consequences of a short run equilibrium is that it reflects not only the most efficient point of operation of each firm able to function in this market but, as we saw, the number of firms is forced by the market (i.e., the invisible hand) to adjust to precisely the ideal number of firms as well.

We indicated above that in the long run in principle average total costs could steadily fall, stay constant, or rise. In Adam Smith's world, however, the long run average costs of production had to rise, otherwise the number of firms would not stay big enough to be called 'competition' (many sellers). That is, efficiency and profit motivated self-interest, and did not move in opposite directions. It is the possibility of falling costs, not contemplated by Smith's invisible hand, and a major sticky wicket for modern day price theorists, that we explore here.

Since 1776, as we all surely know, technological developments have led to enormous increase in machine processes characterized by economies of large scale production. If today we hear much about 'downsizing' it is a relative matter and refers principally to short new adjustments to the number of employees rather than the size of plant. It is a technological question of how much output producing units need to produce for efficiency's sake (minimizing average total costs). As they get larger, still further technological developments may require that the firm be larger still or smaller.

One thing is sure – in the manufacturing sector of a modern economy, as a general rule, the producing units need to be 'large relative to the market.' That is, the producing units need to be so large that typically a 'few' firms could satisfy the market demand. This has led to the creation of 'oligopoly theory' – the consideration of markets in which a 'few' firms produce the entire market output.

Let us consider a good, recent, and well received microeconomic theory text to see how all this is approached nowadays. It is *Microeconomic Theory* by Mas-Colell, Whinston and Green (Harvard economists). We shall therewith illustrate the present state of microeconomic theory. In a section entitled 'Free-Entry and Long-Run Competitive Equilibria' the authors assert:

> Up to this point, we have taken the set of firms and their technological capabilities as fixed. In this section, we consider the case in which an infinite number of firms can potentially be formed, each with access to the most efficient production technology. Moreover, firms may enter or exit the market in response to profit opportunities. This scenario, known as a situation of *free entry*, is often a reasonable approximation when we think of long-run outcomes in a market. In the discussion that follows, we introduce and study a notion of *long-run competitive equilibrium* and then discuss how this concept can be used to analyze long-run and short-run comparative static effects. (Mas-Colell et al. 1995, p. 334)

Note, first, that the authors profess to be introducing a discussion which encompasses long run competitive equilibrium and also a case which 'is often a reasonable approximation when we think of long-run outcomes.' So they follow along with the quotation we considered at the outset, asserting that competition frequently is not too unrealistic an assumption. Is this so?

They next suggest that the discussion can begin by assuming that there are an infinite number of potential firms having access to the necessary technology to produce the good in question. That this supposition rules out most of the actual production processes and units in the manufacturing sector of a modern economy seems clear (there certainly are not an infinite number of steel plants or auto producers waiting to enter those industries), but for the moment let that pass. Long run competitive equilibrium requires that we know *p*, the price per unit which equates demand and supply (and also exists at the lowest point of the firm's average total cost curve), *q*, the output of each firm at that price, and *j*, the number of firms which the market demand will support when operating at these ideal least cost conditions.

> If all firms, active and potential, take prices as unaffected by their own actions, this implies that active firms must earn exactly zero profits in any long-run equilibrium; otherwise we would have either no firms willing to be active in the market (if profits were negative) or an infinite number of firms entering (if profits were positive). (1995, p. 335)[8]

If the industry has constant returns to scale it will be reflected in a long run supply curve which is horizontal. This means that the level of average minimum firm costs never changes, regardless of how many firms enter to meet increases in demand. It requires assumptions of profit maximization, demand equaling supply, and free entry to hold up indefinitely. The authors tell us finally that both the number of firms and the output per firm are indeterminate (1995, p. 336). (With constant costs, output can be produced equally efficiently either by more firms or by larger output per firm.) All that is required is that the output per firm times the number of firms should equal total demand. The only way to get a determinate number of firms is to let the cost curves rise with output (increasing cost case '. . . there must exist a strictly positive output level $\bar{q}$ - at which a firm's average costs of production are minimized . . .' (1995, p. 337).

But realistically, we need also to ask about 'decreasing cost cases' – that is cases in which the firms which make up any given industry can be operating in a range where as they increase output their average costs per unit continue to fall. After all, the economies of scale comprise the major impact which the industrialization of the past two hundred plus years has had on our manufacturing producing units. Recall that Smith's invisible hand worked as it did because the firms were all small relative to the market. Smith did not consider what might happen to the 'hand' were the firms to have market power. But he surely knew. Consider what he had to say about monopoly. Although there is no chapter in the *Wealth of Nations* devoted to monopoly, there are occasional references to monopoly – mostly in trade. At one point he summarizes the effect of monopoly in words which sound very modern. 'A monopoly granted either to an individual or to a trading company has the same effect as a secret in trade or manufactures. The monopolies, by keeping the

8. Recall that these models include 'normal return' in the cost curves themselves.

market constantly under-stocked, by never fully supplying the effectual demand, sell their commodities much above the natural price, and raise their emolument, whether they consist in wages or profit, greatly above their natural rate' (1776/1985, p. 62). What is missing of course is consideration of monopolies which are not 'granted,' but arise in the consequence of powerful firms merely pursuing profits – i.e., when the invisible hand doesn't work. Moreover, he did not hesitate to express his negative opinion of this:

> But the cruellest of our revenue laws, I will venture to affirm, are mild and gentle, in comparison of some of those which the clamour of our merchants and manufacturers has extorted from the legislature, for the support of their own absurd and oppressive monopolies. Like the laws of Draco, these laws, may be said to be all written in blood. (Smith 1776/1985, pp. 324–5)

Ah, what a joy it must have been to write economics in the days before it became a 'positive science!' We argue that the profession in the intervening years has certainly known about market power, but as we shall see in a later chapter, far from joining Smith in disapproving, they have specialized in trying to find ways to defuse the issue.

So, now what do our authors have to say about all this? Well, consider this comment:

> . . . if the efficient scale of operation is large relative to the size of market demand, it could well turn out that the equilibrium number of active firms is small. In these cases, we may reasonably question the appropriateness of the price taking assumption. (Mas-Colell et al. 1995, p. 338).

Our authors conclude that in the case of decreasing cost industries '*no long run competitive equilibrium can exist*' (1995, p. 336, italics in original). This, one would think, introduces a vital new chapter in price theory, but to my knowledge, it has yet to be written.

If we were to assume that historically technological developments have led to steadily increasing scale economies but markets have grown as well, then the changes in the shape of the long run average total cost curve would depend on which changes have been greatest. If firms become larger without their unit costs increasing, the time when average total costs would increase can be postponed. This is undoubtedly what has happened and thus the argument can certainly be made that long run competitive equilibrium models are not very helpful in the modern world for many areas.[9]

This is the lovely world price theorists admire: '. . . when an equilibrium exists . . . the equilibrium outcome maximizes Marshallian aggregate surplus and therefore is Pareto optimal' (Mas-Colell et al. 1995, p. 339).[10]

Thus we see that a major section of the text we review, entitled 'Free Entry and Long Run Competitive Equilibria' comes to the conclusion that only if firms have increasing costs and the proper assumptions can be made do we get determinate results. We shall return to the full implications of this state of affairs. Suffice it to say here that long run equilibrium today signifies a state far different from the simple 'socially optimal results' that Smith got with his invisible hand. Equilibrium is here subject to the constraints which arrive with the assumptions necessary to create the demand and supply curves on which equilibrium rests, on the assumptions back of equating 'welfare' with maximizing the sum of consumer and producer surplus, and on the assumptions necessary to assert Pareto optimality. In short, even before one confronts the impact of modern technology, there are severe limitations to equating equilibrium in current models with Smith's 'best interests of society.'

We add only that it is precisely because the text we used for illustration is a widely respected book, considered one of the best, that it warrants our attention. Its attitude toward monopoly is far more restrained than was Smith's with his talk of 'absurd and oppressive monopolies.'

Today the major question that needs to be asked is: how typical of a modern market economy is the competitive model? (Indeed, we may also ask: how typical is manufacturing?) It is an empirical question. As long ago as the middle of the twentieth century many economists had concluded that 'the ubiquity of oligopoly' was the prevailing empirical conditioner of what price theory needed to explain about the operation of the major industrial economies. In 1949 William Fellner wrote, 'Value theory, as it is usually presented suffers from several limitations which are responsible for its failure to give a sufficiently realistic account of price formation in modern industrialized economies' (Fellner 1949, p. 3). Fellner went on to note that traditional value theory (he

9. We pass over a second assumption – that the demand price is an integer multiple of the minimum cost output per firm. This means that the market demand has to be equal to an amount provided exactly by the number of extant firms each producing at their minimum cost points. As long as the industry remains a constant cost industry the extant firms can continue to increase without efficiency losses as the market expands and so this should not be a problem.

10. The Marshallian aggregate surplus consists of the consumer surplus – all output that consumers would be willing to pay a higher price to get than they have to pay, plus the producer surplus – all the output producers would be willing to sell at a lower price than they in fact get for all the output they sell.

meant price theory) revolved around the 'determinateness of equilibrium' (1949, p. 8).

> In this book, considerable emphasis will be placed on the fact that a significant proportion of the markets with which value theory must be concerned cannot be analyzed in terms of demand functions or supply functions derived from technological data and utility functions alone. Determinate equilibria, in the usual sense, cannot be established for these markets analytically (Fellner 1949, p. 9).[11]

Fellner noted that determinate equilibria could be established for competitive markets, or monopolistic markets. It was most unfortunate, therefore, that it was oligopoly that was ubiquitous. So despite Fellner's statement that much of the economy could not be analyzed in the way that competitive theory required, and despite Fellner's not inconsiderable stature among his fellow economists, his quite devastating reflection on the central thrust of a good deal of then contemporary work in microeconomic theory (just summarized) changed virtually nothing in the character of what his fellow theorists did, then or now. They have continued in their well established ways. The profession took a look at Fellner's perceptive analysis (he was a major economist of his day with a distinguished career at Berkeley and Yale before moving to a Washington DC think tank) and decided that they should stick to what was elegant, what was precise, and what was determinate because (we might intuit) it was aesthetically more pleasing and logically more complete, than a messy theory which could not do better than indeterminate 'ranges' within which price and output might lie – or as we have seen, in which the models themselves might be totally inappropriate.

Oligopolists have market power; they are or might be price makers rather than price takers; they could turn out to be price leaders or price followers as part of their 'price making;' they have much of the flexibility of monopolists and so in pursuing their own self-interest they could most particularly *NOT* be relied upon to contribute optimally to the public interest. That there could be divergence of motive and impact between individual firms and the socially desirable is vividly clear today for tobacco companies and pharmaceutical companies, among others. Fellner's point was that such was most particularly the case whenever fewness rather than 'manyness' was the prevailing structural characteristic in a number of industries.

---

11. We see already that inability to depend on simple demand and supply functions would preclude equating welfare to the Marshallian aggregate surplus which we earlier saw is a critical welfare measure in conventional modern price theory.

The vagueness, the indeterminateness, the messiness was unacceptable to microeconomic theorists. 'Don't confuse us with the facts' became their battle cry (if they bothered to cry about it at all – mostly they simply ignored all this and continued to write about competition, for the reasons alluded to in the quotations at the beginning of this chapter!). It was almost as though the contributions of Fellner, Paul Sweezy (with his 'kinked demand curve' purporting to depict realistically the possible behavior of oligopolists in matching any price decrease by their rivals but refusing to match a price increase), and earlier Joan Robinson and E. H. Chamberlin and many other economists, simply did not exist (Sweezy 1939, pp. 568–73).

Worst of all there was clearly conflict between ideal decision making following efficiency criteria emanating from modern technology on the one hand and the behavior of the oligopolies it produced on the other hand. Efficiency and automaticity were at loggerheads. This was the final – if often unrecognized – nail in the invisible hand's coffin.

The typical price theory textbooks are here represented by Mas-Colell et al., which devotes a single short chapter to oligopoly (52 pages out of 970-odd pages). The number of pages devoted to competition is, of course, far greater. These proportions are noteworthy only because they are typical of microeconomic theory books. And what do they tell us in their short discussions of oligopoly? Earlier they contented themselves with telling us that the outcome was uncertain and necessarily imprecise. Now they have something more to add. 'Competition among firms in an oligopolistic market is inherently a setting of strategic interaction. For this reason, the appropriate tool of analysis is game theory' (Mas-Colell et al. 1995, p. 387). We shall consider the impact of game theory in a subsequent chapter. For now we may note only that, whatever the attractions of game theory may be, it scarcely produces the precise logical outcomes that price theorists have traditionally admired and to which they continue to be addicted.

NORMATIVE AND POSITIVE SCIENCE – CHANGING VIEWS

One of the bedrock assertions of modern mainstream economists is, as we have already noted, that the discipline is a positive, not a normative, science. The discussion we have just concluded has some bearing on this claim. The basic position of conventional economics on this matter was stated baldly by Lionel Robbins in the 1930s.

> Economics is neutral as between ends. Economics cannot pronounce on the validity of ultimate judgments of value.

> . . . Mr. Hawtrey and Mr. J.A. Hobson . . . have argued that economics should not only take account of valuations and ethical standards as given data in the manner explained above, but that also it should pronounce upon the ultimate validity of these valuations and standards. 'Economics,' says Mr. Hawtrey 'cannot be dissociated from Ethics.' Unfortunately, it does not seem logically possible to associate the two studies in any form but mere juxtaposition. Economics deals with ascertainable facts; ethics with valuations and obligations. The two fields of enquiry are not on the same plane of discourse. (Robbins 1932, pp. 147–8)

Thus was born the oft repeated assertion that economics is concerned with 'what is' not with 'what ought to be.' Adam Smith is brought in customarily by stating that in his theological mode, when 'what ought to be' is an appropriate consideration, he wrote his *Theory of Moral Sentiments*, but that in his economist mode, when he wrote *The Wealth of Nations*, he stuck to 'what is.' Earlier considerable doubt was cast here on this argument. In his comments on the Chinese baby drowners, a discussion which clearly arose in a consideration of an economic system, Smith's very words suggest that he was by no means restricting himself to the 'what is' approach. More to the point, his discussion of monopolists, contemplated earlier, would clearly have to be classified as 'normative.' His discussion was replete with his own 'what ought to be' as well.

The argument that economic theory must confine itself to 'what is' not only avoids confronting the view that to take no position is to take a normative position – that of being comfortable enough with the way things are to make no complaint. It has also been a pernicious way to sneak established conventional arrangements into the 'what is' category – therefore beyond debate, when in fact they embody profoundly normative judgements. (Smith was not about to assume the baby drowners were *given* or even more that the 'absurd and oppressive monopolies' were *given* and move on from there.) The proposition that economic theory should take the form of 'If . . . then' reasoning to avoid permitting subjective bias to enter the discussion has been widely and approvingly advanced. Adherents to this view are never very perturbed with the attendant requirement that such theory must be permitted to take various matters as given. Thus, to take an example, the use of Pareto optimality as a welfare standard requires accepting the current distributions of wealth and income as given. Clearly, accepting the prevailing highly unequal distribution of income as given gives a very different normative slant to the analysis than were it based on acceptance as given of, say, a very egalitarian distribution of income. What is accepted as given one can presumably live with reasonably well.

Finally, there is irony in this position as well. Modern microeconomic theory is presumably based on the 'what is' convention required to keep theory positive. To be positive theory must stick to 'what is.' But the heart of microeconomic theory is based, as we have seen, on the appropriateness of assuming that the invisible hand can operate so as to guarantee socially optimal outcomes from personally selfish behavior. Some years ago Amartya Sen raised seriously the appropriateness of basing the discipline on that view of personal behavior. Said Sen:

> In his *Mathematical Psychics*, published in 1881, Edgeworth asserted that 'the first principle of Economics is that every agent is actuated only by self-interest.' This view of man has been a persistent one in economic models, and the nature of economic theory seems to have been much influenced by this basic premise. . . .
>
> I should mention that Edgeworth himself was quite aware that this so-called first principle of Economics was not a particularly realistic one. Indeed, he felt that the 'concrete nineteenth century man' is for the most part an impure egoist, a mixed utilitarian. This raises the interesting question as to why Edgeworth spent so much of his time and talent in developing a line of inquiry the first principle of which he believed to be false. (Sen 1977, p. 317)

If the first principle is questionable, what was done with it may be even more questionable. We reiterate – microeconomic theory is built on the notion that the invisible hand can convert this personally selfish behavior into socially optimal behavior. But that in turn requires widespread competition. And modern industrial economies are characterized by widespread imperfect economies which convert the price takers necessary for the invisible hand to operate into price makers of varying degrees of market influence. The assumption of competition is a requisite for the invisible hand to operate and in fact clearly is *NOT* part of the current scene.[12] Positive microeconomic theory, insisting that it is rooted in strict adherence to 'what is' is predicated on an assumption of ubiquitous competition, which is *NOT* part of the real world's 'what is'!

Out of this emerged a normative confusion that plagues economic theory to this day. Economic theory implicitly asserts that explaining the functioning of the price system is coterminous with explaining the value system. Price theory courses are labeled 'Value Theory.' John R. Hicks, the eminent English economist, wrote a famous book entitled *Value and Capital* which, in fact, is not about value at all but about price and capital. By blurring the arena in which Smith's invisible hand could operate, something Smith did not do, modern price theorists can assume comfortably that by worrying about prices and how they

12. Again, we call attention to Sen's views. He has made the disjunction between the competitive model and the modern world even more obvious. '. . . economics is not concerned only with consumer behavior, nor is consumption confined to 'private goods' . . . In many economic models private goods are the only ones around, and this is typically the case when the "invisible hand" is given the task of doing visible good. But, in fact, public goods are important in most economies,' (Sen 1977, p. 330). Chapter 6 is accordingly devoted to economic theory and the public sector.

operate they are doing all that they, as economists, need to do about the problem we suggested earlier is the real objective of economic activity. It is not about clearing markets but about the degree to which the economy is achieving the objective which Thorstein Veblen described as 'enhancing human life' (Veblen 1994, p. 99). The result of this confusion is that microtheorists write as though market clearing prices are the end result on which enhancing human life depends. In point of fact market clearing prices have their place, but recognizing that place is always the result of societal review of 'equilibrium prices.' It is through a normative review of the resource allocation patterns of emergent prices that the value implications of prices – even equilibrium prices – emerge! We return to normative concerns below.

THE ROLE OF THE PUBLIC SECTOR

A major implication of the continued insistence that the invisible hand does for the modern world what Smith casually mentioned it did in his world is that there is no real or critical role for the public sector, beyond the functions Smith explicitly considers. The public sector is the subject of Chapter 6. Here we note only that if the invisible hand really converts personal selfishness into collective unselfishness then the prices which emerge in free untrammeled markets are also the only value expressions by which society need be troubled. This in the final analysis is the great appeal of the elegant modern invisible hand for today's conventional economists. For those who insist that society must always monitor the results of market allocation via prices in order to assure itself that societal values are being expressed, the answer is clear. If we can take the invisible hand at face value, what emerges from the market is the best expression of societal values possible. In this chapter we have tried to show: (1) that this was not the case even in Smith's time; (2) that thanks to the economic implications of the economies of large scale production it cannot possibly be true today when society has as much interest in equity as in efficiency; (3) competition, not pure let alone perfect, cannot be relied upon to advance societal values without societal review of market performance. To some extent all societies grant this. The modern debate is one of degree rather than kind. Hence, a consideration of the character and role of the public sector will necessarily arise in the chapters to follow.

CONCLUSIONS

A major conclusion of this review of the attitude of the economics profession toward the invisible hand, as we have just seen, is that neither Fellner nor anyone else who has written in the past 50 years has made very much of an impression on that sacred corpus of microeconomic theory which we continue to teach our students as the essential wisdom of how markets work and what the implications are of their operation.[13] On the other hand, not surprisingly, Milton Friedman continues to lead economists in his admiration for the hand. Friedman writing of Smith called him 'the father of modern economics' and added that 'he . . . had the great insight that it was possible to achieve order without central direction, that an ordered society could arise out of the activities of millions of individuals, each pursuing his own objectives without anybody intervening. He used the famous phrase in which he said that an individual who 'intends only his own gain' is 'led by an invisible hand to promote an end which was no part of his intention' (Friedman 1981, p. 7).

There are various rationalizations for why the emphasis continues to be placed on competition – indeed pure and perfect competition.[14] The results which emanate from pure and perfect competition are so logical, so beautiful, so elegant, so ingenious, so wondrous, and lead to such precise market outcomes that to model builders they are well nigh irresistible.

We shall enter into a full fledged critique of these rationalizations in Chapter 4. Here we shall content ourselves with the suggestion that no other discipline, no other field of human knowledge, has so completely surrendered to the lures that lie within the total capitulation to an 'ideal type.' Were sociologists, for example, to surrender to the temptation of assuming that the ideally functioning family was the best model, they, too, would find many attractive features in their paradigm. It would avoid confrontation with virtually all that currently goes wrong in American families. If reminded that roughly half of all American marriages end in divorce (it is 'ubiquitous') there would doubtless be voices raised suggesting that the ideally functioning family is a construct which bears little resemblance to the facts. No one suggests that by advancing 'the ideal family' as one which quietly talks through all disagreements would we get very much help in how to prevent disagreeing couples from ending up in the divorce courts. Similarly, a political scientist who ruminated about the benefits flowing

---

13. We are by no means the first or the only one to question the usual interpretation of Smith's invisible hand. Joseph Stiglitz, took a similar if not precisely identical position, writing 'Smith was undoubtedly right that individuals' pursuits of their private interests lead to social consequences which may be quite different from those intended. But whether it leads to (Pareto) efficient outcomes is a far different matter' (Stiglitz 1991, p. 6).

14. The major innovation in microeconomic theory in the recent past has undoubtedly been game theory. But game theory concentrates on the strategies involved in pursuing self-interest under various sets of circumstances. The outcome of such games is customarily some optimal allocative result. But optimality in game theory usually reflects efficiency. Rarely do games concern themselves with questions of equity. Without introducing equity it is difficult to consider welfare considerations of the sort presumably involved in normative economics.

from an ideally functioning democracy might be forgiven if he or she had a momentary wish that such a system could actually be found in the real world. No one suggests that careful descriptions of the ideally functioning democratic system are very much help in figuring out what to do about lobbies, the influence of large business or labor organizations, or 'soft money,' etc. In the end, they are used like the ideally functioning family, as a starting point – if that.

Often economic theorists fall back on the explanation that we use competitive theory primarily as 'benchmark' theory. The essential matter about benchmarks is to recognize them for what they are. They are not put forth because they accurately describe very much if any of the real world. They are advanced partly as an 'ideal type' against which to describe reality, thereby pointing up the divergences and the difficulties these departures pose. The whole point is to assist in answering the question, 'How can we make this structure or unit function so as to perform more successfully in the actual world the role it was designed to fulfil?' This means, how can it advance life in the real – which is to say flawed – world in which we encounter it?

But in the real world the units as well as the behavior of the units are inevitably much messier and less precise than the benchmark theory continues to make them. They are less appealing to work with than competitive theory. So competitive theory is difficult to utilize even as 'benchmark theory.' The result is that theory applicable to understanding much of the real world is still given short shrift. Neither the implications of oligopoly nor its awkward lack of susceptibility to rigorous quantitative techniques made it particularly appealing to price theorists.

For more than 50 years, in short, the economics profession has devoted itself to creating a complex system for quantifying marginal analysis so that neoclassical economics could be married to differential calculus and sophisticated graphics to display a self-regulating system which was also 'ideal.' Adam Smith's briefly mentioned construct (the invisible hand) was enormously inflated in significance and converted into the Walrasian general equilibrium system to which, lastly, could be attached all the welfare implications earlier mentioned. Not only could they be attached but attached in precise quantitative terms so that the welfare the economy was generating could always be calculated, at least to the extent of saying more than could be generated with any other possible configuration of society's resources. The full mathematical implications of the total utility and total profits generated in any economy can be spewed out! They can, as was intimated, be combined with Pareto optimality to suggest that the particular outpouring of goods and services gets the economy close to the Panglossian ideal of the best possible economy, subject to a few constraints. Economists, as we have seen, say that they use competitive theory as 'benchmark' theory. But the benchmark continues to be the primary market structure subjected to ongoing efforts to improve the theory relevant to it. And the imperfect competition models – 70 years after they were introduced – are still the models given short shrift.

Do I exaggerate? I think not. Gregory Mankiw, author of perhaps the most widely heralded elementary textbook of the 1990s, writes in his introduction,

> In his 1776 book, *The Wealth of Nations*, economist Adam Smith made the most famous observation in all of economics. Households and firms interacting in markets act as if they are guided by an 'invisible hand' that leads them to desirable market outcomes. One of our goals in this book is to understand how this invisible hand works its magic. (Mankiw 2004, p. 9)

This is not the competitive model as 'benchmark' theory! It refers to 'households and firms interacting in markets' – not even competitive markets. It is as if Joan Robinson, Edward Chamberlin, William Fellner, Paul Sweezy and all the others who tried to introduce a bit of realism into microeconomic theory, simply did not exist or at the very least, that what they did was too unimportant to mention alongside a pronouncement of such sweep and power as Smith's 'most famous observation in all of economics.'

For the trend setters among conventional mainstream economics the stakes in the debate summarized here, however abstruse that debate may seem superficially to be, are very high indeed. Some variant of the invisible hand is crucial to the effort to anchor the non-interventionist 'leave it to the market' position in academic respectability. Without it the argument loses the justification for its insistence that self-interest on the part of all participants in the economic game will automatically and without governmental intervention lead to the desired results. That is why microeconomic theorists can continue to focus on the policy implications of pure and perfect competition and grant in the next breath that the likelihood of finding that kind of competition in the real world may be small. For an illustration of this, we saw that a well known recent text could state in one breath that ' . . . if the efficient scale of operation is large relative to the size of market demand it could well turn out that the equilibrium number of active firms is small' we may reasonably question the appropriateness of the price taking assumptions; in the next breath the authors return to embellish the major message being underscored: 'when an equilibrium exists . . . the equilibrium outcome maximizes Marshallian aggregate surplus and therefore is Pareto optimal' (Mas-Colell et al. 1995, pp. 338–9). We pass over the severe limitations of Pareto optimality to act as a stand in for enhancing human life or general welfare. Maximizing the Marshallian surplus and achieving Pareto optimality are so attractive as the end result of economic activity, and so in consonance with the overall *weltanschauung* of the trend setters in the economics establishment that they are simply irresistible.

Therefore, the possibility that the necessary conditions to achieve them may not be present simply has to be dismissed (or ignored as it is in the passage quoted). Theorists end up, in effect, saying, 'Don't confuse me with the facts.'

Thus, by the reasoning process just summarized, have current mainstream economists come to put the invisible hand in a pivotal position not really found anywhere in its original introduction by Smith. I doubt Smith would recognize what has been done to the notion. He surely did not ascribe to it 'the source of economic magic.'

In the end we are forced to conclude that economists continue to assert that the invisible hand is a marvelous instrumentality for producing the ideal welfare economy out of the selfish pursuits of all its individual participants – so marvelous that economists simply ignore the small matter that the real economy diverges from the pure, let alone perfectly competitive economy (critical to the operation of the invisible hand). The divergence is so significant that the invisible hand often cannot function at all, let alone in the ideal fashion so dear to the hearts of economic theorists, who neglect the study of the private visible hand!

REFERENCES

Ahmad, Syed (1990), *Adam Smith's Four Invisible Hands, History of Political Economy*, in Spencer J. Pack, *Capitalism as a Moral System: Adam Smith's Critique of the Free Market Economy,* Aldershot, UK and Brookfield, VT: Edgar Elgar Publishing Limited.

Blaug, Mark (1980), *The Methodology of Economics*, Cambridge: Cambridge University Press.

Bromley, Daniel (1989), *Economic Interests and Institutions*, Oxford and New York: Basil Blackwell.

Dome, Takuo (1994), *History of Economic Theories*, Aldershot, UK and Brookfield, US: Edward Elgar.

Fellner, William (1949), *Competition Among the Few*, New York: Alfred A. Knopf.

Friedman, Milton (1981), *The Invisible Hand in Economics and Politics*, Singapore: Institute of Southeast Asian Studies.

Gregg, Pauline (1969), *A Social and Economic History of Britain, Fifth Edition*, revised London: George G. Harrap & Co. Ltd., *Report of Select Committee on Factory Children's Labor*, 1831–32, **XV**, 192 et seq.

Leftwich, Richard H. (1979), *The Price System and Resource Allocation*, Hinsdale, IL: Dryden Press.

Mankiw, N. Gregory (2004), *Principles of Economics*, *Third Edition*, New York: The Dryden Press.

Mansfield, Edwin (1970), *Microeconomics: Theory and Applications*, New York: W.W. Norton and Company.

Marx, Karl (German Edition 1867, American Edition, 1906), *Capital*, New York: Charles H. Kerr, The Modern Library.

Mas-Colell, Andreum, Michael D. Whinston and Jerry R. Green (1995), *Microeconomic Theory*, New York: Oxford University Press.

Pack, Spencer J. (1991), *Capitalism as a Moral System*, Aldershot, UK and Brookfield, US: Edward Elgar.

Pashigian, B. Peter (1998), *Price Theory and Applications*, *Second Edition*, Boston, MA: Irwin/McGraw-Hill.

Robbins, Lionel (1932), *An Essay On the Nature and Significance of Economic Science*, London: Macmillan and Co. Ltd.

Ruffin, Roy J. (1992), *Intermediate Microeconomics, Second Edition*, New York: HarperCollins.

Sen, Amartya K. (1977), 'Rational fools: a critique of the behavioral foundations of economic theory', *Philosophy and Public Affairs*, **6** (4), 317–44.

Simon, Herbert A. (1997), *Administrative Behavior, Fourth Edition*, New York: The Free Press.

Smith, Adam (1776/1985), *An Inquiry into the Nature and Causes of the Wealth of Nations,* New York: Modern Library.

Stiglitz, Joseph E. (1991), *The Invisible Hand and Modern Welfare Economics*, Cambridge, MA: NBER Working Paper No. 3641.

Sweezy, P.M. (1939), 'Demand under conditions of oligopoly', *Journal of Political Economy*, **XLVII**, 568–73.

Varian, Hal R. (1992), *Microeconomic Analysis*, *Third Edition*, New York: W.W. Norton & Company.

Vaughn, Karen I. (1987), 'Invisible hand', in John Eatwell, Murray Milgate and Peter Newman (eds), *The New Palgrave Dictionary of Economics*, London: Macmillan Press Ltd., pp. 997–98.

Veblen, Thorstein (1994), The Theory of the Leisure Class, New York: Penguin Books.

2. Making progress with theory: do we get what we want or want what we get?

> Newton's law of gravitation, while its principal applications relate to the astrometry of the universe, is rendering constant service to those who are trying to solve the problems of astrophysics: as an instrument of prediction and deduction, as an agency of interpretation; and as a check upon hypotheses. (Campbell 1928, p. 68)

Young scientists early in their careers frequently wrestle with the challenge of how to be objective in their research, especially if it concerns a subject about which they feel passionately. How can you set standards of acceptability in judging the evidence you examine? What should be required for 'proof'? We in the social sciences, at any rate, are all schooled in the 'scientific method' – the notion that one develops a hypothesis, collects data with which to test the hypothesis, and comes to a conclusion (thoroughly grounded in empirical reality) that the data do or do not support the hypothesis. Hypotheses are never proved but if supported by the data they are retained for further research. Thus is 'progress' made in a scientific field.

In the wake of this introduction the young scientists are reassured that pursuit of this technique guarantees, on a wide variety of fronts, that dangers to good and objective research will be avoided. 'Value judgements' however passionately they may be held, can't get in the way and taint 'research.' The distinction between normative and positive will remain; the chasm between the two is broad and complete. 'Is' is permanently and totally separable from 'ought.'

Aspects of existence included in 'is,' however unpleasant, inhumane, despicable, or unspeakable they may be, require no conscious emotion or response (no feelings of guilt need be agonized over) because their inclusion in 'is' (as any good mainstream economist can tell you) means the investigator has received a special inoculation – it is today most often called 'modelling' – which means no personal criticism can flow from taking these matters as 'given.' Guilt free acceptance of 'givens' can presumably be achieved any time anyone puts on the sterile research gown called 'scientific method.'

The extraordinary properties of that gown presumably protect the wearer from getting hung up in all the human emotions that might otherwise destroy the objectivity and, thereby the usefulness, of his or her work. Pursuit of the scientific method, if not a license to kill, is a license neither to worry or to feel guilt about anything that happens in the carrying out of this kind of research. Research predicated on the assumption of things given has the imprimatur of approval by the entire scientific community. As we have suggested, it is designed, among other things, to keep normative and positive analysis in neatly separated arenas and thus to ensure 'value free' economic analysis. Proof in research is guided by this standard.[1]

The conventional contrary approach (the normative approach) is equally recognizable for its pitfalls and its ultimately spineless and shapeless wallowing in emotion. It might be called the 'Don Quixote' approach to scientific investigation. One would begin with strong 'feelings,' 'likes and dislikes,' 'vices and virtues,' 'sins and blessings.' One would set out to 'right all wrongs' – come down on the side of all likes, virtues, and blessings and against all dislikes, vices, and sins. Righting wrongs, healing the ill, strengthening the weak, purifying the corrupt – for scientific research this approach would truly be 'the impossible dream.' Here is a world that would pay no attention to

---

1. The way these questions are conventionally handled in economics involves the field of economic methodology. There is a vast literature in economics dealing with methodology. In a sense economic methodology involves the question of what it means in economics to pursue the scientific method. A major statement of the issues is Mark Blaug, *The Methodology of Economics*. The first edition appeared in 1980 and the second in 1992. A second summary statement of recent debates in economic methodology is Bruce J. Caldwell's *Beyond Positivism*, (1982, revised edition 1994). Major figures in the debate would surely include Karl Popper (especially *The Logic of Scientific Discovery*, 1959 reprinted 1965), I.M.E. Leachates (*The Methodology of Scientific Research Programs,* 1978), Paul Feyerabend (*Against Method: Outline of an Anarchistic Theory of Knowledge*, 1975), and Thomas Kuhn, *The Structure of Scientific Revolutions*, Second Edition 1970). (We comment further on Kuhn in Chapter 8).

It is probably accurate to begin by saying that most economists would accept Popper's notion of falsifiability as the ultimate test of what economics assertions should be accepted. It still holds considerable wide appeal. The falsifiability standard asserts that progress in economics consists of developing hypotheses, accepting them so long as they can't be proven false, and rejecting them when they can.

Both Blaug and Caldwell note in their later editions the tremendous burgeoning of contributions to economic methodology in the years between their two editions. They begin their revised editions by commenting on each other's earlier (first edition) views. Blaug comments that Leachates, Kuhn, Feyerabend, along with a number of others, rejected what he terms Popper's 'ahistorical philosophy of science, and that each 'repeatedly emphasizes the essentially public and cooperative character of scientific knowledge: it is interpersonal test ability, captured by the notion of indefinitely replicable results, that is the hallmark of science and that alone distinguishes it from other human conceptual activities' (Blaug 1992, pp. 37–8).

The debates in economic methodology are today complex and some might say prolix. In the text above we concentrate on only a small aspect of these debates – what can we say about the principal current schools of thought in macroeconomics (where they are more clear cut today than in microeconomics) and what do they tell us about potentially diverse standards of acceptance of hypotheses today? (What do they tell us about how Popper's falsifiability standard is currently applied in macroeconomic theory?)

normative and positive, to 'is' and 'ought.' If all were governed by 'oughts,' in a world of total unreality there would be no positive 'is' at all. This would never do for scientific research. No two people would necessarily see eye-to-eye on the 'correctness' of any findings and total chaos would result. Clarence Ayres likened this 'relativity of mores' to the 'Cretan dilemma.' (The Cretan created an enigma by announcing that all Cretans are 'liars'.) Said Ayres, 'If all values are relative, including intellectual values, then it would seem to follow that modern scientific thinking also is relative to the culture which accredits it, including social thinking, including the principle that all values are relative' (Ayres 1944, p. 208).

The question we come to at last is whether in fact in economic analysis we get the conclusions to which dispassionate analysis ultimately leads us, or do we by a somewhat more devious route get the conclusions which it turns out we wanted all along? How do economists define 'proof'?

APPLYING THE SCIENTIFIC METHOD TO ECONOMICS: A STRICT CONSTRUCTIONIST VIEW

A 'strict constructionist' view of the scientific method would argue that scientific discoveries come first and adjustment to them, whatever it may involve, comes later. A quintessential example is Isaac Newton's 'discovery' of the law of gravity. So I begin by asking, 'What if economics were like physics' (as has always been the cherished dream of many of our theorists)?

Presumably Newton began with no particular normative attitude toward gravitational force – he was neither for it nor against it, he neither liked nor disliked it, he was neither drawn to nor repelled by the idea. This is, of course, an ideal background against which to pursue 'positive analysis.' It is one of the enormous advantages which the 'hard sciences' have over the social and behavioral sciences. The latter involve human beings directly as variables in the analyses, and as such, it is much more difficult to 'feel neutral' about them. Different investigators can, to be sure, have vigorous disagreements about what they study, and feel strongly about their position. But positions pro and con in the hard sciences do not directly speak to human life or human interaction in personal terms and so maintaining scientific detachment may not be so large a challenge.[2]

One commentator has written of

---

2. This is not to say that many scientific discoveries don't affect human life and raise all sorts of normative questions: who should benefit from liver transplants? how much money should appropriately be expended in neonatal medicine to save one tiny premature fetus? etc.

> . . . Newton, pondering alone, alone in that small stone house . . . in the wide countryside . . . [with] intense and concentrated thought in his twenty-third and twenty-fourth year . . . As he sits by the apple tree at Woolsthorpe, Newton's meditations are disturbed by the soft thud of an apple falling on the grass. He thinks of its falling in consequence of the central pull of the earth and then – as far as we can make out – one thought suddenly comes to him, may not the earth, which pulls the apple, also pull the moon? May it not be this pull, suitably weakened by the great distance, that keeps the moon from flying out of its orbit? Would not the moon, if it were at rest, assuredly fall to the earth, like the apple, except that, as the earth is so much larger than the apple, the earth would also measurably fall towards the moon at the same time?
>
> According to what law must the pull of the earth decrease as we go farther away if it is just sufficient to keep the moon in its orbit? Newton deduced that it must weaken inversely as the square of the distance from the center of the earth. (Andrade 1958, pp. 33–8)

Clearly Newton was groping his way toward the notion of centripetal force.[3] As another writer explains, from the falling apple Newton had gotten to the 'extremely plausible . . . hypothesis that the force which keeps the moon and the planets in their orbits is the same force which we experience on earth as gravitation . . .' (Broad 1927, p. 27). This line of reasoning leads to the '. . . extremely beautiful theorem that the attraction produced by a sphere composed of matter which attracts in accordance with the inverse square law is exactly the same at any external point as if all its mass were concentrated in its center' (1927, p. 28). Need we add that this 'inverse square law of gravitation' can be put in a form which will immediately endear it to all modern mainstream economists: 'Two particles, a distance apart, being of mass $\frac{m_1 \times m_2}{r^2}$ attract one another with a force proportional to $m_1 \times m_2$' (North 1967, p. 45).

At the end of the day, we may say that it took Newton more than twenty years after he discovered this 'inverse square law of gravitation' (1665, 1666) before he finally published his work in his *Principia* (1687). For a 'strict constructionist' this illustrates ideal empirical research. Newton began presumably with no preconceptions and reacted to the empirical evidence which 'came to him' (the falling apple). Standards for probability were self-evident.

3. We note in passing that in contemplating the nature of centripetal force Newton did not have to contend with what his parents had taught him as a child about forces, centripetal or otherwise. His friends, his teachers, his minister – the culture around him – all were no doubt wondrously silent on the subject of centripetal force. There was no positive theory ('centripetal force exists'). There was no normative theory ('centripetal force is good'). We may safely say that Newton arrived at his contemplation of centripetal force unencumbered by any emotional or intellectual baggage which might impinge on his de novo views of what he was contemplating.

He reached his general conclusions – seemingly inductively (from the apple to all masses) – on the basis of the evidence before him. We add only that (as is true of the bulk of research leading to scientific progress) they grew out of earlier work (Copernicus, Brahe, Kepler) and led directly to later work (Einstein). For a recent discussion of Newton and his place in the development of insight into gravitational force see (see Gleick 2003.) Note, too, that research in the strict constructionist mode does not have to be concerned, as was earlier implied, with whether it is normative or positive, an advantage which, as we earlier suggested, the physical sciences (up to a point) have over the social sciences. I am not aware that Newton spent any time worrying about whether his work was in positive or normative theory. It is difficult, as we indicated at the outset, to imagine a normative position with respect to gravitational force. One 'approves' of gravity, perhaps, when, for example, thanks to centripetal force, otherwise disparate elements are coordinated into a single smooth functioning whole. One 'disapproves,' perhaps, when again thanks to gravity a young person commits suicide successfully by jumping off a roof. In both cases the normative implications are a stretch. (A would-be suicide takes advantage of gravity. If he drowns himself one can hardly get mad at the lake.) Assuming that gravity exists it is arguably difficult to view it as either a sinful or a virtuous assumption. In model building, assuming that the condition of gravity is 'given' is not a position loaded with normative implications (like, say, the distribution of income in an economic model). The 'scientific method' applied to the hard sciences does not in the first instance then comparably test the emotional attitudes of the hard scientists and their social and behavioral science counterparts.

It is difficult to imagine that a researcher in this field would have preferred a theory which argued that higher masses pull lower masses upwards rather than the reverse. So Newton was able to express his insights mathematically (he had a 'precise quantifiable theory'), and on its basis one can forecast the future for masses placed in motion. To be sure, had one been convinced that the earth was flat, and stuck to this 'given,' it might have severely distorted the findings of a scientist on any subject on which the shape of the earth was a pertinent part of the research problem or its formulation. But even if one began with that hunch, as it has been suggested Columbus did, empirical research (e.g., sailing for weeks in the same direction) ought in time to have disabused one of this notion. In sum, if one follows the strict constructionist position to its logical end it follows that scientific discoveries (originally testable hypotheses) come first, and necessary adjustments to them come later.

We come now to an interesting question in connection with Newton's theory of gravity. We have noted that mainstream economists admire hard sciences such as physics at least in part because one can control the environment (bell jars, vacuums, etc.) and do controlled experiments by setting up testable hypotheses which then are susceptible to precise logical testing by means of deductive logic. (For this reason, for example, striking a tuning fork in a laboratory situation and studying the resultant sound waves is far more appealing to mainstream economists – but for the subject matter – than having to study business fluctuations in the real world. The 'ceteris paribus' approach was 'made' for the former area, and is painfully applied in the latter.) The fundamental distinction we are making is sometimes expressed as the difference between a 'closed system' and an 'open system.' Thus, William Kapp has pointed out that the preferred narrow perspective has 'tended to push conventional economic theory more and more into the direction of a formal, self-contained, closed mechanical analytical system . . .' (Kapp 1976, p. 211). This system, Kapp continues, has been regarded as 'self-contained and self-sustaining (and) isolated from a social and physical environment of which the economic system is a part . . .'.[4] Tony Lawson has devoted an entire book to the implications of this state of affairs.

> The essence of contemporary mainstream economics does not lie at the level of substantive theory, as most critics suggest, but at the level of methodology. Specifically, the most fundamental feature is a generalised insistence on the deductivist mode of explanation . . . And it is in this very essence that the perpetual disarray of the subject is rooted. For, while the generalised usefulness of deductivism is dependent upon a ubiquity of closed systems, the social world, the object of social study, is fundamentally open . . . . (Lawson 1997, p. 282)

We note that Lawson concludes by asserting, '. . . I am arguing for nothing less that orthodox economics' effective demise as a general approach and *mainstream* position' (p. 283, italics in original).

Clearly the closed system approach can be pursued somewhat more facilely in the world of the hard sciences than in the world of the social and behavioral sciences. Mark Blaug put it this way:

> . . . we must now raise a famous question in the philosophy of the social sciences: is there one scientific method applicable to all sciences whatever their subject matter, or must social sciences employ a logic of inquiry uniquely their own? [On

---

4. Kapp contrasts this closed system with an alternative view: '. . . the critics have always considered the economy as an open system in continuous dynamic interaction with a more comprehensive social and political as well as physical system from which economic processes receive important organising (and disorganising) impulses and upon which they exert their own negative and positive impulses (Kapp 1976, p. 213). This alternative view, as currently viewed, is the subject of Chapter 8 below.

p. 42 he answers this question in favor of what he calls 'methodological monism' and continues] . . . we do not mean to deny the relative immaturity of every social science, including economics compared to at least some of the physical sciences. Even if the difference between 'hard' physical and 'soft' social science is only one of degree, that degree is a large one. No social science can boast of the universal laws of modern chemistry, the numerical constants of particle physics, and the predictive accuracy of Newtonian mechanics. (Blaug 1992, p. 47)

We chose Newton's work because it is a quintessential example of research in the hard sciences which mainstream economists admire and, if given the chance, would wish to emulate. In this respect there is an odd aspect to Newton's pattern-to-admire. The famous apple represents the fulcrum of an inductive rather than a deductive approach. He may have traced the consequences of the falling apple deductively, but the falling apple was, by induction, generalized by Newton to apply to all masses moving toward other masses. But there is a crucial difference between Newton and the approach of mainstream economic theorists. Part of the appeal to economists of the hard sciences is that assuming the environment conforms to explicit conditions which can be assumed to be given is not too farfetched (in the world economists idealize experiments can conceivably be conducted under a bell jar and in a vacuum). Newton took the environment – the real environment – as basic to his theory. (For an economic microtheorist to base theory on the real environment would be a real departure. Instead conventional micro-theorists customarily begin with an effort deliberately to imagine a simple play world, to begin with a set of 'givens' – i.e., the necessary assumptions to create the play world and then to set about explaining that world. They even have a name today for what is being explained – it is 'stylized facts!') The falling apple (a real fact) for Newton could trigger his highly useful efforts to understand planetary orbits, etc. Newton, we reiterate, may well have applied deductive logic to that single apple, inductive logic to all falling apples (and by extension to all falling objects).

Newton, in the words previously quoted of Andrade, asked. '. . . may not the earth, which pulls the apple, also pull the moon?' He was making an inductive generalization. In this respect Newton's efforts were not that different from, say, Wesley Clair Mitchell's. Mitchell's efforts were directed toward studying 'what happens during business cycles'. He asked this by focusing on the real world and studying individual real cyclical episodes.[5] By induction he generalized the pattern of interrelationships he found in a number of single episodes to typical

5. Wesley Clair Mitchell left a book, published posthumously, entitled *What Happens During Business Cycles: A Progress Report* (Mitchell 1951).

episodes found in market economies. In doing so he created a highly useful, if scarcely simple, explanation of 'what happens during cycles.' Specifically, Mitchell described business cycles as 'congeries of changes in numerous processes running abreast or following each other' (Mitchell 1927, p. 53). As we have just seen this is very much as Newton generalized (presumably) from one to all falling apples and then to what happens among masses generally. My fellow economists, the conventional ones at least, will be surprised to know that a physicist-mathematician like Newton and Mitchell were methodological brothers! But they were.[6]

Methodologically, as we shall see below, mainstream economists have always admired the possibilities of controlled experimentation in solving problems. They neglected the small matter that controlled experiments are far easier to set up, let alone learn from, for problems not involving human beings. Unfortunately ignoring human beings is rarely if ever a reasonable possibility for economics. Economists think simplification via 'givens' is the most promising path to setting up controlled experiments amenable to inductive reasoning. (Newton could have been looked to for questioning this position, but he wasn't.) As we shall see, real research in real situations (both in economics and elsewhere) more often than not involves a combination of inductive and deductive approaches.

We conclude that economists admired Newton's logic, his precision, and his development of theories which could be expressed mathematically. Therefore, Newton's ability to arrive at precise results and, in consequence, his equations explaining gravitation would resonate well with today's economists. Unfortunately, he also showed the usefulness of induction as well as deduction, and this would be less happily received. As it turns out the solution to any potential confusion this contradictory state of affairs raised would not be hard to find. In typical economist fashion, they would ignore the inductive reasoning and concentrate on the precise results.

Finally we comment on the policy implications of Newton's work. It is doubtful that Newton himself began by interesting himself in the problem of gravitation because of the policy implications, although he might well have found them attractive. (More likely, his interest and his work were motivated by what Veblen called 'idle curiosity'.) What makes his work on gravitation attractive not alone to physicists but to virtually all people was its enormous policy implications. Air flight not only was made possible because Newton, in effect, explained exactly what had to be overcome if objects as heavy as modern

6. Many months after the above section was written, I encountered a comment by Kenneth Boulding: 'Wesley Mitchell has some times been called the Tycho Brahe of economics, recording painstakingly year after year the positions of the economic bodies' (quoted, Moore 1980, p. 3).

aircraft were going to fly through the sky. It explains as well why a policy of having parachutes available in case of accident or technical failure has from the days of the Wright brothers to today been a critical safety measure.

From a Newtonian viewpoint, airplanes are gravity defying machines. Following Newton, mandatory wearing of parachutes is a sensible policy derived from the theory tested and confirmed by Newton's work establishing the law of gravity. Moving beyond Newton to the wider world of theories in the world of the hard sciences, and not forgetting the usefulness of work in 'basic theory,' we may say that at the end of the day a major contribution of theoretical explanations of various phenomena is the tremendous expansion of potentially useful interventionist policies to mitigate the worst aspects of human existence on this planet. Theories have led to policies and instruments to overcome too high temperature, too low temperature, too much humidity, too little or too much rain, etc. After we account for basic theory we may say that the overwhelming function of theory in the world is to enhance comprehension; to assist in improving the comfort, convenience, safety, and productivity of life for humankind on this planet. In most other fields, the discipline's major students are profoundly *NOT* laissez faire. (We pass over without comment the implicit assumption of most human research that the world is and ought to be human-centered.)

In similar vein there are many sensible policies which are derived from insights gleaned from application of the scientific method in the hard sciences: the pasteurization of milk, the vaccination of children against various diseases, the posting of weight limits on bridges, the establishment of structural minima in building construction, the wearing of safety goggles or ear plugs or hard hats in certain kinds of work setting etc. – all these are but the tip of the iceberg of what hard science theorizing has brought to modern human life on the planet. Only in economics, seemingly, is non-intervention raised to a high moral level – and this by 'positive' economists who profess to eschew the use of 'ought' ever!!

Is the scientific method literally applicable in similar fashion to economics? This is the subject for debate in the next section. The short answer is that either this is a complicated question or, perhaps more on target, it is the wrong question.

APPLYING THE SCIENTIFIC METHOD TO ECONOMICS: THE KEYNESIAN CHALLENGE AND THE MAINSTREAM RESPONSE

Having considered what constituted proof for a theory in Newton's world, the obvious question is, what constitutes proof for economists? We have seen that Newton's approach had a directness which attracts in part because it appeals to recursive efforts at corroboration. Scientists with widely differing views and widely differing standards can nonetheless all be impressed by the results of efforts to test the law of gravity. No one has ever observed an item of weight leaving a tree and falling away from the ground. This in time becomes pretty overpowering corroboration of the hypothesis advanced by Newton.

Graduate students in economics all learn about the tenets of the scientific method. They all learn about marshaling facts, stating clearly what they have done and enabling others to replicate their work. Nonetheless there is very much room for asking, 'What is it that economists accept as "proof" of any particular theory?' What makes evidence convincing for them? How can theorists with opposing views ascertain which of competing theories is 'correct'?

We shall concentrate here on theory in macroeconomics because this has been the principal arena for disagreement and controversy in recent years. We shall in later chapters consider problems in microeconomics. It should be clear from the discussion of Smith in Chapter 1 that concern about direction and perspective in modern mainstream economics is by no means a thrust which excludes microeconomic issues.

However, the basic approach long taken in microeconomics has centered on the use of ceteris paribus assumptions. Hence appeal to reality has long since been replaced by appeal to order, relative simplicity, elegance, and precision. Appeal to these characteristics has in microeconomics been its own justification. In this world 'proof' was self-evident – if a theory had precision, beauty, internal logic, and elegance, it did not require proof via a 'reality check.' Hence, the door was open to one charge against microeconomic theory which could not be made against macroeconomic theory. John R. Hicks put it bluntly: 'There is much economic theory which is pursued for no better reason than its intellectual attraction; it is a good game' (Hicks 1979, p. vii).

Game or not, by the last half of the 20th century the failure of microeconomic theory to explain the real world had long since ceased to interest mainstream economists. It had a role as 'benchmark theory' which circumvented any other need for justification and, therefore, was all the 'proof' that was required.

Modern macroeconomics from the start (1930s) was judged in terms of usefulness. Keynes's theory was developed at the same time that Simon Kuznets developed national income accounting. Measuring macroeconomic magnitudes in the 'real' world was present virtually from the introduction of the theory. Keynes we shall see induced great discomfort in economists by suggesting that the macro economy was profoundly flawed. Such explanations as we had could not explain the flaws, and the need for overcoming this state of affairs to develop effective interventionist policy was by the 1930s overpoweringly self-evident. If the mainstream felt that the micro economy really was self-regulating no one then argued this for the macro economy.

Accordingly, we turn to the macroeconomic controversies of the past 70 years in order to inquire in that area what constitutes convincing proof among conflicting theories.

What Constitutes Proof? Three Macroeconomic Theories

Some years ago Friedman suggested there were at least two approaches to proof in economic research

> . . . [an approach will] start with a collection of numerical data bearing on the question under study, subject them to sophisticated econometric techniques, place great reliance on tests of significance, and end with a single hypothesis (equation), however complex
>
> . . . Another way is to examine a wide variety of evidence, quantitative and nonquantitative, bearing on the question under study; test results from one body of evidence on other bodies, using econometric techniques as one tool in this process, and build up a collection of simple hypotheses . . . and finally, test hypotheses on bodies of data other than those from which they were derived. Both ways – and no doubt still others as well – have their use. None, we believe, can be relied on exclusively. (Friedman and Schwartz 1991, p. 39)

Here we shall examine this question by looking at the work of three economists who are taken seriously, John Maynard Keynes, Milton Friedman, and Robert Lucas. One is hard pressed to find three economists more different. All attract fierce supporters and equally fierce critics. Each has had an empirical obstacle to face: Keynes's theory 'cannot explain the stagflation of the 1970s;' Friedman's assumption of stable velocity is brought into question by the instability of velocity in the 1980s; and Lucas's assumption of instantaneous market clearing has a bit of difficulty with the failure of the labor market in the United States to clear for 12 years (1929–1941). None of these matters seems to faze a dedicated adherent to one of these three positions, but they all serve as major avenues of attack for those who disagree with one of these approaches.

Was Friedman surprised with his conclusion concerning the relationship of changes in the money supply and subsequent changes in economic activity? We shall see that the conclusions here did emanate from the examination of empirical evidence. Part of the dispute about monetarism, therefore, concerns the reading of the evidence.

Friedman and Lucas are fierce critics of Keynes and, had he lived, Keynes would probably have been an equally fierce critic of the other two. Friedman and Lucas have not criticized each other extensively although their theories come to quite different conclusions. (The work of either is not fundamentally threatening to the other.) At the end we shall be forced to conclude that the force of logic is only part of a successful effort at 'proving' a theory is credible. We add only that here we shall present no more of each theory than is required to discuss credibility, leaving it to later chapters to consider the theories in greater detail.

Keynesian Theory – Proof and Truth

The great debates about macroeconomic theory today still emanate from the dissension produced by Keynes. That being the case, it is well to begin by recalling that Keynes's theory concerning the determinants of the aggregate equilibrium level of income, output, and employment were an outgrowth of his explicit rejection of the classical theory. An early exposition was L.R. Klein's *Keynesian Revolution* (Klein 1946 and 1961). Recall how Keynes began his *General Theory*:

> I shall argue that the postulates of the classical theory are applicable to a special case only and not to the general case, the situation which it assumes being a limiting point of the possible positions of equilibrium. Moreover, the characteristics of the special case assumed by the classical theory happen not to be those of the economic society in which we actually live, with the result that its teaching is misleading and disastrous if we attempt to apply it to the facts of experience. (Keynes 1936, p. 3)

Keynes is, of course, suggesting that it is pure fluke if aggregate demand equals aggregate supply at the level of income which corresponds to full use of available resources. Keynes's conclusion for the 1930s involved what he called 'underemployment equilibrium' – a state of affairs in which aggregate demand equaled aggregate supply but at a level far below what would prevail were all the available human and non-human resources employed.[7] Underemployment was, therefore, the result of inadequate aggregate demand.

7. Keynes had a straightforward definition of 'under-employment of labour,' '. . . there are men unemployed who would be willing to work at less than the existing real wage' (Keynes 1936, p. 289).

Accordingly the critical aspects of Keynes's theory involved the determinants of aggregate demand. In the end these include household consumption, the determinants of private investment (the marginal efficiency of investment and the interest rate), and government expenditures. These variables accordingly provide an agenda for empirical investigation attempting to prove or disprove Keynes's theory or parts of it. There have been many empirical studies of consumption. The seminal study was Milton Friedman's, *A Theory of the Consumption Function* (Friedman 1957). It initiated a debate about whether the average and the marginal propensity to consume are the same. That is, does the savings rate change over time? The answer (proof of one or another view of this) was sought in survey data, household budget studies, etc. Friedman introduced a complicated aspect of this discussion by questioning whether consumption was more a function of current income ('transitory income') or what he called 'permanent income.'[8]

There have been numerous studies of the relationship between changes in interest and changes in investment. These involve estimating profit expectations; discount rates, capital costs, risk factors, etc. There is a vast literature on these factors.[9] Government expenditures also depend on a diverse set of determinants but in the end the rate of expenditures per period is a known quantity.

It seems clear, therefore, that there has been no dearth of data with which to test Keynes's theory. At least in the case of Keynes, disagreement has not arisen because he based his theory on assumptions upon which empirical verification cast doubt. This is illustrated by noting that Friedman, a major economist who rejected the *General Theory* as an accurate depiction of how market economies operated, did not object to Keynes's formulation of the consumption function. As noted above, he chose only to refine it in greater detail in his well known book (Friedman 1957).

What then are the major bases for criticism of Keynes and his *General Theory*?

Criticism of Keynesianism

Keynes was supporting his theory of unemployment by appeals both to 'the facts' and to logic. We have seen that certainly parts of Keynes's theory can be empirically checked (the consumption function is an obvious case). But much of it rests on acceptance of a chain of logical relationships which may or may not accurately reflect the way the real economy works. The relationships

8. Cf. Mayer (1972) and Darby (1974).
9. E.g., Eisner and Strotz (1964) and Jorgenson (1963).

involved in his 'indirect' link between changes in the money supply and changes in aggregative economic activity can reflect diverse degrees of sensitivity. Keynes assumed one set of sensitivities; monetarists and others have assumed different degrees of sensitivity. The historical record need not support one position consistently. It is true that Keynes's theory could not by itself explain the stagflation of the 1970s. Robert Gordon asserts, 'The old Keynesian theory based on rigid nominal wages had little to say about inflation' (Gordon 2000, p. 548). Inflation was not a problem in the 1930s but Keynesian theory as originally presented was symmetrically capable of explaining both an 'inflationary gap' and a 'deflationary gap.'[10] Keynes' purpose was not directly to explain inflation but to explain why market economies suffered recurring crises and recessions. His 1930s explanation focused on aggregate demand and its recurring tendency to be inadequate. Since his explanation revolved around total expenditures, prices were not stressed. Because his theory focused on aggregate demand does not mean that exogenous events (e.g., OPEC actions) could not destabilize the economy from the supply side. The OPEC quadrupling of oil prices in 1973–74 is given considerable weight in most of the explanations of the price increases and the stagflation of the 1970s in which they figured. I have never understood why this necessarily vitiated Keynes's theory.[11]

To this day there is debate about whether Keynes could get the conclusions he got without assuming 'sticky wages and prices.' The belief that he could not was presumably a major reason that the rational expectations approach has so many adherents. A major line of attack on Keynes revolves critically around this assumption. Many critics have argued that without this assumption Keynes could not have viewed unemployment in the way he does. Very early in the

10. Thus early Keynesians by no means ignored inflation in spite of the prevailing deflation of the period. For example, Alvin Hansen, the leading early American exponent of Keynes, wrote, 'In the absence of private investment outlets adequate to produce full employment, the governmental expenditures could be controlled so as to prevent inflation' (Hansen 1941, p. 178). Dudley Dillard, who wrote the first widely used book explaining Keynesian theory for American students, wrote: '[a] 'general' aspect of the general theory is that it explains inflation as readily as it does unemployment since both are primarily a matter of the volume of effective demand. When demand is deficient, unemployment results and when demand is excessive, inflation results' (Dillard 1948, p. 4). Note that there is no mention of rigid wages.

11. Subsequently later formulations of Keynes (i.e., the AS-AD approach) showed explicitly the role of prices. Oddly, one common explanation for stagflation stressed the manner in which increases in aggregate demand derived from a spending increase or a tax increase, accompanied by a commensurate reduction in private spending. In this case the spending decrease did not result fully in price decreases, but was accompanied by an employment reduction. In this case, the very price stickiness which was one of the factors used presumably to explain underemployment equilibrium could also explain in part stagflation.

General Theory Keynes asks whether unemployment is voluntary or not, and answers

> . . . the contention that the unemployment which characterizes a depression is due to a refusal by labour to accept a reduction of money wages is not clearly supported by the facts. It is not very plausible to assert that unemployment in the United States in 1932 was due either to labor obstinately refusing to accept a reduction of money-wages or to its obstinately demanding a real wage beyond the productivity the economic machine was capable of furnishing. (Keynes 1936, p. 9)

(This is the origin of the 'sticky wage' assumption. Arguably all that need be involved is a failure of labor to be totally mobile.)

Robert Lucas's criticism of Keynes begins by an attempt to refute Keynes's assertion in the quotation above:

> I suspect that the unwillingness to speak of workers in recession as enjoying 'leisure' is more a testimony to the force of Keynes' insistence that unemployment is 'involuntary' than a response to observed phenomena. One doesn't want to suggest that people like depressions! Of course, the hypothesis of a cleared labor market carries no such suggestion, any more than the observation that people go hungry in cleared food markets suggests people enjoy hunger. (Lucas 1981, p. 226)

Lost in the shuffle was one significant question, whether or not sticky wages produce less than ideal results – could it not in fact be true that in the real world wages and many prices are sticky and are likely to remain so? If so, Keynes's arguments remain relevant.

Kevin Hoover has noted that for Lucas involuntary unemployment is caused by a worker charging more than the equilibrium wage (having a higher 'reservation wage' than all 'offer wages'). For Keynes a worker is unemployed when wages paid others *exceed* his reservation wage. Hoover concludes: 'It is not Keynes who has engaged in word-play, but Lucas who, from having paid insufficient attention to Keynes's words, has, misconstrued their clear meaning' (Hoover 1988, pp. 60–1).

For new classical economists proof that 'Keynes was wrong' had tremendous policy implications. Depression as the result of inadequate aggregate demand in the market represented a 'market failure' of enormous significance. Kenneth Galbraith has written of Keynes's diagnosis of the cause of depression,

> With the diagnosis came the cure. No longer could governments wait for self-correcting forces to provide a remedy; the underemployment equilibrium could be stable and persistent. No longer could they wait for unemployment to bring down

> wages; that could lead to equilibrium at a lower level of output and employment. Low interest rates could not be counted on to increase investment and investment spending; perhaps they only reenforced liquidity preference.
>
> There remained one – just one course. That was government intervention to raise the level of investment spending – government borrowing and spending for public purposes. A deliberate deficit. (Galbraith 1987, pp. 234–5)

Here precisely was the point. If the whole Keynesian analysis could be 'proven' to rest on an assumption of sticky wages and prices all these dire consequences could be avoided – most particularly a rational justification for government intervention as the only possible way to improve economic performance. Arguably it was these implications of Keynes's theory that upset people like Lucas quite as much as the theory itself. Therefore, Lucas concludes: 'The onset of the Great Depression did nothing to improve Keynes's equipment for understanding the business cycle, viewed as a recurrent sequence of booms and depressions' (Lucas 1981, pp. 275–6). His final blast, Keynes possibly had some not inaccurate remarks about the difficulty of operating in an uncertain world, but,

> Certainly the likely central role of profit expectations and investment behavior was stressed by virtually every economist who devoted more than superficial thought to business cycles. Economists who find Keynes's style congenial will continue to use his writings as Dennis Robertson did Lewis Carroll's, but surely there is more to the cumulative nature of economics than this. (Lucas 1981, p. 276)

Kenneth Galbraith has reminded us of the ominous significance of Keynes 'underemployment equilibrium' for the laissez-faire views of mainstream economists. The classical position requires that the government play no role. But he quotes Hayek (a quintessential conservative mainstream economist), who wrote, 'The price system will fulfill [its] . . . function only if competition prevails, that is, if the individual producer has to adapt himself to price changes and cannot control them' (Lucas 1981, p. 250). (One wonders how Hayek reacted to, say, public utility regulation.) We suggest, therefore, that Hayek was observing that 'the micro-foundations of macroeconomics' have far wider implications than the mainstream usually contemplates. Without a competitive micro-economy the mainstream assumptions about the economy – micro or macro – cannot operate.

The burden with which Keynes saddled mainstream economists was a rational – even inevitable – necessary role for the federal government. How could that inevitability be demolished? That was what the classical economists searched for from 1936 on and it is what the Lucas followers thought they had finally found. The debate about sticky prices was simply the latest form of a very old debate: is a market economy reliably self-regulating? The attitude toward interventionism is, in the end, a matter of basic value premises.

Lucas, we have seen, has raised the question whether the Great Depression was significantly to be characterized as the result of sticky wages. The 'observed phenomena' which Lucas dismisses so cavalierly, of course, included the statistical fact that in 1932, 25 per cent of the United States labor force was unemployed. No one seriously suggested that the statistics were inaccurate and no one suggested that workers preferred leisure. What Lucas was really implicitly pointing to is the irrelevance of equilibrium to assessing the degree to which any economy is contributing automatically to optimal human existence as the participants in the economy view things currently. It is this perception which distinguishes Keynesian from new classical economists. For a Keynesian, as for heterodox economists generally, equilibria are at best measurements useful in assessing where economies are but not instruments for measuring success in economic activity at a point in time or progress in achieving ideal resource use over time.

Virtually from the outset heterodox economists have criticized the excessive mainstream preoccupation with equilibrium (see Chapter 8). New classical economists in attacking Keynes have arguably outdone their classical predecessors. The emphasis on 'cleared markets' has become the focus in some quarters of a full frontal attack on Keynes. Nowhere is this made clearer than in the macroeconomics text by Robert J. Barro. At the very beginning Barro proclaims:

> Macroeconomics is in a state of flux. The Keynesian model, which was almost universally accepted as the basic paradigm until the late 1960s, has become increasingly less popular. This loss in popularity reflects embarrassment over past economic events, especially the failure of the model to deal satisfactorily with inflation and supply shocks. It also reflects the theoretical and empirical progress of an alternative 'market-clearing approach,' which is more closely related to the macroeconomics that economists use successfully to study the behavior of individual households and businesses. Although some important problems remain, this approach provides a much more satisfactory macroeconomics than the one we had before. By more satisfactory, I mean that the approach avoids internal inconsistencies and also provides a better understanding of the real world. (Barro 1990, p. vii)

The question we ask is, what is being used as 'proof' of the weaknesses in Keynes, severe enough to justify abandoning the central thrust of his analysis, and what is being offered as 'proof' of the alternative model offered? One may quibble about the degree to which the Keynesian model has been supplanted (indeed, in the years since 1984 the pendulum may arguably have swung back somewhat toward a modernized Keynesian theory). The progress of the 'market-clearing approach' has at least been somewhat bumpy in the past 20 years. The main point to note, however, is that Barro suggests theory should be judged by whether or not it gives a 'better understanding of the real world.' Presumably this means that theory should be tested by its ability to explain the real world, that is, by its ability to account for observed factual consequences. But differences arise because of disputes about the facts. Keynes thought that 'the facts' do not support the notion that workers choose voluntarily not to work in depression. This was, of course, the standard of proof suggested by Keynes. (Many of Barro's colleagues would, as we have noted elsewhere, argue that the task of theory is only to explain 'stylized facts'.)

Because Lucas is wed to the traditional definition of a supply curve for labor, that is, he insists that workers choose not to work in depression – they 'must prefer leisure.' How far must one stretch in economics to conclude with unflinching tranquility that the system can work normally and acceptably in such a way that the market can exhibit an equilibrium wage in which nonetheless many workers are deeply dissatisfied and deeply unhappy? Would Lucas be similarly unmoved by equilibria at which many firms exhibited zero (or negative!) profits? A lottery can produce 'equilibrium' (clear the market) in the sense that the number of people holding winning numbers (demanders) equals the number who win (suppliers); it may be one and one. But this tells little about whether a lottery is the ideal way to deploy goods and services among households. We argue, in short, that the argument about sticky wages and prices is largely misplaced. Only by turning economics into a Talmudic pastime can one conjure up a 'stable equilibrium' complete with unhappy workers who, notwithstanding, are voluntarily unemployed. We implied above that all appear to agree that if large numbers of entrepreneurs are unhappy with their (equilibrium) profit rates the system is not working acceptably. The real debate should be about the degree to which unregulated market clearing in markets without societal monitoring is an ideal vehicle for deploying all resources (especially human resources!). Whether or not a given market is in equilibrium – even when expanded to mean 'general equilibrium' – is far less important than whether or not the participants in that market are 'happy,' by which we mean are satisfied that the market is operating in such a way as optimally to enhance their lives. Walras and Dr Pangloss were not on the same wavelength! Whatever one thinks of Dr Pangloss, Walras, in ascertaining the conditions under which all individual markets might clear, was not assessing the truly significant normative yardstick by which the activity ascribed to economies is judged, despite the protestations of Robert Lucas to the contrary.

In the end, the debate about Keynes suggests that the degree to which theory in economics is persuasive depends on the degree to which the tests of persuasiveness are converted into a very selective appeal to facts.[12]

Monetarism – Proof and Truth

Keynesian theory is not the only macroeconomic theory to be challenged. Monetarism has been the subject of a long and often bitter debate. At its peak it was regarded as a viable contender for the place long held by Keynesian theory. One student wrote, 'Keynesianism is defunct. In its place is monetarism, a modern version of the Quantity Theory . . .' (Steele 1989, p. 127).

We shall not try to replicate the debate about monetarism here. We shall instead ask, to what extent has the debate about monetarism been a debate about 'proof' in an empirical sense, or proof in a logical sense, and to what extent has it, like the debate about Keynes, often masked the true debate, which has been about value premises in general and often explicitly about the appropriate role (if any) for interventionism to play in macroeconomic policy?

Some years ago Thomas Mayer, a leading student of monetarism, noted that monetarism was not as monolithic as Keynesianism – it has no *General Theory* (Mayer 1978, p. 1). It may not be monolithic but it is surely associated preeminently with the name of Milton Friedman (doubtless modern monetarists have differing views on a number of issues). Moreover, as Mayer himself notes, he associates Keynesian theory with the views of Duesenberry, Modigliani, Samuelson, and Tobin (Mayer 1978, p. 2). Thus if monetarism is not monolithic neither is Keynesianism.

Mayer notes that there is no authoritative list of Keynesian propositions. He has however attempted a list of monetarism propositions. It provides a good place to start a discussion of monetarism and the possibilities of proof in evaluating theories.

Mayer's list includes:

1. The quantity theory of money, in the sense of the predominance of the impact of monetary factors on nominal income.
2. The monetarist model of the transmission process.
3. Belief in the inherent stability of the private sector.

---

12. Long after this section was written I came across a doubtlessly jocular comment by Mark Blaug. 'The last twenty years have seen an unending series of efforts to produce a decisive empirical test of the Keynesian and the monetarist view of the causes of economic fluctuations. A detached observer might be forgiven for thinking that this discussion has proved nothing but that empirical evidence is apparently incapable of making any economist change his mind' (Blaug 1992, pp. 192–3).

4. Irrelevance of allocative detail for the explanation of short–run changes in money income, and belief in a fluid capital market.
5. Focus on the price level as a whole rather than on individual prices.
6. Reliance on small rather than large econometric models.
7. Use of the reserve base or similar measure as the indicator of monetary policy.
8. Use of the money stock as the proper target of monetary policy.
9. Acceptance of the monetary growth rule.
10. Rejection of an unemployment-inflation trade-off in favor of a real Phillips Curve.
11. A relatively greater concern about inflation than about unemployment compared to other economists.
12. Dislike of government intervention. (1978, p. 2)

We may take this as a reasonably acceptable listing of the essential tenets of monetarism.[13] Seemingly, there is no serious dissent from the list among contributors to the book except to note that monetarists are not monolithic. Different monetarists would assign different weights to Mayer's 12 characteristics. There is reasonable consensus among Mayer's collaborators that the list does an acceptable job of including the factors most monetarists regard as crucial.[14]

Mayer makes it clear that this is an inclusive list derived from the views of a number of diverse economists. The first characteristic obviously derives from the Friedman perspective (commented on below). He obviously has done very much empirical investigation seeking to show the causal role of monetary changes in affecting other economic activity. Taken as a whole we may conclude that many of these characteristics are not directly capable of clear, let alone definitive, empirical investigation. The last is the clearest case exemplifying our contention that monetarism is as much a matter of ideology as of empirically testable hypotheses. After all is said and done, the debate about monetarism has endured for much of the post Keynesian era without either a victory or capitulation. It would be a stretch to say, therefore, that there is a discernible 'proof' to which one can turn in accepting or rejecting their position.

Milton Friedman's seminal modern monetarism is an effort to restore the 'direct link' between the money supply and aggregate economic activity which

---

13. Mayer lists them at the beginning of a book of essays on monetarism which he edited. The book includes contributions by eight prominent economists (prominent monetarists or experts on what monetarism encompasses).

14. The economists in Mayer's volume include: Martin Bronfenbrenner, Karl Brunner, Philip Cagan, Benjamin Friedman, Helmut Frisch, Harry Johnson, David L. Laidler, and Allan Meltzer.

monetarists emphasized before Keynes. In the end his monetarism espouses a 'simple monetary rule' which suggests that the monetary authorities should concentrate on maintaining a stable rate of growth for the money supply based on the estimated real growth rate for the economy. Recently, however, Friedman has written, 'In 1988 I wrote, "No major institution in the U.S. has so poor a record of performance over so long a period as the Federal Reserve" . . . that judgement . . . is amply justified for the first seven decades or so of the Fed's existence . . . it is not valid for the period since' (Friedman 2003). Whether this means that he has changed his long standing view (discussed here) that application of his 'simple monetary rule' is preferable to any interventionist stabilization policy, he does not say. Other strains to his theory involve distrust of the central bank's ability to use discretionary policy with any success and ultimately considerable faith in the ability of the free market to regulate itself reasonably well. Here 'reasonably' means with greater success than would probably accompany any discretionary efforts by government and/or banking agents.[15]

Criticisms of Monetarism

We can vividly illustrate the question posed in the title of this chapter (do we get the theory we want or want the theory we get?) with the evidence frequently marshaled to assess monetarism. The stability of velocity, assumed by monetarists, is widely debated. As we have all learned, Friedman's 'simple monetary rule' is derived from the quantity theory of money which in turn is an outgrowth of the equation of exchange, $MV = PQ$. Classical economists assumed that the quantity of real output (Q) grew only slowly, that P (Price) was passive which meant that price changes were the result and never the cause of what happened to the other variables, and that V (Velocity) was constant. In order to argue that changes in the money supply determined the changes in prices ($\Delta M = \Delta PQ/V$) it is essential to be able to assume that (V) is unchanged. It is a cardinal assumption of monetarism. We have noted earlier that many economists regarded the 1980s as a period that failed to support Friedman's theory. It has become a matter of some importance, therefore, particularly as Friedman himself has insisted that a crucial test for any theory is to test it with

15. While Friedman's views can be found in a long list of books and articles, his basic monetary theories, as well as his efforts at empirical demonstration of these theories can be found in Friedman and Schwartz (1963 and 1970).

data for a different period than the period used to develop the theory originally.[16]

The stability of velocity is questioned by Keynesians and by Keynes himself, in *The General Theory*. He distinguishes three different motives for holding cash, and concludes, 'The strength of all three types of motive partly depend on the cheapness and the reliability of methods of obtaining cash . . .' (Keynes 1936, p. 196). That is to say velocity for Keynes was at least partly a function of interest rates.

Samuelson also makes the point that the stability of velocity is severely undermined by a key notion of rational expectation adherent Robert Lucas which has become known as the Lucas Critique. The breakdown of the stability of velocity in the 1980s came partly in response to the shift in monetary policy in accord with prevailing monetarist thought. During the 'monetarist experiment' the Fed focused on stabilizing the money supply growth directly instead of focusing on interest rates. This supported the Lucas Critique which argues that economic agents modify their behavior in response to policy shifts (cf. Samuelson and Nordhaus 2001, pp. 378–9).

As the formula given above makes evident, calculating velocity for any period is surpassingly easy to do – simply divide nominal GDP by M. A constant velocity is as close to 'proof' as one gets in testing theory against the 'real world' in economics. With all this in mind, we may assert that a comparison of Figure 2.1 and Figure 2.2 tells us Mankiw makes velocity appear very stable; Samuelson makes it look much less stable. In short how you present velocity is crucial!

Figure 2.2 is from the Samuelson-Nordhaus (2001) well known text. Samuelson, known as a Keynesian, after stating that 'one of the tenets of monetarism is that V is relatively stable and predictable,' offers the figure and asks the student, 'Can you think of some reasons why V has grown over time? Hint: How do interest rates affect velocity?' (Samuelson and Nordhaus 2001, p. 715). Clearly Figure 2.2 as presented shows how the stability of velocity broke down after 1980. In contrast, consider the picture presented in Figure 2.1. This is from the recent *Principles* text by N. Gregory Mankiw, hailed as the first post-Keynesian text which reflects the new classical viewpoint. Mankiw concludes on the basis of his evidence in Figure 2.1, 'nominal GDP and the quantity of money have grown dramatically over this period, while velocity has been relatively stable' (Mankiw 1998, p. 617). Indeed velocity for the 20 years

16. '. . . any hypothesis must be tested with data or non-quantitative evidence other than that used in deriving the regression or available when the regression was derived' (Friedman and Schwartz 1991, p. 49).

following 1980 in Mankiw's rendition bears no relation to Samuelson's! It is not hard to find the reasons. The scales are radically different, as are the time periods. Even more important Samuelson relies on *M*1 – 'transactions money' consisting of coins, paper and demand deposits, while Mankiw uses *M*2 which consists of *M*1 plus some 'near monies' (savings, money market funds, etc.). In his original formulation of the principle involved, Friedman did not specify what money he had in mind. Said Friedman in support of his 'direct link' view,

> I know of no severe depression in any country or any time that was not accompanied by a sharp decline in the stock of money and equally no sharp decline in the stock of money that was not accompanied by a severe depression. (Friedman and Schwartz 1963, p. 50. Quoted in Lucas 1981, p. 257)

Were we to search for a monetary category that exhibited unstable velocity it would be an example of what has been called 'ex post theorizing' and therefore not allowed. The term was recently introduced:

> The demand for money defined in any particular way exhibits more instability than Friedman claimed . . . While it is possible to redefine the monetary aggregate to improve the statistical evidence for the new quantity theory of prices, this path opens up potential criticism of ex post theorizing, that is, choosing the definition of monetary aggregate to save the theory in its confrontation with evidence. (Foley 1987)

While clearly Mankiw shows velocity with all the stability that Friedman could wish for, the question is at least raised whether this is an example of 'ex post theorizing.'

There is, therefore, a bottom line of sorts: Samuelson ends up with a diagram which shows instability in velocity, a finding which is consonant with his skepticism about monetarism. Mankiw ends up showing stable velocity, a finding which is consonant with his relatively benign attitude toward monetarism. Thus each ends with the theory they 'want.' We raise the question whether this is an aberrant case, or could it be fairly typical of how theory is judged in our discipline?

Mayer's list reminds us of the long dispute about whether the link between the money supply and aggregate economic activity is a direct or an indirect link. The transmission process is an area which has been extensively subjected to efforts at empirical verification. At the end of empirical investigation of whether changes in the money supply lead or lag changes in economic activity we can read with endless repetition that correlation is not the same thing as causation, but in Figure 2.1, the matter is scarcely resolved. The conclusion hinges partly on the elasticity or inelasticity of the functions involved in an indirect

Figure 2.1 Mankiw – velocity of money

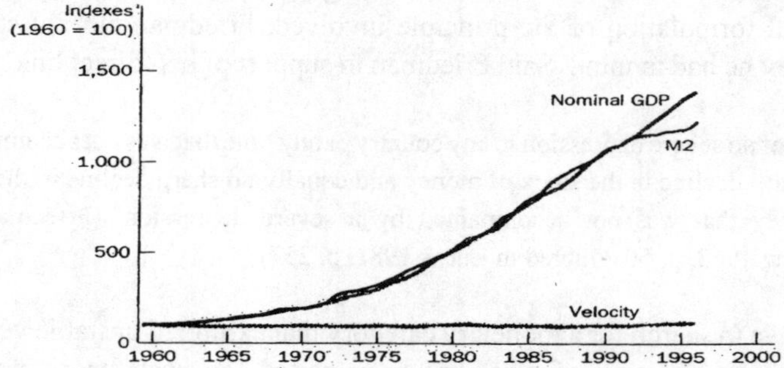

Source: Mankiw (2004), p. 654.

Figure 2.2 Samuelson – velocity of money

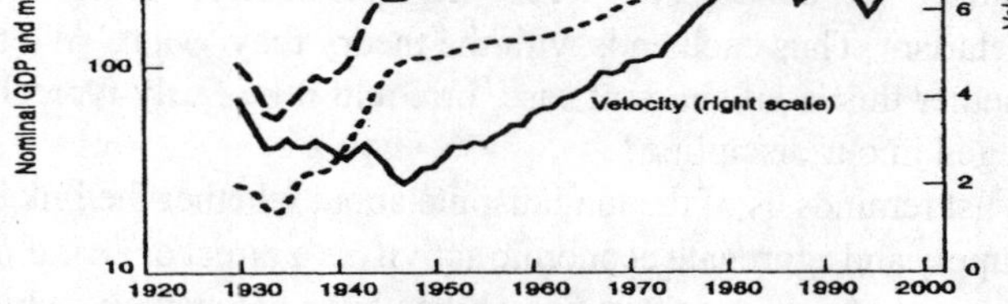

Source: Samuelson and Nordhaus (2001), p. 715.

transmission process. Despite much effort of empirical investigation, the results have, to my knowledge, never been presented in so convincing a manner as to persuade either side that they are in error. Again, Newton 'proving' the law of gravity had it easy.

Many of the other characteristics are simply not possibly subject to empirical verification procedures. In the end Mayer reminds us that it may well be that the difference between monetarists and Keynesians is less about factors subject to empirical verification and more about the value system with which one approaches the study of economic activity. Thus, belief in the inherent stability of the private sector is indeed, as Mayer reminds us, a major characteristic of monetarism, and one not shared by Keynesians. There is no appeal to empirical facts to resolve this difference. (Neither denies or ignores the Great Depression as historical fact!) Just as individuals have varying pain thresholds so that there can be no agreement on what is severe pain, economists cannot agree on how much instability is intolerable, how much inflation is intolerable, or how much unemployment is intolerable. They cannot agree on how long a time comes within the definition of 'self-regulating within a reasonable length of time.'

We need not comment on each of Mayer's characteristics. The point to note is that many are not subject to empirical verification at all. This is most especially true for the last characteristic. Dislike of government intervention may be the most important characteristic of all. It is certainly true that Keynesians can accept (perhaps embrace is the better word) the notion of governmental intervention in order to achieve stable growth rates for the economy. Monetarists cannot. Certainly Friedman has concluded that the record of efforts by the Fed to stabilize the economy is so abysmal that he originally had no hope that it could learn from its own mistakes and do better in the future. The appeal here is to credibility, not empirical proof. Ironically, as we shall see, rational expectations adherents, who conclude that monetary policy is futile unless it is unexpected, probably give the Fed more credit for having rational expectations itself – that is, using all the information at its disposal to formulate monetary policy – than do the monetarists. It is the monetarists who conclude that monetary policy might be effective if applied correctly, but reject the notion that it will be applied effectively. Friedman has never forgiven nor forgotten the monetary policy measures applied during the worst years of the Great Depression. Whether the long expansion of the 1990s has changed his mind at all about the possibility of effective monetary policy he has, to our knowledge, only recently hinted at.

We conclude that while monetarists and Keynesian have never agreed about many matters where empirical proof is at least conceptually possible to obtain, their differences are even greater on those characteristics where such proof is not possible.

In the end the factors that separate some major groups of economic theorists today are not mainly matters of empirical fact, or even matters capable of being appealed to empirical fact. They reflect differences in values. For groups who regard economics as a positive field, to be differentiated from each other by normative matters is an irony worth contemplating. Lucas writes of Friedman with respect and not with the derision he heaps on Keynes. Lucas thinks Friedman's program of stabilization (the 'simple monetary rule') won't work. Lucas quotes Friedman's plan:

> I tried to design a framework that would be appropriate for a world in which cyclical movements other than those introduced by 'bad' monetary and fiscal arrangements, were of no consequence. I then examined the resulting proposal to see how it would behave in respect to cyclical fluctuations. It behaves surprisingly well. (Friedman 1948, 1953, p. 156)

And what does Lucas say about all this?

> The strategy, then, was to design a workable stabilization policy not dependent in any way on detailed knowledge of business cycle dynamics. The program would (I think there is no serious professional disagreement) *fully* protect the economy against sustained inflation. It would *fully* insure against the kind of monetary collapse which was so important a factor in the early stages in the Great Depression of the 1930s. It would entirely eliminate erratic monetary and fiscal shocks as independent sources of instability. Surely these are modest claims . . . In my view recent research has added little to strengthen Friedman's case, except in what might be called a negative way . . . . (Lucas 1981, p. 257)

John Kenneth Galbraith has commented on the monetarist core position – that changes in the money supply are the chief determinant of changes in the macro economy, most particularly prices. After noting the commonly mentioned problem of differentiating cause from effect and the failure of monetarism to explain how changes in the money supply have their impact on prices, Galbraith quotes Friedman to the effect that 'Various relationships in the field of nature and actual science . . . also held true even though they eluded explanation' (Galbraith 1987, p. 272).

Galbraith suggests a 'more grievous difficulty' – we can't clearly define money for the modern economy. It includes cash and demand deposits for sure, but what else? – savings deposits? Lines of credit? etc. (1987, p. 272).

This has led, of course, as was discussed earlier, to the endless debates about which of the various definitions of the money supply should be used in calculating velocity. There is a great temptation to use the one that (if one is monetarist) is most stable and (if one is not a monetarist) to use the one that is least stable. We have seen that this is precisely the kind of question which underscores the difficulty in determining proof in connection with economic theories. The temptation to settle on the definition that leads where one's values point exists partly because there is no clear positive (as opposed to normative) answer to the question, how should we define money? The inability to settle on a definition of money played into Friedman's hands, of course, because while he looked kindly on the quantity theory of money he never believed that the monetary authorities could manipulate the money supply successfully in a counter-cyclical manner. For his own reasons, therefore, he favored a 'simple monetary rule' rather than interventionist monetary policy.

Finally Galbraith suggests where these conflicts and debates can lead. Monetary policy is not 'socially neutral.' 'Monetarism would protect the microeconomic orthodoxy' (1987, p. 273). High interest rates are fine with people who have money to lend, comments Galbraith, 'In so favoring the individually and institutionally affluent, a restrictive monetary policy is in sharp contrast with a restrictive fiscal policy which, relying as it does on increased personal and corporate income taxes, adversely affects the rich' (1987, p. 273). Yet another voice, that of Mark Blaug, is found weighing in among the doubters. Says Blaug, '. . . there is a good deal of evidence that monetarism of the Friedmanite variety has had its day' (Blaug 1992, p. 1994).

Lastly, English economist Nicholas Kaldor has been highly critical of monetarism, arguing that counter-cyclical monetary policy should not focus on controlling the money supply but should instead try to manipulate interest rates so as to encourage stable growth rates. Moreover, despite Friedman's frequent assertions that the relationship between money and aggregate activity is one of the most stable of all economic relationships, Kaldor comments,

> I found most of his 'evidence' (particularly that of his book written with Anna Schwartz . . .) largely worthless or irrelevant. Moreover, I found that contrary to Friedman's frequent assertions, the demand for money as a proportion of incomes (i.e., the reciprocal of the velocity of circulation) is neither 'stable' between countries nor stable over time except in some countries. (Kaldor 1985, p. xviii)

He enumerates countries but the U.S. is not one he finds notable for the stability of velocity. As we have already seen, this relationship is one which ought to be subject to empirical proof, but on which there is by no means a consensus (Kaldor 1985, p. xviii).

Monetarism is especially interesting to consider in connection with the role of and character of proof in economic theory. There are more parts to monetarism that can be empirically tested than is true of many economic theories. This has not made it less controversial. We have seen that there is disagreement about the stability of velocity. Moreover, with Friedman's assertion that the stable relationship between changes in the money supply and changes in economic activity is subject to a 'long and variable lag' the door was open to ambiguity in how the empirical record was viewed. Hence, in the end, as we have said, monetarism is judged to be congenial or not by economists in terms of its value premises as much or more than it is judged by empirical testing (see Mayer's list above). While monetarism is included in any discussion of influential thought among macroeconomists, it is probably safe to say that it is less influential today than it was 30 or 40 years ago when it was widely viewed as the major (and perhaps only successful) group to challenge Keynesian dominance of the field. If its influence has been reduced it is because the proof offered has been less convincing or at least more controversial, as we have seen.

Rational Expectations – Proof and Truth

The last macroeconomic position we shall consider is provided by the rational expectations group. We have already introduced the subject because its adherents are anti-Keynes, and their vocal opposition to Keynes, we have seen, is relevant to discussions of Keynes. We turn now to a critique of this theoretical posture.

The rational expectations hypothesis was introduced by John F. Muth who stated that 'expectations, since they are informed predictions about future events, are essentially the same as the prediction of the relevant economic theory' (Muth 1961, pp. 315–335).

This means that economic agents use all the information available to them (they are 'rational' agents). The economic agent does not merely adjust his or her current forecast in light of changes which have occurred since the previous forecast; he or she always uses all the information to forecast tomorrow. Though introduced into economic discussions by John Muth, it was and is well known and popularized by Robert Lucas and his associates.

Some have argued that rational expectations is an extension of monetarism (though we have seen that they reach different conclusions).

That is, Friedman in his famous Presidential Address to the American Economics Association in 1967 is said to have introduced a view of how the market-oriented macro economy operated based on assumptions of (1) 'market clearing' and (2) imperfect information which produce instability (Friedman 1968). To this group Lucas et al. add a third assumption – the rational expectations hypothesis. (For a recent discussion of all this see Gordon 2000, pp. 548–55.)

As must be clear by now, much of what is called the rational expectations hypothesis consists of criticism of Keynesianism. Lucas does not disagree with the implications of Friedman's perspective, especially its long run implications. For the short run Friedman has long held that the monetary authorities will not manage monetary policy sufficiently well to improve things. Lucas does not necessarily disagree inasmuch as all economic agents are already using all information (including announced monetary actions). Whatever the monetary authorities do in the way of discretionary counter-cyclical action, therefore, will be largely futile, unless it takes the form of unexpected shocks.

Keynes, as noted earlier, is Lucas's principal bete noir. Lucas rejects the emphasis on inadequate demand as well as the focus on employment. Says Lucas about shooting for a target rate of employment – call it full employment: '. . . this way of posing the issue does not lead to an operational basis for unemployment policy, mainly on the ground that economists have no coherent idea as to what full employment means or how it can be measured' (Lucas 1981, p. 240).[17] Lucas goes on: 'Accepting the necessity of a distinction between explanations for normal and cyclical unemployment does not . . . compel one to identify the first as voluntary and the second as involuntary, as Keynes goes on to do' (1981, p. 241). Lucas insists this means the difference has to be one perceived by the workers. He finally concludes: 'In summary, it does not appear possible, even in principle, to classify individual unemployed people as either voluntarily or involuntarily unemployed depending on the characteristics of the decision problems they face. One cannot, even conceptually, arrive at a usable definition of full

---

17. Among those who seemingly had no difficulty defining 'full employment' and who clearly understood about frictional unemployment, was William Beveridge. 'Full employment in this report means . . . having always more vacant jobs than unemployed men, not slightly fewer jobs. It means that the jobs are at fair wages, of such kind, and so located that the unemployed men can reasonably be expected to take them, it means, by consequence, that the normal lag between losing one job and finding another will be very short' (Beveridge 1945, p. 18). Defining full employment in common sense terms (an approach that modern economists often forego for precise elegant econometric formulations) can often lead to useful policy, or so we used to think.

employment as a state in which no involuntary unemployment exists' (1981, p. 243).

Note where this leaves Lucas. There are seemingly no parallel problems about defining or measuring 'sustained inflation.' One might distinguish, say, between prices that start rising when there is still unused capacity from inflation that occurs only when capacity is 'fully utilized.' But these niceties don't bother Lucas. One could distinguish 'cost-push' inflation from inflation produced via inordinate growth in the money supply. One might ask exactly what is meant by 'fully protected' against inflation as opposed to some sort of partial protection. One might ask what is meant by 'full protection' against monetary collapse. It is clear that strong and absolutist language holds no particular peril for Lucas except when it comes to defining, measuring, or attempting to affect policy to cope with people who would like to work and cannot find work. In short, a priori it would seem one could ask as many questions about the clarity, comprehensibility, measurability etc. of 'inflation' as one could about 'unemployment.' It is not usually done.

Doubtless there were thousands who perceived themselves unemployed in the 1930s but Lucas is unpersuaded. He heaps scorn on the Employment Act of 1946 and his pen, dripping with considerable vitriol (especially for a positive economist), adds:

> It would be a difficult and subtle task to trace the effects of the Employment Act on the policy performance of the U.S. government in the postwar years. There is nothing subtle, however, in the effects of the act . . . on the practice of monetary economics in the postwar period. Renamed macroeconomics, this subdiscipline defined itself to be that body of expertise the existence of which was presupposed in the Employment Act, and its practitioners devoted themselves to the development and refinement of forecasting and policy evaluation methods which promised to be of use in the annual diagnosis-prescription exercise called for by the act. (Lucas 1981, p. 250)

In the end Lucas comments,

> As an advice-giving profession we are in way over our heads. The Employment Act of 1946 placed heavy demands on the ability of economists to guide executive authority granted very broad powers. In the early postwar years, and even through the sixties, it appeared that the framework provided by Keynesian theory of income determination was, intelligently applied, capable of meeting these demands. As confidence has ebbed in our ability to use general monetary and fiscal policy to carry out the aims of the Employment Act, professional and nonprofessionals alike have turned to a wide variety of complex, selective

> interventions in individual markets. Even to begin to assess the likely consequences of these policies in anything like a scientific way is clearly well beyond the current limits of our discipline. (1981, p. 259)

Lucas wrote these words in 1980, well before the 'longest peacetime expansion' in the nation's history. With the opening of the new millennium it was by no means clear that monetary policy had been so abysmal during the previous decade, and the reappearance of budgetary surpluses albeit only briefly suggested that fiscal policy could conceivably in time make a comeback as a feasible addition to stabilization measures. If the cycle was by no means obsolete, it gave signs of being tamer than it had been earlier and for longer periods of time. It was by no means obvious in the late 1990s, therefore, that, guided by Keynesian insights, economists were over their heads in reducing the worst manifestations of cyclical instability as Lucas had charged . . . Keynesian theory was at least as good a guide for public policy during the 1990s, say, as any alternative theory.

Oddly enough one of the improvements of the 1990s was the clear evidence that for long periods of time the economy could proceed with both unemployment (however difficult it may be to measure) and inflation well below dangerous levels. Among the notions conceivably becoming historical artifacts were the Phillips Curve and the natural rate of unemployment. The latter was going down, having gone up for some years (assuming it exists at all) and the former seemed increasingly ephemeral in both its short run and its long run incarnations.

Where does this leave our concern with what constitutes proof in economic theorizing? Clearly nothing that Friedman has done in analyzing business cycles and in assessing the role of the money supply in affecting them has disturbed Lucas nearly as much as what Keynes did in analyzing business cycles and in assessing their impact on the employment of labor.

Through rejecting customary definitions or erecting new barriers which old definitions need to overcome, economists like Lucas redefine for themselves standards of proof in empirical economics. The unemployment rates in the 1930s, previously regarded as proof of inadequate economic performance are redeployed to insignificant statistics via redefinition. This is surpassingly fortunate since they fly in the face of the customary rational expectations assumption of instantaneous market clearing. On the other hand no such difficulties arise in connection with the meaning of inflation in the 1970s which Keynesian theory was not well equipped to explain. (One could argue that no theory could be well equipped to explain exogenous events such as the OPEC actions. Exogenous versus endogenous causes of inflation is a refinement rational expectations theories seem not to focus on, but their devotion to the distinction between voluntary and involuntary unemployment is seemingly boundless.)

Lucas makes it clear that he is a great admirer of Mitchell. He likes Mitchell's characterization of business cycles; they exhibit 'conformity.' He likes the stress on the greater amplitude of the production of durables as opposed to non-durables. He approves of the notion that profits are highly conforming and have greater amplitude than other series. Concludes Lucas, 'Though there is absolutely no theoretical reason to anticipate it, one is led by the facts to conclude that, with respect to the qualitative behavior of co-movements among series, *business cycles are all alike*' (Lucas 1981, p. 218, italics in original). '. . . it is easy to forget the remarkable character of the regularities that Mitchell succeeded in discovering and documenting . . . we have lived with them so long that they are simply "facts" which "everyone knows"' (1981, p. 274).

We have seen that the proof of the correctness of a theory for Lucas is derived from its correspondence with 'the facts.' He forgets apparently that he has suggested that the task of economic theory is to produce 'fully articulated, artificial economic systems' rather than to attempt to mirror 'actual economies' (1981, p. 261).

First, what are 'facts' for Lucas? (He now commonly refers to the idea that the challenge of theory as usually seen is to explain 'stylized facts' rather than 'real facts.' Many would think that a far less severe challenge.)

Second, he overlooks the fact that among the series that Mitchell invariably examined, and in which he established conformity and other characteristics deriving from their being part of business cycles, were series dealing with both employment and unemployment. Employment figured prominently in the Burns-Mitchell definition of business cycles ('fluctuations in income, output, and employment'). These labor market series exist and have been available for a long time. They go back monthly at least to 1929. While Lucas, as we have seen, thinks Keynes got hopelessly bogged down in trying to distinguish voluntary from involuntary unemployment, the unemployment statistics have no such problem. They include all the unemployed that can be found and measured without trying to specify the cause of the unemployment.

Lucas chooses what he derides. In the end he apparently thinks it is both clever and telling to say that in suggesting that workers may choose leisure over work in depression 'No one is suggesting that workers *like* depression.' Whether he might try a similar statement about inflation is not clear. How wild a statement is it to suggest that if it is the only alternative to more unemployment some people may choose inflation but this is not to suggest that anyone likes inflation? I suggest that Lucas does not advance our ability to differentiate between facts which further our understanding of, say, business cycles, and those which do not. We have seen this in considering inflation rates where we argued that fluctuations in inflation rates bother him considerably more than fluctuations in employment. He picks and chooses the facts he finds persuasive. Mitchell's work is telling because it produces 'facts' which Lucas finds useful. He never once mentions any unemployment series assessed by Mitchell. In the end, with the exception of the work on the labor series, Lucas labels Mitchell's work useful and presumably useful in advancing our understanding perhaps because it conforms to what Lucas chooses to call the facts. He derides Keynes on the grounds that his work does not conform with the facts, but in what way this is true is never clear. It is at least arguable whether the unemployment series is suspect, as Lucas says it is, because it depends on the individual view of each worker as to whether his unemployment is voluntary or not. (This suggests that the Bureau of Labor Statistics might need to interview each unemployed worker before producing the Unemployment Rate each month!)

Criticism of Rational Expectations

In the years since it was introduced there have been a number of criticisms of rational expectations. Some of the criticism is of the assumptions required by the hypothesis, some is based on the alleged ability of the hypothesis to forecast better than other approaches, some is based on the logic implicit in the hypothesis, and some question the policy implications of the hypothesis.

The major policy implication is the 'policy irrelevance argument' considered earlier. It boils down to the assertion that 'If people have rational expectations, then they use their knowledge of the monetary authority's policy rule to form their expectations of future prices. Consequently, no matter what rate of growth of the money stock the authority uses, it cannot trick economic agents into incorrectly forecasting prices' (Hoover 1988, p. 68). This led Sargent and Wallace to conclude that 'activist monetary policy' would be ineffective (Sargent and Wallace 1975, p. 213). Later students of monetarism are more cautious. Thus, later work has shown '. . . that activist policy has an effect, the problem remaining is now more complicated to evaluate because of the expectations effect' (Snowdon and Vane 1997, p. 13). Holden et al. (1985) note that 'the most powerful criticisms of the rational expectations hypothesis are based on the implicit information requirements of the assumption; agents are assumed to know the correct model of the economy, and solve it appropriately. This assumption is obviously not literally valid' (p. 47). The authors quote R. J. Shiller's comment, 'If economists are only now discovering these models, we cannot seriously propose that everyone else knew them all along' (1985, p. 47).

In addition to this criticism of rational expectations in terms of its underlying logic, Holden et al. survey many studies involving use of the hypothesis in surveys of all sorts and conclude, 'The verdict on the rational expectations hypothesis arising from the consideration of single-equation studies must . . . be one of *not proven*'(1985, p. 142). They summarize their study of various kinds of surveys of expectations. 'The majority of these surveys were found not to meet the *ex post* requirements of the rational expectations hypothesis . . . there is a case for modeling expectations in a way that does not necessarily meet the *ex post* requirements of the rational expectations hypothesis' (1985, p. 175). More generally, the authors conclude, '*a priori* consideration of the marginal costs and benefits of information facing agents in a typical advanced economy leads us to suppose that the rational expectations hypothesis cannot be taken as literally true' (1985, p. 174).

In spite of finding little empirical support for the rational expectations perspective, the authors nonetheless call the rational expectations hypothesis 'Perhaps the single most important hypothesis to have been "discovered" in macroeconomics in the past few decades . . . .' Why? 'The great strength of the rational expectations hypothesis is that it forces us to give explicit attention to the information set which agents are assumed to face' (1985, p. 174). Arguably this is like asserting that the great strength of a Flat Earth Society is that it forces us to pay attention to the shape of the earth.

Finally we may quote Paul Samuelson who says:

> Keynesian economists point to much evidence suggesting that prices and particularly wages move slowly in response to shocks, and few economists believe that labor markets are in constant supply-demand equilibrium. When the assumption of perfectly flexible wages and prices is abandoned, policy will regain its power to affect the real economy in the short run.
>
> Additionally . . . (t)he theory holds that business-cycle fluctuations are 'equilibrium' situations where firms and workers are confused by price and or money shocks. But can misperceptions about wages and prices really explain deep depressions and persistent bouts of unemployment? Did it really take people a full decade to learn how hard times were in the Great Depression? . . .
>
> Finally how can we reconcile the theoretical prediction that cyclical unemployment is produced when workers quit to look for better jobs with the evidence showing that the fraction of job losers rises sharply in recessions . . . . ? (Samuelson and Nordhaus 2001, p. 725)

We have seen that 'proof' in evaluating the rational expectations hypothesis rarely involves testing with historical data. Proof so defined tends to involve asking whether assumptions leading to numbers as estimates derived from applying a theory correspond to the figures eventually produced in the real world. Lucas has attempted to change the terms of the debate by suggesting that theory need not be judged against 'the real world.' Rather simulations which produce 'co-movements' which resemble the cyclically sensitive movements found in the real world are sufficient, at least for Lucas.

While doubtless all economists would not agree with Lucas in this repositioning of the criteria for judging theory, the rational expectations hypothesis has been judged in terms of the reasonableness of the assumption. Thus as a standard of 'proof' in theory all economists do not agree that an assumption of instantaneous market clearing is acceptable for inclusion in a theory designed to be useful. The rational expectations hypothesis is not alone in being judged finally not so much in terms of whether the statistical record supports it as it is in terms of whether the parts of the theory in logic have acceptable credibility.

CONCLUSIONS

We can reach several conclusions. First, macrotheorists do not necessarily characterize each other's theories in mutually consistent ways. Thus, Lucas has written of Keynesian theory, 'Its *central* (italics in original) premises that monetary policy could stabilize interest rates and that inflation could be ignored at high rates of unemployment turn out to be sufficiently bad approximations to reality that the multipliers whose applications rested on them are, quite simply, useless' (Lucas 1981, p. 266). It is doubtful that any Keynesian of whatever stripe would accept that as a correct characterization of the central premises of Keynesianism. It is equally doubtful that Lucas would accept a roughly parallel assertion to the effect that 'the central premise of Lucas's theory is that monetary policy cannot stabilize interest rates and that unemployment can be ignored at high rates of inflation.'

Second, there would doubtless be widespread agreement with Friedman's contention that a good test of any theory is whether it is proven correct in a different time period from that from which it was derived. We noted that monetarists have not been noticeably concerned about the failure of the behavior of velocity to pass that test in the 1980s. Indeed, the failure of velocity to remain stable in the 1980s may have damaged the standing of monetarism more than the failure of the labor market to clear instantaneously in the 1930s did the credibility of the rational expectations position. We have suggested that the rational expectations group rather successfully deflected questions concerning their assertions about the unemployment picture to a debate about how correctly to define involuntary unemployment. This was never matched by any comparable debate about how correctly to define inflation although inflation is perhaps no more, but certainly no less, ambiguous a term than is 'involuntary unemployment.' There has certainly been a continuing debate about what to include in measuring inflation.

Third, relatively few debates about acceptable proof in evaluating macroeconomic theories are resolved by appeal to the statistical record. The debate about the stability of velocity is one of the relatively few times this was the case (and it did not end the disagreement). Debate about appropriately defining the variables being considered obviously can make questions about their measurement more complicated than at first blush one might expect.

Finally, the appeal to usefulness in fashioning effective stabilization policy has been pretty well crushed as a judgmental standard. This shows up most vividly in the 'policy irrelevance' discussion in connection with rational expectations. Friedman's 'simple monetary rule' is designed among other things to suggest in the monetarist perspective the fairly narrow limits for potential success with interventionist policies. The rational expectations assertions concerning policy irrelevance go much farther. They raise the whole question of why we wish to improve, in this case, macroeconomic theory. Lucas says it is merely to understand why intervention is futile (Lucas 1981, p. 235). Most economists would find this unsatisfactory as a reason for improving theory. In this economists need to follow Newton: understanding why the apple falls was never enough. It was merely crucial to critical policy (e.g., preventing airplane crashes, preventing structural collapses, etc.). If interventionist policy is as irrelevant as the rational expectations position claims then no matter how clever the theory, how elegant the math, how internally logical the exposition, advances in theory are remarkably small accomplishments.

If better understanding is definitionally unrelated to improving performance then 'proof' in examining theories is not critically important, except as an academic exercise. We would not care particularly about advances in medical research if they were not judged as potential contributions to better health.

The implications of the argument presented reflect the widely held belief that 'proof' is more convincing when it is presented in work with which one agrees than when it is presented in work with which one disagrees.

In short, we see once again that the disputes between Keynesian and new classical economists including monetarists have never been principally about matters that can be settled by empirical proof. While much is made of the 'failure of Keynesianism to explain stagflation in the 1970s' and the 'failure' of monetarism to account for the volatility of velocity in the 1980s such appeals to 'facts,' we have argued, aren't the primary determinants of the appeal of these two schools. Mayer's last characteristic (dislike of government intervention) we have noted is perhaps the most important and has little if anything to do with the empirical record or empirical proof. Dislike of government is a normative position, not a positive position.[18] Ironically the economists who insist the discipline of economics must be positive are held together mainly by this common normative conviction. Non-interventionists never liked Keynesianism, no matter how persuasive the chain of reasoning, because they didn't like the interventionism to which it led. Keynesians never liked monetarism, no matter how much presumptive empirical evidence was brought to bear, because of what they regarded as its too facile acceptance of the misery of unemployment (Keynes 1936, p. 209). Robert Gordon has called the Keynesian position 'monetary impotence' (Gordon 2000, p. 225).

In the end the factors that separate some major groups of economic theorists today are not matters of empirical fact, or even matters capable of being appealed to empirical fact. They are differences in values. For groups who regard economics as a positive field, to be differentiated from each other by normative matters is an irony worth contemplating.

Thus, Lucas is impressed by Mitchell and not impressed by Keynes. He professes to judge the usefulness of economic theory by an appeal to facts. We have noted that had he chosen to pillory Mitchell for trying to measure unemployment he could have done so and used some of the arguments he uses against Keynes's efforts to measure and analyze unemployment.

There is an explanation for why Lucas never comments on Mitchell's emphasis on the importance of unemployment. Lucas is absolutely correct that Keynes's efforts at macro-economic theory were always ineluctably bound up with his wish to improve macroeconomic policy. Mitchell had no such aim, except very indirectly. The National Bureau of Economic Research, which Mitchell founded, was devoted to the unassailable

18. We have said that normative and positive are indistinguishable. That is to say, that every position, whether advocating change or merely acceptance of the status quo (e.g., the current distribution of income and wealth), becomes as normative a position as advocating a change in them. There is no conflict between this view and the truth of the proposition that to begin by assuming that all government intervention is generally a bad idea represents an ideological (that is, normative) statement.

proposition that economists of all stripes would benefit if they had 'the facts' and by the facts Mitchell meant accurate data, said data organized so as to reflect as accurately as possible whatever meaning for the state of the economy they contained. The Bureau technique for presenting time series dealing with the business cycle was designed to make as clear as possible co-movements, common trends, similarities or differences in amplitude and or timing. The development of public policy to deal with all this Mitchell very carefully always left to others. One can at least raise the question whether or not this characteristic of Mitchell's is what endeared him to Lucas and enabled him to overlook the sin of looking for business cycles in unemployment rates. Keynes looked for cycles in unemployment rates, thought they could be meaningfully interpreted, and also wanted to derive macroeconomic policy which, among other things, would lead to more stable and more rapid growth in economic activity with consequent reduced fluctuations in the labor market indicators.

Differences can continue not only because different economists have different views of what is convincing corroboration of a theory or convincing failure to support a theory. Along with such differences in standards there is an all too human tendency to have different standards depending on whether the theory supports or fails to support the views one already has.

Finally we may note that while this chapter has focused on macroeconomics it has done so only because divergent schools of thought are currently more differentiated in macroeconomics than microeconomics. (In microeconomics, one can distinguish 'interventionists' from 'noninterventionists' but beyond that it becomes complicated.) However, the same problems of how proof is recognized and related to truth can be found in microeconomics. Making progress in economic theory, as in other fields, involves complicated relations between theorist and the field to which the theory presumably applies. Increasingly, economists have distinguished themselves principally by in effect saying, 'Let's play a different game, and by rules of our own choosing.'

REFERENCES

Andrade, E.N. da C. (1958), *Sir Isaac Newton*, Garden City, NY: Doubleday Anchor.

Ayres, Clarence E. (1944), *The Theory of Economic Progress*, Chapel Hill, NC: University of North Carolina Press.

Barro, Robert J. (1981), 'The equilibrium approach to business cycles', in Robert J. Barro (ed.), *Money, Expectations, and Business Cycles*, New York: Academic Press, pp. 41–78.

Barro, Robert J. (1990), *Macroeconomics*, *Third Edition*, New York: John Wiley and Sons.

Barro, Robert J. and Stanley Fischer (1981), 'Recent developments in monetary theory', in Robert J. Barro (ed.), *Money, Expectations, and Business Cycles*, New York: Academic Press, pp. 3–37.

Beveridge, William (1945), *Full Employment in A Free Society*, New York: W.W. Norton and Company.

Blaug, Mark (1980, 1992), *The Methodology of Economics, Second Edition.* Cambridge: Cambridge University Press.

Broad, C.D. (1927), *Sir Isaac Newton*, London: British Academy Oxford University Press.

Caldwell, Bruce J. (1982, revised 1994), *Beyond Positivism: Economic Methodology in the Twentieth Century,* London and New York: Routledge.

Campbell, William W. (1928), 'Newton's influence upon the development of astrophysics', in *Sir Isaac Newton, The History of Science Society*, Baltimore, MD: The Williams and Wilkins Company.

Darby, Michael R. (1974), 'The permanent income theory of consumption – a restatement', *Quarterly Journal of Economics*, **88**, 228–50.

Dillard, Dudley D. (1948), *The Economics of John Maynard Keynes: The Theory of a Monetary Economy*, Englewood Cliffs, NJ: Prentice-Hall.

Eisner, Robert and R.H. Strotz (1964), 'Determinants of business investment', in Daniel B. Suits, et al. (eds), *Commission on Money and Credit*, *Impacts of Monetary Policy*, Englewood Cliffs, NJ: Prentice-Hall, pp. 59–223.

Feldstein, Martin (1985), *Supply-Side Economics: Old Truths and New Claims*, Cambridge, MA: National Bureau of Economic Research.

Feyerabend, Paul (1975), *Against Method: Outline of an Anarchistic Theory of Knowledge*, Cambridge, MA: Humanities Press.

Foley, D. (1987), 'Money in economic activity', in John Eatwell, Murray Milgate, and Peter Newman (eds), *The New Palgrave, A Dictionary of Economics*, London: The Macmillan Press, Ltd., **III**, 524.

Friedman, Milton (1948), 'A monetary and fiscal framework for economic stability', *American Economic Review,* **38**, 245–64. Reprinted in *Essays in Positive Economics*, Chicago: University of Chicago Press, 1953.

Friedman, Milton (1957), 'The supply of money and changes in prices and output', in Kurt R. Leube (ed.), *The Relationship of Prices to Economic Stability and Growth*, Joint Economic Committee, Washington, DC: U.S. Government Printing Office.

Friedman, Milton (1957), *A Theory of the Consumption Function*, Princeton, NJ: Princeton University Press.

Friedman, Milton (1963), *Capitalism and Freedom*, Chicago: University of Chicago Press, Phoenix Books.

Friedman, Milton (1968), 'The role of monetary policy', *American Economic Review*, **58**, 1–17.

Friedman, Milton (1986), 'M1's hot streak gave Keynesians a bad idea', letter to the *Wall Street Journal*.

Friedman, Milton (1987), 'Notes on quantity theory of money', in Kurt R. Leube (ed.), *The Essence of Friedman*, Stanford, CA: Hoover Institute Press.

Friedman, Milton (2003), *Wall Street Journal*, 19 August, editorial page.

Friedman, Milton and Anna J. Schwartz (1963), *A Monetary History of the United States, 1867–1960,* National Bureau of Economic Research, Princeton, NJ: Princeton University Press.

Friedman, Milton and Anna J. Schwartz (1970), Monetary Statistics of the United States, Estimates, Sources, and Methods, New York: distributed by Columbia University Press.

Friedman, Milton and Anna J. Schwartz (1991), 'Alternative approaches to analyzing economic data', *The American Economic Review*, **81** (1), 39–49.

Galbraith, John Kenneth (1987), *Economics in Perspective*, Boston, MA: Houghton Mifflin Company.

Galbraith, John K. and Paul W. McCracken (1983), *Reaganomics: Meaning, Means, and Ends*, New York, London: Free Press, Collier Macmillan.

Gleick, James (2003), *Isaac Newton*, New York: Pantheon Books.

Gordon, Robert J. (2000), *Macroeconomics, Eighth Edition*, New York: Addison-Wesley Longman.

Hansen, Alvin (1941), *Fiscal Policy and Business Cycles*, New York: W.W. Norton & Company.

Harrod, Roy F. (1951), *The Life of John Maynard Keynes*, New York: Harcourt Brace and Company.

Hicks, John R. (1979), *Causality in Economics*, Oxford: Blackwell.

Holden, Kenneth, D.A. Peel and J.L. Thompson (1985), *Expectations: Theory and Evidence*, New York: St. Martin's Press.

Holmes, Cooper B. (1990), *The Honest Truth about Lying With Statistics*, Springfield, IL: Charles C. Thomas.

Hoover, Kevin D. (1988), 'The new classical macroeconomics', in Brian Snowdon and Howard R. Vane (eds), *Reflections on the Development of Modern Macroeconomics*, Oxford: Basil Blackwell, pp. 60–61; p. 68; pp. 234–5.

Jorgenson, D.W. (1963), 'Capital theory and investment behavior', *American Economic Review*, **53** (2), 247–59.

Kaldor, Nicholas (1985), *The Scourge of Monetarism, Second Edition*, Oxford: Oxford University Press.

Kapp, K. William (1976), 'The nature and significance of institutional economics,' *Kyklos*, **29**, fasc. 2.

Keynes, John M. (1936), *General Theory of Employment, Interest, and Money*, New York: Harcourt Brace and Company.

Klein, L.R. (1946 and 1961), *The Keynesian Revolution*, New York: Macmillan and Co.

Krugman, Paul R. (1994), *Peddling Prosperity: Economic Sense and Nonsense in the Age of Diminished Expectations*, New York: W.W. Norton & Company.

Kuhn, Thomas (1970), *The Structure of Scientific Revolutions, Second Edition*, Chicago: University of Chicago Press.

Kydland, Finn and Edward C. Prescott (1980), 'A competitive theory of fluctuations', in Stanley Fischer (ed.), *Rational Expectations and Economic Policy*, Chicago: NBER University of Chicago Press.

Lawson, Tony (1997), *Economics and Reality*, London and New York: Routledge.

Leachates, I.M.E. (1978), *The Methodology of Scientific Research Programs*, Cambridge: Cambridge University Press.

Leube, Kurt R. (1987), *The Essence of Friedman*, Stanford, CA: Stanford University Hoover Institution Press. Adapted from Milton Friedman, 'Quantity theory of money', in John Eatwell, Murray Millgate and Peter Newman (eds), *The New Palgrave: A Dictionary of Economics*, New York: Macmillan Stockton Press.

Lucas, Robert E. (ed.) (1981), *Studies in Business Cycle Theory*, Cambridge, MA: MIT Press.

Lucas, Robert E. (1981a), 'Equilibrium search and unemployment', in Lucas (1981).

Lucas, Robert E. (1981b), 'Understanding business cycles', in Lucas (1981). Originally in Friedrich von Haek, *Road to Serfdom*, Chicago: University of Chicago Press, 1944.

Lucas, Robert E. (1981c), 'Unemployment policy', in Lucas (1981).

Lucas, Robert E. (1981d), 'Towards full employment and price stability, a report to the OECD by a group of independent experts', A Review: by Paul McCracken et al. in Lucas (1981). Originally in Friedrich von Haek, *Road to Serfdom*, Chicago: University of Chicago Press, 1944.

Lucas, Robert E. (1985), 'Wages, employment, and inflation', in Robert E. Lucas (ed.), *Studies in Business Cycle Theory*, Cambridge, MA: MIT Press.

Lucas, Robert E. (1985), 'Methods and problems in business cycle theory', in Robert E. Lucas (ed.), *Studies in Business Cycle Theory*, Cambridge, MA: MIT Press.

McCloskey, D.N. (1985), *The Rhetoric of Economics*, Madison, WI: University of Wisconsin Press.

Mankiw, Gregory (1998), *Principles of Economics*, New York: The Dryden Press, Harcourt Brace College Publishers.

Mankiw, Gregory (2004), *Principles of Economics*, New York: The Dryden Press, Harcourt Brace College Publishers.

Mayer, Thomas (1972), *Permanent Income, Wealth, and Consumption*, Los Angeles: University of California Press.

Mayer, Thomas (ed.) (1978), *The Structure of Monetarism*, New York: W.W. Norton & Company.

Minford, Patrick (1997), 'Macroeconomics: before and after rational expectations', in Brian Snowden and Howard Vane (eds), *Reflections on the Development of Modern Macroeconomics*, Cheltenham, UK: Edward Elgar, pp. 103–27.

Mitchell, Wesley Clair (1927), *Business Cycles: The Problem and Its Setting*, New York: National Bureau of Economic Research.

Mitchell, Wesley Clair (1951), *What Happens During Business Cycles: A Progress Report*, National Bureau of Economic Research, NY: Columbia University Press.

Moore, Geoffrey H. (1980), *Business Cycles, Inflation, and Forecasting*, National Bureau of Economic Research, Studies in Business Cycles No. 24, Cambridge, MA: Ballinger Publishing Company.

Muth, John F. (1961), 'Rational expectations and the theory of price movements', *Econometrica,* **29**, 315–35.

North, J.D. (1967), *Isaac Newton*, Oxford: Oxford University Press.

Popper, Karl (1959 reprinted 1965), *The Logic of Scientific Discovery*, London and New York: Routledge.

Robinson, Joan (1971), *Economic Heresies*, New York: Basic Books.

Roll, Eric (1942), *A History of Economic Thought*, New York: Prentice-Hall.

Samuelson, Paul and William Nordhaus (2001), *Macroeconomics*, *17th Edition,* NY: McGraw-Hill Irwin.

Sargent, Thomas J. and Neil Wallace (1975), '"Rational" expectations, the optimal monetary instrument, and the optimal money supply rule', *Journal of Political Economy*, **83**, 214–54.

Sheffrin, Steven M. (1996), *Rational Expectations*, *Second Edition*, Cambridge: Cambridge University Press.

Simon, Herbert A. (1997), *Administrative Behavior*, *Fourth Edition*, New York: The Free Press.

Snowdon, Brian and Howard R. Vane (eds) (1997), *Reflections on the Development of Modern Macroeconomics*, Cheltenham, UK and Lyme, USA: Edward Elgar.

Steele, G.R. (1989), *Monetarism and the Demise of Keynesian Economics*, New York: St. Martin's Press.

Wanniski, Jude (1983), *The Way the World Works*, New York: Simon and Schuster.

3. Lowering the learning in economics, 1950–2000

THE QUANTIFICATION REVOLUTION TAKES COMMAND: FALLOUT FROM DIVERSE SOURCES

> There is much in economic theory which is pursued for no better reason than its intellectual attraction: it is a good game. (Hicks 1979, p. viii)

> The contemporary theorist is not only well-grounded in mathematics, but finds it the natural medium for expressing his professional ideas: the proof has replaced the argument. (Ward, 1972)

> The mathematical prerequisites for use of the book are a basic knowledge of calculus, some familiarity with linear algebra (although the use of vectors and matrices is introduced gradually in part I), and a grasp of the elementary aspects of probability. Students also will find helpful some familiarity with microeconomics at the level of an intermediate undergraduate course. (Mas-Colell, Whinston and Green 1995, p. xiv)

> Books on technical economics are no longer even superficially accessible to lay people; and young economists overvalue a narrow, and occasionally silly, ingenuity of technique. But the main cost is not so often noticed. It is that during their conversion to a mathematical way of talking the economists adopted a crusading faith, a set of philosophical doctrines, that makes them prone now to fanaticism and intolerance. (McCloskey 1998, p. 4)

> Before the contemporary period of the past five decades, theoretical physics had been an inaccessible ideal toward which economic theory sometimes strove. During that period, this striving became a powerful stimulus in the mathematization of economic theory. (Debreu 1991, p. 2)

We come now to a subject which has had a huge impact on all three of the areas with which we are concerned. (1) The 'Quantification Revolution' has severely affected virtually every aspect of economic theory. Whatever else it has done it has made it extremely difficult for the uninitiated to understand what is being argued. But more than that, it has altered the way in which theory is developed, what is required for it to be convincing to economists themselves, and the attitude toward theory taken by theorists. (Their pride in it has multiplied, if that is possible!) (2) It has drastically affected the teaching of graduate economics, certainly in the United States. It has changed both the curriculum, the way in which the subject is taught, and what students are expected to bring with them to a graduate program in economics. (3) Finally, it has affected the relationship between economic theorists and the development of economic policy. Before we are done, we shall have to consider all three of these interrelated areas.

The first two quotations with which we begin this chapter seem to encapsulate the story of modern economics and its development during the past 50 years. If it is true that economic theory has been turned into an intellectual game, it is indeed reduced to 'lower learning.' The fourth quotation advances a critical view of the outcome, which surely bodes ill, if true, for the future of the discipline. The last quotation, by a leading mathematical economist, states with some pride precisely what those who deplore the mathematization of economic theory view with alarm. Together the quotations lay out the territory we need to explore in this chapter.

THE MATHEMATICS REVOLUTION

When I was a graduate student I remember vividly Robert A. Gordon telling a group of us that we had better take econometrics so we could read the appendices to articles in the *American Economic Review*.

In only a very few short years it had become the case that without econometrics one could not read the articles themselves. (Thus, as I used to remind myself, did I emerge from Berkeley, PhD in hand, the youngest anachronism in the profession.) Gerard Debreu, a leader in quantitative economics, has summarized this shift admirably, if approvingly. He chronicles the rise of the journals devoted to mathematical economics; from 1933 to 1959 there were but two such journals, *Economica* and the *Review of Economic Studies*; these two grew explosively after 1944. The *International Economic Review* was begun in 1960 (Debreu 1991). In 1964 the *Journal of Mathematical Economics* got its start; in 1969 the *Journal of Economic Theory* began.

Meanwhile older journals like the *American Economic Review* underwent radical transformation. As Debreu tells us, in 1940 less than 3 per cent of the pages included even rudimentary mathematical expressions whereas by 1990 close to 40 per cent of the pages did so. Today the percentage is doubtless even higher.

Meanwhile Debreu tells us of the rapid rise to prominence in the profession of mathematically sophisticated economists: the Presidents of the American Economic Association were increasingly likely to be Fellows of the Econometric Society; the Nobel Award in economics and similarly the John Bates Clark medal in the US increasingly went only to economists with high mathematics credentials (cf. Debreu 1991, pp. 1–3).

To be fair, before he is done Debreu makes reference to those who were not sure all this represented genuine unqualified progress. He himself thought the advances were perhaps ambiguous. As he wrote, 'Ceteris paribus, one cannot prefer less to more rigor, lesser to greater generality, or complexity to simplicity; but other things are not equal, and in the estimate of many members of our association the cost of that mathematization sometimes outweighs the benefits' (1991, p. 5).

He notes that both W. Leontief and R.A. Gordon, in their presidential comments to the American Economic Association, had reservations about the mathematization of economics. He grants that their reservations are still relevant, but asserts,

> . . . in spite of their authorities, enhanced by the platform from which they were speaking, and in spite of the wide diffusion of their critiques, neither Leontief (1971) nor Gordon (1976) altered the course of the developments they were assessing. In the past two decades, economic theory has if anything been carried away further by a seemingly irresistible current that can be explained only partly by the intellectual successes of its mathematization. (1991, p. 5)

Part of the transformation he attributes to the reward system in economics today, to which we turn later in this chapter, as well as in a later chapter, and partly it is because, in our view, there are limitations to what the mathematization of economic theory has accomplished that economists like Debreu simply fail to see. We turn to these later in the chapter as well.

We offer one final irony. The form of Professor Debreu's essay on the *Mathematization of Economic Theory* is a rarity nowadays; it is an article in the *American Economic Review* written entirely in old-fashioned words! What was he thinking of?

If alpha is conclusion, *z* – profoundly, and *j* – ironic, we may say, 'ceteris paribus' (how economists love that notion!), alpha = *zj*!

The McCloskey quotation raises one aspect of the story vividly. Critical discussion of the pros and cons of the use of mathematics in economics is practically unheard of today. If economic theorists regarded their field as 'the Queen of the Social Sciences' as long ago as the end of World War II – because of its elegance, its precision, its internal logic and its overall neatness – and all at a time when it was still said in words rather than in numbers, it takes little imagination to realize that today when virtually all statements can be expressed in equations, all sets of interrelated statements (hypotheses, theories) can be put in sets of equations, the pride (arrogance?) and pleasure (ecstasy?) with which our theorists contemplate their work must be genuinely extraordinary. There should be a title higher than Queen of the Social Sciences to bestow on such a thought system.

Actually the basic problem is much older than the mathematics revolution. Not only have economists carried Adam Smith's invisible hand to heights Smith never dreamed of, as we suggested earlier, but the whole concept of economic man has similarly been carried farther than, arguably, made sense. We shall examine this carefully in this chapter in connection with the work of George Katona. Mathematics, we shall argue, was not the instrumentality for diverting economic theory from a solid realistic psychological base. That was done long before the quantification revolution. Mathematics simply played into the hands of mainstream economists because it enabled them to take the discipline even further precisely where they had been pushing to take it all along, but with far more primitive tools.

Gains and Losses from the Mathematics Revolution

Debreu makes the case for what the mathematization of economics has accomplished and, in our view, unwittingly also makes the case for what it has failed to accomplish.

In making the case he notes that the price system can be viewed as a 'point in the linear price space, dual of the commodity space, whose dimension is also the number of commodities' (Debreu 1991, p. 3). He continues:

> In those two linear spaces, the stage was set for sometimes dazzling mathematical developments that began with the elements of differential calculus and linear algebra and that gradually called on an ever broader array of powerful techniques and fundamental results offered by mathematics. Thus the three roles of prices given earlier as instances were illuminated by mathematical theorems: the first, the achievement of an efficient use of resources, by results of convex analysis; the second, the equalization of supply and demand for commodities, by results of fixed point theory; the third, the prevention of the formation of destabilizing coalitions, by results of the theory of integration and nonstandard analysis. In those three cases the lag between the date of mathematical discovery and the date of its application to economic theory decreased over time . . .

> The last, and most recently developed, of the three instances can be chosen, as can either of the other two for a more detailed illustration. Competition is perfect when every agent's influence on the outcome of economic activity is insignificant. The influence of their totality on that outcome is, however, significant. It is to solve the problem of aggregating negligible quantities so as to obtain a nonnegligible sum that integration was invented. In this perspective, the application of integration theory to the study of economic competition is entirely natural. (1991, p. 3)

This passage illustrates almost perfectly our basic thesis. Economic theory (microtheory) in its old-fashioned verbal mode had the grave defect that it revolved almost entirely around competition (or, on occasion, its equally rare opposite, monopoly). The possible exception to this statement is the application of game theory in modern industrial organization theory. These models customarily revolve around efficiency criteria and exclude equity considerations. The real world, in contrast, was (and is) typically characterized by various kinds of oligopoly. Oligopoly has significant equity (that is, welfare) implications.

What Debreu makes abundantly clear is that the process of transforming that theory into mathematical form has perhaps increased its precision, almost surely reduced the number of pages it takes to state it, but retained the emphasis on competition in virtually unchanged form. It may well be that the application of integration theory to the study of economic competition is 'perfectly natural.' But where does that get us if the typical market structure is almost never economic competition? In most real world markets we are most definitely not adding negligible quantities together to get non-negligible sums in the market but adding non-negligible sums from the outset to get non-negligible market sums.

In the entire article in which Debreu admirably recognizes that all economists have not happily bought into the mathematics revolution he never once uses the word oligopoly, never once mentions concentrated economic power, and never worries about whether what human beings do in pursuit of economic activity can truly be reduced to 'treating the set of agents of an economy as the rich collection of the points of an interval of real numbers.'

Among mainstream economists there is virtual unanimity concerning what has been accomplished. Perusal of advanced texts in economic theory today gives ample evidence that virtually the entire corpus of conventional economic theory has now been reconfigured so as to be expressed mathematically by a set of equations. Modeling is the only appropriate way to advance economic theory. This is equally true of both microeconomic and macroeconomic theory. The gains to research and understanding of this rewriting are touted by virtually all who contribute today to contemporary economic theorizing. Thus, Nancy L. Stokey and Robert E. Lucas (1989) begin their book *Recursive Methods in Economic Dynamics* with these words:

> Research in economic dynamics has undergone a remarkable transformation in recent decades. A generation ago, empirical researchers were typically obliged to add dynamic and stochastic elements as afterthoughts to predictions about behavior derived from static, deterministic economic models. Today in every field of application, we have theories that deal explicitly with rational economic agents operating through time in stochastic environments. The idea of an economic equilibrium has undergone a similar evolution: it no longer carries the connotation of a system at rest. Powerful methods are now available for analyzing theoretical models with equilibrium outcomes described by the same kinds of complicated stochastic processes that we use to describe observed economic behavior. (Stokey and Lucas 1989, p. 3)

There can be no question that many of the technical obstacles and limitations to operationalizing various economic theories previously available only in verbal form into the newer form of mathematical models have been eliminated, thanks to modern electronic computers. The combination of correlation, calculus (both single variable and multi variable), probability, and time series analysis, with the use of the electronic computer has literally eliminated physical limitations on what could previously be done. Where before one might have hesitated to posit, say, an 800 variable model on grounds that, among other things, solving 800 simultaneous equations was unimaginable, today such solving is a matter of seconds, at most, minutes.

One comes away from all this, therefore, forced to ask, have we invented a brilliant and efficient technique for expressing classical economic theory in a way which justifies the unanimity with which modern economists embrace it? Or could it be true that, despite its precision, its economy, and its ability to be subjected to deductive logic, the technique we have so proudly applied to virtually all of economic theory leaves many if not all the core deficiencies of that theory intact?

We suggest that the answer to the first question may be more in doubt than is ever really suspected and the answer to the second question may be in the affirmative. Moreover, we further suggest that the virtually total recasting of theory in mathematical terms adds the disadvantage that these deficiencies are all but impossible to illumine unless one has the mathematical knowledge and insight to decipher what is being asserted. The inability of the uninitiated to penetrate the haze is, for the initiated, one of the great if unsung virtues. Today there is a mathematical wall between economic theory and the public. In its present form does it easily pass muster in cost benefit analysis?

Modeling and the Use of Models

We can illustrate the basic problem with a simple comparison. It is doubtful that one part of our illustration has been modeled heretofore. First, we turn to a rarely mentioned figure from the past.

Ricardo became famous, among other things, for his differential rent theory. The idea that one could apply the law of diminishing returns to plots of land classified by their fertility (productivity) made it possible to postulate that a given farmer contemplating the steady increase in demand for his output of crops would classify his land by fertility and apply units of labor and other inputs successively to the highest quality land until the marginal product of such land became equal to the marginal product of the initial input on the second best land, in which case the farmer would stop cultivating the first grade land more intensively in order to apply inputs to the second best land. As diminishing returns set in on the second best there would ultimately come an output best supplied by applying inputs initially to the third best grade of land. This process would continue until the market demand was satisfied.

It was a very neat theory because the cost of producing on the last unit of land required in order to meet the market demand was the unit which determined, in conjunction with the supply, what the price of the crop per unit could be. Obviously all the units produced with fewer inputs produced a surplus above the last unit's marginal cost. This was, of course, 'rent.' The example is ideally suited to being put in a mathematical model because the behavior involved is 'recursive' – the farmer repeatedly applies the same inputs to the land and gets varying outputs. How his output diminishes can easily be expressed in equation form. All the 'switching' amounts of demand (when the farmer would switch from higher grade land to a lower grade because of diminishing returns) can be calculated in advance. The model would give precise results helpful to the farmer in planning his production, and helpful to the government officials interested in how adequate food supplies would be and how affordable to the participants the prices would be. All in all, this is a nice modest task for an econometrician to produce a mathematical model illustrating the differential rent theory in action.

It would be nit picking to point out that probably farmers even in Ricardo's time would have been non-plussed if asked to state how many different grades of land they had. It could, of course, be argued that no farmer in the real world ever divided his land up into N distinct neat qualitative packages with homogeneous land in each one and that he then could neatly apply the law of diminishing returns precisely to each one so as to find the unit of output at which he was indifferent between continuing on grade x of land or producing the first unit of output on grade $x - 1$, the next lowest grade of land. But no matter. It was neater than could be reasonably justified, but it was perfectly logical, and it was precise (too precise!). And it was not really bad as a means of describing what logically a farmer might do. It was arguably a not bad rough and ready characterization. Besides as a theory requiring suspension of belief because of its lack of total realism, Ricardo's theory could not hold a candle to some of those of his successors!

Our main point, however, is that as an example of an economic agent confronting an economic challenge it was reasonably well suited to the approach Ricardo took and so in turn it was an ideal candidate for being converted into a mathematical model.

For comparative purposes, now imagine that we are not economists but psychologists, or sociologists, or marriage counselors trying to explain the marital behavior of Jane Smith. At last count she had had ten husbands, but the number is irrelevant. We postulate that she marries out of a combination of attractive potential possibilities – passion, high interest in her prospective mate, and a strong anticipatory feeling that life after marriage will be richer and fuller and more satisfying. (We can summarize all these factors as alpha.) On the other hand, after she is married she finds a number of unattractive features that gradually mount in importance – she is bored, irritated by habits and traits previously unnoticed, increasingly angered by being crossed, taken advantage of, etc. (We may summarize all these factors as sigma.) At any time the state of any given marriage can be calculated as net alpha (alpha minus sigma). When net alpha is negative most people would call it quits, presumably including Ms Smith. But her case may be more complicated than this. We may postulate a Smith differential marriage theorem which tells us that increasingly over time the favorable marriage factors (alpha) with husband number N (presumably the most appealing person around) have diminished while the unfavorable factors (sigma) are increasing all the time, so that net alpha is diminishing over time. A point is reached where the net alpha with husband number N is lower (it could still be positive) than the perceived net alpha with husband number $N + 1$ (presumably and initially the next most appealing man around). The most recent (and alas the last) net alpha with husband no. N need not be negative – only lower than the initial contemplated net alpha with husband number $N + 1$. Note that there is no reason that the initial alpha with husband number $N + 1$ cannot be lower than the initial alpha was with husband N. There is indeed a high probability that this will be the case. Thus, there is a switching point at which it pays her to divorce N and marry $N + 1$, even though net alpha might not be as promising at the outset as initially it was with number N. No. $N + 1$ could, nonetheless make her feel that a day's effort on the new marriage will make her happier and cause her less anguish than another day being married to number N. She has found the point where it pays her to switch from number N to number $N + 1$. Presumably she has gone through a process that can be described in these terms eight times by now. The speed with which she remarries has abated somewhat (modern economists have a name for this, naturally – it is 'search time'). Because of lengthening search time, she increasingly finds it necessary to factor it in, in determining her switching points.

The Quantification Revolution – The Missing Heart

What has this comparison of Ricardo's differential rent theory and Ms Smith's marital history accomplished? Institutional economists have long insisted that a major problem with conventional microeconomic theory is its tendency to internal logic, neatness, and precision at the expense of realism. In the case of the differential rent theory we alluded to some of the same charges are potentially applicable. But in the end we suggested that as an approximation of how a real farmer might go about deciding when to stop intensive farming in one area and begin on a new field it is perhaps not a bad approximation of the actual process he goes through. It seems, as we underscored, a natural candidate, therefore, for the application of mathematics. The elements entering into it could be reduced to declining or increasing rates (in this case of productivity) which make a certain amount of sense economically and can be neatly summarized mathematically (differential calculus). It does assume that all labor is identical – perhaps a huge assumption which in the real world makes the calculations problematical at best. Still it helps explain how declining productivity is factored in and the utilization of mathematics does little further violation to the facts than was done by Ricardo's original formulation. Ricardo's differential rent theory, in short, is not a bad candidate for Debreu's 'mathematicization.' It is probably no less realistic in quantitative form than it was at Ricardo's hands.

Ms Smith presents more problems. Her behavior has certainly been recursive, but our ability to incorporate all the relevant factors in modeling that behavior has surely been less successful than in the case of the farmer. Our *verbal* description is less adequate than was the case with Ricardo's farmers.

Here we get to the nub of the problem. The differential rent case is basically a recursive mechanical exercise. The personality of the farmer is never introduced because the problem can be set up so that it is irrelevant. (If you think of it, microeconomic theory has always been most comfortable when dealing with homogeneous inputs producing homogeneous outputs. In the real world that is a quite rare combination!) To begin with, it is probably appropriate (more or less) to describe the farmer as a 'rational economic agent.' The behavior that Ricardo was describing, if viewed as a rough approximation, was not in grave conflict with what real farmers do. Profit maximization as an overall summary of their objective is not grossly untrue. Making the profit seeking farmer's personality exogenous, therefore, does little violence to how the model should be constructed nor should it affect the forecasting ability of the economist utilizing the model to forecast the immediate future behavior of the producing unit. Moreover quantifying different parcels of land by their productivity is a manageable objective.

Ms Smith is different. It is somewhat more problematic to describe Ms Smith as a rational economic agent. It is the quality of her responses to various stimuli, including those which are represented by her economic activities, which are hard to treat as mechanically as one can treat the slow but steady deterioration in soil productivity.

The absurdity in the Smith example lies in the failure to recognize that while her behavior bears a superficial resemblance to Ricardo's farmer (they both exhibit switching behavior), no one should pretend that marital choices can be reduced to mechanistic interactions. This in turn reflects the fact that the farmer's problem and measurement thereof is reflecting the differential productivities (output per inputs) of qualitatively different pieces of land. They can be quantified. Quantifying Ms Smith's alpha and sigma, not to mention differential marginal net alphas per unit of time from two successive husbands is a far different proposition! Since that is true, attempting to model her behavior mathematically is an idiotic idea to begin with. But would mainstream economic theorists agree with this assessment? Would they choose to distinguish the problem facing Ricardo's farmers from that confronting Ms Smith? This in turn raises the question, how far can we get in modeling household behavior as that of rational economic agents?

Perhaps few would pretend that in selecting mates human beings can be treated as 'rational economic agents.'[1] How different in ultimate explanation

---

1. We do not even suggest that economic reasoning cannot usefully be applied to non-economic problems involving human beings. Nobel prize winning economist Gary Becker has brilliantly demonstrated that this can indeed be done (Becker 1966, 1981). Another who has done work parallel in some ways to Becker's is Anthony Downs. Downs has attempted to apply the logic of microeconomic theory to the world of political science (Downs 1957). We do not question that there

is the rest of what households do? The construct of economic man has always been criticized as a gross over-simplification and many argue that it has always needed a large dose of reality to make it truly useful. A major point we make is that the introduction of mathematics in general and modeling in particular has pushed economists into an even less realistic treatment of human behavior than was their tendency before. So 'rational economic agents' today are even more mechanistic (if multi-variate) and simplified than the 'economic man' which they have superseded. (Contemplation of the buying habits of Ms Smith, instead of her marital behavior, might underscore this point.)

The comparison of Ricardo and Ms Smith, we have asserted, illustrates the basic problem we face. The human beings who populate this world including its economies are just that – human beings. They are, alas, *NOT* 'rational economic agents operating through time in stochastic environments.' Oh, how economists wish that they were! They wish it so badly that they cope with this state of affairs by the simplest of expedients – they simply assume that they are. (Along with their recent decision to devote economic theory to explaining 'stylized facts' economists have always dealt with 'stylized people'!) It is so much simpler. It is so much neater. It makes mathematical modeling possible. It renders 'the economic problem' capable of very elegant, very precise solutions from which, among many other things, many wonderful welfare implications emanate. Along the way economists have not only raised the bridge, they have lowered the river. As was just noted, they have simplified their task by setting out with their theory to explain not real facts but 'stylized facts,' not the real world, but a simulated world, and they have done it all by peopling their world not with real people but with carefully cleaned up prettified 'rational economic agents' – the modern version of 'economic men.' They have then converted all that they wish to say about how these creatures interact into various carefully orchestrated interrelationships (stochastic; linear or non-linear; dynamic or static, often restricted to two-person-two-good economies, etc.). They have said all they wish to say about the resulting interactions among the creatures they discuss by 'modeling' them – that is, reducing their interactions to a

---

are useful insights to be had by regarding education as investment in human capital or that there are insights to be had into the operation of the political system by applying economic logic or methodology to these problems. But the complexities of human motivation and the subtleties in human thinking, we would suggest, go considerably beyond what can be mathematically reduced to fairly simple generalities about human interaction. The remainder of this chapter suggests the limits to what can be accomplished by assuming rationality and utility maximization as primary determinants of human (including economic) behavior.

series of simultaneous equations, often extremely complex, often difficult to dissect, and done with a 'sky's the limit' attitude toward mathematical complexity.

Even this is not the end, of course. The quantifiers have also destroyed the link between economic theory and economic policy. If, after all, 'leaving it to the market' ends up being the preferred strategy, there is little or no need for interventionist policy and so the fundamental importance of theory is drastically reduced. Lucas tells us that all we really need theory for is to understand and be able to explain why intervention is unnecessary or bad. As we have noted earlier, the public would scarcely be satisfied were it told that the purpose of medical research is to understand why we get cancer or heart disease. Making the human body function better is, as we say, the bottom line for the public.

Reinforcing the Wrong Path

In sum, then, we are surveying a story which ends, in our view, in elegant but futile frustration. While much has been gained in technical sophistication, more – much more – has been lost in focus, in purpose, in objectives, and in the view we economists collectively take toward both our field and the economy itself. We come at last to the basic question – does modern economic theory ever confront the actual economy? Here we examine the state of both the microeconomy and microeconomic theory.

As we do so it is only fair to tell the reader the perspective being applied. We believe that economics is serious business – that the economies of the world are redolent with vast and serious problems. As such they present grave challenges to the world in general, and to economists in particular, to develop policies to ameliorate the problems and to enable economies better 'to enhance human life' (as Thorstein Veblen put it) in ways that are acceptable to the cultures in which these economies are housed. If Sir John Hicks is correct that economics itself is merely 'a good game,' in the end its theory is a fairly mindless game at that. Long after the man who gave us *Value and Capital* had completed that famous volume, he must have realized that he had been contributing to a house of cards. The quotation from Mas-Colell et al. (1995) at the beginning of this chapter well illustrates the profound distortion to economics which Hicks was contemplating. Recall what the authors said: the 'mathematical prerequisites' for this graduate microeconomics course at Harvard are mentioned first and, almost as an afterthought, the authors suggest 'some familiarity with microeconomics' might be helpful. I can hear my colleagues in mainstream America telling me I have lost my reason, but nonetheless I ask what is the dog and what is the tail here? Consider were I to read a statement which said, 'This is a book designed for advanced philosophy. The prerequisites for the course are demonstrating some knowledge of vocabulary, grammar, and spelling. Students will also find knowing some philosophy at the intermediate level helpful.' Or consider a French course in which the students were told that the major requirement was to memorize irregular verb conjugations, but 'some familiarity' with expressing yourself in the French language might be nice as well. I repeat – what are the tools and what is the ultimate purpose?

There is an odd bifurcation in economics today. On the one hand, theory has married mathematics so thoroughly that virtually all the thinking is embedded in systems of equations and the models which result. 'Writing well' or 'writing clearly' in economics no longer refers to the gracefulness with which one uses language, but to the clarity and precision with which one develops equations so as to reflect one's thoughts. At the same time, thanks to the electronic computer, our ability to process masses of data in applied economics has dwarfed anything that used to be possible.

In short, the opportunities which math and computers offer to develop sophisticated oligopoly theory, for example, are largely passed over. Game theory is a different sort of approach and it is not clear whether our ability to theorize about how oligopolistic firms think and act has gotten more accurate, not to say useful, than Samuelson's kinked demand left it, or not. (It has clearly gotten more complex.) We shall return to this problem.

Economic theorists love math and what can be done with computers to develop more and more elegant and precise ways to explain 'stylized facts', and equilibrium has the same pride of place it always had. It is odd that the potential for greater accuracy (read realism!) is seen in applied economics, but the potential for that same accuracy read as greater realism in theory is largely ignored.

Care must be taken here. We need to consider carefully what this mathematical approach adds potentially to the process of understanding economic activity, but we need also to consider what is lost. A clear potential gain is that to the extent that human activity in pursuit of economic gain can be reduced to behavior governed by clear, unvarying, and explicit principles these principles can be pursued to their logical ends – N prioritized reactions to β different stimuli – with precision, clarity, and appropriate and consistent weights reflecting the theorist's best perception of the importance of various motivational forces on the final results. It is not clear that this is currently the principal use to which mathematics in economic theory is put. But the potential is undoubtedly there.

What is lost, of course, are all those factors which emerge only if one grants that there is no real room in a mathematically oriented model for that rich influence of non-economic (narrowly defined) factors which go by the names of culture and personality (the Smith illustration again). In fact culture and personality are the major ingredients lacking in the approach taken in attempts to explain how economies function in modeling terms. Much of this was, my generation was taught, reduced to behavior under competitive or monopolistic conditions. On occasion imperfectly competitive conditions were contemplated, mostly with results that were imprecise. Behavior was, so we learned to accept, inadequately captured because much of the richness and complexity even in the economic aspects of human interaction were of necessity lost or at least glossed over. But we nonetheless found it possible to be comfortable with the notion that economic activity is embedded in a larger culture.

THE BEHAVIORALIST CHALLENGE

Our example of Ms Smith exemplifies the difference between human beings and rational economic agents that economists generally assume away. Economics has always had a tendency to simplify to excess. The complexities of love and marriage are obviously beyond the useful limits of the economic man construct. But that observation raises the more important question of whether or not the economic decision making processes are also too much for that simple construct.

In general, economists, as we have just seen, have preferred simply to define much of what goes on as 'non-economic' and therefore of no interest to the economist. Whether the line between economic and non-economic behavior can be so rigidly drawn is an important but difficult question. The quantification revolution has, as we have noted, pushed mainstream economists to ignore it whenever possible.

'Say It With Numbers' is clearly the theme song of modern economics. In the very first sentence of the Mas-Colell et al. (1995) microeconomic theory text previously referred to the authors begin, 'A distinctive feature of microeconomic theory is that it aims to model economic activity as an interaction of individual economic agents pursuing their private interests' (p. 3). The prevailing view in the discipline is increasingly that everything worthy of discussion can be discussed within economic modeling. To regard economic activity as totally explicable by examination of the interaction among agents is to suggest that in their economic behavior agents in models are like robots – that is, entities that behave logically and consistently given the assumptions made at the time they are launched in whatever it is they do. That there may be areas of economic decision making for which this is an accurate description may be true. But there are many where it clearly is not. All economic behavior is not mechanized. Robots do not have human reactions – they cannot get discouraged or appallingly lazy. They cannot be superstitious or crafty. They cannot be imaginative or contemplative. They cannot be lustful or defeatist. They cannot be shy or bold. They cannot be humorless or fey. They cannot be impulsive or foolish. They cannot get their feelings hurt, they cannot be excessively ambitious (driven!). They cannot, in the term introduced earlier, exhibit a personality. Closer to the economist's 'have' – they cannot innovate, invent, or confront technological progress. Do these things matter? One can at least ask whether the human beings who become economic agents in models are reasonable approximations of the human beings who stumble and bumble through life and in the process of coping with, among other things, their economic challenges, allocate resources in myriad directions with vastly complicated and interactive consequences. In this sense we all resemble Jane Smith more than we resemble parcels of land. Human beings, in our view, are not adequately reduced to economic agents. We have, however, been at pains to suggest that this view is scarcely the mainstream view.

We suggest that the mainstream view, on the other hand, has by no means been held universally among economists. There has for a very long time been a movement called behavioral economics. It preceded the mathematical revolution. Despite the fact that it is obvious that, at least up to the present, behavioral economics has scarcely slowed the invasion of economic theory by mathematics, it still is worth paying attention to what it has always asserted.

Herbert A. Simon once wrote,

> . . . we need to augment and amend the existing body of classical and neoclassical economic theory to achieve a more realistic picture of economic processes as well as a more accurate understanding of the equilibrium toward which these processes move.
>
> Behavioral economics is the name we give to the research enterprise that seeks to meet those needs. Alfred Marshall of *Industry and Trade* (1919) could well have labeled himself a behavioralist. And, of course, behavioral economics can claim John R. Commons, Thorstein Veblen, Joseph Schumpeter, George Katona, and many other distinguished economists of past and recent generations. (Simon 1986, p. xvi)

It is clear from Simon's comment that behavioral economics has much in common with American institutional economics, of which both Commons and Veblen are recognized as founders. The behavioralist challenge is also the institutionalist challenge. (Whatever it is called, mainstream economists are mostly comfortable ignoring it.) Chapter 8 is devoted to institutional economics.

We would disagree slightly with Simon who appears to restrict Marshall's behavioralism to one of his less well known books. In Marshall's *Principles*, he states on page 1 in discussing 'man's character,' that 'the two great forming agencies of the world's history have been the religious and the economic. Here and there the ardour of the military or the artistic spirit has been for a while predominant but religious and economic influences have nowhere been displaced from the front rank even for a time . . . ' (Marshall 1949, p. 1).

We may go further. Economic man, that favorite construct of mainstream economics, is mentioned exactly once in Marshall's *Principles*. And what does he say? He writes,

> . . . economists study the actions of individuals, but study them in relation to social rather than individual life . . .
>
> In all this, they deal with man as he is: not with an abstract or 'economic' man, but a man of flesh and blood. They deal with a man who is largely influenced by egoistic motives in his business life to a great extent with reference to them; but who is also neither above vanity and recklessness, nor below delight in doing his work well for its own sake, or in sacrificing himself for the good of his family, his neighbor, or his country; a man who is not below the love of a virtuous life for its own sake. (1949, pp. 21–22)

Indeed, one can argue that Marshall was too generous to his fellow economists. We mention all this here because the customary view is that, thanks to the quantitative revolution, economists can pursue the view they have always taken, but pursue it better. It would appear that Marshall disagrees with what 'mankind in the ordinary business of life' does both with Nassau Senior's 'pleasure pain machine' view and with today's new classical economists who focus on economic activity as carried out exclusively by 'rational economic agents.'

If behavioral economics can, therefore, be traced back to Marshall, it was clearly given a very large lift by George Katona. In his first book he asserted:

> In this book we shall cut through the time-honored boundaries of two disciplines, economics and psychology. We shall look at economic processes as manifestations of human behavior and analyze them from the point of view of modern psychology. We shall find that the investigation of spending, saving, investing, or determining prices of the size or output has much in common with

> the study of other human activities such as learning, thinking, voting, or getting along with one's employees or one's wife. (Katona 1951, p. 3)

Katona spent his professional life at the Survey Research Center at the University of Michigan. He devoted himself to the common boundary of economics and psychology. Trained in both, the psychological assumptions underpinning economic theory were troublesome to him virtually from the start. Rational economic man was never a congenial basis for thinking about economic problems for Katona. He wrote:

> . . . Human beings do not react to stimuli as automatons. It is necessary, but not enough, to know about the objective circumstances in which people behave differently. People's attitudes, motives, and frames of reference shape their perception of the environment as well as their behavior. In order to understand economic processes, as well as other manifestations of behavior, subjective variables must be studied. (Katona 1951, p. 3)

Katona, in consequence of this perspective, devoted his life to trying to get his fellow economists to understand that economic behavior, though confined to one aspect of life, was not governed by behavior that was totally unrelated to all other kinds of human behavior. It is not clear that economists in general ever fully focused on this point. Early game theorists, for example, studied behavior by letting subjects express their views with play money. The implicit assumption was that attitudes involved in economic decision making (or decisions involving the deploying of resources) could all be expressed through prices. While this may work well for many kinds of economic decision making there are also clearly economic decisions that cannot be reduced to this decision making basis.[2]

One area which always interested Katona was the role played by expectations. As Katona noted, 'Behavioral economics collects data that explain trends predicted by the measurement of attitudes and expectations. The reasons for the changes in expectations need to be known. Such

---

2. As an example we might raise the question whether a particular premature infant ought to be saved by modern technological intervention. Whether from a societal view point this represents a good expenditure of resources could scarcely be resolved by asking the parents 'what price' they would pay and comparing it to the price that others might pay for specified alternative uses of the resources. In this case values are not easily translated into comparative prices. (It is hard to imagine a 'game' between parents of a premature baby and a person in desperate need of a heart transplant to 'decide' who should be treated. One thing is certain: it would not be left to the owner of the medical expertise to 'sell' it to the highest bidder!

information is regularly supplied by the survey data collected' (Katona 1980, p. 8).

In order to get at the reasons alluded to above, the Survey Research Center has for many years published results of a monthly survey, the Consumer Sentiment Index.[3]

By the 1950s Katona was urging economists to learn more about expectations formation. It is odd that many years later economists were told that the rational expectations hypothesis was 'Perhaps the single most important hypothesis to have been discovered in macroeconomics in the past few decades . . .,' and 'The great strength of the rational expectations hypothesis is that it forces us to give explicit attention to the information set which agents are assumed to face' (Holden, Peel, and Thompson 1985, p. 174). Many years before rational expectations came along Katona was, in effect, urging economists to use all the information they could obtain to understand human behavior. It is odd that 'using information efficiently' has been so persuasive a concept recently as offered by the adherents to rational expectations, but in developing economic theory there has always been a rule of parsimony – assume away as much information as possible.

Following Katona came a whole host of economists congregated around two economists who advanced the behavioral economics movement to a significant degree. They are Daniel Kahneman and Amos Tversky, who collaborated for many years. Both (like Katona) were trained in psychology but applied much of their attention to trying to put the psychological assumptions of economic theory on a basis more consonant with the findings of modern psychology. To this end they were long involved in various kinds of psychological experiments designed to more closely identify various kinds of motivation behind human decision making so as to get us beyond merely assuming maximization of either profits or utility by rational economic agents.[4]

Stanley Kaish has characterized the approach taken by Kahneman and Tversky as follows:

> The microeconomic theory of business decision making stresses evaluation of all results, their probability of occurrence, and calculation of expected value . . . (In all this) the assumption of a nonlinear utility function, choice by subjective expected utility (SEA) does produce a reliable and practical guide. Its reliability

3. For details of the survey, see Norman Frumkin (1990), pp. 51–7.
4. The results of their efforts were published in many articles. These studies were collected and published, along with those of their colleagues, in several volumes (Kahneman, Slovic, and Tversky (eds) 1982; Kahneman and Tversky (eds) 2000; and Kahneman 1973).

> lies in its compliance with two axioms of ordinary utility theory: dominance and invariance. Dominance requires that if choice A is as good as choice B in every respect and better than B in at least one, A should be preferred to B. Invariance requires that the way the choices are described, that is the way the outcomes are 'framed,'should not determine the preference ranking of the choices.
>
> The empirical work of Amos Tversky and Daniel Kahneman . . . has demonstrated that neither axiom can be relied on. They have demonstrated that preference depends more on how the choices are framed to the decision maker than on the underlying probabilities and outcomes. (Kaish 1986, p. 38)

More recently behavioral economics has been invigorated by the approach taken by Thaler (1991, 1992, 1993); Laibson (1996); and Mullainathan and Thaler (2000). They have all in various ways come to question the behavioral assumptions which lie behind the conventional economic model of a self-regulating economy moving through time through the efforts and actions of rational participants in economic activity.

In sum, what has been said illustrates the approach of behavioral economics. It subjects the assumptions of conventional micro and macroeconomic theory to experimental verification by setting up ways to find out under the appropriate circumstances how real agents in the appropriate test environments will behave. As such it represents a challenge to the psychological assumptions which lie behind rational economic man.[5] Whatever changes there have been in microeconomic theory since Marshall, those assumptions have until recently been quietly accepted by most economists. They are still not widely challenged, although behavioral economists constitute distinctly a minority view which does challenge them.

---

5. A modern effort to make market interacting more realistic, but far more elegant than behavioral economics goes by the name of game theory. Introduced by Von Neuman and Morganstern (1944) it starts with the huge advantage of 'being mathematical.' It revolves around 'thinking strategically' meaning realizing that your opponent in the market is trying to outdo you just as you are trying to outdo him.

Game theorists undoubtedly don't appreciate what they probably regard as the crudeness and imprecision of behavioral economics, which merely has some realism in its favor. Game theory models can be highly complicated, often elegant, but manage somehow to end up well within the boundaries of the conventional approach taken by economic theory. (A favorite outcome is 'Nash Equilibrium': '. . . no player can improve his or her payoff given the other players' strategy' (Samuelson and Nordhaus 2001, p. 215).

This tells us, therefore, where cigarette prices, if left to a strong smokers' association and the cigarette companies, might come out. It tells nothing about the more important question of what should be the societal approach to a proven carcinogen, if prices ought to reflect all the relevant factors involved in 'enhancing human life.'

In short, we reiterate, game theory continues the longstanding predilection of the mainstream to favor elegance at the expense of realism in economic theory.

We bring this up in a discussion of the quantification revolution because the attractions which lie back of that movement have merely intensified the tendency of mainstream economists to cling to their traditional assumptions. Mathematical modeling of the behavior of rational economic agents is facilitated greatly by those assumptions. (Therefore, mathematical modeling has greatly enhanced the appeal of holding to them.) To question these assumptions, therefore, is to raise yet again and in another form the whole debate about realism and relevance in the development of economic theory.

We may add that institutional economics has always questioned the behavioral assumptions of mainstream theory. Many years ago Clarence Ayres noted that 'Since economic activity is a part of the whole of human behavior, the analysis of that activity must comport with the analysis of behavior generally . . . A valid way of thinking in economics must derive from a valid conception of human nature' (Ayres 1944, pp. 89–90). In a very real sense the discussion of behavioral economics, just concluded, dealt with the search for a valid conception of human nature. That conception is distinctly not what rational economic man embodies, and it is not, therefore, what the quantification revolution has bonded even more closely to mainstream thinking or theorizing. We shall, therefore, need to consider behavioral economics in this book.

THE MODERN EFFORT TO RECAST ECONOMIC ACTIVITY IN A DYNAMIC FRAMEWORK

Modern dynamic economics presents the challenge raised by the quantification revolution in vivid form. One way to frame the question is to ask: what if anything would be different in focus or perspective in a book on, for example, calculus, which relied on the area of economics for its examples and a book on economic theory which relied on sophisticated econometric models? In the second case there is clearly one very great potential gain. Modern econometric models can capture much human behavior more realistically when the models are dynamic. (Whether they have taken advantage of this potential gain very realistically or not is another matter.) If economics has traditionally longed to emulate physics, that longing customarily was limited to statics. But being able to think in dynamic terms opened the possibility that economics could be refashioned in ways closer to say biology, allowing economies like living organisms to grow and develop as well as 'allocate.' We have tried to show that because the view of human nature never changed (or developed) that chance, in our view, has largely been squandered.

To the uninitiated it is difficult to distinguish discussions of complex issues in econometric methodology from complex discussions of economic problems, said discussions being carried forth entirely in terms of econometrics. Econometrics has been followed by psychometrics and sociometrics. Political scientists have their quantitative experts but they muddle through with 'quantitative methods!' Anthropologists seem similarly mired in the awkwardness of 'quantitative analysis of anthropological data.' All this raises a very interesting question. Is it in fact true that the subject matter of economics is more quantitative, or lends itself more to the numerical approach than is true of all other social sciences, or is it in fact merely 'ahead' of them as it has always insisted (the 'Queen of the Social Sciences')? The economics journals do not appear to be filled with discussions of this question. However, it is noteworthy that a long line of scholars, particularly those we have just been considering, all of whom have demonstrated their great interest in economics, have given testimony in their writings which argues that economics in basic content is no more quantitative than any other social science (e.g., Veblen, other institutionalist economists, Katona, Ruth P. Mack, the behavioral economists, etc.).

The mainstream economics response to this line of thinking has for at least the past 50 years been simply and steadfastly to ignore it and persevere in the opposite direction, all the while making the discipline more quantitative with the result that the 'economic agents,' as we have demonstrated in this chapter, have become, if anything, more mechanical, more robotic, and less like real people making economic decisions along with all their other decisions. In this connection terminology is a dead giveaway. Economists are fond of referring to both households and firms as 'rational economic agents.' It is the latter, we have suggested, that economic theory manipulates. Political scientists refer to voters, or possibly 'citizens' (merely descriptive terms). It would at least be eye catching were they to rename them with a distant and uninvolved label such as 'political unit' or 'political agent.' The same thing can be said of sociologists and, psychologists, who might in experimental psychology refer to 'subjects' and in clinical psychology might refer to 'patients.' None appear to dehumanize their subjects quite as completely as the economists' 'economic agents.'

It is an old charge that economists in referring to economic man are trying to isolate human beings in their economic activities from all other things in which human beings engage. Economic activity can arguably be 'modeled' or described in a series of equations more successfully, as we noted earlier, if the recursive character of the behavior can be clearly separated from other kinds of activity motivated in more complicated ways.

In the end it is as impossible in mathematics as it was in words limited to 'economic man' to say all that needs to be said about how human beings interact with respect to economic activity (allocation, production, consumption, etc.). Both in old-fashioned words and in new econometrics, individuals for economists have to interact by well recognized and definable laws. There is no way, accurately reflective of what flesh and blood people do, to model idiosyncratic behavior.

The conclusion seems inescapable that mathematics per se is not the problem; it only exposes the problem with painful clarity. We can say that, thanks to the quantification revolution, the myopic view of human beings previously taken in microeconomic theory is not only preserved but virtually enshrined. That view, underscoring a point we made earlier in connection with Jane Smith, has been well stated by Randall Bartlett:

> Throughout my professional life I have been bothered by the narrow economic vision of 'society' as a 'place' where persons transact, but do not otherwise interact . . . Economists examine markets and exchange . . . The institutional structures of the real world, and of its markets, are far richer and more complex than the mythical ones of the abstract model. (Bartlett 1989, p. ix)

An advanced textbook on economic dynamics by Stokey and Lucas illustrates Bartlett's fear clearly. They say early on, 'Today in every field of application, we have theories that deal explicitly with rational economic agents operating through time in stochastic environments' (1989, p. 3). The awkward question to pose is the one posed earlier in this chapter: 'Is the real world peopled by rational economic agents operating through time in stochastic environments?' Alternatively would it be more useful to describe the world as peopled by fallible human beings, filled with various often conflicting impulses trying to learn as they go and doing the best they can in the face of all sorts of uncertainty? Later the authors suggest that 'most of the results in Chapter 4 carry over almost without change to situations in which the return function is subject to stochastic shocks and the objective is to maximize the expected value of discounted returns' (1989, p. 165). To be sure Keynes had his entrepreneurs trying to maximize discounted returns in his marginal efficiency of capital, but it was not quite as mechanical as it appears in this more recent incarnation. 'Maximizing profits' as an entrepreneurial objective sounds recognizable as human behavior, but becomes much less meaningful when that recognizable objective is put through the purifying process of the economists' ceteris paribus assumptions, rendering it in a mathematical formula as a very precise recursive guide to behavior which becomes infinitely more precise than human behavior is ever likely to be.

In the real world it has long been recognized that 'maximizing profits' might be a 'long run' objective which in the short run can get muddled with various good will activities (fighting disease, sponsoring cultural events, etc.). The latter activities might be included in the verbal description of entrepreneurial behavior but will almost certainly be reduced to an error term or some similar device in a set of mathematical equations.

In economics, mathematics not only permits precise expression of how people behave but it strips the explanations of human behavior down so that the precision is derived from the consequences of precise but recursive behavior. Economists love the precision and the equilibria which they produce and forgive the distortion and over-simplification of human behavior which the math requires, just as they overlooked the somewhat less extreme assumptions which the verbal predecessors of the current mathematical 'economic agents' required. Contrast this view with that of Ruth P. Mack, who contributed to the behavioral economics literature many years ago the following characterization of what influences consumption:

> In twentieth century America, virtually everything that influences what a person is and how he got that way – a process of constant interaction between the evolving individual and his social field – influences what and when and how much he buys or saves . . . Currently his buying is a function of what he is, what he has, the recent history of his purchases, what others have or buy, what he expects, what he hopes, the habits that he has established and very nearly anything else. The dynamics of consumption is in our society coextensive with the dynamics of personality. (Mack 1952, p. 15)

We are back to square one. The problem is not with the use of math per se, but with the construct of economic man and the relentless indelible adherence to that perspective by economists for generations. Ruth Mack is describing human economic behavior in a way which we believe is realistic, but which is inadequately captured both in traditional economic man and even more in the mathematically convenient construct, rational economic agent. Mathematics, we have underscored, serves to express that perspective precisely and elegantly but to hide the inherent limitations of this perspective generally and for certain from those whose knowledge of math is limited. But this perspective also renders it more difficult to make economic theory more realistic by hiding the premises from the view of all but the students of math even as it presents the theory with a pseudo precision and elegance that makes it look as solid and unassailable as – well, Newton's theory of gravity.

Stokey and Lucas assert that 'Powerful methods are now available for analyzing theoretical models with equilibrium outcomes . . .' (1989, p. 3). But they are frank also to say often that they are confining their attention mainly to 'recursive competitive equilibria.' They are indeed following in the footsteps of Arrow, Debreu, et al. It is a time-honored tradition in mainstream economics and it is the kind of approach which lends itself ideally to mathematical modeling. This is what they mean when they talk about the 'widespread' applications of their work to the real world. There are applications in the world of competitive equilibria and they are judged in welfare terms from the perspective of Pareto optimality. When they use expressions like 'powerful tools' they mean tools that can be applied to the world of competitive equilibria and Pareto optimality. This is not really the real world.

As we discuss elsewhere, including Pareto optimality in a system of 'positive economics' does serious violation to the meaning of 'positive' because it requires accepting the current distribution of income and wealth, whatever they are, without question. In any real world system, to accept the distribution of wealth and income without question is surely not a positive view but a normative affirmation!

The basic difference, of course, is that the world that Stokey and Lucas's rational economic agents inhabit can be delineated mathematically, and the world that Ruth Mack sketches cannot. Adherence to reality gets us closer to Mack's world – the world we live in. Adherence to precision, and consistency in analysis leads us to Stokey and Lucas. (We are back to Jane Smith, human being, but not exactly 'rational economic agent!')

In sum, we have asserted that the limitations of mainstream economics existed before its mathematical conversion. The mathematics revolution more fully isolated economists from non-economists, it set off economists even more completely because mathematical formulations had a power and rigor and elegance which earlier economic analyses could only approximate. Thus a book like Hicks's *Value and Capital*, which already contains a considerable amount of math, would be a 'better' book were it written today by an up to date mainstream economist because what is in the book has an excessive amount of verbiage. It is, therefore, 'inefficient.'

Econometric modeling has been described as follows:

> Economic theory is typically crisp and unambiguous. Models of demand, production, and aggregate consumption all postulate precise *deterministic*, relationships. Dependent and independent variables are identified, a functional form is specified, and in most cases, at least a qualitative statement is made about the effects that occur when independent variables in models change. Of course,

> the model is only amplification of reality. It will include the salient features in the relationship of interest, but will leave unaccounted for influences that might well be present but are, for our purposes, unimportant . . . . (Greene 2000, pp. 1–2 emphasis in original)

This is precisely the world to which Randall Bartlett (1989) is objecting. It is clearly a world that is thought to be peculiarly amenable to being expressed in mathematical terms. The conventional modern textbooks dwell on the gains achieved from the mathematics revolution. We have acknowledged what we consider genuine gains, but we ask, what are the losses? We consider this question more fully below.

Mathematics Beyond Economics

We have suggested that the problems of concern to behavioral economists and others antedated the quantification revolution. We further suggested, that in spite of the gains which came with quantification and which we freely acknowledge, there were losses. One was the greater difficulty others found in comprehending what was being done. By now the revolution has gone so far that often little or no effort is made to refer to economic problems at all. We have already noted that it is by no means uncommon nowadays for the math and the accouterments of math to be presented more prominently than any underlying economic problems to which the material under review might pertain.

We present an example, selected more or less at random, from the *Journal of Economic Theory*, one of the newest (1969) of the highly prestigious journals (at least in the United States). The article is entitled 'Continuous approximations of stochastic evolutionary game dynamics.'

The abstract of the article is as follows:

> Continuous approximations that are ordinary differential equations (ODEs) or stochastic differential equations (SDEs) are often used to study the properties of discrete processes. We show that different ways of taking the continuous limit of the same model may result in either an ODE or an SDE and study the manner in which each approximates the discrete model. We compare the asymptotic properties of the continuous equations with those of the discrete dynamics and show that they tend to provide a better approximation when a greater amount of variance of the discrete model is preserved in the continuous limit. (Corradi and Sarin 2000, 163)

We select this abstract, not because there is anything unusual about it but, on the contrary, because it seems quite typical of what one will find in this journal. There does not appear to be one scintilla of a reference to any specific economic subject or problem in this article. It is all about econometric method. It is not unlike writing a piece in the old days (when economists still fumbled with words) which might have read:

> Prose sentences in essays on economic subjects might be declarative or exclamatory. Declarative or exclamatory sentences (DS or ES) are often used to describe the shocking properties of a given interrelationship. We show that the shocking aspects of a given interrelationship can be highlighted either by using ES or by using colorful adjectives in DS. We study the manner in which each highlights that which is shocking. We compare the flexibility that one acquires from the use of a variety of adjectives with the succinct properties which one finds are attached to a short ES. We consider whether succinctness or adjectival variety offers a better approximation of the reality which is inherent in the interrelationship under consideration.

It can be left to the reader to consider whether or not the comparison is a fair one. (At least we refer to 'economic subjects' which is more than the original abstract does!) We suggest that rhetoric can enhance verbal prose in roughly the same way that econometrics can enhance numeric discussion. Economists have never been renowned for their interest in the written word, although they surely have developed interest in econometric presentations. Surely no economics journal would ever have been devoted to improving the written word in economics presentations, and I could never have gotten the perceptive paragraph above published.

The comparison seems appropriate because just as rhetoric can improve writing on many subjects of which economics is but one, it seems clear that the subject of the abstract presented might be applied to many fields besides economics where differential equations can be appropriately employed.

So we end much as we began with a consideration of whether the tail and the dog can be distinguished in current discussions of mathematical presentations of economic subjects.

THE IMPACT OF THE QUANTIFICATION REVOLUTION ON ECONOMICS AS AN ACADEMIC DISCIPLINE

By now the 'quantification revolution' we have been describing has swept away virtually any reservations any economists may have had. It permeates the thinking of major figures in the profession, as we have shown.

It has also transformed the teaching of economics in American graduate schools considered in far greater detail in Chapter 7. We have summarized some of the more important changes in Table 3.1. The table displays some of the essential features of the quantification revolution and its impact on graduate education in 16 of the most prominent graduate programs in economics currently available for prospective future economics students to consider.

The curricular triumph of quantification is the most impressive finding of the table. Fully one third to one half of the required core courses in the graduate schools under consideration involve quantification skills. But the student will become well aware of the stress on quantification skills even before being accepted into a graduate program in economics. No university makes this more unmistakable than Harvard. We have previously mentioned the remarkable stance taken in the graduate microtheory text used at Harvard. It reflects almost perfectly the catalogue stance toward the importance of math. In discussing the mathematics requirement, their catalogue announces: 'Students are expected to have a strong background in linear algebra and calculus upon entering the program; knowledge of differential equations and statistics is also very helpful.' This contrasts strikingly with their attitude toward being admitted to the program at all. 'Concentration in economics is preferred but not required.' And again they add, 'Students will need a strong undergraduate training in mathematics.' In short if you are a mathematician and know no economics they will consider you. If you are an economist and know no math, they won't. We ask once more, what is the tail and what is the dog? The parallel here to our earlier analogy would be telling a student applying for admission to a PhD program in French and being told, 'Students must be able to conjugate irregular verbs. Reading and speaking ability in French is preferred but not required.' I leave it to the reader to ask whether there are any fields of knowledge in which the subject matter of the discipline is less critical than the research methodology tools. 'Learn the tools first – you can always find a subject to apply them to later.' (To be fair, most of the programs included in the table suggest that entering students are expected to know micro and macroeconomic theory at least at the intermediate level.)

Table 3.1 Core PhD requirements in 16 American economics departments

		PhD CORE REQUIREMENTS						
	University	Micro	Macro	Econometrics	Other	Quantitative fields	Is Econ. History offered?	Is Hist. of Economic Thought offered?
1.	Univ. of Chicago	1 year (3 courses)	1 year (3 courses)	1 year Quant. Meth. (3 courses)	None	Math. Econ.	Yes	No
2.	Harvard	1 year (2 courses)	1 year (2 courses)	1 year (2 courses)	None	Advanced Econometrics	Yes	No
3.	M.I.T.	1 Year (2 semesters)	1 year (2 semesters)	1 year (2 semesters)	Economic History (1 semester)	Stat. Methods in Econ. (1 sem.)	Yes	No
4.	Princeton	1 Year (2 terms)	1 Year (2 terms)	(1 year)	None	Advanced Econometrics	No	No
5.	Stanford	3 courses (15 units)	3 courses (15 units)	3 courses (15 units)	None	Advanced Econometrics Math. Econ.	Yes	No
6.	Northwestern Univ.	1 year (3 units)	1 year (3 units)	1year (3 units)	Econ. History (1 unit)	Advanced Econometrics	Yes	No
7.	Yale	1 year (2 courses)	1 year (2 courses)	1 year (2 courses)	Adv. Micro (1 course) Adv. Macro (1 course) Econ. Hist. (1 course)	Advanced Econometrics Math. Econ. Statistics	Yes	No
8.	University of Pennsylvania	1 year (2 courses)	1 year (2 courses)	1 year (2 courses)	Math for Economists (2 courses)	Advanced Econometrics	No	No

Table 3.1 cont.

9.	University of California (Berkeley)	1 year (8 units)	1 year (8 units)	1 year (8 units) (2)	Math Tools for Economists (4 units) Econ Hist (3 units)	Advanced Econometrics Math Economics	Yes	No
10.	University of California, Los Angeles	1 year (3 courses)	1 Year (3 courses)	1 year (3 courses)	Math Methods in Econ (1 course)	Advanced Econometrics Math Econ.	Yes	Yes
11.	University of Wisconsin	1 year (2 courses)	1 year (2 courses) (3)	1 year (2 courses)	Math Econ (1 course) Quantitative Econ. Policy (1 course)	Advanced Econometrics	No	No
12.	Columbia University	1 year (2 courses)	1 year (2 courses)	1 year (2 courses)	Math. Methods for Economists (1 course) Advanced Econometrics (1 course)	Advanced Econometrics Advanced Math Methods	Yes	No
13.	Rochester	1 year (2 courses)	1 year (2 courses)	1 year (2 courses)	Math. Econ. & Statistics (2 courses)	Advanced Econometrics	No	No
14.	Cornell University	1 year (2 courses)	1 year (2 courses)	1 year (2 courses)	Math (1 Course)	Advanced Econometrics	Yes	No
15.	University of Minnesota	1 year (4 units)	1 year (4 units)	1 year (4 units) (4)	(4)	Math. Econ.	No	Yes
16.	University of Michigan	1 year (2 courses)	½ year (1 course)	½ year (1 course)	Statistics (1 course) Mathematics (1 course)	Advanced Econometrics	Yes	No

Table 3.1 cont.

Notes:

(1) Most of the universities included in the table have a variety of advanced workshops, in addition to regular courses, in which generally graduate students are expected to participate. We have made no effort to include them here.

(2) Berkeley does not explicitly say econometrics is a requirement but the implication is clear that two introductory statistics and econometrics courses are generally taken by all students. Both courses are combined econometrics and statistics.

(3) At the University of Wisconsin the field of macroeconomics is combined with money.

(4) The University of Minnesota catalogue exhorts students, 'There is no specific econometrics requirement for graduation, but most economists confront issues of extracting information from data throughout their careers . . . . Moreover, faculty are unsympathetic to students who skip the course but then seek help with econometric issues in writing a thesis. In other words, take this course sequence'.
On the other hand there is a notice in their catalogue that in 1999–2000 there was no econometrics field (presumably beyond the core) being offered! That surely makes Minnesota unique. They have a number of econometrics courses listed in the catalogue.

Source: Unless otherwise specified data are from the 1999–2001 catalogue of each university.

The mathematics revolution shows up in other ways as well. In virtually all the universities in the table econometrics or mathematical economics (or both) show up outside the core as an elective field for more work by the student.

We note that much of the work in virtually every field in economics today involves applying econometrics and other mathematical skills to the subject matter of the field. In certain fields, e.g. game theory, the math is central. Thus it is possible not only to be required, as we have seen, to spend perhaps half the first year on quantitative skills but in the later period when students elect fields they can stick even more to the quantitative approach by the choice of elective fields. Thus the per cent of their graduate school time spent on quantification skills can exceed half of their time. Is there any other discipline in which you could get a PhD by spending the bulk of your time on tools rather than the discipline itself?

Another feature which emerges from the table is the realization that there is very little difference among these programs in their central content. If not 'perfectly homogenous', to use the lingo of our discipline, there is very little product differentiation.

What of the losses which have accompanied the addition of all this mathematics? Some universities (four in our group) no longer offer economic history (although in some – e.g., MIT, Northwestern, Yale, Berkeley, some work in economic history is required for the PhD). We have the impression that work in economic history was quite commonly required in the middle of the twentieth century.

In general it is probably fair to say that, again like many fields, concentration on historical episodes as examples of various theoretical constructs in economics is not a favored approach. One cannot imagine a course, say, in meteorology which would contemplate earthquakes without devoting considerable attention to the historical record. One can, however, write at length about various theories on, say, business cycles with remarkably few allusions to the historical record. (The 'Great Depression' is perhaps an exception.)

The biggest loss has clearly been in the availability of courses in the history of economic thought. None of the universities in the table offer this as a graduate field. There is one graduate course at UCLA, and one at the University of Minnesota. (There is a course on the books at Princeton 'not currently offered.' There is also an undergraduate course offered at Berkeley.) Fifty years ago this state of affairs would have been unimaginable.

It is difficult to imagine that other fields are so disinterested in their own past. Imagine a philosophy program that ignored Plato and Aristotle, or a music program disinterested in Bach and Beethoven, a German literature program that was constructed without Goethe, an art history program that proceeded without da Vinci. Mainstream economists embrace classical and neoclassical economics, but they do not feel you need to study what the founders of these traditions actually said. It is quite enough to read what current economists say they said. Even Keynes need not really be read.[6] In any case the primary function of Keynes, for many economists today, is as Exhibit A in economic thinking gone wrong. The disinterest in history of economic thought is the other side of the coin on which we find the emphasis in graduate theory programs mostly (and increasingly) on what has been written (or calculated!) in the very recent past.[7]

Blaug wrote:

> No idea or theory in economics, physics, chemistry, biology, philosophy and even mathematics is ever thoroughly understood except as the end product of a slice of history, the result of some previous intellectual development . . . So it is . . . with all economic theories. Economic knowledge is path-dependent. What we now know about the economic system is not something we have just discovered, but it is the sum of all discoveries, insights and false starts in the past. Without Hayek and Robbins and Pigou, no Keynes; without Keynes, no Friedman; without Friedman, no Lucas; without Lucas no . . . . (Blaug 2001, 156)

From this point of view it is possible to argue that one consequence of the quantification revolution is that it has obliterated as insignificant virtually everything that was ever previously (say before 1970 or 1980) said about the subject by earlier generations of contemporary economists. It is so creaky, so imprecise, so crude that it is now as irrelevant to the subject as is a Model T to a modern automobile. If Blaug is right (and for example a Model T was surely a necessary precursor to a modern car) then the link between quantification and the present perspective of mainstream economics is close indeed. Along with their admiration and self-satisfaction with what can be done via econometric modeling has come:

1. an easy dismissal of pre-econometric thinking and the thinkers who were involved,

---

6. In working on the earlier discussion of Keynes, I had to get his *Treatise on Money* out of Interlibrary Lending.

7. After the above was written in first draft, an article on this decline in interest in *History of Economic Thought*, by Mark Blaug, came out. He detected some rise in interest in the subject (more journals devoted to the subject, etc.) at the same time that the course continued to disappear. He attributed this anomaly partly to the fact that the history of thought 'appeals to a different type of mind from that of the average mainstream economist' (Blaug 2001, 147).

2. a fixation on the most recent contributions and a corresponding inflation of their importance. (How many graduate courses in economic theory concentrate on work done since – name your own recent date – 1980, 1990, etc.?)
3. A third consequence is, perhaps, truly serious. The discipline has been reshaped to conform to and reflect what can be done via modeling. Not only do economists today stick to what can be quantified, but they will insist almost literally that if it can't be quantified, it can and should be ignored. This assertion runs through the very heart of contemporary economics. 'What you can't count, forget.' Even before the quantification revolution economists felt most comfortable when they asserted that for economics there was no difference between happiness and summing utilities. Because one can sum utilities so brilliantly econometrically the loss has mattered less and less. Economists are not only addicted to the detail that can be spelled out numerically, but they have contempt for the nuances and subtleties which can be expressed, if at all, only verbally. Such subtleties, we assert, are part of the world the economy and, therefore, economists must address. Subtleties are far from unimportant!
4. The ultimate tragedy is that, properly incorporated, there can be little doubt that there is a legitimate and highly useful role for mathematics in the development of economic theory. We have stated this earlier. The ability to make theory dynamic involves utilizing the possibility that all functional relationships need not refer to the same time period – x can be a function of yesterday's y. There is the possibility that one can involve as many dependent variables in an explanation as is required and there is the possibility of being able to describe interrelationships that are more complicated than can readily be explained in words. These are but a few examples of the genuine contributions toward more realistic, therefore more useful, economic theory which mathematical tools open up. But instead of attempting to apply these tools as ancillary aids in gaining insight into reasonably realistic situations, the discipline, as we have attempted to demonstrate, has insisted on applying them wholesale and, moreover, has insisted rigidly on sticking to competitive structures, or if not to playing games (two-person, two-commodity games are popular). And as we have stressed the rigid insistence on modeling only for rational economic agents judged against Pareto optimality – all these and similar rigidities have offset the potential for genuine progress that the introduction of quantification opened up.

We have, in a sense, come full circle. The decline of the history of thought is tied to the rise of quantification and to the triumph of the perspective which sees economics entirely as the study of rational economic man optimizing measurable utilities in a competitive world with perfect knowledge. Economists adore that world. Math enables them to pursue study of that world as they never could before. Why should they contemplate any other world?

One answer might be to suggest by analogy that just because, thanks to the march of scientific progress, wars can be so much more efficiently fought than ever before, seeking peaceful alternatives is both not natural (against human nature) and unnecessary. So we are left with this question: is the tiny toehold for the history of economic thought at UCLA and at the University of Minnesota the last gasp of the past, or the first wave of the future? We suggest only that the answer to that question is tied up with whether or not quantification alone will continue to reflect virtually the only acceptable methodology – all that economists admire; or whether the currently tiny doubts (and cries for change) will move past their current position on the fringes of 'respectable' work in economics.

CONCLUSIONS

We have argued that insisting that economic agents are rational and that their behavior can be analyzed as microeconomists have always done, in terms of relatively simple maximization of 'utility' and profits, reduces human beings to virtual robots in their economic activity and keeps economists from confronting many important real world problems, at least with their theory. We shall return to these problems in detail in later chapters.

Here we need only add that the mathematization of microeconomic theory has left these deficiencies more or less intact and added new difficulties in terms of our ability to communicate both with non-mathematical economists and with the outside world.

It is important to note that this change has affected the teaching of economics in American graduate schools (and to a significant extent in other countries as well), and has, in our judgment, narrowed and warped the scope of scholarship in economics in ways that bode poorly for future progress.

No less an authority than Gerard Debreu has listed many of these consequences. Debreu notes:

> 1. When a theorist . . . judges his scholarly work, . . . values . . . may play a decisive role. The very choice of the questions to which he tries to find answers is influenced by his mathematical background. Thus the danger is ever present that the part of economics will become secondary, if not marginal to that judgement.

> 2. The reward system of our profession reinforces the effects of that autocriticism. Decisions that shape the career of an economic theorist are made by his peers. Whether they are referees of a journal, or of a research organization, members of an appointment or of a promotion committee, when they sit as judges in any capacity their verdicts will not be independent of their own values . . . If he believes that they rate mathematical sophistication highly, and if he can prove that he is one of the sophisticates, the applause that he expects to receive will condition his performance.
> 3. The same effects are also amplified by the relentless pressure to publish exerted by his environment . . . The environment of a scholar demands papers, and the temptation to supply them without restraint may become overpowering to an economic theorist who has developed proficiency in his research style. The precocious development of that proficiency is a comparative advantage that a mathematical approach bestows on him.
> 4. The spread of mathematized economic theory was helped even by its esoteric character. Since its messages cannot be deciphered by economists who do not have the proper key, their evaluation is entrusted to those who have the code. But acceptance of their technical expertise also implies acceptance of their values. (Debreu 1991, 5–6, numbering added)

Debreu recognizes these dangers but is seemingly not particularly alarmed by them. He is mostly very proud of what can be done by presenting conventional economic theory in a mathematical way. In the dozen years since he made his assessment, the trends he notes have only gotten more pronounced. Debreu has not deflected the discipline from its obsession with math any more than did the warnings of Leontief or Gordon before him.

In a sense long before the quantification revolution mainstream economists had expressed a clear preference for a deductive approach to developing economic theory which required putting a very heavy foot on the ceteris paribus pedal. So exaggerated was this tendency that in economics more than in any other social science the theory that emerged applied to a reality that had been specially tailored to fit the theory rather than the other way around. As we have noted earlier, only recently have economists openly granted that their theory was designed to explain 'stylized facts.' The biggest stylization has always been rational economic man himself. One of the (unintended?) consequences emerging from the quantification revolution was to stress this distortion even more. The fit between what can be done with econometrics and its application to rational economic man instead of to the stumbling, bumbling, well meaning but often irrational pursuits of flesh and blood people trying to solve economic problems was so perfect that the flight from reality simply accelerated. Why worry about realism or relevance when the interrelationships depicted econometrically are so elegant, so precise, so internally logical? Modern economic theory is thus still further removed from the world to which policy makers have to apply theory![8] The disjuncture has been further hidden by luck. Had the world suffered a major depression the fact that theory was not giving much assistance to the policy makers would have been clear (and perhaps even worrisome) to everyone.

We can try to make this important point one other way. We underscore once again that we are in no sense anti-quantitative or opposed to the use of mathematics and mathematical reasoning in economic theory. We are concerned only that the methodology now rules the discipline rather than serving it. We have witnessed the longstanding tendency of economic theory to alter the world to suit the theory. This tendency, which began long ago with a 'few simplifying assumptions' had pretty much gotten out of hand before the quantification revolution came along. That revolution simply enabled the problem to be exacerbated even as we all recognized the legitimate advantages which mathematics, perhaps especially econometrics, had to offer. It is rather like the impact on a drug addict of introducing a new and presumably irresistible form of packaging or gift wrapping. What was already an addiction was made even more irresistible. Today one finds, therefore, as we have seen, as many scientific papers concerned with problems in econometric theory or methodology as with problems in economics. The discipline is seriously warped, in consequence, with more and more of its best minds devoted to improving aspects of the packaging and fewer and fewer devoted to the increasing disjunction between the severe and challenging economic problems faced by all our economies and the degree to which economic theorists spend time trying, however indirectly, to help ameliorate them. But the complexity and difficulty in making clear to any but the initiated what is being done has gotten worse, decade by decade. Standing in the shambles, proud of every complexity, every indication of advanced and impressive erudition, are the leaders of quantitative economics (everywhere so recognized as we shall see (Chapter 7) – they run the major departments, the major journals, etc.), ruling supreme over all they survey –

8. One economist who argued that all the elegance and precision did not change the fundamental thrust of mainstream economics was Benjamin Ward. Referring to what he called 'the formalist revolution,' he wrote: '. . . there is one striking and anomalous feature to the whole transformation of economics: it was essentially methodological rather than substantive. If one accepts the Keynesian revolution as a phenomenon of the 30s and 40s, and the formalist revolution as a phenomenon of the 50s and 60s, there just are not any fundamental substantive changes brought about by the latter. The core of theory remains the price system, and right at its heart is still to be found the competitive regime of production and exchange' (Ward 1972, p. 43).

the theory they presumably serve, the non-interventionist policy that theory ostensibly clarifies, and the economies they inhabit. For most people seeing the changes emanating from the quantification revolution is not easy. The trend setting mainstream economists wouldn't have it any other way!

All of this would seem to be corroboration of the basic theme we develop. The distortions in economic theory brought about by the way economists develop it, the distorting effects which that method has on the teaching of economics, especially at the graduate level, and the strictures which all this places on how economic research is organized in the end run headlong into the clear signs that economic theory as it has developed in the United States is far from providing the kind of support to the economic policy makers which they have a right to expect. But let us be very clear. We have underscored in this chapter that none of what has been said is meant to suggest that the application of econometric and other mathematical approaches to economic analysis does not make many useful things possible that cannot be accomplished in any other way. Rather we suggest only that there is very little balance and even less tolerance for methodological diversity among contemporary economic theorists. Impressive as the accomplishments in quantitative economics are, the intolerance for all else is equally impressive and to those so impressed it is a source of enormous pride to the practitioners (who spend little if any time worrying about their intolerance) and considerable distress to the non-practitioners, who are mostly well advised to keep quiet about their distress if they wish to flourish in academia. That their lacks make such flourishing very difficult to achieve adds to their frustration, but leaves the mainstream remarkably unmoved. For the devout quantifiers the Queen of the Social Sciences is doing spectacularly well, making all kinds of progress every day. That these practitioners care little what the mathematically challenged and verbally fixated economic obsoletes think is what adds self-satisfaction to the pride already noted. Whether or not, therefore, the comment of McCloskey with which this chapter began is appropriate is a question we can leave to the reader.

For most people – the mathematically challenged among us – seeing the changes emanating from the quantification revolution is not fully appreciated. Mainstream economists wouldn't have it any other way!

REFERENCES

Ayres, Clarence E. (1944), *The Theory of Economic Progress*, Chapel Hill, NC: University of North Carolina Press.

Bartlett, Randall (1989), *Economics and Power*, Cambridge: Cambridge University Press.

Becker, Gary (1966), *Human Capital: A Theoretical and Empirical Analysis with Special Reference to Education*, New York: National Bureau of Economic Research/Columbia University Press.

Becker, Gary (1981), *A Treatise on the Family*, Cambridge, MA: Harvard University Press.

Blaug, Mark (2001), 'No history of ideas, please, we're economists', *Journal of Economic Perspectives*, **15**, 145–64.

Corradi, Valentina and Rajiv Sarin (2000), 'Continuous approximations of stochastic evolutionary game dynamics', *Journal of Economic Theory*, **94** (2), 163–91.

Debreu, Gerard (1991), 'The mathematization of economic theory', *American Economic Review*, **81** (1), 1–7.

Downs, Anthony (1957), *An Economic Theory of Democracy*, New York: Harper and Row.

Frumkin, Norman (1990), *Guide to Economic Indicators*, Armonk, New York: M.E. Sharpe.

Greene, William H. (2000), *Econometric Analysis, Fourth Edition*, Upper Saddle River, NJ: Prentice-Hall.

Hicks, John R. (1979), *Causality in Economics*, Oxford: Blackwell.

Holden, K., D.A. Peel and J.L. Thompson (1985), *Expectations: Theory and Evidence*, New York: St Martin's Press.

Kahneman, Daniel (1973), *Attention and Effort*, Englewood Cliffs, NJ: Prentice-Hall.

Kahneman, Daniel, Paul Slovic and Amos Tversky (eds) (1982), *Judgement Under Uncertainty: Heuristics and Biases*, Cambridge and New York: Cambridge University Press.

Kahneman, Daniel and Amos Tversky (eds) (2000), *Choices, Values, and Frames*, New York, Cambridge, UK: Russell Sage Foundation Cambridge University Press.

Kaish, Stanley (1986), 'Behavioral economics in the theory of the business cycle', in Benjamin Gilad and Stanley Kaish (eds), *Handbook of Behavioral Economics*, Greenwich, CT: JAI Press, B, p. 31–49.

Katona, George (1951), *Psychological Analysis of Economic Behavior, First Edition*, New York: McGraw-Hill.

Katona, George (1980), *Essays on Behavioral Economics*, Ann Arbor, MI: Survey Research Center, Institute for Social Research, University of Michigan.

Laibson, David (1996), *Hyperbolic Discount Function, Undersaving, and Saving Policy*, Cambridge, MA: National Bureau of Economic Research.

McCloskey, D. (1998), *The Rhetoric of Economics*, Madison, WI: University of Wisconsin Press.

Mack, Ruth P. (1952), 'Economics of consumption', in Bernard Haley (ed.), *A Survey of Contemporary Economics,* **2**, Homewood, IL: Richard D. Irwin, p. 15.

Marshall, Alfred (1919), *Industry and Trade*, London: Macmillan.

Marshall, Alfred (1949), *Principles of Economics*, *Eighth Edition,* London: Macmillan [First Edition 1890].

Mas-Colell, Andreu, Michael D. Whinston and Jerry R. Green (1995), *Microeconomic Theory*, New York: Oxford University Press.

Mullainathan, Sendhil and Richard Thaler (2000), *Behavioral Economics*, Cambridge, MA, National Bureau of Economic Research.

Samuelson, Paul and William Nordhaus (2001), *Macroeconomics, 17th Edition*, New York: McGraw-Hill Irwin.

Simon, Herbert A. (1986), 'Preface', in Benjamin Gilad and Stanley Kaish (eds), *Handbook of Behavioral Economics*, Greenwich, CT: JAI Press.

Stokey, Nancy L. and Robert E. Lucas (1989), *Recursive Methods in Economic Dynamics*, Cambridge, MA: Harvard University Press.

Strumpel, Burkhard, James N. Morgan and Ernest Zahn (eds) (1972), *Human Behavior in Economic Affairs: Essays in Honor of George Katona*, Amsterdam and New York: Elsevier Scientific Publishing.

Thaler, Richard (ed.) (1991), *Quasi-Rational Economics*, New York: Russell Sage Foundation.

Thaler, Richard (ed.) (1992), *The Winner's Curse: Paradoxes and Anomalies of Economic Life*, New York and Toronto: Free Press, Maxwell Macmillan Canada, Maxwell Macmillan International.

Thaler, Richard (ed.) (1993), *Advances in Behavioral Finance*, New York: Russell Sage Foundation.

Von Neuman, John and Oskar Morganstern (1944, Second Edition 1953), *The Theory of Games and Economic Behavior*, Princeton, NJ: Princeton University Press.

Ward, Benjamin (1972), *What's Wrong With Economics*? New York and London: Basic Books.

4. Trivialization and elegance I: the world of microeconomics

> The evidence on price behavior is sufficiently inconsistent with the simple theories of market clearing that industrial economists should be led to explore other paradigms. The most useful extensions of the theory will be those that recognize that marketing is a costly activity, that an impersonal price mechanism is not the only device used to allocate goods, and that price methods in conjunction with non-price methods are typically used to allocate goods. (Carlton 1998, 943)

> The once widespread assumption that changing theories reflected contemporaneous events was part of a more general school of thought – half economics, half sociology, and all mush – known as 'institutional economics.' (Sowell 1993, 788)

THE GLOBAL VIEW

In the first chapter we saw that the modern discipline of economics was set by Adam Smith on a path which had a role for the invisible hand, provided that the market structures were what Smith called competitive. Smith was indeed ready to 'leave it to the market' to allocate resources for much of the economy when competition prevailed.

His famous pin factory extolled the gains in productivity emanating from the division of labor. While such gains could exist, as he saw, in very small firms, he failed to anticipate what would happen to the economies of scale with technological progress. As we shall consider in this chapter, they threatened both the viability and the feasibility of pure competition and left the invisible hand in a far more ambiguous position.

We earlier saw Smith mentioned the invisible hand only once, and devoted considerable space and attention to the public sector. Succeeding generations of economists took the competitive world to which much of Smith's analysis pertained and added marginal analysis, Walrasian general equilibrium, and eventually mathematical modeling to present us with the modern competitive model to which our students are thoroughly exposed. All students, undergraduates but especially graduate students, learn to know and love the competitive model for its precision, complexity, elegance, internal logic, and neatness. No other theory in any social science can come close to it. It can be combined with Pareto optimality to produce a standard for judging welfare and its maximization for the households and firms which inhabit this world. This standard will enable the well trained economist to pronounce on how the component units of a competitive economy epitomize the closest thing that any of us could hope to see to the Panglossian best of all possible worlds.

We showed that an initial problem with this view of the Smithian world was that once the economies of scale became a major factor, which was in process of occurring virtually from when the *Wealth of Nations* was published, the invisible hand ran into a major snag. The conflict became inexorably greater between the efficiency requirements of modern industrial processes and the automaticity which necessarily had to accompany the operation of the system if the invisible hand was to deserve the accolades which economists like to give it. (We reiterate that agriculture and manufacturing do not even predominate any longer in the modern industrial economy. Services have surged.)

The obvious answer to this dilemma was to find devices through which it could be argued that the real world behaved *just like* a competitive world, even if it wasn't strictly true. The ingenuity of economists in pursuing this line of reasoning, not only in microeconomic theory but, as we shall see in the next chapter, in the macroeconomic equivalents of the competitive model, has been impressive indeed.

In this chapter, therefore, we consider 'trivialization' in modern microeconomics, saving the macroeconomic equivalent for the next chapter. We argue that the 1930s was a watershed for economic theory. What Robinson and Chamberlin did for microeconomic theory, Keynes did for macroeconomic theory. Both aspects of modern economic theory were given a chance to come to grips with the modern world and to recognize that, however precise or elegant, theory in any social science has to bear sufficient resemblance to the real world so that it can be helpful in devising useful public policy. The theorists must, therefore, make some effort to explain the economy as it in fact is, 'warts and all.' Instead of building on the advances of the giants of the 1930s all too many economic theorists have devoted themselves either to simply ignoring what was frequently done (all too often this was the case in microeconomics), or to denying the importance or relevance of what was done (the route, we shall see, taken by many 'new classical macroeconomists'). The result was trivialization of economic theory, by which we mean deliberately turning one's back on the efforts to make theory more realistic and in effect frequently severing any links between theory building and policy by suggesting in various ways that the task of theory in any case has nothing much to do with improving economic policy.

It is understood that all theory requires some simplification. But we suggest that confronting the real world in some reasonably recognizable way is at the very least the first requirement in developing economic theory. Only then can it serve as a prelude to better understanding of the real world, which is invariably the first step in improving public policy with which to enhance the flow of real income. We shall see that 'theory as benchmark' can early run into diminishing returns.

In both macroeconomics and microeconomics the major goal of the last half of the twentieth century in economics was, it can be asserted, not to develop better public policy. It was to find a way to restore in both the notion that 'self-regulation' was in general the best policy. For the macroeconomy we spell this out in the next chapter. For microeconomics generally it meant returning to a former *weltanschauung* in which assuming pure competition was not so far-fetched an assumption. Mainstream economists wanted nothing so much as to be able to continue admiring what presumably transpired in that marvelous state they called equilibrium in which neither time nor place exist.

By the start of World War II it seemed clear to many (notably Robinson, Chamberlin, Keynes and their followers) that economic theory as received from its classical and neoclassical expositors was a poor guide to public policy in the modern world.[1]

How did economics manage to squander the great chance for more realistic theory given it in the 1930s? Our discipline has devoted more than 60 years to a desperate search for ways to trivialize economic theory in both microeconomics and macroeconomics. Why? This chapter and the next are devoted to seeking answers. We begin, therefore, to follow economics' yellow brick road.

1. Of course, some economists do not agree that aiding in improving public policy is the ultimate purpose of theory in the discipline. To that group there is an obvious question to be addressed. Does the field of economics, judged by the criterion economists admire above all others when applied elsewhere – namely, efficiency – justify the resources currently devoted to it in teaching and research?

TRIVIALIZING MICROECONOMICS

The field of industrial organization was originally and frequently referred to as 'applied microeconomic theory.' It developed out of the conflict we have been discussing between the economies of large scale production, on the one hand, and the automatic self-regulating production which, guided by the famous invisible hand, allegedly converted personal greed into social welfare without any sacrifice of technological efficiency.

We noted earlier that this meant that in a sense microeconomic theory has been in a never-never land virtually since the beginning. It has always stressed the wonders which flow from a purely competitive economy when in fact the market-oriented economies of the industrialized world could never be competitive in that way because among other things the modern economies of scale would preclude their being efficient (as economists conventionally use the term).

The seminal works which attempted to incorporate these critical aspects of reality into economic theory were, of course, Joan Robinson's *Economics of Imperfect Competition* (1933) and Edward H. Chamberlin's *The Theory of Monopolistic Competition* (1933). Other efforts followed; the last perhaps was William Fellner's *Competition Among the Few*, which came out in 1949. Fellner, in that widely (and we would assert under servedly) ignored book, attempted to put the focus of inquiry working on oligopoly theory. He wrote:

> . . . a significant proportion of the markets with which value theory must be concerned cannot be analyzed in terms of demand functions and supply functions derived from technological data and utility functions alone. Determinate equilibria, in the usual sense, cannot be established for these markets analytically. It is, however, wrong to say that for this reason theory must 'fail' in its discussion of these markets . . . Theory may 'succeed' in a different (and perhaps somewhat more modest) sense, even if it does not establish uniquely determinate prices and outputs from such data alone. (Fellner 1949, pp. 9–10)

We recall all this only to make a major point: for a relatively brief period mainstream economics was willing to contemplate a microeconomic theory that was at least crudely reflective of the world to which it presumably pertained.[2] Many years ago J.K. Galbraith contemplated what had been added to the theoretical work of Robinson and Chamberlin in the subsequent 15 or so years and concluded '. . . little was added in the way either of fundamental

2. When I was a graduate student at Berkeley at mid-century the core 'value theory' course, while it certainly began with competitive theory, included a heavy dose of Robinson, Chamberlin, et al.

revision or noteworthy extension . . . The basic theoretical system emerges largely intact' (Galbraith 1948, p. 103).

We can consider Galbraith's 1948 assessment of the way in which microeconomic theorists had incorporated imperfect competition theory into their work as it pertains to the contemporary treatment of microeconomic theory. We have previously introduced *Microeconomic Theory* by Mas-Colell et al. (1995) as representative of the best and certainly one of the most widely accepted of the current treatments of microeconomic theory. We would argue that it surely is much more sophisticated in its use of mathematics than any of the old price theory texts.

But we may ask, 'to what extent does the Mas-Colell text reflect the changes that Fellner suggested?' Fellner's book, after all, was an effort to reposition microeconomic theory to the reality of a modern economy. That reality involves most particularly oligopolistic indeterminacy in the outcome of market interactions. Because what a given oligopolist does depends on what his rivals do (which depends on what he does!), the oligopolist can set up neither a simple supply function nor a demand function, with the result that the market price and quantity can be determined only within ranges (they are indeterminate). Fellner most particularly argues that 'A theoretical apparatus that "explains" certain processes . . . is preferable to one that does not explain them at all' (Fellner 1949, p. 7). He even thought that 'the willingness to accept reduced standards of rigor' might be less than assumed.

Mas-Colell et al. have nothing if not high standards of rigor. 'Indeterminateness' appears exactly once in the index. The book itself, they assure us, covers 'the full range of topics taught in a typical first year course' (1995, p. xiii). The book concentrates heavily on demand functions and supply functions and the technological processes and utility functions from which they are derived. It thus deals with the world in a traditional way which Fellner suggested was of limited applicability in the modern world, but in far more rigorous fashion than was traditionally done. The emphasis on competitive models is still overwhelming. As we note later in this chapter, oligopoly, the authors tell us, is today mostly dealt with via game theory. If the strategies reflected in game theory games do revolve around questions of efficiency more than questions of equity there are indeed many questions raised by ubiquitous oligopolies that simply cannot be contemplated. Thus, for example, a sampling of questions Fellner suggests need to be raised in assessing the impact of oligopoly on the functioning of an economy would include:

(a) 'The long run consequences of violating accepted value judgements' (Fellner 1949, p. 24). Fellner points out that the point where actions are viewed as 'exploitation' 'depends on the society in question' (p. 25). He writes of the impact of 'quasi-ethical considerations and their impact on the value judgments of society' (p. 25).

(b) Fellner considers the consequences of stalemate on relations between parties with significant market power. He suggests that stalemate adversely affects the public interest. Then he talks about oligopolists or bilateral monopolists who reach agreements 'objectionable from the social point of view' (p. 276).

In short for Fellner consideration of the way in which oligopolistic firms reach their decisions is conditioned by a set of institutional parameters far wider than those which condition the admittedly complicated, elegant, and sophisticated ways in which firm (and household) behavior is depicted in *Microeconomic Theory*. While all would grant that elegance and sophistication abound in this graduate microtheory text, could it not still be said (with Galbraith) that 'the basic theoretical system remains largely intact' as laid out long ago in neoclassical price theory? Is there any room in *Microeconomic Theory* for 'quasi-ethical considerations,' societal value judgments, or for that matter for concern about the impact of market power on societal values and tastes?

Galbraith himself nearly 30 years ago made a major effort at refocusing the thinking of the discipline on the problem of concentration. He suggested that perhaps half the economy consisted of small shopkeepers, barbershops, family size farms, etc. Their behavior was not too badly described by conventional theory. (But they received quite a lot of governmental help – e.g., farm price supports, etc.) The other half of the economy, however, consisted of what he called the planning system – large firms in concentrated industries. The planning system had what he called a 'capacity for radical change.' It did not at all conform to conventional neoclassical thinking (Galbraith 1973, pp. 44–6).

Galbraith's view, like much of his work, was insightful and provocative. It was greeted by his colleagues with a new and even more vigorous round of abstruse mathematization and abstraction.

If the theory of imperfect competition was also a very imperfect aid in creating public policy, at least mainstream economists, certainly at least in part under the impact of Chamberlin, Robinson and their associates, worried at that time about the implications for the real economy of concentration. Any number of mainstream economists worked actively at improving the interface between imperfect competition theory and the problems being presented by imperfectly competitive industries. There were voices in the discipline which agreed with President Franklin Roosevelt who asked Congress in 1938 to investigate concentrated economic power, saying:

> We have witnessed the merging-out of effective competition in many fields of enterprise. We have learned that the so-called competitive system works differently in an industry where there are many independent units, from the way it works in an industry where a few large producers dominate the market.
>
> If private enterprise left to its own devices becomes half-regimented and half-competitive, half slave and half free, as it is today, it obviously cannot adjust itself to meet the needs and demands of the country . . . . (Stocking and Watkins 1951, p. 52)

This, of course, was precisely the point subsequently elaborated by Fellner. Fellner was principally a theorist, while Stocking and Watkins were applied economists.[3] The President's request resulted in the setting up of the Temporary National Economic Committee, which resulted in an extensive investigation into the structure and operation of many aspects of American economic activity. Today it is largely forgotten along with much of the work of economists of that era. Many economists joined the wave of mainstream attention to concentration in industry in the aftermath of Robinson and Chamberlin.[4] The seminal text in industrial organization focusing on economic concentration and its implications was Joe S. Bain (1959).

The Bain approach in industrial organization is known as 'the structure-conduct-performance paradigm' (SCPP). It has now been replaced in industrial organization by what is called the 'new empirical industrial organization' (NEIO).[5] Bresnahan (1989) refers to Bain's work as 'the extreme 'structuralist' view' (p. 1013). Whatever interpretation one puts on that, Bain's approach can scarcely be called anti or even a-empirical. The NEIO approach is surely more econometric than earlier work.

In view of the generally acknowledged 'ubiquity of oligopoly' in the 1940s and beyond, it may not be too far-fetched to suggest that had the discipline followed Fellner's lead, the gulf between mainstream economists

---

3. George W. Stocking and Myron W. Watkins quote Roosevelt because they came to much the same conclusion in a scrupulously careful and detailed study of concentration in American industry. It was done for the Twentieth Century Fund and published in three volumes (Stocking and Watkins 1946, 1948, 1951).
4. One thinks immediately of A.A. Berle and Gardiner C. Means (1932) and A.R. Burns (1936), and a whole host of books on concentration of economic power which came out subsequently in the 1930s and 1940s. Major empirical additions to the literature were the three volumes produced by Stocking and Watkins just mentioned.
5. Cf., for example, T.F. Bresnahan (1989).

and heterodox economists might not have grown ever wider.[6] Instead there might even eventually have been a rapprochement – at least both groups would have been focused, more or less, on trying to understand how resources get deployed in the real world. Instead, as we are here arguing, mainstream economics has moved from a fixation with competitive markets to ever more abstruse techniques for deflecting economic theory further from real world problems.

Almost from the beginning, economic theorists, having introduced the theory of imperfect competition, failed at improving it and going beyond it, failed at making it a more useful aid to developing public policy. Instead they focused on work which had the effect of rationalizing the need to follow such an approach. The theoreticians of the discipline, in effect, asked, 'How can we rationalize a continued fixation on competition' and 'a denigration of the consequences of imperfect competition?' Their impact on policy makers contributed to the change from the vigorous anti-trust activity of the Department of Justice under Thurman Arnold in the late 1930s (hard on the heels of Chamberlin and Robinson), to the relatively restricted use of anti-trust in recent times.

We can suggest the change in perspective this way. In 1949 Corwin Edwards stated well the view among many economists in the aftermath of Chamberlin and Robinson and the applied economists we have mentioned above. He observed that

> The competitive policy presupposes that unchecked private power will ordinarily be used to bring about exploitation and restriction of output; but in striking at extreme departures from competition it does not necessarily aim at an atomized competition such as was envisaged in the older economic theory. The grounds for the policy include not only dislike of restriction of output, and of one-sided bargaining power, but also desire to prevent excessive concentration of wealth and power, desire to keep open the channels of opportunity, and concern lest monopolistic controls of business lead to political oligarchy. These aims are almost platitudinous. Historically, they antedate conceptions of economic equilibrium and of the role of competition in achieving it. (Edwards 1949, pp. 8–9)

If this view was indeed platitudinous in the late 1940s, it was anything but by the later years of the twentieth century. Thus did Robert Bork reflect the view of many concerning the policy implications of modern microeconomic theory. In his 1978 book *The Antitrust Paradox*, he writes:

6. See Chapter 8 for a consideration of heterodox views.

> The thesis of this book has been that modern antitrust has so decayed that the policy is no longer intellectually respectable. Some of it is not respectable as law; more of it is not respectable as economics; and now I wish to suggest that, because it pretends to one objective while frequently accomplishing its opposite, and because it too often forwards trends dangerous to our form of government and society, a great deal of antitrust is not even respectable as politics. (Bork 1978, 1993, p. 418)

It is a long road from Chamberlin and Robinson, reinforced by the empirical work of Berle and Means, Burns, Stocking and Watkins and others to Bork. Bork reflects, it is fair to say, both the failure of modern microeconomic theory to confront such real world problems as concentrated economic power, and the demise of any regrets about it. Bork, of course, is a leading jurist of the current scene. Edward Mason, as long ago as 1937, wrote, 'Lawyers and economists are . . . rapidly ceasing to talk the same language' (Mason 1937). He would doubtless be surprised to find that many economists today probably would mostly agree with Bork's assessment. After all, self- regulating entities don't need governmental regulation.[7] Thus did the process of trivialization in microeconomic theory get started while opportunities for greater realism presented by work in the 1930s and 1940s were abandoned.

Clarifying Trivialization

There is, we have been at pains to suggest, inherent conflict between the logic behind the competitive model, forcing firms to be efficient to stay in business, and the economies of scale, forcing firms to be bigger than pure competition can encompass.

The essential conclusion of conventional competitive theory is that competitive firms (firms small relative to their market), strive as they might to maximize profits, are nonetheless thwarted by their lack of real market power. This is the real invisible hand which keeps them socially acceptable, but economically inefficient. Monopolies are definitionally large relative to their markets, therefore, and so presumably exhibit up to some point economies of scale. But with their size comes also market power and so they can act in anti-social ways in the process of exercising market power and can act in anti-social ways in the process of maximizing profits. This familiar

7. As this is written, the collapse of Enron is still a hot news item. Whether in light of this financial disaster, and the rethinking that will inevitably follow, the beauties of self-regulation will seem less seductive to the public, economists, or government leaders remains to be seen.

story sets up the essential conflict noted earlier with which competitive theory has always wrestled – how to keep the maximization of efficiency, which was grounded in economies of scale, and not suffer the virtually unfettered market power that all too often goes with firms of sufficient size to be efficient.

What we mean by trivialization in microeconomics, therefore, is the effort which has been expended by economic theorists over the years to persuade themselves and others that with various often ingenious lines of argument, and despite the failure of pure (let alone perfect) competition to appear very often in the real world, competitive economic theory is still the principal market form on which to focus. Few would dispute the argument that the competitive model is useful as 'a benchmark.' Like a child's training wheels, it is useful, probably even critical, in getting started in gaining understanding of how resources get deployed in the real world. Generations of price theory textbooks have detailed the usefulness of competitive theory as 'benchmark' theory. But far too often these texts never got beyond the benchmark. (A manual on competitive racing which still had training wheels in place in the last chapter would no doubt cause quite a stir in the racing world. To carry the analogy one ridiculous step further, if the second edition of the manual included mathematical restatements of all the critical relationships – gear to wheel speed ratios, wind resistances, etc. – but left the training wheels in their central place in discussion, it would seem even more bizarre.)

In microeconomics, admiration for the logic, precision and elegance of the benchmark, especially when it is realized that the logic of the whole system rendered it amenable to restatement as a set of equations, precluded instituting any major efforts to develop theory which came even a tad closer to explaining the problems of the real world. One of the objectives of this chapter is to illustrate how poorly what theory we have has served historically in coping with the 'real world.'

This process of trivializing theory can be done in two ways. One can redefine critical terms or aspects of one or more essential parts of the theory so as to render it harmless, harmless being defined as theory which leads to policy ineffectiveness. The second way is to find ways of ignoring the proffered changes in the theory which would enable it to become an effective guide to better public policy.

Trivializing efforts – possible candidates

Inter-product competition The ingenious solution, representing the first approach to trivializing microeconomic theory described above, was one which early on came to devotees of competitive theory: redefine the market.

This approach was an interesting if minor chapter in defanging economic theory. It emerged as an outgrowth of a critical problem we have previously noted was recognized virtually from the outset: what made competition so powerful was that with 'many sellers' consumers had alternatives to which they could turn if any producer should try to do bad things. 'Bad,' of course, meant that the firm tried to act like monopolist, raising the price, restricting the output, etc. so as to be able to mark up the price and make excessive (i.e., non-competitive) profits.

The oft-stated sentiments concerning the anti-social behavior of the stereotypic monopolist were ultimately codified in the Sherman Anti-Trust Act of 1890. Section 1 of that act, we all learned in beginning economics, outlawed monopoly and Section 2 made the behavior which constituted 'monopolizing' illegal. Hence price fixing, setting up market shares, collusion, and a whole host of related activities were presumable as illegal under the Sherman Act.

Very early it was realized that a crucial aspect of defining monopoly and monopolizing and relating both to economic power had to do with 'the extent of the market.' Size was not the same thing as monopoly because, as we were constantly reminded, a small one-chair barber shop could be a monopoly in a small town while large firms with millions of dollars in assets did not necessarily have a dangerous degree of power if they operated in a very large market.

This ancient beginning lecture in industrial organization is pertinent because it early occurred to economists that if monopoly were dependent on 'size relative to the market' this offered a way not to have to worry about monopoly: simply redefine the market. This was one way to reach the conclusion that the real economy is adequately encompassed by competitive theory even if, as was most readily observable, in the real economy there were few major products produced by 'many sellers.' The problem can be turned into a definitional question – sellers of what? Thus if Alcoa was a threat to the economy because at the end of World War II it was the sole producer of aluminum, one could create competition by introducing more aluminum companies as was in fact done after World War II. But – far easier – one could get 'competition' by redefining Alcoa – as no longer an aluminum producer but a 'building materials producer.' By suggesting this simple switch, Alcoa was part of a far bigger market than the aluminum market. As such, Alcoa was in competition with cement, steel, glass, and other alternative building materials.

Mainstream theory early on had a means of testing all this. The ease with which people could substitute one product for another was measured by the cross-elasticity of demand.[8] If it was high the products competed. I would suggest that the concept of cross-elasticity of demand is easier to conceptualize than it is to measure accurately in actual situations. The concept can soothe worries of monopoly power perhaps. But in practice one must ask, does it really reduce market power to refer to the construction materials industry, the romantic gift industry (candy, flowers, jewelry, etc.) the apparel industry (shoes, coats, underwear, etc.)? While there may be merit in some circumstances in referring to these larger categories as 'industries,' in reality except for extreme comparisons it is hard not to conclude that today, say, Alcoa is more limited in its marketing by the existence of Reynolds or Kaiser than it is by the presence of glass, steel, or concrete. It is hard not to think of the number of florists affecting the market power of a flower shop more than the number of candy stores.

Putting forth the 'buildings materials market' as a principal category for study and as a means of not worrying about the commanding position which Alcoa historically had or presently has in relation to other aluminum producers becomes in the end a means for contributing to the trivialization of microeconomic theory. A demand curve for building materials is conceivable on paper. As a guide to public policy in assessing, say, total impact on the economy, it is not very useful. That is to say, technically economists can offer a concept like the 'cross-elasticity of demand' between aluminum and glass or steel. Is it helpful in assessing the significance of the market power which allegedly Alcoa once enjoyed and which was carefully and famously considered in the Alcoa Case in the 1940s (United States vs. Aluminum Co. of America, 148 F. 2d 416, 428, 429, {2d cir. 1945})?

Let us be clear. There is nothing wrong with the concept of cross-elasticity per se and there is nothing wrong with computing it. To clarify the link between market power and the range of alternatives from which a seller can select, it can be useful. But as a means of arguing that even if 'competition' is rare in the real world we can nevertheless continue to focus on competitive theory as though it were adequate to cover real world market situations is to contribute to the trivialization of microeconomic theory.

8. Cross-elasticity of demand is the responsiveness of demand to a change in the price of other commodities. It may be stated as:

$$\frac{\text{The percentage change in the quantity demanded of A}}{\text{The percentage change in the price of B}}$$

(Taylor 1966, p. 55).

Workable competition – aid or hindrance to clear thinking? Sadly, one of the earliest efforts to clarify the meaning of competition was also one which might have escaped the trivialization label and become a genuine path to more useful microeconomic theory. It may have been flawed as some charged. That is to say, it may have fuzzed the parameters of acceptable performance and so made it more difficult to 'maintain competition.' But I am persuaded that it was not originally offered as a way of circumventing the objectives of our anti-trust laws, and it could have helped clarify real problems.

Called 'workable competition,' it was introduced by J.M. Clark in 1939 and died sometime during the decade of the 1990s, although it had been seriously ill for some years before that.[9] If you ask graduate students today about workable competition, the chances are good they never heard of it.

Clark began from the premise that 'perfect competition' does not and cannot exist and presumably never existed (Clark 1940, p. 241). Clark noted, as Scherer and Ross remind us, that 'the competitive model of theory affords no reliable standard for judging real-world market conditions' (Scherer and Ross 1990, p. 53). As a point of departure this is worth remembering: oligopoly theory has always been regarded as unsatisfactory because it leads to imprecise conclusions. Workable competition can best be regarded as an effort to narrow the range of imprecision and thus to make the outcome of interaction in oligopolistic markets both less uncertain and, therefore, more useful for the development of sound public policy. As Clark himself put it, instead of endless nostalgia which he labeled 'historic homesickness' for perfect competition, it would be a step forward if among imperfect forms of competition found in the real world '. . . we can find, after due examination, that some of these forms do their jobs well enough to be an adequate working reliance – more serviceable, on the whole, than those substitutes which involve abandoning reliance on competition' (1940, p. 242).

Clark, therefore, began from an eminently practical and empirically grounded position – what did we need to insist on if industrial performance was to conform more or less to what that competitive model had promised and how could it be accomplished without sacrificing either the automaticity of the system or the efficiency provided by the economies of large scale modern production?

Clark's work is in the tradition of mid-century industrial organization. That is, it begins with an analysis of market problems from the perspective of structure, conduct, and performance. Scherer and Ross present the following

9. It was originally presented in a paper to the American Economics Association in 1939 and published in the *American Economic Review* of June 1940, 241–56.

schema to sumarize the kind of criteria that can be included under the rubric, workable competition.[10]

1. Structural criteria

   *The number of traders should be at least as large as scale economies permit.

   *There should be no artificial inhibitions on mobility and entry.

   *There should be moderate and price-sensitive quality differentials in the products offered.

2. Conduct criteria

   *Some uncertainty should exist in the minds of rivals as to whether price initiatives will be followed.

   *Firms should strive to attain their goals independently, without collusion.

   *There should be no unfair, exclusionary, predatory or coercive tactics.

   *Inefficient suppliers and customers should not be shielded permanently.

   *Sales promotion should be informative, or at least not be misleading.

   *There should be no persistent, harmful price discrimination.

3. Performance criteria

   *Firms' production and distribution operations should be efficient and not wasteful of resources.

   *Output levels and product quality (that is, variety, durability, safety, reliability, and so forth) should be responsive to consumer demands.

   *Profits should be at levels just sufficient to reward investment, efficiency, and innovation.

   *Prices should encourage rational choice, guide markets toward equilibrium, and not intensify cyclical instability.

   *Opportunities for introducing technically superior new products and processes should be exploited.

   *Promotional expenses should not be excessive.

   *Success should accrue to sellers who best serve consumer wants. (Scherer and Ross 1990, pp. 53–4)

There is no question that making some of these dicta operational could be difficult (e.g., how big do profits need to be to cover, but just, investment, efficiency, and innovation?) Theorists always disliked 'oligopolistic indeterminacy,' but it would seem they might have seen merit in making explicit where the indeterminacy lies so that it might be reduced to a minimum.

10. Their schema is based on the extensive work of Stephen Sosnick, whose doctoral dissertation involved an extensive review of the workable competition literature (Sosnick 1958).

Clark's workable competition utilized the 'structure-conduct-performance' approach in applied industrial organization. It had as its basic premise the view that efforts to translate the perfect competition paradigm into a realistic guide to evaluating industrial performance could best be done by judging separately the structure, the conduct, and the performance of industrial firms. It granted that competitive theory was a far from ideal guide to empirical work and to establishing public policy. It did not deny that received theory fixated on simplistic, rarely encountered, market structures, assumed the invisible hand automatically channeled conduct into only socially desirable directions, and insisted, when it focused on the real world at all, that ideal performance was really there for all to see. It was the reality of all this, of course, which Clark began by questioning. Whatever else, Clark's article produced what Scherer and Ross describe as 'an explosion of articles' (1990, p. 53).

It is always easy to criticize requirements fleshing out the criteria for acceptable structure, conduct, and performance listed above as filled with ambiguities and replete with ranges of acceptability rather than the precision the conventional competitive price theory model exhibits. However, it can also be said to make reasonably specific a number of important characteristics of market operations that we could characterize as broadly acceptable of what we need to require of our resource deploying system if we are to develop an economy which can enhance life in a democratic and efficient society.

George W. Stocking has noted that some perceptive lawyers 'saw the doctrine of workable competition [as] a crude tool for blunting the impact of antitrust statutes' while others saw it as 'a delicate instrument for separating socially desirable from anti-social business practices, and good market structures from bad' (Stocking 1961, p. 251). Stocking himself sided with those who concluded that on balance the principle of workable competition led to 'a low estimate of the value of remedial action designed to increase the number of sellers and reduce monopoly elements in industrial markets' (1961, p. 260). Nevertheless, he also concluded that 'Although I do not regard the principle of workability as an acceptable guide to antitrust cases, I do believe that the criteria that economists have developed for determining workability – structure, conduct, and performance – can serve a useful, perhaps indispensable function in determining the existence of monopoly' (1961, p. 276).

By the 1960s workable competition was clearly a dying possibility even for discussion. Nonetheless, its demise as a vehicle for improving the realism of price theory was, not surprisingly, not mourned by all. Thomas Sowell reminds us that 'When asked . . . one day what it meant . . . George Stigler

(1993) replied, "It means such competition as pleases the economist who is talking" (Sowell 1993, p. 787). Such dismissal takes little effort and raises the question, what approach would be better? In the case of workable competition, no one ever claimed it was more than a step in the right direction. Whether game theory, for example, can be relied upon not to 'blunt the impact of antitrust statutes' and to serve as a vehicle for determining sound public policy is a question worth pondering.

Whatever else, consideration of the concept of workable competition was in a sense a high water mark in the effort begun by Robinson and Chamberlin to interject greater realism into microeconomics by developing theories of imperfect competition and suggesting they could become useful guides for public policy. But as Stocking put it in speaking of Chamberlin and Robinson, 'As their theories gained in refinement and precision, they lost in reality' (Stocking 1961, p. v). This is always the challenge in social science theory. This was almost the last voice raised worrying about keeping theory close enough to reality to serve a useful purpose by improving public policy. After that the policy makers were pretty much on their own.

The rebuttable presumption against bigness: a forgotten possibility Many years ago Corwin Edwards summarized succinctly the potential danger in large firms. Said Edwards:

> Standards are . . . needed to cope with excessive power derived from excessive overall size rather than from monopoly in particular industries. The power of the business giant consists in ability to coerce others, to close channels of opportunity, and to obtain special privileges in its dealing with those who should serve all comers impartially: for example banks; common carriers; law courts; government executives; and legislatures. A concern is too large when it has coercive power or is habitually able to obtain discriminatory privilege. (Edwards 1949, p. 130)

In the end, size and even size relative to the market is not coterminous with market power, as the quotation from Edwards makes clear. Microeconomic theory has never given very satisfactory (i.e., socially useful) guidance to policy makers in ways to deal with economic power and its concentration. The fixation on competition has been a major reason for this, but not the only one.

Edwards argued that there should be laws against concentration of economic power that leads to the kind of coercive power he described. He doubted the Sherman Act approach – writing a general law that could be applied case by case to individual firms – would work in the case of excessive power. He had another suggestion, however.

He called it 'a rebuttable presumption against bigness.' If economic power rather than 'mere size' was, in the final analysis, the evil to be dealt with Edwards saw a way to deal with it through a simpler approach to size. Laying aside our concern with the deleterious effects of coping by redefining the market, economics has had a long history of confusion about how large relative to the market a firm had to be in order to constitute a potential threat to welfare. The most famous statement on this was that of Judge Learned Hand, offered in the Alcoa case. He concluded that Alcoa was indeed a monopoly, in terms of share of the relevant market, because 90 per cent 'is enough to constitute a monopoly; it is doubtful whether 60 or 64 per cent would be enough; and certainly 33 per cent is not.'[11] Hand's '30–60–90 per cent' dictum was widely quoted.

In Edwards' view the Hand approach was too simplistic. There are too many factors, often intangible, which impinge on the real impact of actual firms on economic activity to make it very simple to generalize about the size-economic power relationship.

Edwards' suggestion was 'to establish a rebuttable presumption against bigness in excess of some relatively high level of size. Assuming that bigness is typically dangerous and therefore objectionable, such a policy would tolerate the large enterprise only where bigness could be shown to be necessary to the public interest. It would place the burden of proof upon the large enterprise to justify its existence' (Edwards 1949, p. 131). That, of course, was its distinctive feature.

Putting the onus on the firm to prove its size was necessary would bring some of the technique used even now in the case of public utilities to bear on the governance of all business firms. More generally, Edwards detailed a lengthy list of changes which he argued would make it more difficult for firms to retain and exercise market power not justified by the requirements of scale economies. Detailing all these suggestions would take us too far afield here. Suffice it to say that the direction in which Edwards was pointing 50 years ago was for our purposes a major attempt to tighten the link between developments in microeconomic theory and in the development of sound public policy. At bottom this requires implicit recognition of the critical link – guiding public policy is a major challenge to theory, in this case microeconomic theory. This proposition is not necessarily accepted by mainstream economists today. Certainly those who argue that in general a firm's activities can almost invariably be left to the market do not accept the necessity to monitor such activity or improve public policy.

---

11. U.S. vs. Aluminum Company of America et al., 148 F.2d 416, 424 (1945).

In the end the suggestion that we establish a rebuttable presumption against bigness beyond some size represented, like workable competition, a possible path for strengthening the theory–policy link. It was rejected by neglect more than by repudiation. But its rejection contributed to the trivialization of microeconomic theory in general. One can indeed argue that the entire structure-conduct-performance orientation in industrial organization in the middle of the twentieth century facilitated the effort to revise theory so as to improve policy. The rebuttable presumption is today a forgotten possibility. It was never tried. Whatever else one may say, the reception it received corroborates our view that the mainstream was intent on coping with the challenges to received microeconomic theory by finding ways to ignore them. As such it contributed to trivializing microeconomic theory in general.

Contestable markets – a step in the right direction – will it be taken? The basic idea behind the notion of contestable markets is that whatever the actual structure of the market may be there is a possibility of competitive pressure being exerted by potential entrants. How large a possibility is the critical question. The seminal work on contestable markets was by Baumol, Panzar and Willig, and appeared in 1982 (Baumol, Panzar and Willig 1982). At first blush it appears that it might have been a sort of generalized fudge factor to enable markets that are far from competitive to be deemed acceptable because they could in some sense be said to face competition from *potential* entrants. In a world where competitive markets are deemed acceptable and imperfectly competitive markets are suspect, it helps rationalize the status quo if the pool of acceptability could be enlarged by adding the possibility of competition to some markets clearly not now competitive.

In fact contestability was quite carefully and explicitly defined so that arguably applying it as a guide to public policy could have led to assisting in developing sound policy. Specifically contestability was advanced by asserting that there are three conditions required for a market to be declared a contestable market:

1. There must be 'no significant entry barriers' in markets deemed contestable.
2. There can be 'no significant excess profits' in these markets.
3. The industry 'must be efficient in its pricing and in its allocation of production among incumbent suppliers.' (Willig 1987, p. 619)

The critical notion in contestable markets is, therefore, that regardless of how many firms are in the industry, 'it is potential competition from potential entrants rather than competition among active suppliers that effectively constrains the equilibrium behavior of the incumbents' (Willig 1987, p. 618).

One reason contestable markets were viewed with suspicion may have been because, as Willig, asserts, 'One of the principal lessons of the analysis of PCM [perfectly contestable markets] is that monopoly does not necessarily entail welfare losses' (1987, pp. 621–2). The truth of this depends entirely, of course, on the genuineness of the threat of entry, even for a monopoly.

What is the status of contestable markets theory today? Baumol himself says it was widely cited when it first came out, but then was 'wrongly cited' by some lawyers who implied that 'we believed all markets are highly contestable so real antitrust issues are virtually nonexistent.' He thinks it is on the rise again.[12] One thing seems clear. Contestable markets, like the rebuttable presumption, is rarely if ever mentioned in the most widely used current microeconomics texts.[13]

The status of the confrontation today

We have examined a variety of ways in which the potential impact of theory on the economy could actually be blunted (that is the theory could be trivialized) as well as some ways that, although they may have looked superficially like trivialization, actually were an effort genuinely to clarify the implications of theory.

What is the status of the connection between microeconomic theory and the economy today? Inter-product competition clearly redefines markets in a way which, if paid attention to, would make anti-trust violations harder to prove. It blurred, but did not remove the structural challenge involved in the conflict between scale economies and their efficiency requirements, on the one hand, and the automatic congruence (as per the invisible hand) of profit seeking and societal welfare in competitive markets on the other.

Workable competition could have helped focus on how imperfectly competitive markets acquire the power to threaten societal goals. (Stocking worried that it may have made it more difficult to see violations of the law, although he also thought it a necessary effort at clarifying enforcement efforts.) As we said at the beginning, in our opinion workable competition was a significant and realistic effort to make microeconomic theory a genuinely useful guide to improving public policy. Instead it was ultimately

---

12. Private communication with Baumol, 2002.

13. In Mas-Colell et al. there is one minor reference suggesting that contestable markets might provide a formalization of one of their models (Mas-Colell et al. 1995, p. 411). Hal Varian's *Microeconomic Analysis* (1992) has no discussion of contestable markets.

rejected if not forgotten, thereby removing a possible obstacle to the trivialization of economic theory which, in our view, has largely characterized the most prominent mainstream efforts in recent years.[14] Its death, in any case, has prevented any possibility of it helping to clarify inconsistencies between price theory and societal objectives.

Edwards' rebuttable presumption against bigness greater than an arbitrary per cent of the market was a suggestion that made sense in logic and indeed which might have been useful (Edwards 1949, p. 131). So far as is known, it was never tried. I don't think it was even discussed seriously. It added to the trivialization process only in that it constituted one more piece of evidence suggesting that the basic conflict we have tried to consider, which lies at the base of price theory, has never worried price theorists.

Contestable markets, as we have said, have been contemplated but there has as yet not been a significant move to introduce this standard into active and consistent use.

Game Theory and 'The New Industrial Organization'

Actually, as was mentioned earlier in this chapter, by the last quarter of the twentieth century, virtually all efforts to build on the introduction of theories of imperfect competition to make microtheory more realistic, thus allowing it to be of greater potential assistance in developing useful public policy, were swept to one side by the rising tide of game theory which inundated virtually all fields of economic theory.[15] Workable competition is nowhere mentioned in either volume of the *Handbook* (Schmalensee and Willig 1998) and contestable markets are mentioned but briefly, in connection with game theory experiments.[16]

The *Handbook* tells us that game theory has led to 'the new industrial organization' and this approach has three key features: 'The emphasis is on specific industries. The focus is on developing models of firm behavior. Empirical work is based on well-founded models of firm behavior' (1998, p. 10).

---

14. Workable competition is not even mentioned in the index to the most comprehensive industrial organization book in current use (Schmalensee and Willig 1998).

15. For example, a recent textbook, *Industrial Organization, A Strategic Approach* tells us, 'By the late 1970s it was clear that the extensive analysis carried out within the framework of the SCP [structure-conduct-performance, ed.] was yielding diminishing returns . . . At the same time an upsurge of interest occurred in the application of game theory to economics in general and to industrial organization in particular (Church and Ware 2000, p. 10).

16. In view of the fact that Volume II is co-edited by Robert Willig and the first chapter in Volume I is written by John Panzar, Baumol's two co-authors in the 1982 book on contestable markets, the references can be regarded as minimal indeed.

It is worth pausing briefly to consider Church and Ware's '. . . completely new and comprehensive book that systematically presents and makes accessible the advances and new learning of the past twenty years' (2000, p. vii). We do not focus on them because they have written a bad book. Rather they have written a book which has the same perspective as the Schmalensee and Willig *Handbook* and can be regarded as typical of industrial organization texts now. It is undoubtedly a well done example of this approach.

There can be no gainsaying that many interesting situations involving the strategic decisions of self-interested players in hypothetical market situations can be dissected and assessed with game theory. It thus has surely played to the similarities of economic theory to chess which years ago, we saw earlier, caused J.R. Hicks to describe economic theory as 'a good game.'

We have used the word 'trivialization' in connection with economic theory partly to refer to the tendency to sever the link between economic theory and economic policy. We noted earlier that game theory described the outcome of bargaining between self-interested players under various circumstances. The outcome of such bargaining leads to 'optimal' allocative results, provided one views optimal in terms of efficiency. Only rarely would questions of equity be taken into account. The whole field of normative economics involves considerations of questions of equity. Mainstream economists may consider the debate as to whether economics is a normative or positive discipline as settled but economic policy is ineluctably concerned with normative questions. Chapter 8 raises the question of how given societies determine equitable allocative results. When heterodox economists suggest that it is difficult to differentiate normative and positive they refer to the use of given assumptions in economic theorizing. To assume that a distribution of income is 'given' is to finesse the complicated but critical question of what distribution or distributions of income are equitable in a given society. Acquiescence is a value laden attitude just as are acceptance or rejection.

Game theory is so constructed as to finesse questions of equity. By replacing the structure-conduct-behavior approach with a game theoretic approach it becomes more difficult to introduce questions of equity. If theory is regarded as having its raison d'etre principally in guiding policy makers it is not difficult to see how the switch to game theory in industrial organization, the applied field of microeconomic theory, has not led, say, to vigorous and extensive reliance on anti-trust policy.

Clearly the game theory perspective is consistent with Church and Ware's view that the structure-performance-conduct approach, which grew out of workable competition, was 'yielding diminishing returns.' This, of course, contrasts with the view several decades earlier typified, say, by Stocking who, we have seen, pronounced it 'possibly indispensable in defining monopoly,' as recently as 1961. Nevertheless, Church and Ware can dismiss it. Like the *Handbook*, one does not even find it mentioned in the index. In contrast there are many entries in the index relating to Bertrand and Cournot. Their 'new and comprehensive book' begins its discussion of oligopoly by carefully considering the Bertrand equilibrium, introduced in 1838, and described as 'a simple static game devoted to homogeneous products and assuming no entry, etc.' They pay similar attention to Cournot's equilibrium, introduced 45 years after Bertrand, and as we saw earlier a model hedged with different but equally restrictive assumptions. Unlike workable competition (1949), neither Cournot (1883) nor Bertrand (1838) presumably has yet started producing diminishing returns to the likes of Church and Ware.

Similarly, they find room for the Stackleberg game (1934), ('probably the oldest and simplest strategic game in economics' (Church and Ware 2000, p. 467)). They rely on Pareto notions of welfare at various points. As is usual, removing the distribution of income and wealth from the list of matters to be considered is not mentioned, but does simplify things. In short, there is much of the conventional classical or neoclassical world in their approach along with a commendable introduction of actual cases from the real world. (They tell us they use anti-trust applications and cases as 'a constant "reality check" (Church and Ware 2000, p. 467, p. vii).) (It may not be altogether insignificant that they choose to show a chess piece by way of illustration on the cover of their book. An alternative might have been an unemployed steel worker. Do I digress?) The critical link between various games and their simplification for public policy is not easy to isolate or summarize.

Stocking's fairly skeptical take on workable competition seems nonetheless more reasonable even now in light of what we know in the early years of the twenty-first century than that of those who have dismissed totally and seemingly out of hand the structure-conduct performance view.

Even if for economists the structure-conduct-performance approach yielded only diminishing returns, the same cannot be said for the approach taken by lawyers. We repeat Edward S. Mason's view that 'lawyers and economists are . . . rapidly ceasing to talk the same language' (Mason 1937). Mason suggested so very long ago that increasingly lawyers were concerned with developing public policy to further the 'public interest' while economists were ever more concerned with 'the analysis of market situations.' Lawyers like Bork agree with the diminishing returns view of modern economists. The thrust of modern game theory would appear to be directed toward the 'analysis of market situations' rather than the development of public policy.

If mainstream economists are largely in agreement with the diminishing returns views of Church and Ware, there are interventionist lawyers moving in the direction Mason suggested much earlier. Thus in his *Principles of Antitrust Law*, lawyer Stephen F. Ross begins by expressing the public interest view explicitly. Ross notes that anti-trust law 'should primarily focus on preventing consumers from having their wealth taken by misconduct of sellers' (Ross 1993, p. v). This is clearly not the language of the economist, and it may also not be the focus of game playing economists, but as a description of the ultimate objective of sound economic policy, vintage 1950, and reduced to the simplest terms, it is not bad. One is struck immediately by the similarity in Ross's organization of the subject and that of the workable competition approach. Thus an early chapter is devoted to 'market structure and monopoly power.' His book is also concerned with such matters as exclusionary conduct, efforts to monopolize, agreements to divide markets, vertical restraints, mergers (horizontal, vertical, conglomerate), price discrimination. While some of these matters appear in the *Handbook*, the general approach is far more reminiscent of mid-century industrial organization books than of the 'new industrial organization.'

The rebuttable presumption against bigness, as noted above, in our view still has attractive features although large firms have now overrun many areas of the economy. While 'downsizing' has become a favorite catchword, and there is some evidence that in some areas firms are bigger than scale economies of production require, the rise of multinational corporations has put firm size much of the time outside the control of national governments. If we were to guess we should suggest that the next major effort at enforcing constraints on large firms in the name of social control might well be an international effort at some sort of anti-trust enforcement. (The European Union, for example, has been moving in this direction.)

In all these empirical efforts to put enforceable teeth into the implications of competitive theory for its applications one difficulty remains. A virtue of the simple Smithian world was that good behavior was not gained at the *sufferance* of the firms but because the system *compelled* it. With the possible exception of the entry threat in contestable markets, the other efforts lack the teeth that were provided by that threat.

APPLYING THEORY IN THE REAL WORLD

The story we have told thus far is one of opportunities missed to take received microeconomics and modernize even the smallest aspects of its inflexibility and rigidity in order to increase its relevance to the problems being faced in the real world. We have seen (Chapter 3) the willingness and even eagerness of theorists to make theory more quantitative and, therefore, in the eyes of its devotees more precise, more elegant, and more logical. These have been the objectives of the past 50 years. The voices which have been raised to ask how useful all this has been in enabling the theory to address the real problems of the real world have been pretty much drowned out – mostly by simply ignoring them.

Arguably, most of the efforts which have been on display in the real world to apply anti-trust laws have arisen under an umbrella very much like the workable competition efforts. But theorists have pulled away from the moorings of the workable competition possibility, as we have seen, in favor of game theory and the highly mathematical approach favored in all of economics. We have seen that this has meant that the gulf between mainstream economic theory and anti-trust law as it has evolved has gotten steadily wider.

This book is entitled *Economics Confronts the Economy* and we come now to a major aspect of this confrontation. We have thus far argued that microtheorists turned their backs on the opportunities of the 1930s to make theory more applicable to real life situations. We have also argued that microeconomic theory has most particularly chosen to go down a different road, a road making perhaps for even more elegance and precision, a road that makes economic theory more like the hard sciences than ever it had achieved before. This we have just seen widened the wedge between microtheory and its applied field, industrial organization. The latter has been infected with the same game theory-cum-quantification virus that has afflicted the rest of economics, with the result, it can be charged, that economic theory as applied gives less guidance and support to improving the operation of the real economy than ever before.

We suggest that the views of Clark, Bain, Edwards, Stocking, Watkins, Mason, and others writing between the end of World War II and the late 1960s at least tried to build on the imperfect competition work of the 1930s by making anti-trust guidelines clearer and more useful. Since that time, we argue, the many applied economists working in the field of regulation and anti-trust have gotten precious little help from the theorists. Into the vacuum they have left, administrators in general have fallen into accepting a new standard de facto for dealing with bigness. In the absence of guidance from theorists, administrators have devised rules of their own. The one which has emerged most clearly asserts that often firms are 'too big to let die' while small firms and certainly individuals are customarily 'too small to save.' This is nowhere written in statute and certainly not in economic principle. Yet in the vacuum, this principle frequently rules the day. It is to exemplify this de facto policy that the rest of this chapter is devoted.

As is often the case, the policy has emerged from a series of decisions concerning events in the real world. It is important to remember that de facto policy develops where de jure policy is thwarted. We have attempted above to give evidence of this thwarting.

Diverse Economic Units: too big to die, too small to save

Bailing out the biggies – too big to die One of our conclusions in Chapter 1 was that the invisible hand and bigness, especially bigness relative to the market, have never been comfortable together. We have noted that the economies of scale made efficiency incompatible with structural competition in many markets. We have argued that microeconomic theory has really never come to grips with the consequences of this conflict. Conventional price theory copes with this problem partly by customarily assuming technology to be given. This postpones but does not really avoid the problem. Automaticity and efficiency can prove difficult or impossible to reconcile. (Some people naturally raised the question of national security as well.) The resultant vacuum has always posed problems for theory as a guide to public policy. One way in which this failure has been highlighted has been by the treatment of large firms which get into various kinds of financial or other difficulties. Neither Adam Smith nor any other classical price theorist ever suggested that the invisible hand meant some firms were too large to fail. That notion, informal perhaps, but clearly in use, seems to be one of the recent contributions of economists and lawyers to public debate.

The saga of Lockheed – example number one One empirical example of 'economics confronting the economy' involved the Lockheed Aircraft Corporation, which got into severe financial difficulties and was bailed out by a loan of $250 million by the Federal government, which was approved by the Emergency Loan Guarantee Board in September 1971. This was during the Nixon Administration. If you want to know what is meant by being 'too big to fail' consider the view of then Secretary of the Treasury, John Connally. We are told that he announced in May of 1971 'that the White House will ask Congress to guarantee $250 million in bank loans to Lockheed, inasmuch as 24,000 jobs and $1.4 billion in investment are involved.'[17] How did this come about? Bear in mind what has previously been said about competition and the invisible hand. Relevant, too, will be the

17. The quotation is from Walter J. Boyne (1998, p. 360).

discussion in Chapter 6 of the views of 'public choice economists' who insist that the market is preferable to the public sector because the public sector has a perchance for corrupting people. We see here that Lockheed and Chrysler, not to mention more recently Enron, did not exactly bolster ethical standards. We are told that the Lockheed executives for most of the 30 years prior to 1971 generally had admired Dan Haughton, head of the corporation in this period.

> However, all agree that Haughton did make at least one major error . . . he failed to take the necessary steps to purchase Douglas Aircraft Company before McDonnell did so in April 1967.
>
> The prospect of Lockheed's acquiring Douglas had been carefully reviewed by upper management. It was economically feasible, and the elimination of competition from the market would have made Lockheed a much stronger player against Boeing . . . One reason given for the decision not to buy was a desire to let Douglas go under and then pick it up for a bargain price. (Boyne 1998, pp. 350–351)

Boyne continues, '. . . according to many . . . Haughton declined to take action primarily because Lockheed did not want to build aircraft someone else had designed . . . Thus corporate chauvinism, pure and simple, carried the seeds of disaster. It might not have been Haughton's only mistake, but it was a sufficiently grievous error' (Boyne 1998, p. 351). One can't help contemplating whether this description would have caused Adam Smith to wonder about the generality of his pin factory example. He would, of course, have been on target had he related Mr Haughton to his businessmen having lunch.

The details of the Lockheed affair would take us too far afield. However, certain broad statements of position taken by the principals are germane to the argument we need to make. It was in connection with a transport plane, the C–5A, that Lockheed was building for the Air Force that it got into serious financial difficulty. Specifically Lockheed ran into 'cost overruns' amounting to something over $200 million. Moreover, Lockheed's financial situation was complicated by the fact that it had loan arrangements with 24 different commercial banks. The *New York Times* reported that 'both the defense department and Lockheed are negotiating on the assumption that [the] government intended to rescue [the] company from bankruptcy by ultimately providing funds for continued work on C–5As and other military programs' (*New York Times* 1971, January 7, 1:3). Lockheed eventually agreed to the defense department demand that it accept the $200 million loss. The *New York Times* editorialized that 'Lockheed has demonstrated [a] degree of managerial inefficiency unusual even for a defense contractor; it would be better for the government to let the company "go under" and reorganize in bankruptcy' (*New York Times* 1971, January 8, 30:1).

President Nixon approved the loan to Lockheed. According to the *New York Times*, '. . . President Nixon will ask Congress for $250 million in long-term financing to rescue Lockheed from possible bankruptcy; . . . (notes) company plays important role in safeguarding national security and holds present state of economy had persuaded Administration that the company should not be allowed to go bankrupt' (*New York Times* 1971, May 7, 1:5). Ultimately, the loan was approved by the Senate by a vote of 49–48 on August 3, 1971.

Representative Moorhead, who was a member of the House Banking and Currency Committee, charged that the aid was 'scandalous,' and said the 'government was under no obligation to subsidize Lockheed's corporate errors.' He went on that Chairman Haughton 'has intimidated the government with threats of corporate suicide while absconding with taxpayers' money,' Haughton asserted that government aid 'should be expected when competition is so fierce' (*New York Times* 1971, May 13, 67:8). (Interestingly, our theorists remained silent, failing even to mention the invisible hand, in the face of this blast.) The *New York Times* had an editorial charging that the administration violated its own principles in seeking to rescue Lockheed (*New York Times* 1971, May 14, 40:2).

Subsequently, Lockheed was involved in a complicated affair involving charges that as a large company operating internationally, it had been involved in a series of payments to foreign leaders and officials. At hearings before Senator Frank Church's Senate Sub-Committee investigating the behavior of multi-national corporations, Senator Church charged in his opening statement, 'The bribes and the payoffs associated with doing business abroad represent a pattern of crookedness that would make, in terms of its scope and magnitude, crookedness in politics look like a Sunday School picnic by comparison . . .' (quoted in Boulton 1978, p. 266).

So in the end Lockheed got its help from the government. While there was criticism and objection to the aid from some quarters, to our knowledge no public choice economists, no lawyers of the Bork school of thought, no game theorists, no new empirical industrial organization economists, no non-interventionists in general raised any hue and cry to the effect that 'government should be gotten off Lockheed's back.'

The story of Chrysler – example number two The story of the Chrysler bailout is somewhat less complicated. In the first quarter of 1979 the company lost $53.8 million. This was only about half what it had lost in the first quarter of the previous year, but was 'more than market analysts had anticipated.' The Chairman of the Board, John J. Riccardo, and the President, at the time, Lee A. Iacocca, predicted the second quarter losses would be even larger (*New York Times* 1979, May 4, IV, 1:3). Chrysler's financial difficulties were attributed partly to the expense of meeting the government's regulatory standards (involving such items as fuel efficiency and clean-air standards). In this connection, it is interesting to note that neither of the other two of the 'big three' in automobile production in the US were in financial difficulties. Thus 'operations problems' must have figured rather prominently in the difficulties as well.

The Carter Administration 'may ask Congress to give substantial financial aid to Chrysler Corporation; says overall economy of U.S. would be shaken if the company failed' (*New York Times* 1979, August 1, IV, 3). (Here is the 'too big to fail' view, expressed in its starkest terms.) In any case Chrysler decided to ask for $1.5 billion in federal aid. In their request Chrysler apparently noted the $250 (million) loan the government had made to Lockheed (*New York Times* 1979, August). In connection with all this the comments of the President, Lee Iacocca, are not without interest. He wrote, '. . . it was clear that only drastic measures could save the Chrysler Corporation.' 'Believe me, the last thing in the world I wanted to do was turn to the government. But once I made the decision, I went at it with all flags flying.'

> Ideologically, I've always been a free-enterpriser, a believer in survival of the fittest. When I was president of Ford . . . I went to the capital for only one reason – to try to get the government off our backs. So naturally, when I was back in Washington as chairman of Chrysler to make the case for government help, everybody said; 'How can you? How dare you?'
>
> What choice do I have? I answered. It's the only game in town. (Iacocca and Novak 1984, p. 192)

(Iacocca here manages somehow to suggest that getting aid from the federal government was the patriotic thing to do.) Again Smith's invisible hand was nowhere to be found. If union demands for wage increases are invariably labeled 'inflationary' not a word about inflation was mentioned in these deliberations.

One student of the economy, writing on the extent of the previous year's losses, is more revealing if less than elegant: 'Chrysler's problems were exacerbated by poor management and lousy engineering. On November 2, 1978, the day that Lee Iacocca joined the company, Chrysler reported a quarterly loss of $159 million, the worst in its history' (Waller 2001, p. 25).

Another view, agreeing with the one just presented, was that of Senator Gary Hart, who wrote,

> I opposed the Chrysler bailout as I did most of the others. It was not an industrial policy; it was an ad hoc response to an immediate, urgent need. The Democrats – and I have been critical of my own party in this regard – have been a party that responds to companies, individual companies if not whole industries, that find themselves in trouble primarily because of international competition, poor management, or poor agreements among management and labor. They find themselves on the threshold of disaster; and they come, as someone once said, as a dinosaur to the public doorstep; and they say, 'Feed me or I'll die and stink up the place.' (Hart 1986, p. 223)

Whatever the merits of the case, the Carter Administration was prepared to consider aiding Chrysler (*New York Times*, June 23, 27:6). The Congressional Budget Office studied the matter and concluded that the collapse of Chrysler could trigger widespread instability and loss of jobs (*New York Times* 1979, August 12, 33:6). In the end Congress approved loan guarantees to Chrysler worth about $1.5 billion, which was the biggest government bailout ever to a private corporation. Once again, so far as is known there were no cries of an outrageous intrusion by big government into the enterprise economy.[18]

Bigness and our changing views The Lockheed and Chrysler sagas express only one side of our tendency governmentally to find big firms 'too big to let fail.' More generally we may say that the official attitude toward anti-trust activity in the years since the passage of the Sherman Act in 1890 has itself been cyclical. There have been times characterized by relatively strict enforcement and other times characterized by quite lax enforcement. There was an upsurge in the late 1930s, very possibly under the influence of the introduction of imperfect competition theory. After World War II there was another brief surge. Three anti-trust cases stand out in this period. The first concerned Alcoa and the aluminum industry. In the New York court Judge Learned Hand made a widely quoted statement to the effect that if a firm had 90 per cent of the market it surely constituted a monopoly and was illegal. If, however, it controlled 60 or 64 per cent of the market it was 'doubtful' that it could be accused of monopolizing the market. Finally if it controlled only 33 per cent it would 'certainly' not be illegal (Bain 1959, p. 309). Relief was

18. Quotations in this section, unless otherwise cited, are from *New York Times Index* covering the Chrysler Corporation in the news for 1979.

postponed until after the war when Alcoa was forced to sell some of its facilities, which ultimately became Reynolds Aluminum. The second (1946) concerned the tobacco industry and suggested that it is possible 'to infer monopolization without evidence of unreasonable practices driving competitors from the market.' It was said that it came close to making the mere possession of monopoly power illegal (Scherer and Ross 1990, p. 456). The third case involved the motion picture industry (1948) and was directed 'against several motion picture exhibition chains, charging them with monopolizing first-run exhibition . . . (they threatened not to exhibit certain producers' films in towns where they operated the only theaters unless producers gave them first-run preference in towns where they faced competition)' (Scherer and Ross 1990, p. 456). Scherer and Ross conclude that in all three of these cases 'the Supreme Court ruled that illegal monopolization existed' (1990, p. 456).

In recent years there have also been relatively few cases but among them, there have been several notable cases. The IBM case filed in 1969 and settled in 1978 has been characterized as having become 'a historic relic,' and the government had good reasons for withdrawing. Yet by doing so, it set a bad precedent: it rewarded anti-trust targets who, by fighting a war of attrition, delayed the administration of justice until the issues were overtaken by events (Scherer and Ross 1990, p. 462). On the other hand, the AT&T case, filed in 1974 and settled in 1981, involved the rather special problem of alleged predatory pricing in an industry which was already regulated. It was decided against AT&T, which was forced to separate its local (monopoly) business from its long distance business, although it was allowed to keep its research and development arm (Bell Laboratories) which in September 1996 spun itself off and renamed itself Lucent Technology.

Another case receiving much attention was the Microsoft case, in which it was alleged that Microsoft used its dominant position in the production of operating systems to strengthen its position in other markets such as the browser market. A breakup into two companies was ordered by the appeals court in June 2000, but the order was reversed in June 2001. The Microsoft case was not unlike the AT&T case – a large firm using its monopoly position in one area to gain greater strength in other areas.

In general, with these few exceptions, anti-trust has not been actively intrusive into the activities of large firms in recent years.

Should Big Firms be Immortal? We introduce all this here only to make a few fairly obvious points. First, large modern corporations like Lockheed and Chrysler, capable of negotiating at the highest levels with the highest officials of both domestic and foreign governments, obviously have and exercise kinds of power which go far beyond anything conventional price theory even attempts to confront.

This does not mean that what is under discussion is not properly of concern to economic theorists. Indeed, economists of an earlier era attempted to confront some of these challenges as they presented themselves then. The disjuncture between theory and policy as it affects what happens to large firms has, if anything, widened in the recent past. Improving policy has not been high on the agendas of the theorists.

We argue that despite the Lockheed story, the Chrysler story, and other such sagas – and despite the rise of the multi-nationals and the challenges they present for public policy in many market economies, Galbraith's 1949 assessment is remarkably close to the truth even now. Microeconomic theory has changed remarkably little in its coverage or its extensions. Arguably, therefore, those charged with codifying laws with respect to the operation of business enterprises have gotten less guidance from economic theorists in recent years than they got, say, in the 1930s. For corroboration one has but to peruse current highly regarded microeconomic theory books. There are many descriptions of multi-national corporations and their actions in international business or finance books, but if one looks in modern price theory textbooks for the 'noteworthy extensions' to which Galbraith made reference, one is hard-pressed to find any dealing with multi-national firms and their impact on economic performance. Modern price theory books have not tried to become significantly more attuned to the real economy. (The modern texts are, of course, vastly more sophisticated mathematically and they pay much attention to game theory.) Otherwise, in coverage, they are similar to the price theory texts of my undergraduate days. The competitive model is laid out in great detail. They include brief attention to monopoly, leading to reduced output and raised prices. They still usually pay little attention to oligopoly. One looks in vain for any thoughtful consideration of economic concentration. One finds virtually no reference to multi-national corporations and consideration of cartels is almost non-existent.

Whether this constitutes all the help applied economists dealing, say with OPEC, can legitimately need or can expect from economic theorists is a question to be pondered. It seems essentially correct to note that economists writing in the middle of the twentieth century were more concerned with concentration and its economic consequences than their counterparts in recent years have been. If, for example, Stocking and Watkins, not theorists at all, but applied economists, nevertheless devoted a book length study to major cartels as they impacted on the market economies of the mid-century, the OPEC activity of the 1970s, though widely discussed in macroeconomics as a cause of inflation, has received remarkably little attention from microeconomists, certainly not from microtheorists. At the very least, OPEC activity must be a useful illustration of some aspects of firm behavior which price theory ostensibly confronts. For example, Varian's book, originally published in 1978, but in a third edition by 1992, seemingly finds no occasion to use OPEC as an example of anything relevant to the concerns of price theorists. He refers once briefly to cartels 'where the firms collude to some degree in setting their prices and outputs . . .' (Varian 1992, p. 303). What we find for OPEC is also true for the Lockheed and Chrysler stories. The major anti-trust cases are seemingly illustrative of no price theory questions worth mentioning in a theory text. But the appeal of Bertrand and Cournot and Edgeworth to microtheory textbook writers is, we have seen, apparently eternal. So, too are the attractions of multiple (Walrasian) equilibria, potential Pareto improvements, etc. Coverage is much the same in virtually all the most widely used price theory texts. They provide via ceteris paribus assumptions and by other means a thick protective shield against real world firms and their problems. The texts come with a virtual guarantee: 'Any resemblance to actual firms is purely coincidental.' Not often do these texts reflect firms grappling with what is going on in the real economy. Arguably, if at least occasionally problems emerging in the real world could be successfully confronted by applying to them policy derived from theory, we could say that economics was contributing significantly to improving the lives of real people. Industrial organization economists after Stocking and Watkins have moved steadily away from the approach pioneered by Joe Bain and increasingly, as we have noted, have followed the rest of economics into game theory, abstruse quantification, etc. The field has never dealt adequately with multi-national firms and cartels and the challenges they pose. They have not even tried to do this, e.g., neither is mentioned in Scherer and Ross, in the 1990 edition of their book, nor are they mentioned by Church and Ware, in their text which came out in 2000 (after the game theory deluge in industrial organization).

The Lockheed, Chrysler, and multi-national firms stories are, we suggested, illustrative of the stuff of which challenges in the modern microeconomy are made. We argue that there is a disjunction between what the microtheory texts choose to expostulate on (reflected in what the applied field texts consider), and what the real world microeconomies are churning up to perplex policy makers. The modern theory texts and to a large extent the applied texts as well, will certainly pay attention to game theory and there might be chapters dealing explicitly with the increased importance of mathematics and its applications. However, the basic emphasis is seemingly timeless. It is endemic in the perspective taken in microeconomics. In most disciplines one might expect to find real world examples in theory texts illustrating what is being discussed. In medicine, for example, no matter how abstruse or complex the basic research may be, sooner or later someone takes the results to a hospital and asks how they might be applied to improving the prognosis for real patients afflicted with real diseases. (Medical texts are replete with pictures showing patient *X* with disease *Y*. Economists are not so disposed. They never have been.)

One could, in short, argue that in the case of a huge corporation, with assets dwarfing those of many countries' GDP, whose activities significantly affect national security, but whose leaders are quite as flawed as the public officials the public choice economists describe so vividly, all these developments would cry out for the noteworthy extensions to price theory that Galbraith suggested were not very prominent half a century ago! We suggest here that they are still rare.

All of this is, of course, central to one theme of this book. It is to suggest that the traditional state of microeconomic theory, particularly since World War II, has been concerned with some new areas, yes (game theory, mathematical modeling, etc.). But it has never been fond of building discussions around historical episodes culled from the real world. Judge Gary in his day was not discussed in price theory texts, so we are not surprised that the texts of today ignore the Lockheed and Chrysler episodes, the problems in banking caused by South American debt defaults, or OPEC activity. It is not surprising that they ignore multi-national firms and the implications of what their impact has been on market operations for firms in many fields. Little wonder that administrators devise their own guidelines even if 'too big to die' may be a flawed guide.[19] Price theory is distanced from market activity in the real world. The basic texts continue to give short shrift to oligopoly even just as a conceivable type of market structure and, as we have seen, pour their attention increasingly into areas not easily focused on improving public policy. Mason's 1937 point that economists are more interested in analyzing abstract market situations than in assisting in improving public policy seems truer today. In short, our theorists don't appear to be overly fascinated with the real world and they have, as we have tried to show, busied themselves with tasks other than achieving greater realism in their work.

Is it really out of order to ask, 'Are the questions theorists ask today the questions that perusal of the economic scene today compels us to ask?' Is it irrelevant to ask, where is the discussion of theory which might help sort out

---

19. The problems of Enron revealed in early 2002, though as of this writing still not totally clear, may not, we noted earlier, be an exception to what has been said. It may be that the financial blundering was simply too large for those disposed to help to be able to find a way to do so.

the complexities of Lockheed or Chrysler et al.? Do multi-national firms pose any threats or obstacles to economic performance against which we can all rest assured the public interest is protected or even taken into account? Are these questions the results only of a disgruntled mind nit-picking?

Corwin Edwards in 1949 wrote, 'The contention here is that the classical case of monopoly is relatively unimportant and that the significance of the monopoly problem is to be found primarily in phenomena that lie outside the central focus of traditional theory' (Edwards 1949, p. 112). Plus ca change, plus c'est la meme chose!

Too Small to Save

If firms in the real economy can be considered 'too big to die,' we can ask, what happens at the other end of the spectrum? There we find that by invariably assuming income and wealth distributions to be given and by couching most of the considerations of welfare in a world limited by Pareto optimality, mainstream microeconomic theory deals equally inadequately with small firms and individuals who are, by the de facto rules of economic reality, regarded as 'too small to save.' During the Reagan Administration, which put special emphasis on getting the role of the government, particularly the federal government, scaled down to the appropriate size for 'a proper market-oriented economy,' we began hearing about the social safety net and holes in the net through which individuals might fall.

These are the people we speak of now. Price theory does not address itself to the 'have nots.' It would, unfortunately, take us far too far afield to deal adequately with this subject. But we can sketch in the dimensions of the problem in order to make a point. If one examines what happens in the real economy, one sees what the absence of clear and feasible guidelines dealing with bigness leads to. The failure to confront the fate of small units, especially individuals, is equally unfortunate. Because conventional microtheorists insist that theirs is a 'positive' rather than a 'normative' perspective we can only assume that what we here discuss and the flaws in our system which it reveals can be swallowed whole and without comment by the mainstream theorists of whom we speak.

Still the fate of 'little guys' in the United States has been of concern in many quarters for a long time. (Economic theorists can define away the problem with a couple of assumptions: e.g., tastes and income are 'given.' Assumptions never disturb positive analyses!) In 1987, for example, the Council of State Governments published a document entitled *Mending the Social Safety Net: A Responsible Agenda for the 100th Congress*. It contained a paper by Mitch Snyder and Mary Ellen Hobs dealing with homelessness which concluded:

> The Reagan administration has stated its position quite clearly: Homelessness is strictly a state and local problem. We must quickly come to grips with federal inaction and indifference, and we must overcome it.
>
> We cannot move into the 21st century with millions of Americans eating out of trash bins and living on the street. Our security, and very possibly, our survival as a nation may depend on our ability – and our willingness – to come to grips with the contradictions and inconsistencies contained and made manifest by the problem of homelessness in America. (Snyder and Hobs, 1987)

I hear the voices already informing me that homelessness is not a fit subject for economic theory, let alone a criterion for judging welfare. I grant that the presence simultaneously of homelessness and market equilibrium can pass all the tests, including Pareto optimality. Homelessness is a long way from the parameters on the table for discussion in, say, a class considering the welfare implications of a market clearing solution or even general equilibrium. If income is so distributed that some individuals are homeless, there is no necessary contradiction with the requirements for Pareto optimality. So shall we change our standards for determining Pareto optimality, our standards for what we mean by homelessness, or our parameters for deeming a problem a fit subject for economic theory to confront? I need not take a position to make the point. I'm not sure I have ever seen that question raised in any economics book. Yet the notion of holes in the social safety net arose within the Reagan Administration, scarcely a bastion of far out economic reasoning. Recognition in that case clearly preceded real concern, but it was (is) a necessary first step.

For many years the problem of poverty in Europe, was as we saw in Chapter 1, regarded as a problem for the churches mostly. Still, we saw that Adam Smith had no compunction about writing in highly normative terminology rather than 'positive' terminology, in discussing such things as unemployment or poverty. Modern economists insist that they are invariably part of a discipline based on a positive theoretical base and they prefer to stick to less colorful language. Thus the problems of unemployment and poverty are customarily handled with carefully neutralized terminology. Instead of the language Smith employed in discussing Chinese poverty, for example, economists today are far more apt to refer to situations characterized by a high Gini coefficient. This is a good deal less upsetting than a Smith-like depiction of the misery of poverty. As for unemployment, as we shall see in the next chapter, confronting the impact of job loss on the quality of economic life squarely is far more likely to be painful than if one confines oneself to the consideration of high structural unemployment or a consideration of 'natural' unemployment, which, since it sounds natural, is probably not so bad. In any case, in this chapter we have sketched the view taken of big units in economic difficulty. Before we close the chapter, it is only fair and appropriate to contemplate the view taken of small weak units in economic difficulty.

Unless one wishes to argue that economic theorists have absolutely no impact on societal attitudes toward the subjects they consider, the tendency to keep at arm's length the consequences of our present economy as it unfolds for individuals at the bottom end of the economic ladder and to refer to the poor in colorless terminology (e.g., as 'outliers') may well have impact on how 'little guys' get treated. It would clearly take us too far afield to delve very deeply into the state of the social safety net, or the size of its holes. But there are some fairly obvious ways to characterize current US attitudes toward the 'have nots,' especially relative to the attitudes held in other countries to which the US might reasonably be compared. (That we may also compare these attitudes to the attitudes toward units 'too big to fail' (just examined) goes without saying.)

One simple way to contemplate the state of the 'have nots' in the United States is to make some simple comparisons between what happens to them in the United States and what happens to them in other more or less comparable countries. This means, obviously, that we stay away from third world countries whose overall resource levels (and, even more, resource levels per capita) are vastly lower than those found in the US. Thus in Table 4.1 you will find the United Sates compared to a number of industrialized European economies, as well as a few major advanced Asian economies. We include 18 countries and the US. We begin with a very obvious point. The GNP per capita, as adjusted for differences in the purchasing power of the monetary unit in each country, is a simple and reasonably accurate indicator of the relative level of potential economic activity per capita in a country. Thus the fact that GNP per capita is a great deal larger in the United States than in any other country in the table suggests that as a rough measure of the ability of the US to protect its least affluent citizens from the ravages of poverty and what it brings with it, the US resources to cope are certainly as large and very probably a good deal larger than is the case for any other country in the world.

How does this advantage translate into measures of survival and thriving for its citizens? The United States, for example, for a recent year had the highest infant mortality rate per 1000 live births of any country included in the table. It seems reasonable to suppose that, relative to the other countries in the table, the US suffers no obvious and huge disadvantage – its climate is moderate, its food production is enormous, its potential for producing the most advanced medical care currently possible has no obvious factors which should hold back potential improvements. We conclude that 'the market' (for whatever the reasons which are currently guiding it) has chosen not to deploy sufficient resources and in such a way as to reduce infant mortality to the level to which it has been reduced in other developed economies. Arguably this and all other such social indicators for the US could be as or more impressive than they are in other comparable countries. That is, in view of the advantage indicated by the US adjusted GDP per capita we could have the highest quality of life as reflected by these indicators. Instead there is evidence to suggest in short that the 'little guys' by quite a few measures fall through the holes in the social safety net in greater numbers in the US than is true in 18 of the other advanced countries, comparison to which with the US is reasonable. No economist to my knowledge has ever suggested this be labeled a 'market failure,'or even a 'market idiosyncrasy.' (A common definition of market failure – 'the inability of a system of private markets to provide certain goods, either at all or at the most "optimal" levels', Pearce (1986, p. 264.) Yet it does not appear a distortion of the language to suggest that the lowest possible infant mortality rate might be labeled the 'optimal level.' For economists the problem is only that 'the market' chooses not to produce what is optimal. Economic theorists don't appear to worry that the theory has any weaknesses. Economists seem content, it is fair to say, to deflect questions about all this by insisting that the problems or questions raised are 'non-economic.' Arguably, producing a steady, possibly growing supply of viable and potentially increasingly productive little human inputs for ultimate employment in the economy is the most basic of economic activities. Yet the richest and most powerful economy in the world is not doing this input production very well and it is not a problem which appears especially to challenge mainstream economic theorists.[20]

How well do human inputs fare at the other end of the journey, in terms of life expectancy? Only two countries in our list show lower life expectancy than the US. (There are several with the same expectancy as the US.) There is no reason intuitively why 14 countries including such countries as Italy, Australia, Japan, or Belgium should exhibit longer life expectancies for both men and women than the US, but they do.

In a different test the table suggests that if one considers measures such as numbers of television sets per 1000 inhabitants, the United States can lead by a whopping margin. Here is a challenge that our market system is

20. They may well regard income distribution as a normative question while aggregate income is a positive question.

Table 4.1 Living standard indicators

Rank by column 3	Country	GNP/per capita adj. PPP vs $	Infant mortality rate per 1000 live births 1998	Life expectancy at birth years, 1998[a]		% Share of income		No. television sets per 1000 Inhabitants 1998
				Men	Women	Lowest 10%	Highest 10%	
(Col. 1)	(Col. 2)	(Col. 3)	(Col. 4)	(Col. 5)	(Col. 6)	(Col. 7)	(Col. 8)	(Col. 9)
1	US	$30 600	7	74	80	1.8	30.5	855 (97)
2	Switzerland	27 468	4	76	82	2.6	25.2	419 (95)
3	Norway	26 522	4	76	81	4.1	21.8	433 (96)
4	Denmark	24 280	5	73	78	3.6	20.5	574 (94)
5	Belgium	24 200	6	75	81	3.7	20.2	340
6	Japan	24 041	4	77	84	4.8	21.7	684 (95)
7	Austria	23 808	5	75	81	4.4	19.3	331
8	Canada	23 725	5	76	82	2.8	23.8	714 (95)
9	Netherlands	23 052	5	75	81	2.8	25.1	497 (95)
10	Australia	22 448	5	76	82	2	25.4	495 (95)
11	Germany	22 404	5	74	80	3.3	23.7	415
12	France	21 897	5	75	82	2.8	25.1	360
13	Finland	21 209	4	74	81	4.2	21.6	519 (95)
14	UK	20 883	6	75	80	2.6	27.3	448 (95)
15	Sweden	20 874	4	77	82	3.7	20.1	378
16	Italy	20 751	5	75	82	3.5	21.8	273
17	Ireland	19 140	6	73 (87)	79 (87)	2.5	27.4	409 (95)
18	Spain	16 730	5	75	82	2.8	25.2	404 (95)
19	New Zealand	16 566	5	75	80	0.3	29.8	295

Notes:

1 GDP is adjusted for Purchasing Power Parity

[a] 1998, except as shown in parentheses.

Sources: Basic Sources: *Attacking Poverty: World Development Report, 2000/2001,* World Bank, New York and Oxford: Oxford University Press, 2001. Col. 1, Table 1, p. 274, Col. 2, Table 7, p. 286, Cols. 5 and 6, Table 2, p. 277.Cols 7 and 8, Table 5, p. 282. Col. 9, OECD, *Basic Statistics: Living Standards*, 2001. (Included at back of all 2001 Country Reports). We used Belgium.

superbly equipped to confront. Poverty and its attendant evils, homelessness, malnutrition, high infant mortality, low life expectancy etc. are in the end tied to the way in which income is distributed. (If we ask about the per cent of total income going to the lowest and the highest 10 per cent of the income distribution Table 4.1 shows that the distribution of income in the US in the 1990s was more unequal than for any other country. Not only did the top 10 per cent have the highest share of total income (over 30 per cent, with the exception of New Zealand) but the lowest 10 per cent had less than 2 per cent. This means that despite the great wealth of the US, which dwarfs that of any other country, we were, if not content – certainly not very exercised about income inequality. A bottom 10 per cent that got only 2 per cent of the income, as we have just seen, caused little comment. It indicated, nevertheless, the quality of life for these people is very low indeed. It is obviously not as low as it is in some countries, particularly Third World countries low in resources, etc. But mainstream economists never tire of pointing out that economics is all about 'opportunity costs.' We have the resources to improve the lot of these have nots were we of a market-oriented mind to do so.[21]

It is no doubt highly unusual for economists to be reminded that having the knowledge of resource deploying potential which their training presumably offers them, they have some obligation to point out to the policy makers what could be done. A major contention of this book is that far from taking this obligation to heart, economic theorists have increasingly turned their attention elsewhere. There is considerable evidence to suggest that both the degree of inequality in income distribution and the per cent of the population living in poverty have not changed in many years (perhaps they are slightly worse now). The way one measures poverty is crucial in firming up this conclusion.

There has at the same time in recent years been much talk of getting people off the welfare rolls, and replacing welfare with work. If the inequality has remained steady, in the end this objective, if realized at all, could only increase the misery among the group in poverty. We have elsewhere talked about the increasing attention theorists pay to the micro foundations of macroeconomics. There is some evidence of the reverse – the macro foundations of microeconomics. Thus one student of unemployment has suggested, 'There is little question . . . that high levels of unemployment

21. To those who choose to point out that I am talking here about 'sociology' or some other fuzzy subject rather than economics, I point out that what has been under discussion is of a piece with the discussion in Adam Smith's *Wealth of Nations* concerning conditions in China considered in Chapter 1. Much can be said for the insights to be gleaned from Smith's great book, if one reads beyond the mention of the invisible hand (Smith, 1776/1985).

are a standard part of government policy – to "cool off the economy and to brake soaring inflationary wages"' (Nelson 1982, p. 74). If this is true the policy surely can be traced to advice – implicit or explicit – macroeconomic policy makers have been getting from economic theorists. Among other severe consequences, it suggests that in addition to the initial inequality, already higher than in other similar countries, the pain associated with fighting inflation is considered appropriately deployed when transferred disproportionately to the lower income groups, thus allowing inflation to exacerbate even more the effects of the initial inequality.

CONCLUSION

All this leaves discussants about the economy in something of a quandary. At the same time that there are economists who argue that the anti-trust laws are no longer viable or feasible or appropriate so that wealth and power gained through monopoly and monopolizing (or oligopoly and oligopolizing) occur without comment from these theorists, the fate of the have nots at the other end is similarly not commented on.

In pronouncing that they assume technology, the distribution of income, and the distribution of wealth are 'given,' our 'positive economic theorists' manage to sweep quite a lot under the proverbial rug. We have not here compared the performance of the US economy to that of impoverished Third World countries, but to countries which, like the US, are fairly well developed, have resources, trained labor, etc. Relative to what the US could do, were it of a mind to enhance the lives of all up to their potential, the application of current economic theory to the task of fashioning sound equitable and effective public policy is largely left absent.

We raise complicated questions, we grant. Those economic theorists who argue for 'leaving it to the market' put themselves in a difficult position. In the case of Lockheed or Chrysler or other large firms they do not argue that the proper role for the economist is to 'keep the government off our backs.' Only in the case of the have nots – the impoverished, the homeless, the infants, etc. do they, by their silence, suggest that this state of affairs is satisfactory. 'Positive' economic theorists carefully stay away from all real world situations including both of these.

There is, then, a vacuum – a normative vacuum, if you will, produced by the current state of microeconomic theory. Because there is a vacuum it has been filled de facto by the 'too big to fail, too small to save' perspective considered in this chapter. This perspective we noted has surely never been explicitly asserted by any responsible theorist. It emerges implicitly via a perspective based on the knowledge of what resource deployment can achieve. That simple perspective is left as the only guide to public policy. In mainstream macroeconomics, as we shall see in the next chapter, we have at least contemplated what 'potential output' might be like. But in microeconomics what the quality of life might potentially look like were the market monitored by efficient and democratically sensitive public policy, remains an open question in a country such as the US. Microeconomics, as we have suggested, is stuck in a Pareto optimality general equilibrium time warp.

Somehow, as the next chapter will suggest, intervening to avoid inflation has received the blessing even of some economic theorists who don't believe in intervention. Neither other macroeconomic objectives (we shall see) nor microeconomic objectives in general (as we have seen in this chapter) have received that endorsement.

REFERENCES

Bain, Joe S. (1959), *Industrial Organization*, New York: John Wiley & Sons.

Baumol, William J., John C. Panzar and Robert D. Willig (1982), *Contestable Markets and The Theory of Industry Structure*, New York: Harcourt Brace Jovanovich.

Baumol, William (2002), Private communication to author.

Berle, A. and Gardiner C. Means (1932), *The Modern Corporation and Private Property*, New York: Macmillan.

Bork, Robert H. (1978, 1993), *The Anti-trust Paradox*, New York: The Free Press (original, Basic Books).

Boulton, David (1978), *The Grease Machine*, New York: Harper and Row.

Boyne, Walter J. (1998), *Beyond the Horizons, The Lockheed Story*, New York: St Martin's Press.

Bresnahan, T.F. (1989), 'Industries and market power', in Richard Schmalensee and Robert D. Willig (eds), *Handbook of Industrial Organization, Volume 2*, Amsterdam: Elsevier Science, pp. 1011–57.

Burns, A.R. (1936), *The Decline of Competition*, New York: McGraw Hill.

Carlton, D.W. (1998), 'How markets clear', in Richard Schmalensee and Robert Willig (eds), *Handbook of Industrial Organization*, Amsterdam: North Holland.

Chamberlin, Edward H. (1933), *The Theory of Monopolistic Competition*, Cambridge, MA: Harvard University Press.

Church, Jeffrey and Roger Ware (2000), *Industrial Organization, A Strategic Approach*, Boston: Irwin McGraw-Hill.

Clark, J.M. (1940), 'Toward a concept of workable competition', *Proceedings*, American Economic Association, June 30, pp. 241–56. Reprinted in American Economic Association, *Readings in the Social Control of Industry*, Philadelphia, PA: Blakiston.

Edwards, Corwin (1949), *Maintaining Competition*, New York: McGraw-Hill.

Fellner, William (1949), *Competition Among the Few*, New York: Alfred A. Knopf.

Galbraith, John K. (1948), 'Monopoly and concentration of economic power', in Howard Ellis (ed.), *A Survey of Contemporary Economics*, Philadelphia, PA: Blakiston.

Galbraith, John Kenneth (1973), *Economics and the Public Purpose*, Boston, MA: Houghton Mifflin.

Hart, Gary (1986), 'Comments', in Claude E. Barfield and William A. Schambra (eds), *The Politics of Industrial Policy*, Washington, DC: American Enterprise Institute for Public Policy Research.

Iacocca, Lee A. and Lee Novak (1984), *Iacocca, An Autobiography*, New York: Bantam Books.

Mas-Colell, Andreum, Michael D. Whinston and Jerry D. Green (1995), *Microeconomic Theory*, New York: Oxford University Press.

Mason, Edward S. (1937), 'Monopoly in law and economics', *The Yale Law Journal*, **47** (1), November, 34–49. Reprinted in American Economic Association, *Readings in the Social Control of Industry*, Philadelphia, PA: Blakiston, 1949.

Nelson, Joel I. (1982), *Economic Inequality: Conflict Without Change*, New York: Columbia University Press.

New York Times (1971), January 7, 1:3.

New York Times (1971), January 8, 30:1.

New York Times (1971), May 7, 1:5.

New York Times (1971), May 13, 67:8.

New York Times (1971), May 14, 40:2.

New York Times (1979), May 4, IV, 1:3.

New York Times (1979), June 23, 27:6.

New York Times (1979), August 1, IV, 4:3.

New York Times (1979), August 12, 33:6.

Pearce, David W. (1986), *The MIT Dictionary of Modern Economics, Third Edition*, Cambridge, MA: MIT Press.

Robinson, Joan (1933), *Economics of Imperfect Competition*, London: Macmillan.

Ross, Stephen F. (1993), *Principles of Anti-trust Law*, Westbury, NY: Foundation Press.

Scherer, F.M. and David Ross (1990), *Industrial Market Structure and Economic Performance, Third Edition*, Boston, MA: Houghton Mifflin.

Schmalensee, Richard and Robert Willig (eds) (1998), *Handbook of Industrial Organization*, Amsterdam: North Holland.

Smith, Adam (1776/1985), *The Wealth of Nations*, New York: Modern Library Edition.

Snyder, Mitch and Mary Ellen Hobs (1987), 'Sheltering the homeless: An American imperative', in Council of State Governments, *Mending the Social Safety Net: A Responsible Agenda for the 100th Congress*, Washington, DC: Government Printing Office.

Sosnick, Stephen (1958), 'A critique of concepts of workable competition', *Quarterly Journal of Economics*, **2**, 380–423.

Sowell, Thomas (1993), 'A student's eye view of George Stigler', *Journal of Political Economy*, **101** (5), 784–92.

Stigler, George (ed.) (1993), *Journal of Political Economy*, **101** (5), entire journal dedicated to George Stigler, articles written by different of his students.

Stocking, George W. (1961), *Workable Competition and Anti-trust Policy*, Nashville, TN: Vanderbilt University Press.

Stocking, George W. and Myron W. Watkins (1946), *Cartels in Action*, New York: Twentieth Century Fund.

Stocking, George W. and Myron W. Watkins (1948), *Cartels or Competition*, New York: Twentieth Century Fund.

Stocking, George W. and Myron W. Watkins (1951), *Monopoly and Free Enterprise*, New York: Twentieth Century Fund.

Taylor, Philip A.S. (1966), *A New Dictionary of Economics*, London: Routledge and Kegan Paul.

Varian, Hal R. (1992), *Microeconomic Analysis*, *Third Edition*, New York: W.W. Norton & Company.

Waller, David (2001), *Wheels on Fire*, London: Hodder & Stoughton.

Willig, Robert D. (1987), 'Contestable markets', in Eatwell, John, Murray Milgate, and Peter Newman (eds), *The New Palgrave, A Dictionary of Economics,* London: Macmillan Press, 618–19, 621–2.

5. Trivialization and elegance II: the world of macroeconomics

> The prestige of theoretical work is so secure in our profession that its proponents too rarely find themselves on the defensive . . . (Lucas 1981, p. 11)

> The core of most undergraduate macroeconomics courses is the IS-LM model, which has not been taught in graduate schools for 20 years. Graduate students of macroeconomics learn models that are dynamic; undergraduate students are taught models that are static. Graduate students learn general equilibrium theory; undergraduates are taught Keynesian economics. Many undergraduate treatments have lost touch with data from the real world that our subject was developed to explain (this is also true, to a regrettable extent, of many graduate programs). (Farmer 2002, p. v)

The microeconomic story we have just told is at bottom a tale of great but ultimately muffed opportunities to make microeconomic theory more connected to reality and hence a more useful adjunct to public policy. The story we now turn to is essentially a parallel story. A major advantage in this task is that we can build on what has been said in Chapter 2. We there considered macroeconomic theory at some length because it is there that schools in economics can be differentiated most clearly. We examined the assertion that schools of thought can be identified in part by their attitude toward the relationship between theory and policy. In the last chapter we examined the relations between several divergent views of microeconomic theory as they have developed and the public policy alternatives with which each view can be identified. We tried to show that in microeconomics the broad division between interventionists and non-interventionists can be seen once again. In Chapter 2 we made the point that while the automatic market adjusting economy was originally a construct of microeconomic theory, the modern schools which share a non-interventionist perspective are most clearly identifiable in macroeconomics where Keynesians of one stripe or another constitute the interventionists and the new classical school, which reflects the divergent responses to the Keynesian challenge (all designed, as we saw in Chapter 2, to defang Keynes) represents the non-interventionist perspective. Accordingly, in this chapter we examine the trivialization process as it pertains to macroeconomics in somewhat greater detail, following on the discussion of Chapter 2. In particular we made the point that 'new classical economics' encompasses a variety of views – monetarism, supply side economics, and rational expectations all of which come (but by divergent paths) to the conclusion that intervention to improve macroeconomic performance is a mistake.[1]

Just as public policy in microeconomics has mostly been developed by applied economists in the learning-by-doing world, so, too, we argue here, the same thing has happened in macroeconomics. Theorists have been busy, as we saw, getting rid of Keynes's influence. Now, in the belief (mistaken?) that this effort has been successful, they have moved on to more esoteric pursuits.

Here we consider how these efforts as a launching pad for mainstream attitudes toward public policy have unfolded in macroeconomics just as we previously assessed them in microeconomics. Here the discussion must ultimately focus on the two major kinds of interventionist policy which have evolved – monetary policy and fiscal policy. The discussion of monetary policy can build on what was said about this in Chapter 2. The last part of this chapter will be devoted to a consideration of fiscal policy. In both, we shall see how economic theorists have managed (but by quite different routes) not to contribute significantly to developing better interventionist policy. The policy makers are, in consequence, left to their own devices.

The 1930s proved to be a watershed decade for both micro and macro economic theory. In Chapter 4 we asserted that the seminal contributions of Robinson and Chamberlin and Keynes opened the way to ridding economic theory of the excessively constraining world of 'economic givens' on which classical and neoclassical theory had relied. The 'ubiquity of oligopoly' as a fact of life emerged in microeconomics as did 'under-employment equilibrium' in macroeconomics. (Each suggested that theory to be useful should not stray too far into simplification.) Each paved the way potentially to making theory more relevant. Each was ultimately rejected in favor of sticking with the beauty, logic, and precision of the conjectural orthodox cocoon in which most of our theorists have always preferred to operate.

Schools of thought in macroeconomics we repeat are somewhat more clear cut than they are in microeconomics, which is why in Chapter 2 we relied on macroeconomics. A major point we made was that it is far easier

1. Monetarism, it will be recalled, in the hands of Friedman argued that the Fed is as likely or more to get interventionist monetary policy wrong as right and therefore is very likely to make things worse. This was, of course, the classical view toward public policy, but it was developed mostly in the world of microeconomics.

for non-interventionists – those who are comfortable with the status quo – to insist that ours is a positive science. Those who like 'what is' are less concerned with the difference between 'what is' and 'what ought to be.' Those who find fault with the status quo are apt to have the distinction before them much of the time. So in macroeconomics, the non-interventionists (monetarists, supply siders, rational expectations adherents, etc.) are more content with the present state of the economy than the Keynesians (of all stripes) and other heterodox economists. The latter, we saw, are more apt to regard economics as a normative science.

Here we focus directly on the character of the trivialization process as it manifests itself in macroeconomics. If in microtheory trivialization grows out of obsession with the competitive model, in macroeconomic theory it primarily takes the form of finding ways to reject Keynes or at least to reduce his influence on policy makers. Some of the ways this can be done have been considered in Chapter 2. Here we consider theoretical claims that trivialize critical aspects of the effort to make macroeconomic theory more realistic. There has been a parallel process of escape from realism in macrotheory, comparable to what we saw earlier in microeconomic theory.

The past 50 years have witnessed a vigorous effort to undo the Keynesian revolution. Less than fully employed economies are as ubiquitous as oligopoly and both threaten the centrality and dominance of the mainstream theoretical perspective. The process of trivialization was used against each. In many ways the process was even more prominent in macroeconomics. We have seen that in microeconomics it often took the form of denouncing suggested ways to make theory more realistic in favor of methodical characteristics deemed more crucial by microtheorists (precision, internal logic, neatness, etc.). In macroeconomics we find the assault has been far more direct. The competitive assumptions were never declared to be correct reflections of the real world in microeconomics. They were necessary to make the theoretical world analytically manageable. (Assumptions, after all, are always necessary in constructing theory. The critical question becomes one of degree.) In macroeconomics the denigrative assertion was not based on the need for simplification; it was based on claims that Keynesian theory was simply incorrect. The world, we were told, really was (after some critical redefinitions) as mainstream macroeconomics showed it – 'naturally fully employed.' 'Many buyers and sellers' was the microeconomic standard – the microtheorists had to settle for 'benchmark theory.' In macroeconomics full employment (well, as full as we can tolerate!!) was no benchmark – by God, that is the way the world really is!

There is one difference in the perspective taken in microeconomics from that taken in macroeconomics. What has always appealed about competitive theory, we repeat, is its claim to precision, plus its elegance, and its logic. These qualities have always endeared themselves to those who saw economics as the best hope in social science for a discipline based on a theory as rigorous as that found in the hard sciences. As we suggested in Chapter 2 it was expedient and prestigious to convert to mathematical modeling. The appeal of mainstream macroeconomics is somewhat different. If fully employed inputs is the natural condition of the macroeconomy then surely non-intervention is the best policy. In microeconomics in contrast the natural world might be Darwinian, hence not too attractive to contemplate. Thus it is more appealing to focus on the end result rather than the process. If one accepts all the assumptions lying behind the welfare implications of competitive microtheory, the emerging picture is very attractive. The process is less disturbing in macroeconomics and hence it is easier to regard it as 'natural.' As we have seen, Keynes raised the specter that what was really natural was not necessarily attractive and that indeed such results in macroeconomics far from being 'natural' might be a rare fluke.

We can identify the difference between the appeal of micro and macro in one other way. Competitive microtheory would appeal to a compulsive housekeeper – everything is related precisely to everything else, movement is like clockwork, and nothing is left to chance. Macroeconomics on the other hand would appeal to the happy camper – all is wonderful in nature because you can enjoy the moon and stars and being in the outdoors. Nature is the world at its best. Forgotten are the times when it rains, is very cold, is blistering hot, is replete with flies and bees, etc. It is a churlish person indeed who insists on forcing us to look at all that is unpleasant in nature. The appeal of one is its precision and the appeal of the other is its naturalness. One is a Swiss watch; the other a sunset.

So in effect even if pure competition is as rare as full employment, mainstream microeconomists focused on the competitive case for reasons other than their insistence that it really existed. In macroeconomics, we shall see, through artful and careful redefinition and other maneuvers, full employment has been redefined and reinstalled, at least to the satisfaction of many mainstream economists, as the natural state of the world after all.

TRIVIALIZING MACROECONOMICS

We have previously suggested that theory can be trivialized two ways. Critical terms can be redefined so as to render the theory harmless, harmless meaning that it leads to either policy ineffectiveness or futility. The second way is to ignore proffered changes in the theory which might make it a better analytical guide to public policy. In microeconomics we found more of the second than the first technique. In macroeconomics we shall find the reverse.

Redefining Full Employment

Arthur F. Burns wrote in 1963,

> During the nineteenth century, full employment was just a dream of a small band of reformers. Today it is a firmly established objective of public policy, through the greater part of the world, including our own country . . . This moral commitment to full employment has been reaffirmed time and again by successive Presidents and successive Congresses. There can be no doubt that it expresses faithfully the prevailing sentiment of the American people. (Burns 1969, p. 175)

Trivialization via redefinition is seemingly always tempting. Full employment may have been 'a firmly established objective' in 1963. It may have been a 'moral commitment,' and it may have been clear to the American people, but it wasn't so clear to mainstream economists. At the very least it was far too simple and straightforward. They were about to begin embroidering 'full employment' in a major way. Therefore, very soon it would be virtually impossible for non-economists to understand what were the objectives of our 'Full Employment Act' as now refurbished.

At least in the 1940s there was no confusion about the term full employment. When William Beveridge entitled his best seller *Full Employment in a Free Society* he correctly assumed there would be little confusion anywhere about 'full employment.' Said Beveridge, 'Some frictional unemployment there will be in a progressive society however high the demand for labor. Full employment means that unemployment is reduced to short intervals of standing by, with the certainty that very soon one will be wanted in one's old job again, or will be wanted in a new job that is within one's powers' (Beveridge 1945, p. 18).

In the United States, the full Employment Act of 1946 suggests only that it is 'the continuing policy and responsibility of the Federal Government to use all practical means . . . to promote full employment . . .' (Full Employment Act 1946, 1985). The congressmen did not engage in extended debate about what full employment meant. They seemed to understand that more or less it meant people who needed and/or wanted to work could find jobs for which they were qualified in a reasonably short period of time.

Keynes gave several definitions of full employment, but at least one is pretty straightforward: full employment is 'a situation in which aggregate employment is inelastic in response to an increase in the effective demand for its output' (Keynes 1936, p. 26). That seems clear enough – if employers want to employ more labor and there is no more labor to employ, the economy must be 'fully employed' already. Presumably allowance here could be made for frictional unemployment and perhaps for seasonal as well. Arguably, it also includes structural unemployment – there would be no increase in the effective demand for labor which was inadequately trained to produce the output that was demanded.

Mainstream macroeconomists have trivialized the problem of unemployment initially by renaming the variable involved. They no longer speak of full employment; instead they speak of 'natural unemployment.' As a concept, full employment (reasonably full employment) and its twin concept, unemployment (reasonable unemployment) are easily understood, and those who lean toward interventionist policy can study and make potentially useful policy suggestions.

From the Great Depression until the 1960s economists recommended 'full employment policies.' Even macroeconomic theorists thought in terms of the 'policy implications' of their work. Then the trivializers got hold of 'full employment' and delivered macroeconomics into the hands of the non-interventionists as best they could. The process involved conceptual hair splitting, adding aspects that could not be measured accurately or in some cases at all, and revamping the terminology.

Milton Friedman, by no means the worst offender, but probably the best known, illustrates the process of trivialization. He begins by renaming the problem variable 'the natural rate of unemployment' and redefines it thus:

> The natural rate of unemployment . . . is the level that would be ground out by the Walrasian system of general equilibrium equations, provided there is embedded in them the actual structural characteristics of the labor and commodity markets, including market imperfections, stochastic variability in demands and supplies, the cost of gathering information about job vacancies and labor availabilities, the costs of mobility, and so on. (Friedman 1968, p. 8)

Friedman, with this definition, accomplishes several things. First, by calling the unemployment in question 'natural' he suggests it is not something we ought to have to worry about. Things that are 'natural' are frequently things that one cannot truly influence. They are non-discretionary. If my students are 'naturally stupid' I need not worry about whether or not I am a good teacher, naturally or otherwise. This is true even if the things under review are catastrophic, like terminal cancer. Pancreatic cancer is perfectly 'natural' – it occurs spontaneously in previously healthy individuals and kills them in fairly short order. It is not pleasant but its outcome, in the present state of our knowledge, is unavoidable. That does not prevent researchers from searching for a cure, but we get ahead of our story.

Second, 'natural,' in fact, is the ideal adjective to apply to an economic process to which seeking remedial public policy is to be defined as futile. Things found in 'nature' like natural disasters are clearly, we reiterate, unavoidable. Meteorologists do not spend their time seeking ways to avoid hurricanes or tornadoes. (Seeding clouds is perhaps a modest exception.)

Third, promoting improvement in processes which are natural must perforce be interpreted in ways which avoid absolutist interpretations. When doctors are said to seek 'to promote full health' we are expected to realize that this does not mean that there will not be days of illness in one's life, or that illnesses will come along which find them helpless. In fact, no reasonable user of the term 'full employment' has, to our knowledge, ever assumed it meant absolutely full employment. Thus, Burns comments that 'All economists recognize . . . that if the concept of full employment is to serve public policy constructively, it must at least allow for seasonal variation in economic activity and for the familiar frictions of the labor market' (Burns 1969, p. 185). He suggests that full employment really must mean 'maximum employment.' If he does not explicitly include structural unemployment there is room in his common sense approach for so doing.

Fourth, a category of employment which can be defined as beyond the ability of even enlightened public policy to affect is a great boon to those who wish to declare that the macroeconomy we have, 'au naturel,' is the best we can have a right to expect. To those who regard interventionist policies as futile the more of the manifestations of unhappy interventionist macroeconomic occurrences which can be put in this box the better the remaining macroeconomic performance will look. As we shall see, these macroeconomists reserve to themselves one big exception to this line of thought: inflation. Inflation is the only unfortunate occurrence to which modern non-interventionists very often urge intervention. Friedman himself with his 'simple monetary rule' is more restrained here than many non-interventionist economists. (We shall return to this exception below.)

Fifth, the most obvious and perhaps the simplest thing Friedman accomplished was also the most fundamental. Friedman's efforts here, as in so many places, served as the launching pad for very many mainstream forays into the complexities of full employment as a concept for today. Beveridge we have seen had no trouble finding a reasonable definition of full employment. He defined the problem simply and directly and, most importantly, in terms that could be potentially translated into public policy. When Friedman got through defining it, 'full employment' was so convoluted, so abstruse, and so filled with complications and abstractions that no policy could be easily and possibly ever appropriately formulated to deal with the problem. Indeed arguably it could not with any ease even be measured! But macrotheorists had grist for many an article, graduate students in economics had many hours of difficult theory to study, and doors for many PhD exam questions and dissertation topics were beautifully opened. What more could be wanted?

After Friedman, defining the natural rate of unemployment became something of a cottage industry. Modern macroeconomics concentrates, therefore, not on full employment but on something less than full employment. 'Natural unemployment' is objectionable for all the reasons listed above. However, relatively few mainstream economists ever raised these objections but a number ultimately did come to see that the term was obfuscating, or at least was imprecise.

We can go further. If the natural rate of unemployment represented a conversion of a fairly simple objective into a difficult-to-understand objective, the second point to make is that not all economists agreed as to the definition of the natural rate. Recent definitions of the natural rate of unemployment include the following:

1. A fairly typical definition of the natural rate of unemployment is that of Robert Barro. He tells us that the natural rate of unemployment is, 'The average unemployment rate that prevails in the economy, depending on the average rates of job separation and job finding' (Barro 1990, p. 562). Job separation and job finding would clearly encompass frictional unemployment. Recessions enter as greater than average separations. Job separations can occur due to seasonal, frictional, structural, or cyclical factors while job findings can occur similarly from all four of these factors. Barro's approach is all inclusive but not helpful in sorting out the reasons for unemployment.
2. 'That natural rate of unemployment is the rate of unemployment arising from labor market frictions[2] that exist when the labor market is in equilibrium' (Dornbusch and Fischer 1990, p. 485).
3. 'The natural rate of unemployment consists of only frictional and structural unemployment' (O'Sullivan and Sheffrin 2001, p. 120). They define it again – 'the level of unemployment when there is no cyclical

---

2. Many modern discussions of unemployment allow for the 'costs of search' because, unlike a perfect classical labor market, finding suitable workers in tight labor markets today is not costless. The relatively few unemployed workers, therefore, who are regarded as too costly to find are thus part of those 'naturally unemployed.'

unemployment' (2001, p. 120).

4. A final attempt at definition would be: 'the normal rate of unemployment around which the unemployment rate fluctuates' (Mankiw 1998, p. 779).

In sum, the consensus (O'Sullivan and Sheffrin are exceptions with a narrower definition) seems to be that the natural rate of unemployment, however defined, refers to some rate of unemployment greater than one would have found in, say, Beveridge's day, when frictional and seasonal unemployment were certainly recognized, along with cyclical unemployment and probably some structural unemployment. It refers to that unemployment greater than Beveridge would have seen which exists and is the price of not having the economy so close to capacity as to loose an unacceptable acceleration in inflation.

Here we wish first to focus only on the degree to which the labor force is employed because the notion of 'full employment' began life as a straightforward statement of one of the most basic and universal expectations of what an economy should be held responsible for – providing jobs for those who participate in the economy. So a major point we make here is that a very straightforward objective of any economy – to provide jobs for its participants – at the hands of Friedman and others became so adumbrated with complexities that it was not easy any longer to understand, much less to measure. That state of affairs is, as we have seen, not all bad if you advocate doing nothing to affect employment levels as a matter of principle. For those who did advocate intervention, early policy measures revolved around job retraining, better job advertising, reducing 'search time' in other ways, creating public works 'shelves' of planned public projects, etc.

Next economists added the notion that unemployment was tied to inflation. The inflation connection led to rechristening the problem with a carefully calibrated substitute; the 'Non-Accelerating Inflation Rate of Unemployment' – or NAIRU, for short. We consider this term more fully in connection with the Phillips curve, to which we turn in the next section.

A number of definers attempt to make this connection. Thus Gordon writes: 'The natural rate of unemployment designates the level of unemployment at which the inflation rate is constant, with no tendency to accelerate or decelerate' (Gordon 2000, p. 9).

Similarly Samuelson and Nordhaus give essentially the same characterization. They define NAIRU as 'That unemployment rate consistent with a constant inflation rate. At the NAIRU, upward and downward forces on price and wage inflation are in balance so there is no tendency for inflation to change. The NAIRU is the lowest unemployment rate that can be sustained without upward pressure on inflation. The NAIRU is the unemployment rate at which the long-run Phillips curve is vertical' (Samuelson and Nordhaus 2001, p. 771). Samuelson and Nordhaus at least add, 'The original name for the NAIRU was the "natural rate of unemployment." This term is unsatisfactory because there is nothing natural about the NAIRU' (2001, p. 696). In the fifteenth edition of their book (1995) they still call it the Natural Rate of Unemployment (Samuelson and Nordhaus 1995, p. 591). By the sixteenth edition (1998) they have switched to calling it the 'Lowest Sustainable Unemployment Rate' (LSUR) (Samuelson and Nordhaus 1998, p. 591). Few other economists bother with this distinction (cf., for example, the definition by Barro, above).

The difficulty with the Gordon-Samuelson view is that one can never ever know whether or not there is pressure one way or the other on the inflation rate until some later period of time. If the inflation rate went up then (by definition) the unemployment rate at the beginning of the time period under review must have been 'below its natural rate.' If the inflation rate went down the reverse must have been true. As a policy guide such a view of unemployment would always be available only when it was too late to be useful. As we have seen, however, the natural rate of unemployment was not primarily introduced as a policy guide. Many of those who find the NAIRU concept useful are generally inclined against interventionist public policy. But they may make an exception for policy to keep inflation rates low. Often they are less concerned about policies to keep unemployment low, regarding the latter as 'the price of keeping inflation under control.'

A 1997 issue of the *Journal of Economic Perspectives* devoted considerable space to a Symposium on the Natural Rate Hypothesis. Roughly half the papers supported the idea and half were highly critical. The critics got empirical support when the natural rate – if it exists – began to fall after 1984.

In the introductory paper to the Symposium Joseph Stiglitz asserts, 'I have become convinced that the NAIRU is a useful analytic concept' (Stiglitz 1997, p. 3). Robert Gordon in the second paper says, 'Whether the goal is steady inflation or lower inflation, the Fed needs to know the value of the NAIRU' (Gordon 1997, p. 11). This suggests a certain reality to the NAIRU.

Staiger, Stock and Watson, in contrast, look at the evidence and conclude, '. . . the NAIRU appears to be imprecisely estimated. Moreover, forecast errors of more than one percentage point in average annual inflation based on this regression are common. A policy maker would understandably hope for a better predictor of inflation . . .' (Staiger, Stock and Watson 1997, p. 35). They add, referring to their study, '. . . these results reinforce the common sense, if unexciting, view that monetary policy should be informed by a wide range of variables, not just unemployment' (1997, p. 48). Note, we underscore, that while presumably unemployment is a real number, the NAIRU is for them 'an estimate.'

Blanchard and Katz in yet a fourth paper survey progress in studying the natural rate of unemployment and insist that there has been much progress in this area in the previous 30 years. A major conclusion they reach is that '. . . the nature of the relations between firms and workers leads to wage setting that often differs substantially from competitive wage setting. This in turn is likely to result in a different level of unemployment that differs from the efficient frictional level' (Blanchard and Katz 1997, p. 51). They thus attribute the difference between what is presumably the natural rate of unemployment and the rate that reflects an efficient economy entirely to workers getting 'excessive' wages. This seems excessive in view of the decline of union strength. Moreover, it assumes no conflict between competitive units and achieving efficiency. This suggests a different perspective toward the oft-repeated view of the importance of the microfoundations of macroeconomics. (See the previous chapter!) They do end with a plea for greater cooperation between labor economists and microeconomists in general on the one hand and macroeconomists on the other in seeking the causes for the perceived behavior of the natural rate of unemployment.

Richard Rogerson quotes a number of definitions of the natural rate of unemployment and then draws from them the following:

> If transitivity is assumed to hold then the above list of quotations would tell us something like: long run, frictional, average, equilibrium, normal, full employment, necessary-steady state, lowest sustainable, efficient, Hodrick-Prescott trend, natural. [From all this Rogerson reaches a conclusion with which we certainly concur.] It would seem doubtful that any concept that is sufficiently ambiguous as to promote this many different uses can be helpful in guiding scientific inquiry (Rogerson 1997, p. 74).

Finally James K. Galbraith in an essay entitled 'Time to ditch the NAIRU' so argues on grounds that there is no compelling case for the NAIRU, that 'the empirical evidence for a vertical Phillips curve and the associated hypothesis that lowering unemployment past the NAIRU leads to unacceptable acceleration of inflation is weak, . . . (that) attempts to estimate the location of the NAIRU have become a professional embarrassment' (and that) 'adherence to the concept as a guide to policy has major costs and negligible benefits' (Galbraith 1997, p. 93).

That the costs being high (conveniently?) leads to the conclusion that interventionist policy is futile and the benefits are negligible is illustrated in Romer's wording of the natural rate:

> . . . the natural-rate hypothesis states that there is some 'normal' or 'natural' rate of unemployment, and that monetary policy cannot keep unemployment below this level indefinitely. The precise determinants of the natural rate are unimportant. (Romer 1996, p. 226)[3]

This is interesting because we still do not have any very precise definition of 'normal unemployment.' Arguably, what we need to know is that in the natural rate enthusiast's view the Promised Land is where one does not have to focus on sufficient jobs for all who are able and willing to work. Romer has told us that 'monetary policy cannot keep unemployment below this [the natural, ed.] level indefinitely.' Romer here suggests implicitly why the role of monetary policy is so complicated in the modern world.

It is no doubt a bad but nonetheless irresistible analogy to point out that we expect doctors to continue looking for ways to improve our diverse ailments even though we recognize that 'medical intervention cannot keep us 'in better-than-dead' health indefinitely.' 'Economists are a long way from having a good quantitative understanding of the determinants of the natural rate, either across time or across countries' (Blanchard and Katz 1996, p. 2). They add,

> . . . we feel that a divide has grown between macroeconomists and labor economists, at least on this side of the Atlantic. Too much theoretical work on the natural rate of unemployment by macroeconomists is divorced from microeconomic evidence, and too much microeconometric work seems in search of a broader theoretical framework for interpretation. This is unhealthy. (Blanchard and Katz 1996, p. 28)

No one should be surprised that hypothetical time series are more difficult to verify empirically than 'actual time series.' There was a time when economists contented themselves merely with writing about 'stylized facts.' Now they want to support them empirically.

Ambiguity arose not only from how the theory was formulated but also in

---

3. The reader may wonder, does Romer have a role for fiscal policy? The answer is that the term appears on exactly one page in his book, if the index is to be believed. His comment appears in connection with his discussion of a model which highlights the role of money in creating hyper-inflations. Says Romer, ' . . . the model explains the central role of fiscal problems in causing high inflations and hyper-inflations, and the role of fiscal reforms in ending them' (Romer 1996, p. 428). That's not a very significant role.

the diverse ways it was estimated for the real world. For example one study of the NAIRU in Canada echoed Rogerson and Galbraith. It concluded:

> The analysis of this paper suggests that considerable uncertainty attaches to the concept of the NAIRU. NAIRU theory suggests that there exists a unique equilibrium rate of unemployment consistent with stable inflation, which is determined on the supply side of the economy. According to this theory, aggregate demand affects unemployment only in the short run. In the long run, the rate of unemployment will always be equal to the NAIRU, and variations in demand will be reflected solely in the rate of inflation.
>
> . . . the theory of hysteresis suggests that no such unique equilibrium rate of unemployment exists: with hysteresis, long run unemployment is sensitive to past and present short run values of the unemployment rate, which are in turn influenced by general macroeconomic conditions, i.e., the state of aggregate demand.
>
> . . . These results imply that the NAIRU is a spurious statistical artifact . . . . (Setterfield 1996, pp. 67–8).

Tersely, Samuelson and Nordhaus, after having, as we have seen, given a fairly comprehensive definition of what they mean by the NAIRU, nonetheless echo the sentiments just expressed by Staiger, Stock and Watson; by Blanchard and Katz; by Rogerson; by Galbraith; and by Setterfield. They illustrate the NAIRU with a chart and comment, 'The NAIRU is shown as a wide band to reflect the fact that it is difficult to estimate the NAIRU precisely' (Samuelson and Nordhaus 2001, p. 699).

This contrasts sharply with the approach taken by Mankiw. He shows a chart which compares the actual unemployment rate to a straight line drawn at precisely 6 per cent and covering the period 1970–1995, labeled 'The Natural Rate of Unemployment' (2004, p. 569). No ambiguity there!

Frequently economists, glossing over the difficulties we have been considering, write about the natural rate of unemployment or the NAIRU as though it were an actual time series to be found, perhaps, in the *Survey of Current Business*. This approach clearly makes the task of empirically verifying theory less difficult, but only hypothetically.

In sum, it is clear that there is considerable controversy over the usefulness, not to say the meaning, of the NAIRU among mainstream economists. We add to this only the observation that the NAIRU is but one more contrivance introduced which, whatever the announced reason, has the effect of lowering the bar which real economic activity has to meet in order to be pronounced 'normal' or 'acceptable' or 'in equilibrium.' We have already seen these devices in microeconomic theory. They have the effect, intended or not, of making the policy objectives that much easier to achieve because they are less demanding.

In any case, to consider adequately the place of the NAIRU in modern macroeconomic theory, we must do so in connection with the Phillips curve, to which we now turn.

The Phillips Curve

In what sense do we include the Phillips curve among the constructs used to trivialize macroeconomic theory (Phillips 1958)? First of all, as we shall see here, it is by no means clear that it exists now, if ever it did. As many have now noted, briefly toward the end of the 1960s and the early 1970s a relationship seemed clear. It was argued that interventionists used a Phillips curve to show that at any given time policy makers were presented a 'menu of choices' from which they could choose the precise amount of unemployment and the rate of change in the inflation rate that seemed best for the economy ('fine tuning' it was called). Overall, the Phillips curve has mainly been an instrumentality of non-interventionists. With it they believed they could demonstrate the futility of trying to affect the unemployment rate by tolerating inflation rate acceleration. As such it raises again the question considered in Chapter 2 – do we want the theory we get or get the theory we want? As an aid in dampening any enthusiasm for applying economic theory to the improvement of economic policy, the Phillips curve is probably the best illustration of all.

Non-interventionists arguably have always made an exception to their 'positive' approach for the view that 'inflation is bad' and intervening to reduce that threat is to be tolerated. (The only disagreement with this exception would come from very strict monetarists who regard any interventionist monetary policy with suspicion.) We alluded briefly in Chapter 2 to the charge that Keynes failed to put sufficient emphasis on fighting inflation as a macroeconomic policy objective. (His theory was charged specifically with failing to explain the stagflation of the 1970s.) While inflation has reared its head from time to time for many centuries, it was not notably prominent in the 1930s on which Keynes was, of course, focused while writing the *General Theory*. In logic as we will see Keynesian theory can be as useful in explaining an 'inflationary gap' (effective demand exceeding what full employment could accommodate) as it can be in explaining a 'deflationary gap' in times of inadequate effective demand.[4]

Indeed thinking about inflation and its impact on macroeconomic activity has undergone a sea change in the past 50 years. Consider the views of Samuelson in the first (1948) edition of his *Economics* text:

> An increase in prices is usually associated with an increase in employment. In mild inflation the wheels of industry are well lubricated and total output goes up. Private investment is brisk, and jobs are plentiful. Thus a little inflation is usually to be preferred to a little deflation. The losses to fixed-income groups are a good deal less than the gains to the rest of the community. Even workers with relatively fixed wages are often better off because of improved employment opportunities and a greater take-home pay; and a rise in interest rates on new securities may partly make up any losses to creditors. (Samuelson 1948, p. 282)

That view was probably not regarded as very controversial when Samuelson expressed it. Today Samuelson still argues that 'most agree that a predictable and gently rising price level provides the best climate for healthy economic growth' (Samuelson and Nordhaus 2001, p. 691). Now low inflation is carefully distinguished from higher rates. But now many disagree with this position. Their thinking is closer to the views of Leon Henderson, Director of the Office of Price Administration during World War II, who was quoted famously (and perhaps apocryphally!) as saying, 'A little inflation is like a little pregnancy. It grows.' Thus, Robert Hall has long considered a zero inflation rate (or close to it) the appropriate target: 'For inflation, it seems clear that the desirable level is near zero' (Hall and Taylor 1986, p. 450).

We can pinpoint the arrival of the Phillips curve as a means for including both inflation rate concerns and unemployment on the mainstream scene. Paul Samuelson makes no mention of the Phillips curve in the fourth edition of his *Economics* text (1958). In the fifth edition (1961) the Phillips curve is introduced. As is well known, the original curve, noted earlier, was introduced by A.W. Phillips and was devoted to demonstrating a close relationship between unemployment and the rate of change of money wages in the United Kingdom for the period 1861–1957 (Phillips 1958, pp. 283–99). We mention this primarily to make clear that the relationship Phillips was concerned with was presumably found over a period of almost one hundred years. In contrast, we repeat, the original modern generalized

---

4. In my graduate school days we learned about both the inflationary gap and the deflationary gap outcomes for the Keynesian model. This was, of course, before the AD-AS model, which features focusing on real income, and became popular as a way to distinguish real from nominal effects.

use of the Phillips curve notion was originally applied to less than a decade.

All the data required for our discussion of the Phillips curve are shown in Figure 5.1. We call attention first to the period 1961–1969, the decade which shows a sufficiently close relationship between the inflation rate and the unemployment rate to explain how all the talk about a 'trade off' got launched. As Samuelson put it (in language which will doubtless strike many readers today as 'quaint'), 'There is, so to speak, a choice for society between reasonably high employment with maximal growth and a price creep, or reasonably stable prices with considerable unemployment: and it is a difficult social dilemma to decide what compromises to make' (Samuelson 1961, p. 383). Note the real concern about the unemployed and the modest terms in which the inflation threat is couched. Before long at the hands of our 'positive' macro-theorists, the threat of inflation was 'accelerating,' and the problem of unemployment had been resolved by introducing an assumed long run where 'full employment' once again 'naturally' prevailed. But we get ahead of our story.

In the early days, depictions of the Phillips curve, based on the 1960s, were doted on by economists of many persuasions. This was true despite the fact that, as one textbook recently stated, the Phillips curve 'provided an important stimulus to the research of theorists working on the neoclassical model' (Farmer 1999, p. 320). Conservatives insisted that the 'difficult social dilemma' (not so difficult for them) must of necessity be resolved in favor of keeping inflation rates down, regardless of what happened to unemployment rates. Interventionists, as was noted above, used the Phillips curve to suggest that there was 'a menu of choices' available and that policy makers could in fact choose with some precision what unemployment rate to shoot for because one could foretell with some precision what the price in inflation would be for any given drop in the unemployment rate, just as presumably one could foretell the cost in rising unemployment of pushing the inflation rate down.

Then all hell broke loose in the United States. After the 1960s, the inflation rate and the unemployment rate produced the maze shown in Figure 5.1. The lovers of abstruse theories had a ball. We were told that what we had seen for the 1960s was a 'short run Phillips curve' and that there were a whole series of these 'shifting short run curves' visible in charts such as we depict. Sometimes in order to accommodate the data, theorists were required to show a shifting Phillips curve for each year. Were a demand curve depicted similarly, with the theorist insisting that in each period the curve 'shifted,' one would be hard-pressed to explain what was the inverse relationship the demand curve was ostensibly portraying. In the case of the Philips curve no one seemed to mind when the curve kept shifting.

Figure 5.1 Phillips curve (1960–1999), United States

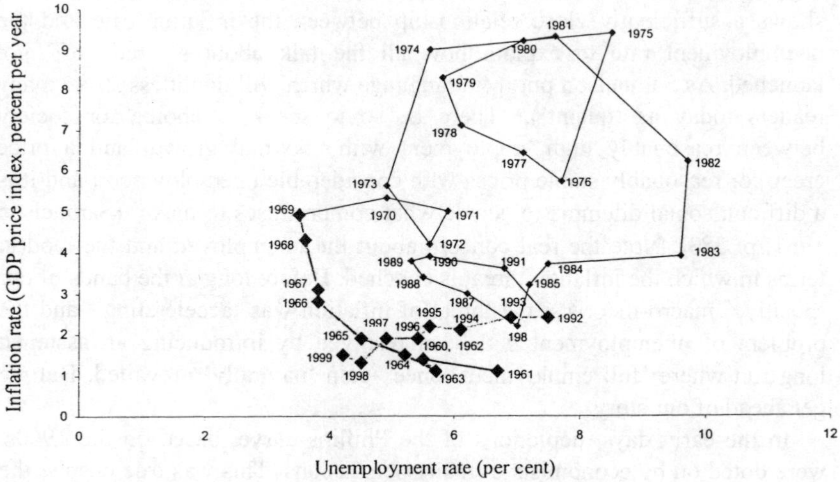

At this point we return to Phelps' (1987) and Friedman's contribution (1968) because together they persuaded many economists that the entire Phillips curve was, as then being depicted, 'short run.' Back of all these short run shifting Philips curves there is a long run Phillips curve and (surprise!) it is found at full employment where there is no trade off at all. Furthermore, since we have returned to full employment via market forces, the only impact which mistaken efforts to affect short run unemployment conditions can have is to force up the inflation rate. Once again we see evidence of non-interventionists 'getting the theory they want' – that doing nothing is best after all. Let the unemployed respond 'naturally' to what happens in the market and in the long run all will be well. It is the macro equivalent of the invisible hand and we are thus returned to the cozy cocoon we contemplated in the first chapter! Not for nothing did the Phillips curve 'stimulate neoclassical theorists'!

Throughout the long years during which economists debated about the puzzling pattern being described by each successive year's inflation rate and unemployment rate, the discussion was invariably couched in terms of why what was happening was so different from what happened in the 1960s. It was rarely commented on that Phillips's original relationship involved unemployment and the change in money wages. It did not directly involve inflation. Legions of specialists in collective bargaining, haggling over the terms of COLAs, can testify that wage changes are only very imperfectly associated with inflation rate changes.

The basic point to be made is that one is on far more solid ground basing a finding on a century of data than on a decade or less. It just happened that the decade of the 1960s behaved in a way that many economists found useful in pushing the position they had mostly accepted earlier. In discussing this, Phelps has said of Phillips's work, '. . . the rate of unemployment required to hold down the rate of wage inflation to the level of normal experience – the average, and accustomed rate is certainly positive, perhaps 2 to 3 percent in the United Kingdom, the domain of Phillips's data, and has not shifted notably over nearly a century of observation' (Phelps 1987, p. 858). In reaching this conclusion Phelps specifically tells us that the ceteris paribus assumptions need to include the rate of change in unemployment, the rate of change in nominal wages, and the (algebraic) rate of wage inflation (1987, p. 858). He does not include the rate of productivity of labor, although this is invariably included in depicting the simpler Phillips curve. It is indicated by showing the rate of wage increase assumed to be compatible with a zero rate of inflation. Constant productivity, among other things, would be required to argue that the rate of nominal wage increase and the general rate of inflation were perfectly correlated.

Even if one accepts Phelps's comment as correct for the century to which he referred, one would have to add that the long constancy to which he refers clearly has broken down in the last 30 years, at least for the United States.

There is one further adumbration we need to add. In their original discussions Friedman-Phelps in their depiction of the Phillips curve, at least in its short run manifestation, declared that each Phillips curve (such as that we see in Figure 5.1 for the 1960s) was based on an assumed set of unvarying expectations. So now we have not only a short run and a long run Phillips curve, but the short run Phillips curve can be 'expectation augmented.' In fact, a recent careful statement of what this trade off is based on tells us, 'The leading framework for estimating the NAIRU arises from defining it to be the value of unemployment that is consistent with a stable expectations-augmented Phillips relation' (Staiger, Stock and Watson 1996, p. 3). It is not, therefore, at all surprising that as we have seen they conclude that 'Our main finding is that the natural rate is measured quite imprecisely. For example, we find that a typical value of the NAIRU in 1990 is 6.2%, with a 95% confidence interval for the NAIRU in 1990 being 5.1% to 7.7%. This confidence interval incorporates uncertainty about the parameters . . .' (1996, p. 2). They add, 'A central conclusion from this analysis is that a wide range of values of the NAIRU are consistent with the empirical evidence' (1996, p. 31). Not surprisingly, their final conclusion from all this is that '. . .

these results raise serious questions about the role that estimates of the NAIRU should play in discussions of monetary policy' (1996, p. 2).

This sets the stage for their view of the NAIRU drawn earlier. It applies in the long run to the level of unemployment that is compatible with no acceleration in the inflation rate. This constitutes the framework within which NAIRU proclaimers can make their argument for the futility of allowing inflation rates to increase in order to accommodate falling unemployment rates. Figure 5.2, similar to the figure Samuelson and Nordhaus use to illustrate the NAIRU, illustrates this futility. We will follow them in calling the lower Phillips curve a short run relationship ($SRPC_1$) based on a low 'inertial inflation rate' at, say, *A* (Samuelson and Nordhaus 2001, pp. 696–8). They then assume there is an expansion so that economic activity increases, unemployment falls below the rate at *A* and the economy moves along the lower short run Phillips curve to *B*. The longer the expanding economy stays at *B* the more difficulty the public has in accepting *A* as the true underlying inertial inflation rate. When the 'inflationary psychology' adjusts to the realization that basically the inflation rate is now higher, (at *B*) it becomes more difficult to maintain that the lower Phillips curve ($SRPC_1$) really represents the economy. When this realization becomes general knowledge (that the underlying inflation rate is now higher) we shift to the upper Phillips curve ($SRPC_2$) based on the higher 'inertial inflation rate' of *D* rather than *A*. As the economy continues at *C* the expansionary forces abate and contraction begins to set in, which means that entrepreneurs no longer support aggregate economic activity at the level subsumed at *C* and, therefore, economic activity slows and then declines so that unemployment is pushed up again along the higher short run Phillips curve ($SRPC_2$) (to *D*). As Samuelson and Nordhaus (and many others) point out, at the higher inertial inflation rate unemployment is once more at the same level but now with inflation accelerating even faster at *D* than it did at *C*. Conclusion – the non-accelerating inflation rate of unemployment shows that there is in principle a level of unemployment below which it is absolutely futile to try and push the economy because all that can be accomplished is to increase the rate of inflation, which of course causes widespread misery in the economy.

There are two problems with this assessment, in our judgment. One involves the implicit use of expectations as they are here used, and the other involves the tilt toward controlling inflation at the expense of unemployment which is a major (if implicit) characteristic of most models in modern macroeconomic theory and the direction in which it has been moving for many years. We shall take them up in turn.

As we saw in Chapter 2, advocates of rational expectations models like to tell us that one of their basic assumptions is that 'economic agents use all information efficiently.' That may be, but assuming information is used efficiently is a far cry from assuming that all economic agents are perfect forecasters. Expectations can be inserted into models as they have been here, so as to support the findings in logic of these models. In passing, note that the ultimate 'finding' of non-interventionist mainstream macroeconomic modeling parallels what we saw in the previous chapter with microeconomic modeling, namely that market-driven economies – both micro and macro – perform as well as we can get them to perform without any interventionist policy. Perfect foresight on the part of economic agents could conceivably help produce this result. Would anyone deny that, however well the economy functions when left to the market, it would work better if all agents had perfect foresight?

We illustrate how expectations are used to further this line of reasoning by quoting Phelps' use of expectations in quite another context. In defining 'the equilibrium price level' for the current period he writes,

> Given the supply of money, there is a nominal price level that is in some suitable sense the equilibrium price level; more generally, there is an equilibrium path of the price level. The equilibrium price level in the current period, *given next period's price level*, is just high enough to reduce the real value of this period's cash balances down to the quantity demanded – figured at the corresponding nominal rate of interest (which is a decreasing function of this period's price level) and output level (which was taken to be independent of the price level if nominal wages were also taken as finding their equilibrium level. (Phelps 1987, p. 858, emphasis in original).

Buried in all this is a wonderful example of how expectations can currently be incorporated into a model. To assume that next period's price level is given is tantamount to assuming it is perfectly known today (i.e., the inflation rate must be anticipated perfectly correctly). This can only mean that the agents in this model have perfect foresight and there are no unexpected shocks, which goes considerably beyond merely assuming agents use information efficiently. One could perhaps justify such an assumption if critical relationships which pertained to the real world were thereby clarified. But so far as we can tell this is not the case here. It simply makes the models work and enables the modeler to impute to 'equilibrium price levels' characteristics and implications which make for a neater world in which to contemplate what has been done. Logic and precision have thereby been enhanced but in the process the model is permitted to eclipse what might be required were we to attempt to apply all this to improving public policy, in this case, monetary policy.

We do not quarrel with the logic, but we do quarrel with the conclusion that this masks. At bottom we can surely say there must be a realization that a world in which there is perfect foresight, therefore no uncertainty, and no exogenous shocks would surely be a world far easier both to stabilize and to forecast. Monetary policy would face far fewer challenges. Conveniently, the world is far simpler. This is but one more example of the self-serving manner in which modern economists all too frequently confront the economy.

The other problem is the implicit tilt toward the notion that avoiding inflation increases is of greater importance than avoiding unemployment increases. The model anticipates the conclusions it reached by suggesting that there is 'an inertial inflation rate' associated with every short run Phillips curve and that there is a 'natural rate of unemployment' below which the economy cannot be pushed. Attempting to reduce the unemployment rate below this 'natural' rate sounds as though it would be futile. Samuelson puts it aptly by suggesting the 'surprising outcome,' the rate of inflation has increased and therefore at the end unemployment is the same and *real* GDP is the same, but prices are rising faster than ever! (Samuelson and Nordhaus 2001, p. 697). Samuelson and Nordhaus in fact suggest that the points ABCD in Figure 5.2 'produce clockwise loops' that look like the loops in Figure 5.1. Does he really suggest that we have been on a 30 year roller coaster involving changing inertial inflation rates and shifting 'natural rates of unemployment?' In any case, the model is designed to demonstrate that inflating one's way out of unemployment is as bad as public policy can get!

I suggest there is an alternative scenario, just as logical (perhaps more so) with a different conclusion to be drawn. But put them both together and we shall try to show why one strategy is as short-sighted and futile as the other.[5]

Figure 5.3 illustrates the second interpretation. Like Samuelson's figure it is not based on any real time period. But it could well have applied to the 1980s. Put the case that there is some inflation rate that can be regarded as the long run 'average' – it will be the maximum inflation rate that can be sustained without generating the 'intolerable' unemployment rates all expect. (We can follow Friedman, Phelps, et. al. and call it 'the Non-Increasing Unemployment Rate of Inflation' (NIURI)). It is clear that whatever else in the previous quarter century ending at the end of the 1980s, the inflation rate in the US had been far above zero. It probably averaged about 3 per cent so we can indeed call this the 'natural inflation rate.' We will not dispute for the moment the assumption in the short run Phillips curve that there is a trade off between inflation rates and the unemployment rate. The actual

5. The following is based on Klein (1990, pp. 293–302).

Figure 5.2 The non-accelerating inflation rate of unemployment (NAIRU): the conventional view

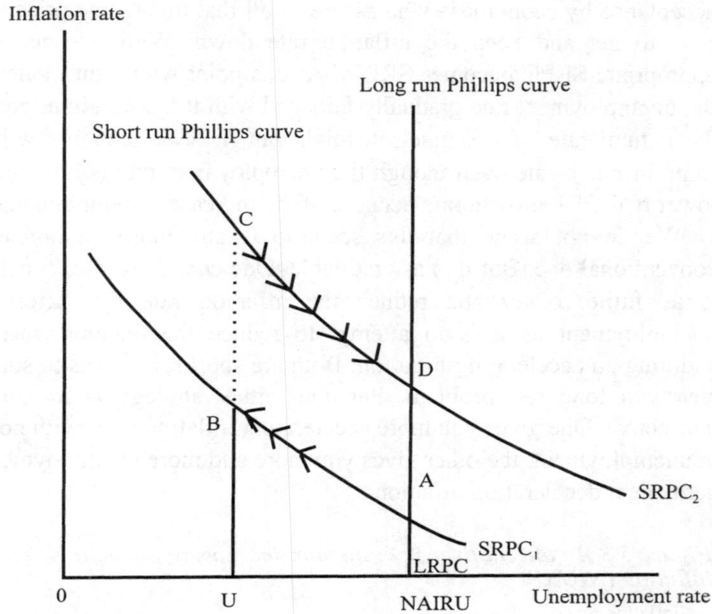

unemployment rate is something that all get accustomed to as well. It depends on what unemployment has been in the recent past. (It would include seasonal, frictional, structural, and perhaps some cyclical unemployment.) In any case, again following Friedman, Phelps, et al. the short run Phillips curve is drawn with an underlying unemployment rate that is accepted, 'the inertial unemployment rate.' (There would no doubt be 'discouraged workers' who look or do not look for jobs in this period based on their attitude toward that unemployment rate. Attributing their failure to search for a job to inertia seems perhaps even more appropriate than applying the word to inflation expectations.) The monetary authorities, we postulate, decide economic expansion is threatening to get out of hand; they fear accelerating inflation in the near future and so concur that it is critical to get the inflation rate down now. They tighten up, with the result that the inflation rate falls below its 'natural rate' of 3 per cent. The economy is pushed along the lower inertial unemployment rate Phillips curve toward *B*. The economy is pushed toward recession. Monetary policy may get credit for a while with successfully reducing the inflation rate, but the longer the unemployment rate stays at *B* (greater than what the unemployment rate was at *A*) the more people accept it as endemic. They are perhaps helped along in this acceptance by economists who assure us all that this is 'the price we have to pay' to get and keep the inflation rate down. With this acceptance the appropriate SRPC becomes $SRPC_2$. At this point with tight monetary policy the unemployment rate gradually falls and with it the inflation rate returns to its 'natural rate.' As Samuelson might put it, 'The economy will have the same inflation rate even though the unemployment rate is now higher and a lower real GDP growth rate because of the increased unemployment.'

We do not argue that this scenario is any more creditable than the conventional one. But it is as creditable. One can, therefore, conclude that it is as futile to try and reduce the inflation rate by suffering greater unemployment as it is to attempt to reduce the unemployment rate by enduring an accelerating inflation. Both are short run efforts to solve what is clearly a long run problem. Pursuing either strategy is in the long run ineffective. One gives you more accelerating inflation rates with no reduction in unemployment; the other gives you more and more unemployment with no permanent decelerating inflation.

Figure 5.3 An alternative view: the non-increasing unemployment rate of inflation (NIURI)

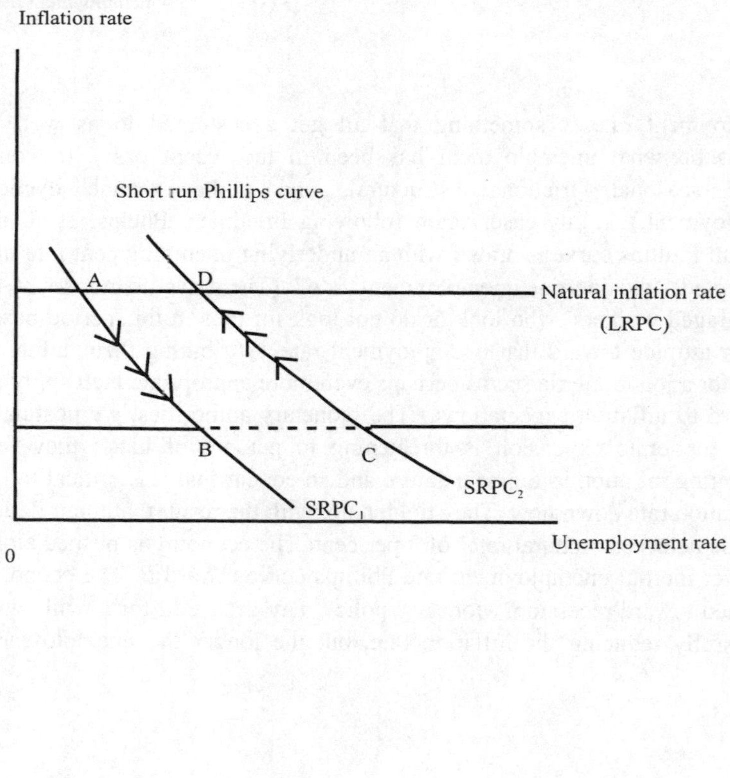

If one thinks about it, the 'Phillips curl' (Samuelson's term) shown in Figure 5.1 corroborates this. Over time until the 1990s the US was gradually suffering accelerating inflation rates and rising unemployment. Clearly what was called for were policies designed to reduce *both at the same time.* One thing was seen correctly. In the long run there is no trade off. While the 'accelerationists' assumed the effort to base policy on the short run would lead to accelerating inflation rates, the alternative suggested here would lead to rising unemployment rates, which was in fact what happened for some years (the rising 'natural rate' which we were told was unavoidable). In Samuelson and Nordhaus's depiction, 'the natural unemployment rate' rose from 1955 to about 1980 and fell more or less thereafter (Samuelson and Nordhaus 2001, p. 699). It is interesting to note that in his widely admired basic text Gregory Mankiw, in contrast to the changing band employed by Samuelson and Nordhaus to represent the NAIRU, simply employs a straight line at 6 per cent, as though the 'normal rate of unemployment' (their words) – never varied (cf. Mankiw 1998, p. 603).

This brings us, of course, to the 1990s. The presumed secular increase in the 'natural rate of unemployment' mysteriously began, we were told, to decline. Inflation increases were for some years pronounced to be imminent, but ultimately some economists began to declare that the inflationary threat was not developing as anticipated.

As for the Phillips curve there have been a few additional efforts to keep the idea viable that should be mentioned before we leave the subject. Some economists distinguish between 'the empirical Phillips curve' and the Phillips curve 'in its natural-rate reincarnation, as the tool by which the natural rate of unemployment is estimated.' (Cf., for example, Gordon 1988, p. 1.) Clearly it is only in its 'empirical form' that one can attempt to relate real time series to the hypothesis. In its 'natural rate form,' particularly when 'expectations-augmented,' it may have useful heuristic properties, but can scarcely serve as a launching pad for empirical testing with real world data. Using data, already less than precise because they depend on ex ante changes in the inflation rate, which now also include an imputed expectations assumption, to estimate a time series which may not exist at all can scarcely be precise and conceivably could have difficulties at times even being approximate.

Nevertheless, the tendency is widespread and strong to derive 'actual' numbers from the 'natural rate reincarnation' and treat them as though they were as real as the numbers derived from the 'empirical' Phillips curve. If Samuelson and Nordhaus treat the natural rate as 'a wide band,'as we have seen, there are many others who produce a precise changing number they label the Natural Rate of Unemployment which they use quite as though it came from actual statistics. Mankiw pronounces the natural rate to be 5.5 per cent (Mankiw 1998, p. 603).

Finally we need to say a word about related developments in the 1990s. With their record of low inflation rates AND low unemployment rates they have not been kind to the Phillips curve in either form. As Figure 5.1 shows the empirical record of the 1990s produces a pattern almost directly opposite to that of the simple 1960s pattern. As for the 'natural rate reincarnation,' unemployment rates below the 'natural rate,' according to Friedman and Phelps, are supposed to produce the evil of accelerating inflation. Since inflation in the 1990s clearly was not accelerating it raised the awkward question of exactly where the natural rate of unemployment was. The honest-to-God actual unemployment rate (if an economist who wishes to be taken seriously can still speak in such simplistic terms) got down to 4 per cent without seemingly producing any tendency of inflation rates to budge let alone accelerate. There were those who insisted that 'the Natural Rate of Unemployment' after years of rising had begun to fall more or less steadily. Robert J. Gordon labeled the 1990s 'the Goldilocks economy' – ('not too hot and not too cold, but just right') (Gordon 1998, p. 2).

What could have produced this strange behavior? Robert Gordon attributes the simultaneous appearance of low inflation and low unemployment in the 1990s to the lower real price of energy, the lower real price of imports, the faster decline in the real price of computers, the slower inflation in medical care, and measurement improvements (improvements in some government indexes removed the previous overstatement of the inflation rate) (Gordon 2000, pp. 264–6). These were in line with his earlier conclusion, contradicting the Phillips curve, that 'wage behavior (is) irrelevant for inflation,' (Gordon 1988, p. 28). He added 'possible additional explanations: demographic changes, higher rates of imprisonment, and the role of temporary help agencies in speeding re-employment' (2000, p. 268).

Katz and Krueger look at changes in labor markets which reflect structural changes and might well prove lasting (that is, might permanently lower the natural rate of unemployment). They consider 'favorable demographic trends, the recent surge in the growth of the prison population, improved efficiency in matching jobs with workers, and greater increased anxiety on workers part about job security' (Katz and Krueger 1999, p. x). This second list is particularly revealing because it suggests that much of the 'good news' from the employment side is scarcely good news for workers. Thus, for example, it may be that an increase in incarcerations will reduce the supply of labor and so reduce the pressure of finding jobs by holding down the size of the labor force. But it is scarcely good news for workers ('Go to jail and avoid unemployment') nor is it fiscally very good news for the economy. Coping with workers fiscally who are unemployed can scarcely cost more than coping with the same workers (now prisoners) in incarceration. Similarly, greater anxiety about job security on the part of the labor force can scarcely be regarded as a salutary development among the work force. Still, one assumes that tough-minded positive economists take evidence where they find it and react accordingly.

Many economists would agree with Gordon that many of the forces which produced the Goldilocks economy could reverse themselves. Still Samuelson and Nordhaus remind us as well that, 'many classical and supply-side economists see the 1990s as yet another nail in the Phillips curve coffin' (1998, p. 700). Others, as we noted earlier, have found an ingenious way to redraw the Phillips curve, this time as a positively correlated relationship between real aggregate output and the inflation rate. How is this managed? One economist who did not care to be a pallbearer at the Phillips curve funeral, has explained the change this way:

> . . . since the rate of change in nominal wages is highly positively correlated with the rate of change in other money prices, and the unemployment rate is highly negatively correlated with the deviation of aggregate economic activity from trend, it should not be surprising that if there's a negative correlation between the rate of change in nominal wages and the unemployment rate, there will also be a positive correlation between the inflation rate and the deviation of aggregate economic activity from trend. Indeed, the term Phillips curve has come to denote any positive correlation between aggregate economic activity and the inflation rate. (Williamson 2002, p. 572)

This new definition of the Phillips curve may come as a surprise to Phillips. Gordon has commented, 'Traditionally wage equations of the Phillips curve variety are the central element that explains inflation in large-scale Keynesian econometric models. . . When the labor's share variable is statistically insignificant, as in almost all the equations estimated in this paper, wage behavior becomes irrelevant for inflation' (Gordon 1988, p. 28). If Gordon is correct and wage behavior is irrelevant for inflation it is difficult to see how the resurrected Phillips curve we just considered can hold up, since it depends upon 'the rate of change in nominal wages.'

An even more devastating comment is made by Lawrence H. Summers: '. . . models containing standard Phillips curves depicting the sluggish adjustment of prices are fatally flawed as Keynes' vision of the economy or of reality' (Summers 1988, p. 12).

In sum, the Phillips curve has had a long and colorful passage through modern macro-economic theory. Whether it is dead or dying or will in fact be resurrected in some new form remains to be seen. That it has proved most useful to those who wished to argue that the inflation threat is the supreme threat to a modern market economy seems clear. It is to this increased fixation on inflation that we next turn for another technique found helpful to those who seek, in this case, to distance macroeconomic theory from any possible application to policy developed to confront unemployment.

The Deification of Inflation

No one would argue that inflation, particularly high rates of inflation, cannot have deleterious effects on any macroeconomy. In that sense to worry about inflation is surely not a trivial matter. But we have argued that there is a clear tendency today for those generally opposed to 'interventionist policies' to make an exception for efforts to fight inflation. And in the name of that fight other objects of concern to interventionists, most particularly the degree of unemployment, are too readily sacrificed. Most especially the effects of the fight against inflation are not frowned on even if they place severe burdens on workers who are, in consequence of that fight, thrown into the ranks of the unemployed. From a number of worthy objectives for interventionist macroeconomic policy, the virtual single-minded fixation holding down on price increases is not without severe and inequitably felt costs. If 'trivializing' is, therefore, a harsh description of these efforts, the priorities back of these efforts seem clearly questionable.

Recall what we said in Chapter 2 concerning Lucas's insistence that, on the one hand 'One cannot, even conceptually, arrive at a usable definition of full employment' (Lucas 1981, p. 243). On the other hand imagine any mainstream economist who wished to be taken seriously concluding (symmetrically?) that inflation was too difficult to define to be an operationally usable term!

Nothing has changed more in recent years than the presentation of the problem of inflation. As is often the case, there is no better way to chronicle the change than to examine successive editions of Samuelson's basic text. The story is familiar but worth reviewing. Thus in the eleventh edition (1980) as in most of the previous editions the reader is treated to two figures – one depicting a 'Deflationary Gap' and the other an 'Inflationary Gap.' They have here been combined in Figure 5.4. The crossings are labeled 'equilibrium' and the significance of each depends entirely on where it is located relative to the 'full employment' level of output $C + I$.[6] They still could form the basis for a relatively straightforward employment goal for macroeconomic policy. In the figure (following convention) GNP is marked on the horizontal axis but is not specified as to whether it is in real or nominal dollars. It was usually discussed as though all the dollar amounts were nominal dollars. The deflationary gap (Y_{F1}) represented the shortfall of total $C + I$ and 'full employment GNP.' In contrast, the inflationary gap (Y_{F2}) was defined as a gap, in which 'full employment falls short of scheduled investment' (Samuelson 1980, p. 229). As both gaps were designed to represent the world as Keynes saw it, Keynesian economics was presumably not then regarded as tilting toward 'depression' as is so often charged today, but could depict with equal facility the world in which aggregate demand exceeded full employment GNP or fell below that level of GNP. The distinctive feature of the Keynesian perspective was that the level of aggregate economic activity depended on the level of effective demand, and this level became the equilibrium level. As all economists know, effective demand was the key to equilibrium. But, unlike the classical equilibrium – here all the resources were utilized – this equilibrium, subject as we say to the level of effective demand could be at any level of income or output. In the 1930s the major economies were plagued with an 'under-employment level equilibrium,' but it could be at an inflationary level as well. Were equilibrium to occur at full employment it would be, therefore, for Keynes, a pure fluke, rather than a market-driven preordained conclusion.[7] My generation of graduate students was taught this and it seemed totally logical and symmetrical to us.

The problem, of course, was one to which Keynes himself had alluded: while in the case of the inflationary gap it was clear that 'filling it' could produce only price increases, the deflationary gap was ambiguous. At less than full employment presumably increased aggregate demand could produce increased real output, increased prices or increases in both, depending on the shape of the aggregate supply curve. Although introduced in *The General Theory*, it was not elaborated to anything like the extent the next couple of decades would witness.

---

6. It is hard to realize that only 22 years ago we still spoke of 'full employment' in straightforward and unambiguous terms. In our earlier discussion of full employment, recall that people like Arthur Burns and William Beveridge spoke of full employment decades ago understanding full well the importance of allowing for frictional, seasonal, and structural changes. In 1968 Burns wrote 'Major structural changes have . . . occurred in the sphere of employment' (Burns 1969, p. 47).
7. As Keynes put it in *The General Theory*, ' . . . whilst a deflation of effective demand below the level required for full employment will diminish employment as well as prices, an inflation of it above this level will merely affect prices' (Keynes 1936, p. 291).

In the twelfth edition (1985) of Samuelson (now with Nordhaus) this inability to distinguish real from nominal output in inflation was corrected. The reader is told, 'We have introduced aggregate supply and demand (AS-AD) as the central approach to understanding overall movements in prices and national output. All major issues in macroeconomics are now analyzed using these new tools. We thereby integrate different schools of thought –

Figure 5.4 Keynes: inflationary and deflationary gaps

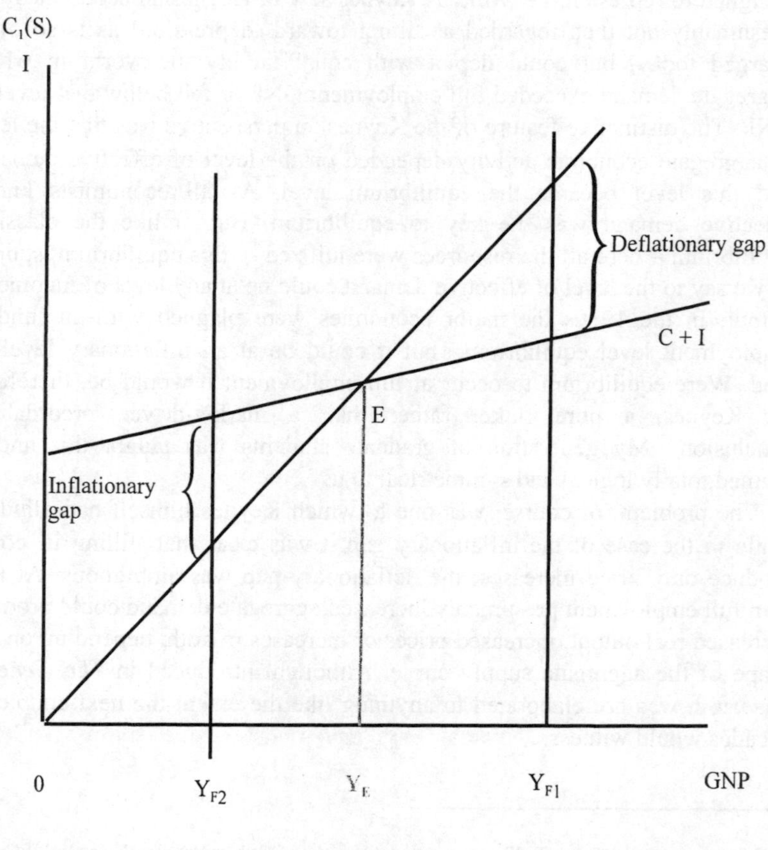

Keynesian, classical, monetarist, supply-side, rational-expectations and modern mainstream macroeconomics' (Samuelson and Nordhaus 1985, p. viii).

Nonetheless, despite the 'ease with which students can grasp it,' by the seventeenth edition Samuelson and Nordhaus change the name to 'lowest sustainable unemployment rate' because 'there is nothing natural about the LSUR' (Samuelson and Nordhaus 1998, p. 591).

Other changes are more subtle. In the eleventh edition (1980) we were told about the 'natural rate of unemployment' (in quotation marks) and it is stated 'It claims: . . . above this critical so-called natural rate of unemployment [then estimated to be 6 per cent, ed.], the rate of inflation will decelerate' (Samuelson and Nordhaus 1980, pp.771–2). Five years later the quotation marks are gone and the natural rate no longer makes 'claims.' It has become an unambiguous concept. 'The natural rate of unemployment is that rate at which upward and downward forces on prices and wages are in balance' (1985, p. 217). The reader is told that 'Students can easily grasp the importance of the natural rate of unemployment, why the natural rate has drifted up in recent years, and what can be done to lower it' (Samuelson and Nordhaus, 1985, p. viii). If it is true as we saw above that the natural rate, at least in its most modern form (the NAIRU), is a 'spurious statistical artifact,' we should indeed be impressed with students who can grasp it easily. For Samuelson a hypothesis offered somewhat tentatively had at least for a time become a credible theory, obviously worth considering, and Keynesian economics had become but one of a number of competing schools of thought, all presumably worthy of considerable attention.

In short, the discipline bought more or less fully into the changed perspective. The attitude toward both inflation and unemployment changed as well. Inflation had become the preeminent concern, unemployment had shrunk for many to a subsidiary worry. Keynesian economics had been transformed (again for many but not all) from an insightful fresh examination of how the macroeconomy functioned to the musings of an economist whose focus was misguided because he was excessively focused on demand shocks – most particularly inadequate aggregate demand, ignoring supply shocks, and reached his gloomy conclusion ('under-employment equilibrium') only by assuming that wages and prices were sticky. Lost somehow was the possibility that entrepreneurs might choose to hire fewer workers if their expectations of selling what they could produce fell low enough. (Funny thing – it was quite acceptable (even critical) in the new macroeconomic environment to argue that workers were 'voluntarily unemployed' but quite seldom was it argued that entrepreneurs might voluntarily reduce production.) In the world which Keynes had attempted to dispatch there was always a price at which goods or factors could be taken off the market (the 'market clearing price'). Among new classical economists, the 'sticky price' explanation was widely adopted. If there were any voices asking why this should be, they were very quiet in the 1980s. If prices were sticky it could perhaps be explained on grounds that entrepreneurs had to protect profits.

Only wage stickiness was commonly assumed to keep costs up and was rarely, if ever, related to maintaining purchasing power.[8] If the reader supposes that there were any parallel remarks offered in commentary suggesting that generous executive salaries, not to mention bonuses and excessive non-labor costs, etc. may also have had something to do with corporate solvency problems either in Europe or the United States, they will look in vain. It was not always thus. In the beginning of concern about inflation, that concern led to consideration of how to control 'cost-push inflation.' Gardiner C. Means long ago (1934) used the term 'administered prices' (Means 1962, p. 77). Today it has been reduced to 'wage-push inflation,' as though wages are the only item in costs and the only possible cause of inflationary pressures (cf. Means 1962, pp. 77–96).

Modern economics has tied consideration of inflation to unemployment, and, as we have tried to show, there has already been the suggestion that as between the two, inflation was the greater threat. Even 'non-interventionists' could be persuaded to 'do something' about inflation. In contrast, unemployment and indeed virtually all other problems in the functioning economy 'could best be left to the market.'

We have, in short, seen that in logic enduring inflation to reduce the unemployment rate is as futile as enduring the unemployment rate to reduce inflation. As the thrust of writing on economic policy tilted more and more toward the single goal of reducing inflation, the indirect result of what macrotheorists were saying increasingly took the form of insisting that high unemployment was an unavoidable major (if for some painful) way to fight inflation. It was increasingly not unlike physicians in their zeal to keep body temperature down insisting on complete permanent bed rest in cooled rooms, totally forgetting that, even if successful in reducing temperature, a life spent in bed is a life of poor quality. (Dying is, of course, one – albeit extreme – way to reduce body temperature! The analogy may be a bit far-fetched but the basic point seems on target. Inflation and unemployment are not symmetrical in their impact on economic life.) Economic activity quintessentially revolves around human beings and the quality of their lives. Inflation is a single measure of an aspect of economic activity that needs to be minimized. The perspective underlying macroeconomic policy, derived as it is from currently faddish macroeconomic theory, is, we would argue, badly warped. A fundamental task of an economy is to provide rewarding

8. By the seventeenth edition (2001) Samuelson and Nordhaus tell the reader, 'Many experts believe that it will be necessary to improve European labor market institutions by reducing the generosity of welfare and unemployment insurance and remove restrictions on hiring and firing practices of firms (Samuelson and Nordhaus 2001, p. 679).

productive work for its participants and to provide them with suitable recompense (i.e., living wages). Absent this activity and even keeping inflation down is far from adequate to garner approval of participants in the economy. (Here is one place where economists, addicted as many are to cost-benefit analysis, fail to apply it.)

In life Keynes began with a model that could explain both inflation and deflation. In death his theory was reinterpreted to suggest that he never considered explaining anything but 'depression,' and he was pilloried in many quarters because his theory 'failed to explain the stagflation' which many countries, including the United States, suffered in the 1970s. This stagflation (falling output and rising prices) was widely attributed to exogenous supply shocks (e.g., the OPEC quadrupling of the price of crude oil in 1972–73 and again in 1978–79 (Samuelson 1980, p. 426). No other macroeconomic theory (e.g., monetarism, rational expectations, etc.) could explain stagflation either – they could only describe it. Theories only coincidentally explain exogenous occurrences! It was as though Dr Ehrlich and his 'magic bullets' were condemned with fury after their discovery and the logical explanation for their effectiveness, because a patient treated with them failed to survive being struck by a car.

If the Keynesian model could be focused on either an inflationary or a deflationary gap, there is no question that Keynes himself focused more on the challenge which the depression of the 1930s presented to the world's major market economies. Unemployment was enormous and the inflationary threat far from in sight in the mid 1930s. That inflation has in recent years become a major source of concern all would grant. But the degree to which economists focus on inflation to the virtual neglect of unemployment is of a piece with what has previously been said: it is part of the world created by what I have called the trivializers. In that world the ways they have found to reduce the condition of unemployment to irrelevance if not extinction is truly impressive. Thus, for example, in the *Economic Report of the President* for 2002, in contemplating the economic outlook, we are told, 'The economy continues to display characteristics favorable to long-term growth: productivity growth remains strong, and inflation remains low and stable' (*Economic Report of the President* 2002, p. 52). It is appropriate to ask whether this summarizes adequately the concerns expressed in the Employment Act of 1946, which in the first place mandated that these reports by the President be made each year. The unemployment rate was 5.8 per cent, the highest since 1994 *(Economic Report of the President* 2003, p. 319). It is the per cent of the civilian labor force unemployed. (The Act, after all, was not entitled The Price Stability Act of 1946). Lest anyone think the omission was accidental, the Economic Outlook section of the report has a subsection entitled 'Inflation Forecast' – there is no explicit consideration of employment prospects. The closest is a comment in discussing inflation prospects to the effect that in 2003 and 2004, '. . . some downward pressure will be maintained on the inflation rate, because the unemployment rate is projected to remain high over that period' (*Economic Report of the President* 2002, p. 54). One presumes this is viewed as good news. In the new environment for macrotheory the role of labor is clear – it can contribute to keeping the inflation rate down (no wild wage demands) and the productivity rate up (work hard)! Clearly, focusing directly on workers (as in an 'Employment Act!') and/or worrying explicitly about the welfare of workers, employed or unemployed, is a hopelessly old-fashioned and simple-minded notion.

Cutting Keynes Down to Size: The Demonization of Fiscal Policy

The story we have just told persuaded new classical economists that they had done a pretty good job of cutting Keynes down to size. Throughout the discussion of the Phillips curve, the discovery of 'the natural rate of unemployment,' the rise of NAIRU, and the discussion of what was termed the deification of the fight against inflation along with the defanging of unemployment as a problem to worry about, mainstream theorists worried less and less about traditional economic problems and more and more about polishing and improving their new tools.

The mainstream consensus was pretty clear. Keeping inflation down was looked on with approval. But beyond that vigorous interventionist policy was policy on which it was difficult to agree. The 'simple monetary rule,' and freeing entrepreneurs to do their thing got varying degrees of support. Keynes, it was charged, thought 'money didn't matter.' Even worse, his theory led to pernicious and explosively dangerous consequences.

Recent discussion of fiscal policy in general and 'Keynesian' fiscal policy in particular has muddled two quite different charges. The first is that Keynes advocated 'big government.' The second is that 'Keynesian fiscal policy' meant irresponsible public spending and big debt.

Keynes, fiscal policy, and government size

Turning to the first question, we can build on what has been said earlier about Keynes. Let us begin with the trenchant comment of Joseph Steindl. He has argued that what Keynes 'stood on its head in economics' was 'the analogy between the individual household and society as a whole' (Steindl 1985, p. 99). While for the individual it may be true that income determines spending, for society as a whole it is quite the reverse – spending determines income. In particular government spending, unlike private spending, does not lead to a 'burden on public debt' (internal debt) like the burden of repayment which clouds private debt. On this confusion rests the critical linkage muddling the two charges just mentioned. The erroneous charge against Keynes: 'Keynesian' fiscal policy means big government and big government means big spending and big spending means big public debt.

Our earlier discussion should make sorting this out easier. Concerning the first question, did Keynes advocate 'big government?' the answer is 'no.' In fact, insofar as can be told, Keynes took no position on the appropriate size for the public sector nor on whether it should be growing, shrinking or staying unchanged. (It would be surprising if he would have found the question, so posed, even interesting!) He did take the position that a healthy economy should employ all its resources and when they were not employed in the private sector the public sector should be substituted for the inadequate private demand. Many years ago Robert Heilbroner and Peter Bernstein gave the appropriate response to the charge that Keynes advocated 'big government.' They wrote, 'To say that the burden of government is too heavy . . . is to imply that we have an excess of teachers, soldiers, policemen, highways, health services, weather forecasters, air traffic facilities, and judges' (Heilbroner and Bernstein 1971, p. 64).

Despite this, the mainstream has worked to convince us that 'fiscal policy' does take a position on government size. In the *Economic Report of the President* for 2003, for example, we have this view of fiscal policy: 'An important goal of fiscal policy is to promote growth by limiting the share of output commanded by the government' (p. 52). Simply, this is a novel definition of fiscal policy.

The next point to make is that while the size of government has nothing to do with fiscal policy, there is a legitimate basis for determining governmental responsibilities which ultimately will at least indirectly determine government size. The original perspective toward fiscal policy deserves being restored. The statement in the 2003 *Economic Report of the President* may be compared with the statement of Edwin G. Nourse, first Chairman of the Council of Economic Advisors. (The Council and the *Economic Report* were both mandated by the Full Employment Act of 1946.) Said Nourse,

> The distinctive character of the Employment Act was that it accepted responsibility on the part of the federal government to make systematic study of its several policies and programs to see that they move consistently toward maintaining the health of the economy and continuous high utilization of the

nation's resources. (Nourse 1953, p. 67)

Note there is no mention of the relation of federal government economic activity to total output. As in all other areas, the responsibilities of the government should determine its size (it should be big enough to accomplish its missions as democratically determined).

Nourse did put his finger on the significant change: for the first time there was in federal legislation an explicit federal responsibility to maintain the nation's economic health and to utilize national resources (including human) as fully as possible. In this way the Employment Act accepted a Keynesian perspective toward the relationship between the political system and economic health. That perspective applied to the US was succinctly summarized in these words:

> The persistent theme was that of unemployment, caused by a failure of private investment to match the level of savings at a full employment income. With the effectiveness of monetary policy reduced by inelastic investment and higher liquidity preference in a sluggish economy, the required level of aggregate demand would have to be provided by fiscal expansion, responded to in the private sector by a multiplier-accelerator process.[9]

All economists do not approve of the Employment Act. Amendments have been suggested, but so far as is known it has been amended but once.[10] Conservatives and liberals, Keynesians and followers of Mises or Buchanan – all types of economists find, as Bernstein and Heilbroner suggest, some role for public spending.[11] The only question is one of degree.

These sorts of expenditures to guarantee the basic health of the economy cover all the expenditures of government unrelated to the stages of the business cycle. That is to say, they are arranged for and carried out by the government, involve revenues and expenditures and so contribute to 'fiscal impact' but are not part of fiscal policy, a term as noted below, best reserved for the deliberate changing of revenues and expenditures so as to affect the level of aggregate economic activity (that means having a deliberate impact on the effects of the business cycle). Presumably a critical role for

---

9. This is the summary written by Richard Musgrave of Alvin Hansen's restatement of Keynes's theory applied to the US economy which led to the passage of the Employment Act (Musgrave 1987, p. 591).

10. In 1978 Congress passed the Humphrey-Hawkins Act (The Full Employment and Balanced Growth Act of 1987). It changed no goals for the Act but attempted to quantify them – the unemployment rate target was to be 4 per cent and the inflation rate target was to be 3 per cent.

11. Recall the discussion in Chapter 1 of Adam's Smith's view of the public sector.

government in a democratic society, and one that has been stressed throughout this book, was what Nourse was referring to. It has to do with societal monitoring of resource deployment in the market and the continual judging of the results of that deployment against current societal values regarding what are acceptable minimum standards of what in earlier work I called 'the higher efficiency' – not only narrow allocative efficiency, but security, equity, poverty, freedom, and compassion, all qualities which all economies exhibit to some degree (from zero to a lot!). How much health, how much security, etc. do all participants in the economy have a right to? At the margin as societal values change, attitudes toward these ('the higher efficiency') are constantly changing, and frequently controversial. But more basically, some degree of all of them is an integral part of any post-barbaric society.[12]

Keynes, fiscal policy, and debt size

This brings us to the second question about fiscal policy. What is its true mission, viewed as an outgrowth of Keynes's theory, and how has it been distorted in recent discussion? The answer is that it involves stabilizing macroeconomic activity. If an objective of economic policy should be to enable the economy to utilize all its resources most efficiently to produce maximum (optimal) output, recurring departures from the rate of production which achieves this optimal output not only thwart the objective, but can cause much human misery as well. So viewed, fiscal policy is a stabilizing instrument designed to improve the health of the economy.

In contrast to the definition of fiscal policy we saw in the 2003 *Economic Report*, the most recent edition of Samuelson and Nordhaus presents a definition of fiscal policy closer to the usual definition one finds: 'Fiscal policy – A government's program with respect to 1) the purchase of goods and services and spending on transfer payments, and 2) the amount and type of taxes' (Samuelson and Nordhaus 2001, p. 764). This definition says nothing at all about the share of output commanded by government – whether it should be big or small, shrinking or growing. A program implies thought out goals.

The stabilizing role of fiscal policy has taken a beating in recent years. It is enough to recall Robert Lucas's general dismissal. He views fiscal policy as the interventionist outcome of macroeconomics. Macroeconomics, we saw earlier, is for Lucas only a 'subfield of economics' that

12. All this, most particularly the higher efficiency, is discussed in greater detail in Chapter 8.

'. . . defined itself to be that body of expertise the existence of which was presupposed in the Employment Act . . .' (Lucas 1981, p. 250). Lucas continued by asserting that the Employment Act led to 'general monetary and fiscal policy' and that 'Even to begin to assess the likely consequences of these policies in anything like a scientific way is clearly well beyond the current limits of our discipline' (1981, p. 29). (If only someone with clout would make a similarly dismissive statement about microeconomics, all economic theorists could close up shop and turn their attention elsewhere!)

The Lucas dismissal of both macroeconomics and fiscal policy is part of the trivialization of economic theory that we have discussed in earlier chapters. The reductio ad absurdum of this position in macroeconomics was that interventionist policy was futile at best and badly operated at worst. In any case sensible economists could readily perceive that macroeconomic resource deployment could safely be 'left to the market' (as the invisible hand had led early economists to conclude for microeconomics!). Lucas, in effect, argues in parallel fashion the same thing for macroeconomics, but goes a step further and gets rid of macroeconomics as well. The story we tell now simply goes one step further than we have before. Along with trivializing interventionist theory, it has seemed useful to show that policy derived from any interventionist theory can't work. We saw what monetarists had to say about interventionist monetary theory. Virtually all new classical economists tried the same approach we see here for fiscal policy.

This second question has a perfectly appropriate basis: what is the role of government taxes and expenditures in offsetting the excesses of the business cycle? We reserve for the last section of this chapter the views of those who deny that there are excesses to the business cycle.

Keynes in fact does not discuss fiscal policy in any detail in the *General Theory*. He certainly does not lay out what mid-twentieth century students were told was 'Keynesian fiscal policy.' The explicit suggestion that the federal budget should be balanced over the business cycle was developed by Alvin Hansen, the leading American early exponent of Keynes's General Theory. One finds comments in the *Economic Report of the President* for some early years that made the counter-cyclical role of stabilizing fiscal policy explicit. For example, the *Economic Report* for 1949 comments,

> The national tax policy should be flexible and should be promptly adjusted to the changing needs of business and consumers in the course of evolving economic events. The same dictates of prudent policy which call for higher taxes in a period of inflation would call for tax adjustments designed to counteract any serious recessionary movement (*Economic Report of the President* 1949, p. 3; Hansen 1964, p. 535). [Hansen quotes the *Report*] It is essential, said the Council

> in its *Annual Economic Review*, to permit fiscal policy to be reversed if recessionary trends should later develop which might call for tax reductions to stimulate business and markets and additional public expenditures. (*Economic Report of the President* 1949, p. 535, quoted in Hansen 1964, p. 535)

The economic reports were born of the same legislation that produced the Employment Act and so counter-cyclical fiscal policy is best viewed as part of the early efforts to take seriously the federal responsibility for lessening the worst manifestations of the business cycle.

Economics students were introduced to this counter-cyclical compensatory policy in the very first edition of Samuelson's *Economics*:

> According to the counter cyclical view, the government budget need not be in balance in each or every month or year; on the contrary, during inflationary times, the budget should show a surplus of tax receipts over expenditures so that the public debt can be reduced. But when bad times come, then the budget should show a deficit of taxes over expenditures, with the public debt returning to its previous level. Only over the whole business cycle need the budget be in balance. (Samuelson 1948, pp. 410–11)

Just in case anyone was left in doubt why all this was necessary, the young Professor Samuelson added, 'The private economy is not unlike a machine without an effective steering wheel or governor' (1948, p. 412). (The proponents of 'equilibrium business cycle theory,' were no doubt still in diapers when Samuelson penned this view.)

As for the implications for the public debt, Samuelson presented a perfectly symmetrical treatment of 'booms' and 'depressions' so that the public debt was unaffected by fiscal policy. Initially we need here note only that 'Keynesian fiscal policy' in the hands of the Americans (Hansen and Samuelson) was tied to the business cycle and was therefore never designed to lead to ever growing public debt.

Fiscal policy in action

If the early *Economic Report of the President* in the beginning regards fiscal policy as an instrument for prescribing the appropriate size of the federal government, the place to introduce the modern fiscal policy controversy is to note that nowhere in any of his writings, insofar as we know, did Keynes ever suggest that the goal of fiscal policy should be to achieve any particular predetermined per cent of GDP over which 'the government had command.' Instead he had a far more modest goal, one that both Hansen and Samuelson have stated far more explicitly than Keynes ever managed to do himself.

The initial point to be made in connection with this examination of our historical use of government taxes and expenditures, as in fact they have been carried out, is that they serve admirably to differentiate what we call 'fiscal impact' from 'fiscal policy.' The simplest examination of the historical record will drive home the point that both the taxes collected and the expenditures made were such as clearly to have consequences of various sorts for the performance of the US macroeconomy. We shall argue here that they cannot legitimately be called 'fiscal policy' because as we just indicated 'policy' requires explicit objectives. In the case of fiscal policy, both Samuelson and Hansen make them clear. The Budget in the United States, which is to say the way in which federal expenditures have been determined and carried out and the way in which federal taxes have been determined and carried out (most especially in the recent past), have demonstrably *not* been determined or decided by attempting to relate either to the (current) stage of the business cycle. We are not saying anyone did a poor job of assessing the current stage of the business cycle or did a poor job of timing expenditure and/or tax changes to have a particular effect on the cycle.[13] The basic relevance of the business cycle to most of the tax and expenditure decisions made in the past 30 or so years is vividly illustrated by Figure 5.5.[14]

Note that an annual deficit or surplus in the federal budget was particularly noteworthy even in the 1960s. Starting about 1970 the annual budget produced a deficit and this continued until the mid 1990s. In the early days Republicans professed to be more alarmed about deficits than Democrats, but they produced deficits as surely as did the Democrats. The largest deficits, run up during the 1980s and the 1990s, produced the period of falling deficits culminating in the three years, beginning in 1998, when we actually produced a budgetary surplus. The most recent years have seen the return to deficits.

The first observation, therefore, is that there is no dramatic difference between budgetary performance in one party versus the other. The point to make is that the deficit record reflects the end result of the maneuvering that produces each year's tax receipts and expenditures. That maneuvering involves not only economic considerations but political and varied random elements. It reflects the net result of conflicting tendencies, e.g., the resistance to taxes, the total inability to avoid certain expenditures, etc. There

---

13. So ironically in the case of fiscal policy it may have been unnecessary to trivialize the relevant theory, as the policy makers were in this case bent on giving a very low priority to carrying out the requirements of good theory.

14. The figure is reproduced from Klein (2003), p. 67.

Figure 5.5 Fiscal policy vs fiscal impact

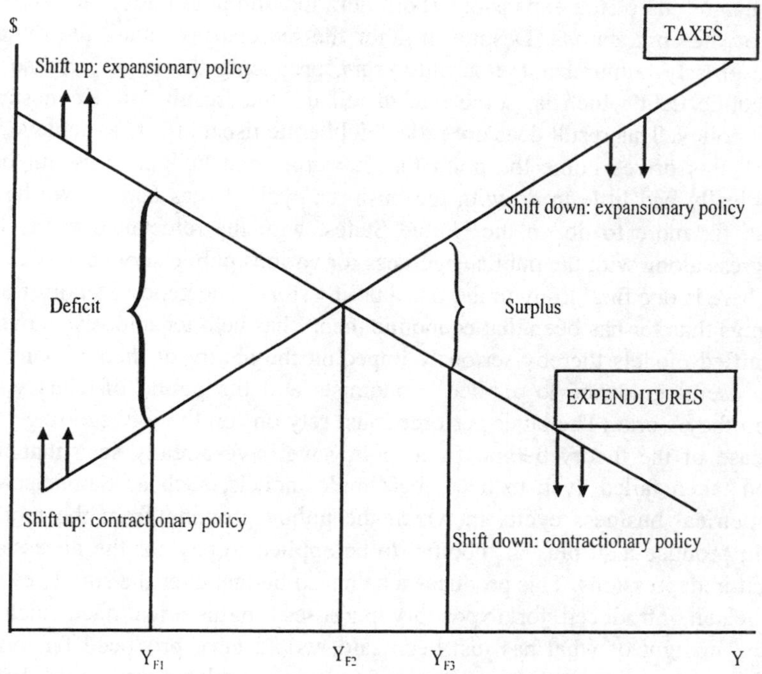

is no overriding theory back of what results. It is in this sense that the results are better labeled 'stance' – simply what results – than 'policy' – a deliberate goal-oriented effort to achieve any particular economic effect on the aggregate economy from the combination of expenditures and receipts in place at any given time. There are aspects of the tax expenditure-receipt system which reflect cyclical considerations, but they do not necessarily predominate. In the end then no one necessarily wants the fiscal system or the budgetary results which in fact we get.

The other point to make is that the counter-cyclical compensatory policy Samuelson referred to suggests that there should be deficits only in contraction and surpluses only in expansions. Allowing for the timing problems that Samuelson mentioned as long ago as 1948, one would still expect to be able to associate surpluses with good times and deficits with bad times. Clearly this has not been the case. Even more important, recall that Samuelson illustrated this policy with a simplified world in which expansions and contractions were equal in impact. This is clearly not the case for a growing economy such as the United States during the last half century. The magnitude of the expansions (both duration and amplitude) far exceeds that of the contractions. Despite this, for the reasons just cited, the deficit years grossly outnumber the surplus years, producing the huge increase in the public debt which is, some like to tell us, the 'result' of 'Keynesian' fiscal policy. This result does not reflect deliberate fiscal efforts to achieve it.

All this drives home the point that how the total budget turns out has historically had little to do with the business cycle. It has had, as we have noted, far more to do, in the United States, with the reluctance to tax by Congress along with the public eagerness for various public services.

There is one final irony in the fiscal policy story. The general tenor of our findings thus far has been that economic theory has held tenaciously to over-simplified models thereby seriously impeding the ability of theoreticians to offer useful guidance to applied economists and the public officials with whom they work. (The latter perforce must rely on 'on the job' training.) In the case of the theory behind fiscal policy we have already seen that the action taken failed even to heed the simple models, such as Samuelson's symmetrical business cycle, in which the policy growing from the model would produce a surplus in 'booms' to be applied to pay for the necessary deficit in depressions. This produces a balanced budget over the simple cycle Samuelson introduced for expository purposes. In historical fact, such a policy, in light of what has just been said, would have produced far more surpluses than deficits and instead of a rising public debt would have produced a falling public debt.

The irony lies in the fact that while the implications of the fairly simple Hansen-Samuelson theory were over-run in this case by public officials who ignored theory for the reasons already discussed, the theory – in contrast to most recent developments in economic theory – has become far more realistic, thereby making it more useful potentially, than it was at midcentury. Were it carried over into policy, the stability of the system might be considerably increased, despite the problems in timing, etc. which have been recognized for more than half a century.

Thus modern fiscal theory clarifies, we underscore, the distinction between 'fiscal impact' and fiscal policy. We can finally illustrate this distinction best by referring to Figure 5.5. Relatively uncontroversial are the federal taxes and expenditures which rise and fall automatically with changes in income. These 'automatic stabilizers' do indeed live up to their name to a degree: when aggregate income rises (falls) those taxes which increase (decrease) and expenditures which fall (rise) automatically stabilize income without need for further congressional action. Together they presumably set at least roughly the slopes of the tax and expenditure functions. The slopes in both reflect the degree of 'progressivity' built into the fiscal system at any given time. Fiscal policy, in line with the Samuelson-Nordhaus definition previously quoted, will cause shifts up or down in the two functions according to whether they add to or subtract from the total taxes and expenditures imposed on any given income group. 'Fiscal policy' then means trying in expansion to shift down the tax function and up the expenditure function, while contraction would stimulate the reverse shifts. (Unlike movements on the two functions, shifts do indeed require congressional action.)

All this means, of course, that simply knowing whether there is a budgetary surplus or deficit tells little about whether the budgetary stance is expansionary or contractionary. The actual surplus or deficit is the result not only of policies set but also by the stage of the business cycle. So if 'full employment' (reasonably full use of aggregate resources) were, for example, at YF1 the stance would be expansionary because there is a large deficit at YF1 even if, thanks to the business cycle, the economy is far above YF1 so that there is in fact a budgetary surplus. On the other hand if there is full employment at YF3 the fiscal impact is contractionary (there is a surplus at YF3) even if, because of a contraction, income is way below YF3 where there is nominally a deficit. The budget has a neutral effect on the economy (with expenditures and taxes in balance) only if (by chance) reasonably 'full employment' occurs at an income level of YF2. In short the impact of the budgetary deficit or surplus is determined by assessing the impact of the extant policies on a fully employed economy. Policies producing a small deficit which might be welcomed in times that were not very bad would not be very helpful in a severe depression where they would represent too little intervention to help lessen the impact of the business cycle. The relationship between the income level where the budget is in balance and the full employment income level is the critical determinant of impact. Economic theorists understand this perfectly well but neither the media nor the public appears to share in this insight. The confusion is carried over to how the results of past fiscal policies are interpreted.

Where does this leave us? In fact, as we have just seen, the balance or imbalance at any given time of expenditures and tax revenues tells one little about whether the impact of extant fiscal activity is expansionary or contractionary. We can tell something, however, over time if we relate the rate of changes in taxes and expenditures to the rate of change in income – that is, to the stages of the business cycle.

Fiscal policy – concluding thoughts

In sum, modern fiscal policy is an outgrowth of Keynesian theory. The Keynesian notion that cyclical recessions were the result of recurring inadequate aggregate demand led naturally to the idea that government expenditures could augment that inadequacy. So fiscal policy has now been turned on its head, so to speak. Instead of being regarded as a possible aid to stability in time of recession it is regarded as the enemy of economic growth. In part this reflects the debate about whether recession (including the Great Depression) was the result of inadequate demand brought about through significant inability to demand consumer goods or on the supply side by inability (or unwillingness) to produce. This is a very old debate. In fact Keynes thought it was brought about by both. Keynes noted, '. . . there are two ways to expand output . . . concentrate effort on increasing consumption (or) increasing the stock of capital until it ceases to be scarce . . . the wisest course is to advance on both fronts at once' (Keynes 1936, p. 325).

I recently began an essay on fiscal policy with these words:

> Fiscal policy is arguably the most explicit embodiment of the institutionalist conviction that there is a constructive role for governmental intervention in the quest for stable satisfactory growth rates in the modern market oriented economy. As such, it is, therefore, at the same time an equally explicit rejection of the conventional mainstream belief that the best course is almost invariably to leave the economy to the not invariably tender mercies of the market. (Klein 2003, p. 47)

We leave a further discussion of the comparison with institutionalist economics to Chapter 8.

Equilibrium Business Cycles

Finally, we must consider the implications of the introduction into common discourse about macroeconomics of the notion of 'equilibrium business cycles' and its twin, real business cycle theory. This perspective on recent developments in macroeconomic theory and their impact on the role of macroeconomic policy follows naturally both from what has just been said as well as what was said earlier in Chapter 2 about the differences among the currently competing schools of macroeconomic thought. We were concerned there primarily with methodological differences among these schools, and in particular how ideology affects thinking about fundamental matters such as whether economic theory is best viewed as normative or positive. Here we are concerned with the explanatory deficiencies which remain on each side as economic challenges to current economists. We shall argue that the recasting of macroeconomic policy debate in such terms as are involved in the equilibrium business cycle in effect trivializes much of macroeconomics and threatens explicitly the inversion of the field from an intellectual endeavor to improve the performance of market-oriented macroeconomies to the polite parlor pastime that has been lurking potentially in the wings for many years. In the end, we shall ask which view of how human beings interact in the economy is most accurate, useful, and analytically significant.

There are several critical threads to the story. As a start we may note that 'equilibrium business cycles' as a descriptive term has been introduced to suggest broadly that the business cycle is just the normal adjustment process which dynamic economies go through in the process of their growth and development. As such, we should not bother about them any more than a parent should be unduly upset if a child has a tantrum or suffers measles, or is rude to an elder. All these are similarly natural occurrences which little humans go through in the process of becoming mature humans. Thus, Long and Plosser in a seminal and widely quoted 1983 paper summarize what they think they have done as follows:

> In this paper we demonstrated in some detail how certain very ordinary economic principles lead maximizing individuals to choose consumption-production plans that display many of the characteristics commonly associated with business cycles. In particular, if both present and future consumption are normal goods in consumer preferences, it is well known that consumers will attempt to spread over many periods the consumption effects of any unanticipated wealth increment. In a multi-sector model such as ours consumers will also attempt to allocate their incremental savings in a way that leads to increased consumption of many different goods. At constant relative policies, this suggests that business-cycle features like persistence and comovement are characteristics of desired consumption plans. (Long and Plosser 1983, 39–69)

At the end of the previous section we saw that modern macroeconomists are fixated on inflation as an evil to be rooted out (fair enough). Here we see that unemployment is nothing to worry about. The perspective toward that condition taken in the Employment Act of 1946 we saw is very much out of fashion. If one asks why the *Economic Report of the President* for 2002 worries about inflation at a time when it is low, but not unemployment – granted it is also low – the answer lies in the attitude toward unemployment taken in modern macrotheory.

Consider the discussion by Robert Barro to be typical of much current macroeconomic theory. An entire section of his macroeconomics text is devoted to inflation; only a brief chapter to unemployment. In the 'equilibrium business cycle' theory the price system would presumably operate in such a way as to clear all markets by ratifying in every market a price where each supply equals each demand – presumably including that of labor. Thus, we are told, 'To explain unemployment and vacancies, we have to introduce some type of "friction" into the workings of the labor market' (Barro 1990, p. 252). It turns out that these frictions can be found in such structures as the unemployment insurance program, the minimum wage laws, labor unions, as well as in some supply shocks. Presumably all these create interferences between the value of what labor contributes to output and what it gets as return (one wonders what Marx would have to say!). This perspective is also the source of the view that unemployment is a voluntary condition, a view encountered earlier in this book. In 'equilibrium business cycles,' the labor market, like all other markets, simply reflects the workings of supply and demand. 'The dynamics of employment and unemployment depend on the rates of job separation and job finding. If these rates are constant, the economy tends automatically to a natural rate of unemployment' (Barro 1990, p. 274).

The policy implication of all this is that if these frictions were removed and the monetary authorities did not make mischief, unemployment would cease to be a problem. No parallel argument on the management side is ever introduced. Unions create wage stickiness, but neither monopolies nor, say, the National Association of Manufacturers, could possibly contribute to inflation (price stickiness in the form of an upward ratchet effect!). The productivity of management is slippery, although Harvey Leibenstein tried years ago to suggest with his 'X inefficiency' that 'firms,' operating with given technology, may not automatically make their optimal contribution to output (Leibenstein 1966, 1976). We are, in short, back to our earlier observation that the factors of production are viewed asymmetrically in the viewpoint taken by many mainstream (non-interventionist) macrotheorists toward the modern macroeconomy.

Moreover, back of all this, in the view taken in many presentations of equilibrium business cycles, is the intimation that consumers are capable of detailed maximizing behavior, carefully calibrated to allot to each time period in their life the appropriate consumption-savings division so as ultimately to achieve diverse, carefully and minutely planned, lifetime financial objectives.[15] Friedman's main point was that consumers change

15. Patterns of consumption and savings have been studied for at least the past fifty years. The best known is, of course (Friedman 1957).

consumption patterns only slowly, basing them on 'permanent income' which for Friedman turns out to be a longer run view of monthly or annual income covering a range of years. So the 'permanent income' version of lifetime income is a complicated sliding scale. It stops a good deal short of a carefully planned lifetime plan for monthly budget items; 'permanent income' views are altered from time to time so that how windfalls affect consumption may differ depending on where in one's life they appear.

Both Modigliani and Brumberg (1954) and Duesenberry (1959) had theories that suggested that people try to maintain the consumption patterns attained at their highest previous income levels. This makes a good deal of intuitive sense. Modigliani did attempt a view of lifetime savings behavior based on lifetime calculations. That younger people setting up households would spend more and retired people less of their income than those in the middle makes rough sense (Modigliani and Brumberg 1954; Ando and Modigliani 1963, pp. 55–84). Duesenberry suggested that how consumers react to income changes may depend on their previous high income and may indeed be different (not merely reversed) when income falls than when it rises.[16]

To suggest the first limitation which occurs to me, unless one knows precisely when one will die, applying the appropriate discount rate to make all this come out appropriately is mathematically very difficult. Second, is it in fact true that consumers will attempt to spread the consumption effects of unanticipated wealth increments over many time periods?

In sum, the conclusion that business cycles may just be characteristic of 'desired consumption plans' would, we suppose, give many economists pause. Can one seriously argue that the Great Depression was just the result of consumers doing what they wanted to do?

A second strand to the story is that however one views the macroeconomy as it unfolds over time, intervention is futile. As Kydland and Prescott put this cheerful view of intervention:

> Even if there is an agreed-upon, fixed social objective function and policy makers know the timing and magnitude of the effects of their actions, discretionary policy, namely, the selection of that decision which is best, given the current situation and a correct evaluation of the end-of-period position, does not result in the social objective function being maximized. The reason for this apparent paradox is that economic planning is not a game against nature but, rather a game against rational economic agents. We conclude that there is no way control

16. Duesenberry (1959) developed the 'ratchet effect' of consumption changes with income changes. None of these appear as sweeping as Long and Plosser.

> theory can be made applicable to economic planning when expectations are rational. (Kydland and Prescott 1977, pp. 473–91)

This, of course, is the famous conclusion loosed on the discipline with the advent of the 'Lucas critique' which told us that positive actions which are rational will be anticipated in advance by rational participants in the economy and will cause economic agents to discount them in advance in planning their own courses of action – thus they will have no effect on policy. As Lucas himself put it,

> . . . given that the structure of an econometric model consists of optimal decision rules of economic agents, and that optimal decision rules vary systematically with changes in the structure of series relevant to the decision maker, it follows that any change in policy will systematically alter the structure of econometric models.
>
> . . . For issues involving policy evaluation . . . (this conclusion) is fundamental; for it implies that comparisons of the effects of alternative policy rules using current macroeconomic models are invalid regardless of the performance of these models over the sample period or in *ex ante* short-term forecasting. (Lucas 1981, p. 126)

All this led, in the words of Edward Prescott, to 'the demise of Keynesian macroeconometric models' (Prescott 1995, 1502) which had been 'ideally suited to evaluate the consequences of alternative policy actions' (1995, 1503).

Prescott asserted that as a result of all this 'economists were faced with a problem of what to do when it came to macroeconomic forecasting and policy advising' (1995, 1503). 'With the failure of the macroeconometric models, atheoretical methods, in particular the vector auto-regression . . . methods . . . came to prominence . . . but how to use them for making policy advice, given the Lucas Critique, is a problem with no solution' (1995, 1503).

No doubt if business cycles are merely part of a normal adjustment process, the fact that there is no solution to the problem of how to make macroeconomic policy effective is of little concern. The question, however, that can be raised is whether in fact economic agents are invariably 'rational' in the Lucas sense, and regardless of the answer to that question, can economists accept the instability that constitutes the business cycle history of all major market-oriented economies as tolerable? Perusal of the post-World War II business cycle history of all the major industrial market-oriented economies reveals that in addition to a number of mild cycles each country has endured at least one major cycle and some quite a few.[17] The business cycle, in short, despite all the recurring pronouncements, is not quite dead!

What the economists quoted here and their colleagues have managed to suggest, of course, is that the modern macroeconomy is basically in equilibrium – indeed, in Walrasian general equilibrium but for the occasional shocks from technological development (the 'real shocks' which produce 'real business cycles'). This leaves us with a conclusion that modern instability arises either from real shocks, the monetary shocks which arise from the misguided efforts of monetary authorities to intervene in an effort to stabilize economic activity, or from some variety of external disturbance. One student, who looked with favor on the impact the real business cycle school has had, has asserted that 'The predominant belief in the immediate post-war period was that business cycles were inefficient, and it was government's role to try and prevent these fluctuations' (Farmer 2002, p. 104). It is to be contrasted with the real business cycle view that 'economic fluctuations are the unavoidable responses of optimizing agents to changing productive opportunities . . . there is no role for policy because the agents themselves cope with economic fluctuation in the most efficient way possible' (2002, p. 105).

This overall is in stark contrast to the Keynesian view because the equilibrium business cycles perspective most particularly denies that the Keynesian system can lead to disequilibrium except through 'sticky wages and prices.' Each of these views involves a characterization of human behavior. At bottom the answer to the question which is more credible may lie in which view of human behavior is more believable. The new classicists say that Keynes's theory is based on an 'animal spirits' view of human behavior. It is true that Keynes explains business cycle downturns as essentially a collapse in the marginal efficiency of investment. Whether this is an 'animal sprits' view of the entrepreneur is at least moot. To Keynesians it suggested the entrepreneurial necessity to keep capacity growing at an ideal rate, which means correctly forecasting future consumer demand, technological progress, weather developments, delivery schedules, etc. This has always been, and still remains, a very tall long run order indeed. Moreover, the confidence which must undergird entrepreneurs' investment decisions, and on which continued prosperity depends, therefore, can ultimately be eroded and that erosion tends to snowball around crises in

17. For confirmation the reader may consult the business cycle chronologies and indicator monitoring records constructed by the Economic Cycle Research Institute (ECRI), 420 Lexington Avenue, New York NY 10170, which at present maintains and monitors the monthly business cycle developments of 17 major industrial market-oriented economies.

confidence. This, to be sure, is a different view of economic agents than the Lucas view in which economic agents use all information efficiently to yield perfect foresight. Here, while they may learn from the past and use all the information they can obtain (that is 'be efficient'), their behavior is nonetheless also colored by confidence, uncertainty, and other factors we considered earlier in connection with the perspective of behavioral economists.

An implication of this difference is that for New Classicists the price system works more or less perfectly to clear markets while for Keynesians it may work reasonably well a good deal of the time but far from perfectly. It is clear to Keynesians that market adjustments are not instantaneous – far from it. How long in fact they can take seems never explicitly to be explored. But inventory levels (or more accurately inventory-sales ratios) are rarely assumed to reflect at all times the collective wishes of entrepreneurs; capacity levels are not assumed invariably to reflect precisely what entrepreneurs would like them to be; and actual deployments of goods and services are rarely assumed to reflect household decisions with respect to the deployment of every last dollar to the ideal use to which the consumers would wish. In short, there is, further, a serious problem with the view that these rational economic agents will naturally gravitate to a Walrasian equilibrium world unless there is a technological (or monetary) shock. (As we have said, such shocks – sooner or later – are highly likely!) In the process of rejecting Keynes because of the alleged 'animal spirits' with which he imbues his people, the question arises, could normally rational people fail to maintain a state of constant dynamic equilibrium? Must Keynes rely on 'sticky prices' to disequilibrate his economy? What seems to get overlooked is the fact that there could well never really be a time when all prices and wages reflect supplies and demands which simultaneously clear all markets. In the typical market economy, prices reflect supplies and demands including all current inventory levels and they are further influenced by the attitudes which economic agents hold toward those inventories. It does not require actual changes in inventory levels but merely changed attitudes toward inventory levels to move the economy away from any equilibria near which markets may have been hovering. Over the cycle changing attitudes toward inventories are major ingredients activating the cycle. (James Tobin characterized the difference between his view and that of Edward Prescott by commenting, 'He [Prescott] thinks fluctuations are moving equilibrium in which supply and demand are equal to each other all the time, and he attributes most of the cycle to productivity fluctuations; whereas I believe that in business cycles, we don't have market clearing. Instead, we do have . . . involuntary unemployment and other situations of excess supply, predominantly. We're losing output that would be valuable to the economy, to society. It's not a moving equilibrium'.)[18] The Tobin explanation clearly does not revolve around sticky prices and wages at all.

The stock market is a case growing out of transactions occurring between both a seller and a buyer, but tracing nonetheless an often unstable and uncertain sales path into the future. There is presumably a market clearing price, but along with those prices are the complex currents and fads, attitudes and fears, that push investors to wish to sell or to wish to buy. In short the changing attitudes toward a given stock affects its price quite as much as (or more than) the actual number of shares being traded.

The behavior of stock investors on any given day (or any given hour!) looks like it is influenced by the kinds of factors stressed by behavioral economists as discussed in Chapter 3. Recall Ruth P. Mack's depiction of what affects the typical economic agent. It is not that economic agents are not rational, as they see it, but to reduce all economic behavior to simple 'optimizing behavior' flies in the face of the conflicting influences on the agent, and of the challenges to a simplistic view of optimizing to which Mack called attention.

The fundamental task of the entrepreneur is to be thinking constantly about whether the plant is being operated at the appropriate rate given anticipated sales in the immediate future and whether the size of the plant (its capacity) is appropriate to anticipated longer term demands. In carrying out this constant adjustment process the appropriateness of any current policy will be buffeted not only by supply shocks of various sorts (including the technological), but by demand shocks as well (the result of misread signals and correctly read signals which prove false in the face of subsequent changes in attitude of those producing the signals). It seems entirely logical, therefore, to assume that these factors can explain many signs of instability, as even the most rational of economic agents stumble and bumble their way to the future. Intelligent sane people engaged in the most stable economic activity they can fashion are nonetheless not the cold detached calculating robots forever keeping supplies and demands in balance into which the new classical view of rationality turns them. Even if they were, there is no reason to suppose that prices and wages are as marvelously flexible as 'instant market clearing' would require.

One thing seems clear. Very many economists would disagree with the view that the principal Keynesian objection to business cycles was that they are an inefficient way to achieve necessary adjustments in economic activity

18. From *The Region*, published by the Federal Reserve Bank of Minneapolis, December 1996, quoted in Farmer (2002), p. 101.

(though they surely are that also!). It surely did not occur to anyone in the 1930s to criticize the Great Depression for its inefficiency. Whether or not by some twisted logic anyone would call depressions efficient at anything, they are far too painful for those who suffer joblessness and all the assorted miseries that accompany that state.

As for the Lucas critique, despite the attention it has received, it is not clear that 'policy-ineffectiveness' has swept the discipline. It may have vast appeal for new classical macroeconomists, but the applied economists – for example, those at the Federal Reserve Board – continue to work on the assumption that counter-cyclical policy can have some effect. As of this writing, the contraction of 2001 appears to have been one of the milder ones in post-war history. That the reduction in the discount rate some 11 times in the previous year may have had some influence is not beyond belief. The reaction of the stock market to those interest rate deductions suggests that even though the investors may have been 'rational,' in the sense that they knew the Fed was likely to reduce the discount rate in contraction, they responded favorably to the actual lowering. (That monetary policy was changed so often suggests that it can be a far from perfect instrument for stabilizing economic activity.)

Finally, as for the view that cycles are just the 'unavoidable response of optimizing agents responding to their opportunities', we have already suggested earlier in this chapter that if there are those who might consign the unemployment problem to this cocoon so well padded against the outside world, there are seemingly few economists who would suggest that we just wait for 'the natural adjustment processes' of our economy, peopled as it is with rational economic agents, to take care of inflation. (One question, of course, is how much pain should be tolerated as part of a normal adjustment process.)

CONCLUSIONS

Macroeconomists often refer to their world as the world of 'stylized facts.' Some jokester, now lost in the mists of anonymity, once defined stylized facts as 'facts we know are not true.' That it is transcendentally easier to analyze and understand a world simplified by various assumptions will surely not surprise a well trained mainstream economist. If microeconomists cling to the pure competition model because it is familiar and comfortable, the macroeconomists have happily occupied a world they have been busy reconstructing for the past 50 years.

David Colander recently differentiated the old from the new

macroeconomics in a review of the new *Handbook of Macroeconomics*, one of a series of new handbooks dedicated to presenting the 'cutting edge' of economics in the major areas. Says Colander:

> The book reflects the revolution that has occurred in macro. Robert Lucas's work, and new classical work more generally, serves as the foundation of the modern approach . . . The question modern macroeconomists are trying to answer, is it possible to specify problems in a dynamic stochastic general equilibrium framework that is consistent with the observed data? is both a more and a less challenging question than the one earlier macroeconomists were trying to answer: Is it possible to design models that will assist in solving macro problems of business cycles, unemployment, inflation, and low growth? (Colander 2002, p. 173)

Whether the new macro faces more or less challenging questions doesn't seem to me nearly as important a question as whether the new questions are as interesting or important as the old. Among those presumably new as well as the old macroeconomists there must be found some who think the question of whether modern market-oriented economies are unstable, suffer recurring unemployment and inflation as well as low growth rates remains a question of some interest. New macroeconomists do not say that we used to have these problems but somehow now they are all solved. Neither do they say that unemployment or inflation of X per cent used to be regarded as the threshold of what cannot be tolerated but now we are tougher. They do not assert that suffering builds character. One way of characterizing our theme in this chapter is to say that we assert that the new questions carry less weight (are therefore, in a real sense more trivial) than the older questions did.

It is true that Lucas has said we cannot define what we mean by full employment. Still it is difficult to believe that we (policy makers in general if economic theorists have abandoned the area) cannot tell when there is considerable evidence that more people are out of work than is tolerable. There is some debate about whether the ideal inflation rate is low or zero, but the state of inflation, like unemployment, can be judged reasonably accurately.

On the other hand the appeal of the new question is not altogether clear to some of us who have not embraced it joyously. Why is the question whether the specification of a problem is consistent with the observed data of commanding interest if it is not hooked to improving economic policy? Put to one side the question whether the unemployed are voluntarily unemployed. We do not need to dwell indefinitely on the question, is it unpleasant to be unemployed? For quite a lot of people it clearly is. Nor is it difficult to find why inflation rapidly becomes worrisome and painful.

On the face of it macroeconomics has traded questions which can readily be perceived as commanding immediate attention for a question which has appeal not unlike the proverbial game of chess. Even if 'progress' can be found, is the accomplishment in the same general ballpark as contributing to economic stability, lower inflation, higher employment, or higher growth?

In its most extreme form the new thinking literally defines traditional macroeconomics out of existence. Along the way quite a few 'stylized facts' come into existence. We have seen that often nowadays the NAIRU is referred to as though it were as literally factual as any statistic reported in the *Survey of Current Business*. An 'expectation-augmented short run Phillips curve' is about as far from real world data as one can get, and yet economists of various persuasions devoted inordinate amounts of time to contemplating its impact on us before theoretical onslaughts from the right and a contrary empirical record in the 1990s made it seem an untenable construct to keep afloat, even in the relatively abstract world that new classical macroeconomists have favored. This chapter has focused on 'stylized facts'; important concepts to conjure with involve such relatively recent, not to say novel, ideas as the 'full employment unemployment rate,' the 'non-accelerating inflation rate of unemployment,' 'the expectation-augmented Phillips curve,' 'real business cycles,' 'equilibrium business cycles,' the 'inertial rate of inflation,' and 'the irrelevance result for systematic monetary policy.' No one can accuse new classical economists of forgetting to label their contributions to the field.

Macroeconomists no longer feel any affinity for *The Grapes of Wrath*. They might feel more at home at Alice's Tea Party than with the Joads. On the other hand, Dr Pangloss is a constant companion. German inflation in the inter-war period holds the attention of a few diehard monetarists, but the field on the cutting edge has moved on – they advocate Friedman's 'simple monetary rule' or else urge that we 'leave it to the market.' Seemingly market clearing and long run inflation problems are not compatible. Graduate students are judged by how cleverly they manage to construct models which demonstrate that Marshall's 'men in the ordinary business of life' just might maximize profits by acting so as to let economic variables produce 'co-movements' which look like the cycles we see in the real economy. The Employment Act of 1946 is never mentioned and the monetary authorities in all market economies are fun to trash. Keynes ends up being Much Ado About Nothing.

Do I exaggerate? Robert Barro can tell us unblushingly that he will deal with models in which 'the aggregate consistency conditions hold and this can be done by assuming that the various markets – say for goods and credit –

always clear' (Barro 1990, p. 210). Robert Lucas can tell us reassuringly that 'One cannot, even conceptually, arrive at a usable definition of full employment as a state in which no involuntary unemployment exists' (Lucas 1981, p. 243). Mankiw can tell us about the 'sacrifice ratio – An economy . . . to reduce inflation . . . must endure a period of high unemployment and low output.' The sacrifice ratio is 'the number of percentage points of annual output lost in the process of reducing inflation by 1 percentage point' (Mankiw 1998, p. 749). Seemingly, modern macroeconomists can tell us precisely how much pain we must endure. The pain is asymmetrically distributed, however. Imagine an economist announcing that firms will have to endure six months of low or non-existent profits in order to get the inflation rate down! Mankiw is at least still suggesting that something ought to be done about inflation. Robert Gordon undertakes econometric analysis from which he can tell us, lest anyone thought there was any good news on the unemployment front, '. . . as of late 1987, there is absolutely no basis to support the conclusion that the natural rate of unemployment has fallen below 6 percent. The benign behavior of wage changes merely reflects a decline in labor's share that has not been communicated to price behavior' (Gordon 1988, p. 30). Seemingly, in a world of mostly instantly clearing prices, when they don't clear it won't show up in the prices, but in the wages![19]

So much pain, so much precision, so much complexity! Our portrait of a field where any possible links to improved public policy have carefully been surgically removed is complete. It is at its core, a portrait of a 'positive' discipline doing its quantitative thing. It monitors our self-adjusting world. The 'bottom line' would appear to be that the macroeconomy in the United States since, say, 1990, has performed a good deal better than the state of macrotheory would have suggested. Economics may not do a very good job of confronting the economy, but perhaps the economy is developing a certain immunity to the ministrations of macrotheorists.

---

19. In the 1990s new evidence caused Gordon to change his mind and he characterized our economy as a 'Goldilocks economy' (not too hot and not too cold, but just right). Thus, for the period 1996–99 he comments, 'Despite low unemployment, inflation did not accelerate in response, leading economists and the Fed governors to conclude that the natural rate had fallen substantially since the late 1980s.'

REFERENCES

Ando, A. and Franco Modigliani (1963), 'The "life cycle" hypothesis of saving: aggregate implications and tests', *American Economic Review*, **53**, 55–84. Reprinted in R.A. Gordon and L.R. Klein (eds), *Readings in Business Cycles*, Homewood, IL: Richard D. Irwin, 1965, pp. 398–426.

Barro, Robert J. (1990), *Macroeconomics, Third Edition,* New York: John Wiley & Sons.

Beveridge, William (1945), *Full Employment in a Free Society*, New York: W.W. Norton Company.

Blanchard, Olivier and Lawrence F. Katz (1996), *What We Know and Do Not Know About the Natural Rate of Unemployment*, Cambridge, MA: NBER, Working Paper 5822.

Blanchard, Olivier and Lawrence F. Katz (1997), 'What we know and do not know about the natural rate of unemployment', *Journal of Economic Perspectives*, **11** (1), 51.

Brainard, William C. and George L. Perry (eds) (1999), in *Brookings Papers on Economic Activity*, No. 1, commenting on Lawrence F. Katz and Alan B. Krueger, 'The high pressure U.S. labor market of the 1990s', in same issue, pp. 1–55.

Burns, Arthur F. (1963), 'Economics and Our Public Policy of Full Employment', Lecture at Rice University, published in E.O. Edwards (ed.), *The Nation's Economic Objectives*, Chicago: University of Chicago Press (1994), 55-71.

Burns, Arthur F. (1969), *The Business Cycle in a Changing World*, New York: Columbia University Press for the National Bureau of Economic Research.

Burns, Arthur F. (1969a), 'The nature and causes of business cycles', reprinted in Burns (1969).

Colander, David (2002), 'Review of *Handbook of Macroeconomics*, vols. 1A, 1B, and 1C', *Journal of Economic Literature*, **CL**, Number 1.

Dornbusch, Rudiger and Stanley Fischer (1990), *Macroeconomics, Fifth Edition*, New York: McGraw-Hill.

Duesenberry, James S. (1959), *Income, Saving, and the Theory of Consumer Behavior*, Cambridge, MA: Harvard University Press.

Economic Report of the President to the Congress (1949), quoted in Alvin Hansen, *Business Cycles and National Income*, Expanded Edition, New York: W.W. Norton & Company, 1964.

Economic Report of the President (2002), Washington, DC: Government Printing Office.

Economic Report of the President (2003), Washington, DC: Government Printing Office.

Farmer, Roger E.A. (1999), *Macroeconomics, Second Edition*, Cincinnati: South-Western College Publishing.

Farmer, Roger E.A. (2002), *Macroeconomics, Second Edition*, Cincinnati, OH: South-Western Publishing Company.

Friedman, Milton (1957), *The Theory of the Consumption Function,* Princeton, NJ: Princeton University Press for the National Bureau of Economic Research.

Friedman, Milton (1968), 'The role of monetary policy', *American Economic Review*, **58**, 1–17.

Full Employment Act of 1946, As amended with related laws, Originally Public Law 304, 79th Congress, Joint Economic Committee, 99th Congress, 1st Session, October 1985, Washington, DC: Government Printing Office, 1985.

Galbraith, James K. (1997), 'Time to ditch the NAIRU', *The Journal of Economic Perspectives*, **11** (1), 93-108.

Gordon, Robert J. (1988), *U.S. Inflation, Labor's Share, and the Natural Rate of Unemployment*, Cambridge, MA: NBER Working Paper Series, p. 1, p. 28.

Gordon, Robert J. (1997), 'The time-varying NAIRU and its implications for economic policy', *Journal of Economic Perspectives*, **11** (1), 11.

Gordon, Robert J. (1998), 'Foundations of the goldilocks economy: supply shocks and the time varying NAIRU', *Brookings Papers on Economic Activity*, **2**, 2, 329.

Gordon, Robert J. (2000), *Macroeconomics, Eighth Edition*, Reading, MA: Addison-Wesley Longman.

Hall, Robert and John B. Taylor (1986), *Macroeconomics: Theory, Performance, and Policy*, New York: W.W. Norton.

Hansen, Allan (1964), *Business Cycles and National Income*, Expanded Edition, New York: W.W. Norton & Company.

Heilbroner, Robert L. and Peter L. Bernstein (1971), *A Primer on Government Spending, Second Edition*, New York: Random House.

Katz, Lawrence F. and Alan B. Krueger (1999), 'The high-pressure U.S. labor market of the 1990s', Washington, DC: *Brookings Institution Papers on Economic Activity*.

Keynes, John M. (1936), *General Theory of Employment, Interest, and Money,* New York: Harcourt Brace and Company.

Klein, Philip A. (1990), 'What's natural about unemployment?' in P.A. Klein (ed.), *Analyzing Modern Business Cycles, Essays Honoring Geoffrey H. Moore*, Armonk, NY: M.E. Sharpe, 293–302.

Klein, Philip A. (2003), 'An institutionalist view of fiscal policy', in Marc R. Tool and Paul Dale Bush (eds), *Institutional Analysis and Public Policy*, Boston, MA: Kluwer Academic Publishers.

Kydland, Finn E. and Edward C. Prescott (1977), 'Rules rather than discretion: the inconsistency of optimal plans', *Journal of Political Economy*, **85** (3), 473–91.

Leibenstein, Harvey (1966), 'Allocative efficiency vs. x efficiency', *American Economic Review*, **56**, 392–415.

Leibenstein, Harvey (1976), *Beyond Economic Man*, Cambridge, MA: Harvard University Press.

Long, John B.J. and Charles I. Plosser (1983), 'Real business cycles', *Journal of Political Economy*, **91** (1), 39–69.

Lucas, Robert (1981), *Studies in Business Cycle Theory*, Cambridge, MA: MIT Press.

Lucas, Robert (1981a), 'Econometric policy evaluation: a critique', in Karl Brunner and Allan Meltzer (eds), *The Phillips Curve and Labor Markets, Vol. 1*, Carnegie-Rochester Conference Series on Public Policy, Amsterdam: North-Holland Publishing Company, 243, 250. Reprinted in Lucas (1981).

Mankiw, N. Gregory (1998), *Principles of Economics, Third Edition*, New York: Dryden Press.

Means, Gardiner C. (1962), 'The reality of administered prices', in *The Corporate Revolution in America*, essays by Gardiner C. Means, New York: Crowell-Collier Press, pp. 77–96.

Modigliani, Franco and R.E. Brumberg (1954), 'Utility analysis and the consumption function', in K.K. Kurihara (ed.), *Post-Keynesian Economics*, New Brunswick, NJ: Rutgers University Press.

Musgrave, Richard M. (1987), 'Essay on Alvin Hansen', in John Eatwell, Murray Mitgate and Peter Newman (eds), *The New Palgrave, Dictionary of Economics*, *Vol. 2*, London: MacMillan.

Nourse, Edwin G. (1953), *Economics in the Public Service*, New York: Harcourt Brace and Company. Quoted in Klein (2003).

O'Sullivan, Arthur and Steven M. Sheffrin (2001), *Macroeconomics: Principles and Tools, Second Edition*, Upper Saddle River, NJ: Prentice-Hall.

Phelps, Edmund (1987), 'The Phillips Curve', in John Eatwell, Murray Milgate, and Peter Newman (eds), *The New Palgrave*, *Dictionary of Economics*, *Vol. 3*, London: Macmillan, p. 858.

Phillips, A.W. (1958), 'The relation between unemployment and the rate of change of money wages rates in the United Kingdom, 1861–1957', *Economica*, **25**, 283–99.

Prescott, Edward C. (1995), 'Comment on computable general equilibrium models and monetary policy advice', *Journal of Money, Credit, and Banking*, **27** (4), 1502–3.

Rogerson, Richard (1997), 'Theory ahead of language in the economics of unemployment', *Journal of Economic Perspectives*, **11** (1), 74.

Romer, David (1996), *Advanced Macroeconomics*, New York: McGraw-Hill.

Samuelson, Paul A. (1948), *Economics: An Introductory Analysis, First Edition*, New York: McGraw-Hill.

Samuelson, Paul A. (1958), *Economics: An Introductory Analysis, Fourth Edition*, New York: McGraw-Hill.

Samuelson, Paul A. (1961), *Economics, Fifth Edition*, New York: McGraw-Hill.

Samuelson, Paul A. (1980), *Economics, Eleventh Edition*, New York: McGraw-Hill.

Samuelson, Paul A. and William Nordhaus (1985), *Economics, Twelfth Edition*, New York: McGraw-Hill/Irwin.

Samuelson, Paul A. and William Nordhaus (1995), *Economics, Fifteenth Edition*, New York: McGraw-Hill/Irwin.

Samuelson, Paul A. and William Nordhaus (1998), *Economics, Sixteenth Edition*, New York: McGraw-Hill/Irwin.

Samuelson, Paul A. and William Nordhaus (2001), *Economics, Seventeenth Edition*, New York: McGraw-Hill/Irwin.

Setterfield, Mark (1996), 'Using the NAIRU as a basis for macroeconomic policy', in Brian K. MacLean and Lars Osberg (eds), *The Unemployment Crisis: All for Nought*, Montreal: McGill-Queen's University Press, pp. 67–8.

Staiger, Douglas, James H. Stock and Mark W. Watson (1996), *How Precise are Estimates of the Natural Rate of Unemployment*?, NBER Working Paper Series, No. 5477, Cambridge, MA: NBER.

Staiger, Douglas, James H. Stock and Mark W. Watson (1997), 'The NAIRU, unemployment and monetary policy', *Journal of Economic Perspectives*, **11** (1), 35.

Steindl, Joseph (1985), 'J.M. Keynes: society and the economist', in Fausto Vicarelli (ed.), *Keynes' Relevance Today*, Philadelphia, PA: University of Pennsylvania Press.

Stiglitz, Joseph (1997), 'Reflections on the natural rate hypothesis', *Journal of Economic Perspectives*, **11** (1), 3.

Summers, Lawrence H. (1988), 'Should Keynesian economics dispense with the Phillips curve'?, in Rod Cross (ed.), *Unemployment, Hysteresis, and the Natural Rate Hypothesis*, Oxford: Basil Blackwell.

Tool, Marc R. and Paul Dale Bush (2003), *Institutionalist Analysis and Economic Policy*, Boston, MA: Kluwer Academic Publishers.

The Region (1996), published by the Federal Reserve Bank of Minneapolis, quoted in Farmer (2002).

Williamson, Stephen D. (2002), *Macroeconomics*, Boston, MA: Addison-Wesley.

6. Theory and the role of the public sector

. . . only experience can show how far the common will, embodied in the policy of the State, ought to be directed to increasing and supplementing the inducement to invest; and how far it is safe to stimulate the average propensity to consume . . . (Keynes 1936, p. 377)

Modern capitalism is a mixed economic system. The larger part of national output is purchased by private consumers and investors, and the larger part of the product is produced and supplied by private firms. The distribution of income is determined largely by the ownership of factors of production and by their earnings in the market. At the same time, a substantial share of the nation's product goes to satisfy public wants, a substantial part of private income originates in the public budget, and public tax and transfer payments significantly influence the state of private distribution. Moreover, budget policy affects the level of employment and prices in the private sector. Thus ours is a mixed system, including a sizable and vitally important sphere of public economy along with the market sector. (Musgrave 1959, p. 3)

Whether the views so widely accepted about the effects of fiscal policy be right or wrong, they are contradicted by at least one extensive body of evidence. I know of no other coherent or organized body of evidence justifying them. They are part of economic mythology, not the demonstrated conclusions of economic analysis or quantitative studies. Yet they have wielded immense influence in securing widespread public backing for far reaching governmental interference in economic life. (Friedman 1962, p. 84)

It is now known that the presumption of the efficiency of the market economy is valid only under fairly restrictive assumptions. (Stiglitz, 1988, p. 8)

The sheer mass of our federal government is simply inconsistent with a free society. If nearly half of what you make is spent by someone else, that means half your work time is spent working for someone else. (Armey 1995, p. 29)

INTRODUCTION

In previous chapters we have seen that at bottom the trivialization campaign in both micro and macroeconomics has been directed at asserting that public policy is either irrelevant or futile or both. Friedman would no doubt argue, therefore, that an essential function of economic analysis is to fight off the efforts of do gooders to expand the public sector. Lucas has said it is to understand why interventionist public policy is futile.

In the end both need to consider whether their brand of cost-benefit analysis would justify the expenditures of so many resources, especially human resources, as in fact we do expend on the discipline of economics. So we paraphrase an old joke: 'How many economists ought it take to watch the free market and its invisible hand produce the best of all possible economies without any interventionist public policy at all?' The British would ask, 'How many economists will, thereby, be rendered redundant?'

Economists at places like the University of Chicago (at least in its heyday), the University of Virginia, and George Mason University need to ask, 'How superfluous are our programs in economics? Do we really contribute significantly by turning out more new classical theorists (and if so, contribute to what)?'

In this chapter we shall argue that a great deal of nonsense is circulated about how big and burdensome is the public sector. Furthermore the talk about the size of the public sector is in fact a verbal smoke screen hiding the ideologic bias which many have against the fundamental perspective required to deploy resources for most purposes in the public sector. Mainstream economists who mostly know better are often surprisingly silent in the face of the many things said about the public sector. The reason for the silence, we shall argue, takes us back to the point made in Chapter 2. If we get the theory we want because in fact it is the theory we want, we want it because it leads to the conclusions already favored by many, including many economists. In this case the public sector, we shall see, leads to changes in the status quo and if it is the status quo 'we like,' change is definitionally most unfortunate. As we have noted earlier, to be a positive economist means there is a high probability that one likes the status quo. That is why 'no value position' need be taken toward 'what is.' All that is required is to see to it that little changes in what is. Economists would be regarded like goal keepers in soccer – preserve the status quo, at all costs.

We begin, therefore, with a factual question. Exactly how big is the public sector in the United States?

THE SIZE OF THE PUBLIC SECTOR IN THE UNITED STATES RELATIVE TO OTHER MARKET ECONOMIES – SOME FACTS

The OECD comparisons are as straightforward as these comparisons can be.[1] The only other effort to rank countries according to the size of the total government expenditure relative to GDP is one by the International Monetary Fund reported by Robert Barro (Barro 1997, p. 439). The IMF computed the average size of government expenditures as a percent of GDP for the years 1970–1985. This had the advantage, of course, of minimizing any unusual expenditures which might crop up in a single year. There were 19 countries on their list which duplicated the countries reported in Table 6.1. There were some differences in percentages, as was to be expected. When the rank order of the 19 countries common to both lists was compared, the rank correlation coefficient was .76. This suggests considerable overlap in the ordering of the country size between the two efforts despite the different time periods involved. In the IMF ordering the United States public sector was larger only than that in Japan, Korea, and Mexico, which is precisely what is reported in the OECD ranking. Clearly the conclusion in the text that the US has long ranked near the bottom of comparable market-oriented countries in the relative size of the public sector is well grounded in statistical fact. The story told by Table 6.1 is reasonably clear and very consistent. Judged against a number of industrial market-oriented economies, the public sector of the US economy is small relative to Gross Domestic Product. Perhaps more significantly, it has been small relative to GDP for as far back as the relevant data can be at all accurately measured.

The public sector did not suddenly become small, as some may imagine, during the Reagan Administration. The table shows the relative size of the US public sector even in 1937, toward the end of the New Deal, after the introduction of Social Security and a number of other programs designed to bolster the faltering state of affairs of the private sector to a greater extent

---

1. The earlier (pre-1999) comparisons confronted many of the same problems. Tanzi and Schuknecht (2000) up through 1937 presented 'central government' only rather than 'general government.' For the United States it is difficult, for example, to combine federal, state, and local taxes to get a clean measure of 'general government' because the federal government gives grants-in-aid to the other two levels of government. Unless one is careful the grants-in-aid show up in federal current expenditures as well as in state and local current receipts. Total current government receipts have to be adjusted to avoid double counting. Other countries do not necessarily have precise equivalents of the three levels of government found in the US, but similar problems undoubtedly are encountered in measuring 'total government.' The OECD presumably takes care to see to it that all comparisons are to GDP rather than to GNP, as did Tanzi and Schuknecht in presenting the older comparisons.

Table 6.1 Total government expenditures as a per cent of GDP, various years, 1870–1999

Country	Late 19th Century	World War I		World War II	Post World War II			
		Pre	Post	Pre %				
	About 1870	1913	1920	1937	1960	1980	1990	1999
Sweden	5.7	10.4	10.9	16.5	31	60.1	59.1	52
Denmark								50
Belgium	—	—	—	—	30.3	57.8	54.3	46
Finland								46
France	12.6	17	27.6	29	34.6	46.1	49.8	46
Austria	10.5	17	14.7	20.6	35.7	48.1	38.6	44
Italy	13.7	17.1	30.1	31.1	30.1	42.1	53.4	43
Luxemburg								42
Netherlands	—	—	—	—	33.7	55.8	54.1	42
Norway	5.9	9.3	16	11.8	29.9	43.8	54.9	42
Czech Republic								40
Hungary								39
Canada	—	—	16.7	25	28.6	38.8	46	38
Germany	10	14.8	25	34.1	32.4	47.9	45.1	38
Greece								37
Iceland								36
New Zealand	—	—	24.6	25.3	26.9	38.1	41.3	36
United Kingdom	9.4	12.7	26.2	30	32.2	43	39.9	36
Poland								35
Slovak Republic								35
Spain	—	—	—	—	18.8	32.2	42	35
Portugal								34
Trinidad	16.5	14	17	24.1	17.2	32.8	33.5	34
Ireland	—	—	18.8	25.5	28	48.9	41.2	32
Australia	18.3	16.5	19.3	14.8	21.2	34.1	34.9	31
Turkey								31
United States	7.3	7.5	12.1	19.7	27	31.4	32.8	29
Japan	8.8	8.3	14.8	25.4	17.5	32	31.3	26
South Korea								24
Mexico								17

Note: Table 6.1 for the pre-1999 years presents the size of the public sector measured as general government expenditures as a per cent of GDP. For 1999 it is measured by total tax revenues as per cent of GDP. The table has been updated by the author from Table 1.1 in Tanzi and Schuknecht (2000). Tanzi and Schuknecht (2000) in turn based their work on Fernandez (1976). It is not always clear where data for individual countries originated, but as best as can be determined the explicit country sources prior to 1999 are as follows: Australia – Bureau of Census and Statistics (1938); Belgium – Institut National de la Statistique (1952); United States – United States Bureau of the Census (1975); Norway – Statistisk Sentralbyra (1969, 1978); France – Delorme and Andre (1983); New Zealand – IMF, *Statistical Appendix*. Also: New Zealand – Official Statistics (1938); Switzerland – IMF, *Switzerland Recent Economic Developments*, (1996); The Netherlands – Centraal Bureau voor de Statistiek (1956); Italy – Istituto Nazionale de Statistica (1951); Austria – Oesterreichisches Statisches Zentralamt (1935); Neck and Schneider (1988). Data for other countries as well as some recent data are either from Tanzi and Schuknecht (2000) or from Butlin (1984); Flora, Kraus, and Pfennig (1987); Mitchell (1998). The 1999 data are collected by author from OECD (2002), Table A, p. 404.

than ever before (or since). Even then the US public sector was under 20 per cent of GDP. Of the 14 countries represented for that year in the table, only three had smaller public sectors than the US.[2]

We see as well that even the impact of the tremendous growth in government spending necessitated by World War II did little to change the relative size of the US public sector. In 1960, and indeed thereafter until the end of the century the size of the US public sector relative to GDP continued to be either the smallest of any country under consideration, or close to the bottom.

So as the twenty-first century opens what do we find? We find the past continuing to repeat itself. Far from a bloated public sector, compared to the other 29 OECD countries the total tax revenues which support the public sector is smaller in the United States than for any other country with three exceptions. The two countries with the smallest public sector, South Korea and Mexico, are scarcely known for the lavish public services they provide. The third is Japan, which, of course, up to now has not been permitted since the end of the World War II to spend on military purposes. In point of fact, US National Defense outlays in 1999 were 3 per cent of GDP. So without them the US, too, would have been at 26 per cent of GDP, assuming it did not extract the national defense expenditures from the citizens *(Economic Report of the President* 2002, p. 414).

On the other hand, among the countries with larger public sectors than the US one finds such countries as Finland, Hungary, Greece, Poland, Spain, Portugal, and Turkey. We are not aware that one finds the same degree of vituperation directed at public expenditures in these countries as we shall see below in the United States, nor are they known particularly for coddling their citizens.

We shall see there are frequent charges about the bloated size of the US public sector and there is a popular impression that, thanks to the unremitting efforts of those who point its elephantine size out to us, it has shrunk. It is well to examine the record with some care as we do here.

JUDGING THE SIZE OF THE PUBLIC SECTOR

The literature on the public sector and its role in the economy has burgeoned in the recent past. Much of this interest was a reaction to the impact Keynes had on the thinking of economists. Much, as we noted in Chapter 2, is bound

---

2. Two were Norway and Sweden. Paradoxically, Sweden subsequently began to develop its public sector rapidly and today has the largest of any country included in the list.

up in ideology. That is why we began this chapter with an effort at getting the statistics right concerning the size of the public sector at the outset. What we have tried to show is that the US public sector is and has always been relatively small. While this is fairly easy to show it is remarkably common for writers on the public sector, including economists, to contemplate the US public sector as though that simple factual situation were not so.

A small public sector can mean one of two things. It can signify remarkable efficiency in providing public services, or it can mean that, for whatever reason, a country has decided to provide fewer public services. At near 30 per cent of GDP recently the US public sector is pretty close to half the size of, say, the Swedish public sector. Were the difference to be explained by efficiency, we should have to argue that, if the US had standards for public sector services comparable to those in other countries, then it achieved those standards because its public sector was (is) almost twice as efficient as that of any other country. This in turn would suggest that the public sector in the US must hold an efficiency advantage over the private sector in the US (how else do you explain why the US steel, automobile, and other industries have had increasing trouble meeting competition from other countries in recent years?) If we were to take this suggestion seriously it would surely meet with opposition from Professors Buchanan and Tullock. They have argued particularly that employment in the public sector tends to make workers inefficient, dishonest, etc. as compared to their performance in the private sector. The public choice people most particularly would dispute any effort to suggest greater efficiency relative to other countries in the US public sector. We consider their views at some length at the end of this chapter.

Fortunately for the public choice people, we have other evidence arguing against the greater efficiency explanation for the size of the US public sector. It lies in what economists like to call 'social indicators.' We examined a few of these in Chapter 4 in the discussion of those who are 'too small to save.' Were the size differential to be explained on efficiency grounds the US should excel in the provision of health care, child care, care of the aged, housing, welfare, retirement, occupational safety, etc. It does excel in terms of the adequacy of the infrastructure, especially the highway system. Even without the detailed consideration which the 'social safety net' deserves, we can conclude with reasonable certainty that the areas where the US is near the bottom rather than the top in terms of social indicators suggest that the differential in the size of the public sector for the US vis à vis comparable countries can be explained by a US collective decision to settle for less provision to a sizable part of the lower income distribution groups than in other countries.

If Professor Buchanan is correct that employment in the public sector breeds inefficiency, with our provision of these services in the private sector, which he insists is so much more efficient than in the public sector, the US ought to lead rather than lag among countries in the provision of these services. Presumably we rely on the private sector to provide more of these services than do most of the other industrialized market economies with which reasonably we can be compared. Since it clearly does not, we would ask Professor Buchanan, why?

For our purposes the public sector becomes crucial because along with efforts to provide a social safetynet, it is the source of anti-trust activity, much other regulatory activity, stabilization efforts (we may include the Federal Reserve in the public sector for this purpose), and a large part of the effort to stimulate economic growth. In short the public sector is what one mainly has in mind when one speaks of 'interventionism.' When economics confronts the economy it is through the way in which the public sector is viewed, shaped, and managed that this confrontation comes about. The public sector is at the heart of the confrontation on which we focus in this book.

One of the themes we are suggesting is that many mainstream economists fail in the end to contribute to improving interventionist public policy. They are, in consequence, quite content to see the discipline move in other directions. We have called this trivialization but obviously all economists do not agree.

The Actual Size of the Public Sector and Distorted Rhetoric

We have argued that one may disagree about the impact of the public sector, but public discussion on this could advance more expeditiously if dislike of the public sector were not confused with inaccurate considerations of its size. At times it almost seems that the more commentators dislike the public sector the more 'bloated' they insist it is!

One of the early prominent voices muddying the waters of understanding about the public sector and interventionism was President Dwight D. Eisenhower and his confused view of the public debt. In remarks he made in 1959 he said that the previous year 'I got the idea it would be good for me to write a letter to my own grandson and try to tell him that he should stop supporting me. I would like to get over the idea – I would like each of us to get over the idea to the younger generation, . . . and say: "Whenever we add to the national debt one single dollar, you are helping to support me, because I am living on debt which I am passing on to you", (Eisenhower 1960, p. 763). Thus was born, so far as we can tell, the notion that the chief impact of a rising domestic debt is to put a huge burden on our grandchildren (they have to pay it off) and the idea has been endlessly repeated ever since. So pleased with this formulation was Eisenhower that four years later he was still refining it:

> I say the time-tested rules of financial policy still apply. Spending for spending's sake is patently a false theory . . . In effect we are stealing from our grandchildren in order to satisfy our desires of today . . . Imagine how much better the country would feel if it had no debt at all but a healthy surplus. (Eisenhower 1963, p. 16)

One of the greatest of the clarion callers to the effect that our bloated public sector led to huge debt was former President Reagan. In his first *Economic Report* Ronald Reagan wrote:

> We often hear it said that we work the first few months of the year for the government and then we start working for ourselves. But that is backwards. In fact, the first part of the year we work for ourselves. We begin working for the government only when our income reaches taxable levels. After that the more we earn, the more we work for the government, until rising tax rates on each dollar of extra income discourage many people from further work effort or from saving and investment. (*Economic Report of the President* 1982, pp. 6–7)

Imagine what we would think if parents took this attitude toward the costs of raising their children. This would be particularly disturbing were parents to feel that the more they earned the greater were the possibilities for choosing better schools, better clothes, etc. for their children so that the costs of child rearing rose so that 'the more we earn, the more we work for our children, until rising costs of each dollar earned discourage parents from further work effort because it would just go to their children instead of to them.'

One can imagine the reaction were such comments directed at parents. They don't understand the true meaning of being in a family. They are taking a selfish – perhaps even greedy – attitude toward their parental responsibilities. An often-forgotten aspect of Reagan's plan was reflected in his comment, 'A reduced role for the federal government means an enhanced role for state and local governments' (*Economic Report of the President* 1982, p. 5).[3]

---

3. At the same time that Reagan was suggesting an enhanced role for the state and local governments his Council of Economic Advisors (in the same *Economic Report*) commented, 'Given the large transfers of federally raised funds to the state, and local budgets, federal, state and local

Reagan, as pleased with his thinking on the debt as Eisenhower, also repeated and embellished this position. Contemplating the prosperity of the 1980s, he told the Republican National Convention in 1988

> . . . we intend to ensure this kind of economic prosperity right through the nineties and into the next century by guaranteeing the federal government can never again spend and tax the American people into another economic nightmare. We'll do it by passing the line item veto, the balanced budget amendment, and limits on congressional taxing power. *(Public Papers of the Presidents* 1991, p. 1077) [With the exception of the first, none of these came to pass in the subsequent four years.]

The quotation from Ronald Reagan concerning how many days one must work 'for the government' rather than for 'oneself' is a good example of a commonly used rhetorical attack on the public sector. The public sector is not only separated from individuals but turned in a 'we – they' sort of way into the enemy. In the case of taxation this turns into the exhortation, 'Don't let them take it away.' 'Them,' of course, is the hated enemy – the federal government. One's own income belongs to the individual – it is 'ours.' But as has often been said, we do not similarly refer to 'our' poverty, 'our' infant mortality, 'our' poor conservation, 'our' polluted streams, 'our' inadequate health care, etc. The only possible exception, which in passing confirms the ideological origins of the rhetoric employed for discussion of the public sector, is the case of national defense – there we do talk about the 'common defense.' Thus the only public good or service that is given common recognition as legitimately collective is 'our defense.'

While Reagan may have counted the number of days 'we' have to work for 'them,' I doubt he would have calculated the number of days of social security payment a typical senior citizen must devote to purchasing prescription drugs; how many days of unemployment insurance must be devoted to buying adequate food for the children of an unemployed worker, etc. These questions don't get raised because, the social safety net notwithstanding, these problems are not 'ours' but 'theirs' – the unfortunates without jobs or with large medical expenses. The subtle difference is that, however unfortunate falling through the social safety net may be, it is never 'us' who fall through but 'them.' 'We' are the fortunate; 'they' are the have-

---

deficits should be considered jointly (*Economic Report of the President* 1982, p. 96). Pursuit of Reagan's plan would, of course, require an increase in the size of state and local taxes. These levels of government have proven even more loath than the federal government to raise taxes, although in some states they have increased ineluctably. California with its famous Proposition 13 is the best example of the reaction of states to the idea of higher taxes.

nots and the government. This perhaps explains why 'positive' economists in sticking to 'what is' usually confront only 'we.'

This view of the public sector as the province of 'them' and the implacable enemy of 'us' carries over into the attitude toward the public debt. Selling bonds to the public as a means of raising assets with which to finance activities is 'prudent finance' when carried out by a large – and perhaps irresponsible – corporation. It is invariably reckless and irresponsible as in 'tax, tax, tax-spend, spend, spend!') when carried out by the federal government.

Finally it is perhaps worth pointing out that reducing the size of the federal sector, even as a per cent of GNP, is very difficult to achieve. Reagan wished to do this possibly more than any other modern president. He commented on the program he set before the Congress at the start of his administration, 'Carrying out this program of budget restraint will also halt and begin to reverse the tendency to take an ever-larger share of our economic resources. From a high of 23 per cent of the Gross National Product (GNP) in fiscal 1981, federal outlays are now scheduled to decline to 21.8 per cent in fiscal 1982 and to reach approximately 19 per cent beginning in 1984' (*Public Papers of the Presidents* 1982). He then produced the table shown below as Table 6.2, to which we have added only a column showing what actually happened to federal budget outlays.

In short we have established that the size of the public sector of the economy in the US, relative to its GDP, is certainly not light years larger than is the case in other comparable countries, and indeed there is considerable evidence to suggest that the United States economy has always had one of the smallest public sectors, relative to its GDP, of any economy in the market-oriented world. If we were to examine the statistical record in greater detail we would find that the federal government, which is the recipient of the most vitriolic disparagement, has grown relatively less than either the local or the state governments in recent years. So the denunciations of the 'bloated' federal government are based on ideology, not any statistical record which can be laid out in corroboration of the charge.

Facing the Impact of Ideology Squarely

We pause long enough to consider how a sister social science deals with ideology. Political science may not provide better answers but they have frequently seemed to ask questions more directly than do economists. The impact of ideology in contemplating the role of the public sector is a case in point. More than most questions in economics, debate about the public sector clearly reflects ideology. Clearly, too, this fact conflicts with the presumed

Table 6.2 The federal budget and GNP

Fiscal year	Outlays as a per cent of GNP	Outlays as a per cent of GNP
	(Scheduled by the Reagan Administration)	(Actual)
1981	23	22.2
1982	21.8	23.1
1983	20.4	23.5
1984	19.3	22.2
1985	19.2	22.9
1986	19	22.5

Source: *Public Papers of the Presidents* (1982), p. 121. Actual outlay percentages are from *Economic Report of the President* (2002), p. 414. (The latter figures are all percentages of Gross National Product.)

approach in a 'positive science.'

Societal values are embodied in public policy. (Policy to stay out or to get into an area with public policy reflects societal values also. Both deciding to and deciding not to fund a program with public funds in a field is a normative decision.) We shall need to consider this. Buchanan is, for example, very much in the camp of those who argue that economics is a positive science. Despite this, his profound suspicion of societal good coming from the public sector is consonant with the philosophical predictions of mainstream non-interventionists. They must surely consider themselves positive economists, but their convictions are sharply judgmental. Here we may note merely that in political science these matters are faced squarely. Thus, a political scientist does not hesitate to write:

> Ideologies can bias evaluating and can therefore influence strategies of dealing with broad societal problems. Liberals and conservatives differ in regard to their attitudes toward broad societal problems. . . . Difference in connection with policies related to poverty and education are apparent . . . Conservatives are . . . skeptical about the benefits of government intervention in the economy and believe the free market should be left alone to deal with the problems of poverty and unemployment that exist in our society.
>
> . . . The liberal approach tends to advocate more intervention by the federal government . . . The liberal point of view reflects the democratic ideal that equality must be balanced with liberty and efficiency . . . (Koven 1988, pp.

170–1).

Another political scientist with considerable insight has written,

> In a representative democracy, people will allow government to rule over them so long as they believe it is responsive to their will. Roosevelt deftly played on both the local and national models of citizenship to shore up the crumbling legitimacy of governmental institutions . . . Casting the national state broadly as a source of material benefits set the stage for the full emergence of interest group politics during the New Deal . . . In recent decades, however, with the continued decline of the party system and growth of persistent budgetary deficits and national debt citizens once again are questioning the basic legitimacy of our governing institutions . . . The legitimacy conferred by the budget as a symbol of responsible government has eroded in recent years, and there is nothing to take its place . . . Yet, for all this, as the century comes to a close and we confront the problems of sustaining a viable representative democracy in an increasingly large, complex, and diverse society, we might do well to pause to consider how a group of well-meaning, intelligent, and articulate citizens used budget reform to address similar problems as the century was born. (Kahn 1997, pp. 212–4)

We cannot deny that this approach to confronting the role of the public sector sets up constructs that are difficult to quantify, let alone measure. We have already confronted this head on in Chapter 3. Nevertheless, we think perhaps it would be well to keep the political science perspective in mind, in particular its effort at realism and directness, as we compare it to the efforts summarized here of economists to cope with the comparable overall problems. We may well ask, 'Does the fate of, for example, consumer surplus and the changing nature of 'deadweight loss' actually clarify the economic problem more precisely as well as more manageably for the real world?'

Ideology and Distorted Rhetoric

All in all, we think a strong case can be made for the assertion that terminology commonly used in connection with the public sector is not neutral. It is highly larded over with ideology. This is perhaps not surprising but it raises a fundamental question. What is the relationship between the terminology and the attitudes of economists, especially academic economists? (Do economists have any obligation to contribute to public discussion? Do they have any obligation to correct misunderstandings concerning the relationship of the public sector to the rest of the economy?)

In short, what, if anything, do mainstream economists do to reorient the public in their thinking away from terminology which originates in ideology and toward terminology which focuses on the essential questions requiring public debate? A related question would be, to what extent do economists buy into the prevailing mainstream culture from which emanates the popular ideology insofar as the public sector is concerned?

We have already seen examples of how ideology colors the language of debate about the public sector. Another example would be official economic documents where we encounter the notion of obtaining for the public 'tax relief.' For example, in *The Economic Report of the President* (2002), in a section entitled 'Tax Relief in 2001' we read,

> The President laid a strong foundation for growth in 2001 with the Economic Growth and Tax Relief Reconciliation Act. This package provides a powerful stimulus for future growth, with reductions in marginal tax rates that improve incentives and leave in the hands of Americans a greater share of their own money to spend on consumption, education, and retirement investment. (*Economic Report of the President* 2002, p. 44)

It may well leave a greater share of money in the hands of Americans, but at what cost is not stated. Presumably it means that the public sector will have less revenue to spend on 'free public education,' ostensibly guaranteed in state constitutions, or less on health care, etc. Were the language neutral one might regard the fiscal changes as the imposition of 'tax pain' because private expenditures on health care, education, etc. will necessarily need to be increased. As for defense, there is, of course, no way in which this quintessentially public expenditure can be turned over to the private sector. We need not belabor the point that the terminology surrounding this budgetary item is distinctly different from all other items. Defense expenditure is never 'inflationary;' it is never 'robbing consumers of discretion' or 'entrepreneurs of incentive,' or 'adding to the burdens on our grandchildren.' It surely never prevents tax relief! All of these charges are regularly leveled at most budgetary expenditure items by those who, for ideological reasons, refer to the necessity for 'tax relief' which will force less public spending on these items.

The point to note is very simple and widely ignored. The moving of expenditures from the public sector to the private sector or from the private sector to the public sector is not a matter of substituting pain for relief or relief for pain. It is entirely a matter of where costs are best – that is, most efficiently – incurred. The word 'costs' is the basic economic term, hence presumably without psychological overtones, and raises the question of balancing of cost with benefit. The essential public debate, to which presumably economists through their discipline might have a great deal to contribute, has to do with where services are most efficiently provided. One may begin with the assertion that some services are most efficiently provided in the public sector and some in the private sector. Sorting out which belongs where is a critical topic requiring public debate.

In short, the terminology obfuscates the real debate. One would be regarded as demented were one to refer to 'education relief' or 'defense relief' or 'health benefits relief' ('relief' being interpreted, as in tax relief, to mean a smaller expenditure being reserved for these items). Yet it is a matter of simple arithmetic to note that to the extent that these services are not provided in the public sector via 'unrelieved taxes ' they have to be provided in the private sector (presumably by the assumption of 'unrelieved expenditure pain'). Put this way it is clear that the real debate is not over the necessity for making such things available to households in a 'civilized' society/economy but where are they most efficiently provided (i.e., where the pain is least, and the service provision most productive).

We have already seen that ideologically tinged terminology is widely found in political discussion. While arguably many economists attempt to convey correct views of, say, the burden of the public debt, there is a widespread public perception, requiring enlightenment, that the debt is a great real burden on our grandchildren. Economic theorists have devised a number of artful (and perhaps artificial!) theoretical contrivances which play into the hands of those who would demonize the public sector.

It is to sorting out these views that the remainder of this chapter is devoted. We begin by underscoring again the assertion that an appropriate view in economics must be that the public sector is 'all of us.' That is surely the view we take of the elected (public) officials in a political democracy. The President is 'the president of all the people,' – not elected to desert 'us' and join 'them.' There is a perfectly legitimate debate which economists – perhaps particularly the theorists – need to be a part of concerning the appropriate role for the public sector in considering what can best be done in the private sector and what in the public sector. But we argue that economists do their discipline and the economy a disservice when they contribute to the demonization of the public sector and/or the sanctification of the private sector.

We start from a position which we regard as both objectively and subjectively appropriate. We assert that it is possible to expend resources efficiently or inefficiently in the public sector. An essential part of the economist's job is to determine how much must be spent to achieve certain results in the public sector vs. the private sector. A secondary question is, if it can be determined that the public sector is the appropriate site for expenditures to be made, are they provided most efficiently at the federal, the state, or the local level? If some resources are most efficiently deployed in the public sector, there is no disagreement with the mainstream assertion that many times resources are most efficiently deployed in the private sector (through the free market). This suggests that we have no disagreement with the assertion that where goods and services can be most efficiently produced needs to be determined on a case by case basis.

Aside from the caveat just introduced, we may begin by asking, what contrivances have been introduced which play into the hands of those who would demonize the public sector? Is 'demonization' too strong as a description of what we have in mind? We think not. We just recalled above, that it was Reagan who asserted that he intended to guarantee that, ' . . . the federal government can never again spend and tax the American people into another economic nightmare.' What exactly was the nightmare? When exactly did this nightmare occur? If it did occur, what is the evidence that it was not a failure of households to consume or firms to invest that produced it? If the public debt per se can be alleged to be an economic nightmare 'demonization' seems an apt description of what is being done.

CONVERTING THE PUBLIC SECTOR INTO A TRIVIAL PURSUIT

The relatively narrow scope frequently reserved for the public sector and 'public goods' is said to derive from what is non-controversially distinctive about goods which are 'public.' As conventionally described they are '*non-rivalrous*' or '*non-depletable*' (consumption of them by one person does not reduce the ability of another person to consume them – like national defense. They are '*non-excludable*' (when one person consumes them it is impossible to keep another person from consuming them). Again national defense is the most obvious example – making one citizen secure cannot avoid making another citizen – or all citizens – secure. Sometimes a third characteristic is mentioned – '*non-rejectibility*' – no citizen can reject the proffered service. Beyond this, says the mainstream, the role of the public sector rapidly gets murky.

In earlier chapters we have seen that if we study the work of mainstream economic theorists we shall soon 'see' (at least through their eyes) the futility of intervening in the microeconomy with regulatory policies or in the macroeconomy with stabilization policies or efforts to affect the growth rate. These efforts, which in effect ask us to sit back and relax and watch the wonders of the market unfold before our eyes, we called 'trivialization' efforts because the true measure of their success is the degree to which they render efforts to improve theory, so as to make interventionist policy more effective in its impact on the private sector, nugatory.

Ah, you say, that still leaves efforts to improve public performance through the public sector. Not a chance! Our 'new classical' colleagues have not forgotten to consider direct public investment and other actions which might be taken by the government, particularly the federal government, to improve economic performance. By now no reader should be surprised to learn that these efforts, too, are doomed to failure. Either they make things worse, or have no effect at all. Mainstream theorists are an inventive lot. They have saved some of their most ingenious trivializations for proffered efforts to improve economic performance through the public sector. We detail some of the more important of these efforts in the pages below.

The Ricardian Equivalence Theorem

The Ricardo Equivalence Theorem argues that whether the government finances its expenditures by borrowing or by taxing is a matter of supreme unimportance because either way the households will regard their net wealth as unchanged and so direct expenditure through the public sector will have no significant impact on the consumption function. Thus, if the government finances one million dollars of new expenditures by taxing, so that disposable income is reduced by one million dollars, and if one goes along with Keynes (a not very common reaction in a typical modern new classical economist!) consumption would fall accordingly. On the other hand if the one million dollars is financed by going into debt (issuing bonds) the Keynesian reaction is that households will regard their disposable income as augmented by one million dollars and so their consumption expenditures will increase. The Ricardian Equivalence folks say, 'No! Households all know that the bonds one day will come due and have to be repaid.' So they set aside what will be required to pay off the bonds. This will, of course, reduce disposable income by the same amount as was the case for taxation, with the exception of the interest payments which would be provided for in the sinking fund that paid off both principal and interest. As exponents of the theorem typically conclude, '. . . household behavior is invariant to the switch between tax finance and debt finance for a given amount of government spending' (Abel 1987, p. 175). If true, why, for example, would a household ever feel free to buy a car with a loan, knowing the loan would have to be repaid?

Nonetheless, this theorem has had enormous appeal to a large number of economists.[4] What is clear is that this is probably a good example of the kind of controversy out of which a remarkable number of promotions and tenure decisions could be secured in today's academia, things being how they are. Here we see one of the phenomena lurking behind the genesis of this book. One may get tenured or promoted in, say, physiology, by finding a new way to reduce the incidence or severity of some disease. In economics it is difficult to estimate how many promotions and tenure decisions have been bolstered in major American departments of economics in the past half century through efforts, not unlike those we have been considering, which are esoteric in the extreme. The reader may think I digress. I don't! We shall return to this in Chapter 7.

If in fact households pay attention to increases in the public debt because they know that the bonds issued to effect such an increase will need to be repaid, the 'equivalence theorem' means that household consumption is unaffected by public expenditures financed by borrowing. If this is indeed true, a Keynesian, beginning from $Y = C + I + G$ would have to grant that if every increase in G is offset by a decrease in C, then, of course, any real change in Y is non-existent. Equivalently, the argument would be that aggregate demand is unaffected by public spending financed by debt. If true, this is one of the most devastating arguments we have yet seen leading to the 'intervention is futile' conclusion so dear to the hearts of new classical economic theorists.

While we have seen earlier that dedicated trivializers don't really like to be confused by facts, a shot of empirical reality does seem especially appropriate here. Consider the 1980s in the United States. As more than one economist has pointed out, the decade of the 1980s saw a huge increase in the outstanding public debt (from $711.9 billion in fiscal 1980 to $2411.8 in fiscal 1990 (*Economic Report of the President* 2002, p. 413). This amounts to about a three and half-fold increase in the debt in a decade. Were the Ricardian Equivalence Theory in fact applicable we should have noted a

---

4. It was Robert Barro who originally called attention to this position, but he did not attribute it to Ricardo until Buchanan called his attention to Ricardo's argument to this effect (cf. Buchanan 1986, pp. 337–42). Barro now attributes this theorem to Ricardo (Barro 1997, p. 522). To get all the credit spread correctly around, Gerald O'Driscoll weighed in by writing that while Buchanan correctly criticized Barro for not giving due credit to Ricardo, he argued that Buchanan did so because he interpreted Ricardo in the conventional way. In point of fact, O'Driscoll said, Buchanan and many others have misinterpreted Ricardo, who really had a 'non-equivalence theorem' rather than an equivalence theorem. That is, O'Driscoll argued that Ricardo did not in fact think that increasing the public debt and increasing taxes were equivalent in the impact on the economy. For our purposes all this raises only the question whether Ricardo was or was not an early trivializer. As we saw in Chapter 1 it is not clear that modern economists correctly interpret Smith. Why should Ricardo be any different?

massive change in household behavior. Household saving would have had to increase by a like magnitude. Instead household saving as a per cent of disposable income, which had been 10.2 per cent in 1980 by 1990 had fallen to 7.8 per cent. By the year 2000 it had dwindled to 1.0 per cent. If American consumers were worried about having one day to cough up the wherewithal to repay the debt which the government incurred in the 1980s they had an odd way of showing it. A three and a half-fold increase in government debt was matched by a ten-fold decrease in saving as a per cent of disposable income, by the most recent figures available.[5]

If the 1980s, therefore, presents empirical evidence which could be regarded as overwhelming, not all economists are convinced. Thus, Andrew B. Abel concludes that 'The existing literature that attempts to test empirically whether the theorem holds has produced mixed results, some claiming to show that it holds, and others the opposite.' He goes one step further, arguing that from a policy point of view the question is whether departures from the theorem are 'quantitatively substantial.' Even here he asserts, 'Existing empirical work has not yet produced a consensus on this question' (Abel 1987, p. 178). On the other hand, no less a student of the subject than James Buchanan writes, 'The empirical evidence gained from straightforward observation of modern politics points clearly toward rejection of the equivalence theorem. Taxation and debt are not treated as identical by voting constituents . . .' (Buchanan 1987, p. 1045).

Even this is not the end of debate about the Ricardian Equivalence Theorem. Even if one grants that today's consumers might be worried about the need to repay current debt one day and would wish to modify their current consumption so as to have the wherewithal available for the required repayment, there is a small and awkward problem. People die. Bonds issued this year may be due God knows when – most often, people who worry about the debt as a problem talk, as we have noted, about 'the burden of debt on our grandchildren.' Presumably, therefore, we are talking about 40 to 60 years in the future. Depending on a number of demographic factors, when our grandchildren are doing this grappling with debt repayment 'we' may be long gone. Clearly a way has to be found, therefore, to make 'us' feel financially responsible for 'them' – ideally, all the 'them' who may appear. Not to worry! As Abel so ably informs us, Robert Barro presented an ingenious argument which extends the Ricardian Equivalence Theorem to cover the case in which consumers die before future taxes are increased to compensate for the current tax cut (Abel 1987, p. 176).

Barro's solution is to impute to his consumers 'altruistic motives.' Most

5. The savings percentages are reported in *The Economic Report of the President* (2002), p. 356.

particularly he contemplates the behavior of what he has labeled 'inter-generationally altruistic consumers.'[6] 'Inter-generationally altruistic consumers' as a construct may be necessary to cope with the awkwardness of death, but I permit myself to digress long enough to point out that a major – perhaps THE major – assumption around which neoclassical microeconomic theory revolves is self-interest as the motivating force in all economic activity. Hence, were we to assume altruism as a major motivator, none of the welfare implications of the basic price model could be counted on, beginning with the invisible hand. Of course what is being attempted is, we would be told, not so much an abandonment of self-interest, as a broadening of self-interest to extend beyond a given economic agent so as to encompass all future generations of that agent. So broadening the notion of the economic agent at the very least blurs the distinction between selfishness and altruism. We claim merely that any blurring of this line would at the very least open a major can of worms, because, were it widely adopted, it would constitute a major reorientation of price theory (certainly competitive price theory) and its implications.

'Inter-generationally altruistic consumers' have been rechristened 'overlapping generations' for modeling purposes. Here we can pause only to note that such models have proliferated in the past half century to include all sorts of economic situations. The term was introduced by Paul Samuelson in 1958 and, in the words of one economist, 'has developed into what is without doubt the most important and influential paradigm in neoclassical general equilibrium theory outside the Arrow, Debreu economy' (Geanakoplos 1987, p. 767). For Samuelson overlapping generations models meant thinking of consumption as a process involving agents who live for two periods (young and old). If they acquire commodities when young but not when they are old Samuelson found they would be better off if they gave half their goods to their predecessor (an old father) and got half from their successor (a young son). The problem with this welfare optimizing solution apparently is that the old have nothing to exchange to the young for their part in the exchange. Hence, the 'market' would not work. The profession stewed about this for some time. Seemingly it was unnerving to find that a market solution did not work.

Ultimately, we are told, the 'Samuelson suboptimality paradox' was solved with the realization that the problem was not one of market failure at all: 'Exactly the same equilibrium allocation would be reached if all agents, dead and unborn, met (in spirit) before the beginning of time and traded all consumption goods, dated from all time periods, simultaneously under the

6. The phrase is from Abel (1987), p. 176.

usual conditions of perfect intermediation' (Geanakoplos 1987, p. 767). For its sheer breathtaking quality this vision surely must take the prize for 'stylizing' as in 'stylized facts.' There are some minor problems. If 'overlapping generations' ever stopped overlapping, it seems money would lose its value, because for money to have 'positive value' there must be confidence that it can continue to represent the value of whatever we put a price on. The last generation would find money useless because to the non-existent 'next' generation money would have no value (there would be no one there to assume it had value!) At least this was the reasoning of overlapping generations thinking. There would be no one there to appreciate the flow of services from products either. Would they, therefore, lose 'positive utility'? It is not clear that anyone has ever said.

It can surely be argued that economists might well refrain from such apocalyptic worrying while the economy of the here and now is so problem-ridden. There is a conclusion to be reached about the enormous outpouring of interest in overlapping generations models. It is not that they are without value or interest. They exhibit both. But while they may contribute to sorting out the internal logic of the theory to which they are applied, they do not contribute to the improvement of public policy for the here and now.

This means that assuming that subsequent generations of oneself continue indefinitely can simplify the development of economic theory in precisely the same way that the development of a new and distinctive opening move can contribute to a better chess game. Paul Samuelson in the path breaking paper mentioned earlier which began the development of overlapping generations models is explicit about this. At the conclusion he comments, 'I do not pretend to pass judgement on the policies related to all this. But I do suggest for economists' further research the difficult analysis of capital models which grapple with the fact that each and every today is followed by a tomorrow' (Samuelson 1958, p. 482). Calculating both costs and utilities for eternity is indeed a daunting challenge. Fortunately meeting it can be postponed.

Barro's approach should indeed be called 'ingenious.' It is one of the best of all extant examples of trivializing theory with elegance. Barro begins with the assertion that

> The assumption that government bonds are perceived as net wealth by the private sector is crucial in demonstrating real effects of shifts in the stock of public debt. In particular, the standard effects of 'expansionary' fiscal policy on aggregate demand hinge on this assumption. (Barro 1973, p. 1095)

Twenty-two pages later he concludes that

> It was shown that households would act as though they were infinitely lived, and hence, that there would be no marginal net-wealth effects of government bonds, so long as there existed an operative chain of intergenerational transfers which connected current to future generations.
>
> The basic conclusion is that there is no persuasive theoretical case for treating government debt, at the margin, as a net component of perceived household wealth . . . If, in fact, the marginal net-wealth effect were negligible, the implications for monetary and fiscal analysis would be far reaching. In particular, . . . a change in the stock of government debt would have no effect on capital formation, and . . . fiscal effects involving changes in the relative amount of tax and debt finance for a given amount of public expenditure would have no effect on aggregate demand, interest rates, and capital formation. (Barro 1973, pp. 1116–7)

What could be sweeter music to the ears of a true believer in leaving it all to the market?

One or two more comments on overlapping generations models may be in order. The flavor of the world of these models is perhaps conveyed by the comment that when they are compared to the Arrow-Debreu model of general equilibrium 'there is a profound difference in their equilibria' (Geanakoplos 1987, p. 767). The overlapping generations models may be 'Pareto sub-optimal' and 'money may have a positive value' (1987, p. 767). If one thinks Pareto optimality is vastly over-used as a normative criterion, as we have suggested earlier, the difference is perhaps not so large. Secondly, despite the tremendous amount of attention paid to Arrow-Debreu models it is worth noting that a sympathetic student of the approach still feels obliged to add, 'In reality, it is very rare to find a market for a pure Arrow-Debreu commodity' (1987, p. 116). This is not so surprising when it is recalled that this same sympathetic student of Arrow-Debreu has also written, 'The Arrow-Debreu model of general equilibrium, based on agent optimization, rational expectations, and market clearing, is universally regarded as the central paradigm of the neoclassical approach to economic theory' (1987, p. 767). It is odd the way reality keeps intruding into a world otherwise allegedly so useful heuristically as the one in which neoclassical price theorists dwell.

Finally, it is interesting to note that most of the papers written on overlapping generations models and their implications devote themselves to spinning out the mathematical logic of the model but almost never include any conclusions. What one is supposed to glean from these efforts is, therefore, left somewhat unclear.

If overlapping generations models have proven to be a boon to expositions of the Ricardian Equivalence Theorem it is probably appropriate to conclude our considerations of the Equivalence Theorem with this highly relevant comment by one student of the problem: 'Although the Ricardian view is not widely held by policy makers, the theory is very popular among academics' (Farmer 2002, p. 327). This is, of course, a principal point we have been underscoring – increasingly our theorists have lost interest in policy matters altogether. This explains the frequent use of the word 'elegant' to describe what they do. Elegance no doubt has its place – but as a total substitute for relevance and empirical usefulness, it does leave something to be desired.

In the real world people don't live forever, but many problems outlive any given generation. Most people outside the relatively small world of Ricardian Equivalence believers would argue that perhaps we should make room for at least a few carefully thought out policies based on what economists have been able to learn in the last 60 years. There might be an outside chance of rounding up a few economists who would insist that it is worth trying to improve if not perfect such reality-derived policy so that it can be applied it to the real and problem-ridden world in which we live.

By way of conclusion, we may quote David Romer's useful summation of the debate:

> What in the end, should one make of the Ricardian equivalence debate? Economists take a wide range of positions on the issue. At one extreme is the view that Ricardian equivalence is a theoretical abstraction so unrelated to reality that it is of little interest. At the other extreme is the position that despite the many reasons for it not to hold exactly, it is nonetheless a good first approximation. A reasonable middle ground is that Ricardian equivalence is a useful theoretical baseline but not a useful empirical one. It is valuable as a theoretical baseline because it is so simple and logical. (Romer 1996, p. 71)

Alas, Professor Romer has inadvertently repeated the old canard about something which may be all right in theory but not in practice. I thought Paul Samuelson disposed of this once and for all in the first edition of his *Economics*. In 1948 he wrote, ' . . . when a student says, "That's all right in theory but not in practice," he really means "That's not right in theory," or else he is talking nonsense' (Samuelson 1948, p. 8). I have believed all these years that Samuelson was right. I still do. It must be wrong: if a position is not a useful empirical one it can't be a useful theoretical baseline. Unhappily, logic and simplicity don't help. All the logic and simplicity in the world not hooked to reality or veracity are still useless. Professor Romer has inadvertently put his finger on a major reason that modern economics has such difficulty confronting the modern economy. Could there be a book in this?

The 'Crowding Out' Argument

One of the earliest rites by which theorists surveying the macroeconomic scene argued that interventionist policy was a futile pursuit goes by the name of 'crowding out.' Olivier Blanchard has broadened the concept to cover the waterfront – so he defines it as referring to 'all the things which can go wrong whenever fiscal policy is used to affect output' (Blanchard 1987, p. 728). As such the Ricardian Equivalence argument which we have just considered would fall under this rubric. Barro defines crowding out as 'The decrease in private consumption and investment that results from an increase in government consumption' (Barro 1997, p. 463). This too may be too broad as it may well be the case that the decrease in private consumption and investment which results from an increase in government consumption can be zero, but we get ahead of our story. A better but still broad definition suggests that crowding out is: 'The possibility that an increase in one form of spending may cause another form to fall' (Black 1997, p. 104). Three possibilities are suggested:

1. If the government increased spending in the form of say, public works this may create scarce resources (e.g., engineers) causing delays in investment projects already planned.
2. If the increase in government activity causes inflation this could lead to tighter monetary policy and force cuts in alternative spending.
3. If the increase in government debt makes private investors nervous, the increase in public works could scare off other private investment. (Black 1997, p. 104)[7]

The most common and explicit definition of crowding out states that it refers to 'The reduction in demand that results when a fiscal expansion raises the interest rate' (Mankiw 2004, p. 719). The term certainly originated in the consideration of monetary policy and was introduced to suggest the expansionary powers of Keynesian fiscal policy could be limited if such policy resulted in tightening the money supply, thereby raising interest rates. The increased cost of private investment could more than undo whatever good the expansionary fiscal policy could accomplish. As such it was one of

7. These possibilities are enumerated under 'Crowding Out', Black (1997), pp. 104–5.

the earliest and remains one of the most popular of the techniques designed to trivialize interventionist policy.

The first thing to note was that as originally conceived, the crowding out effect was a consequence of efforts to introduce the expansionary impact of fiscal policies utilized when the economy was at or very near full employment.

The crowding out arguments can get very exotic. The fundamental point that we would make is that the notion of crowding out when the economy is at full employment suggests a failure to understand counter-cyclical fiscal policy. (Keynesians would argue that at full employment there is no need for any expansionary fiscal policy.) It also points to the impact of increased federal expenditures on aggregate economic activity when undertaken for reasons outside the effort to utilize counter-cyclical fiscal policy.

In the first case fiscal policy as an outgrowth of conventional Keynesian analysis involves utilizing the federal government as a spender of last resort. When aggregate demand is inadequate (fails to provide for full use of the economy's resources) one can substitute government expenditures for private expenditures. Obviously when the resources are fully employed there is no need to do this. One can manufacture scenarios in which government spending causes interest rates to rise. This implies that, thanks to monetary mismanagement, the monetary authorities have fixed the money supply at a level too small to permit all resources to be employed at reasonable interest rates. If one defined Keynesian fiscal policy as one in which federal revenues and expenditures are balanced over the cycle rather than over the calendar (or fiscal) year, the impact of federal activity ought to be no greater than that which can support full employment. In principle, any impact on the 'fixed money supply' would have to be because the money supply was fixed at too small a level.[8]

We shall see below that the crowding out argument is also very much a part of the argument about whether or not the debt is a burden on future generations.

Public Debt 'Burden'

We suggested earlier in this chapter that expostulating on the burden of

---

8. More precisely the money supply needs to grow at a rate at least approximating the real growth rate of the economy. This is, of course, the essence of Friedman's 'simple monetary rule.' Samuelson terms the simple monetary rule 'The cardinal tenet of monetarist economic philosophy: (set) the growth of the money supply at a fixed rate and hold(s) to that rate through thick and thin' (Samuelson and Nordhaus 2001, p. 770).

public debt was one of the most common techniques for adding to what we called the demonization of the public sector. That demonization is the other side, of course, of the effort to reduce most if not all interventionism to as close to insignificance (either via futility or negative consequences) as possible.

Accordingly we need to pause at least briefly to consider the impact of government expenditures on the health of the macroeconomy. The first point that needs to be underscored is that the impact of government expenditures financed by tax revenue is fundamentally different than the impact from expenditures financed by increased government debt. We have considered the former and its treatment by many mainstream economists in the discussion of the Ricardian Equivalence Theorem. A point that is often made is that no one objects to a business selling bonds to finance its expenditures but when the same tactic is pursued by the government, especially the federal government, it is irresponsible, and therefore a cause for anguish. Thus, Robert Gordon reminds us, 'No one has ever accused AT&T of creating a burden on future generations by issuing bonds, and for good reason' (Gordon 2000, p. 353). Gordon goes on to argue that any investment should be judged by whether its stream of benefits exceeds the government's borrowing rate, or not. He argues that when the interest payments exceed the future benefits a 'true burden on future generations' has been created. He cites as an example the cost of current meals consumed by the armed forces. It would appear to be an unfortunate choice as an example. If the object of the exercise of fiscal policy should be to refrain from adding to the burden on future generations the only logical position to take is that as a matter of policy we must refrain from all armed conflict. That is to say, examination of the growth of the public debt in the United States at least will show that it has risen dramatically in each war in which we have engaged, and fallen only partially to its prewar level after the war is over. The obvious explanation is that 'we' have never paid for a war with tax revenues in our entire history.

An alternative, which this writer at least finds more persuasive, is to define future benefits somewhat more realistically, which some will interpret only as more generously. To take an obvious example, one could fairly easily make the case that, had 'we' not chosen to fight World War II the US would have been annihilated. Is it too much of a stretch to argue that preserving the integrity of the US as a country constitutes a 'future stream of benefits' – perhaps even higher than the interest rate paid on the bonds which were sold to pay for the war? Still, Professor Gordon, taking a position which undoubtedly would endear him to many an accountant, asserts that 'The government must pay interest to keep bondholders happy, just as AT&T must pay interest . . . yet there is no future benefit or income to pay interest.

Future taxpayers are forced to hand over extra payments to government to cover the interest on the debt, and the tax payers receive no benefit in return' (Gordon 2000, p. 354).

We have argued in effect at various points in this book that economic activity can be assessed meaningfully only if it is always and everywhere placed in a cultural or societal context. Professor Gordon has, paradoxically, illustrated the 'burden' of the public debt with an example from virtually the only expenditure category that is relatively uncontroversial. When we say, as indeed often we do, that national security is something that 'we' need to purchase 'regardless of cost' we are in effect saying that for this category at least the conventional economic calculus which requires that the benefits always equal – if they do not exceed – costs, must be suspended. Better yet, it needs to be interpreted realistically, which in this case means recognizing that even in economics there are transactions of great importance which cannot be reduced to the calculus that does so much for us in the market. (The strict market calculus: always leave it to the market! Everything has a price.) Were it otherwise, economists might have to deal with the following situations, or some like them: Father to Doctor: 'Doctor, my wife and I have thought it over, and while we are sure you are a good surgeon and that Junior's brain operation is well worth $43000 unfortunately that's a good deal more than Junior is worth to us.' Or: Husband to Wife: 'How much do I love you? Well, I considered carefully and were you a prostitute I would pay you $463 a night. That's how high is my sky and how deep is my ocean.' Finally there is the classic Jack Benny joke: Crook to Benny: 'Your money or your life.' Long painful pause while Benny considers the choice. The point is clear. It's all well and good to push for 'leaving it to the market.' But only up to a point. Determining that point is what the great debate is all about. To the market everything has a price. No question! Cost-benefit analysis, so useful in many situations, in some critically important areas is clearly (if tacitly) considered out of bounds.

It is clear that the burden of the public debt is closely related to the crowding out argument, considered above. The argument just made amounts to suggesting that at least in national defense, among other consequences, the 'crowding out' argument loses all its force because whatever might be 'crowded out' by government expenditures is considered far less vital to the health of the society – including its economy – than whatever expenditure it may be which is being 'crowded in.'

National defense is simply the most obvious and overwhelmingly uncomplicated example of a case where the calculus of the market – the price system if you will – is an inappropriate guide to resource deployment. This is another way of noting a point made here before – the economy at bottom is not an entity for positive analysis, useful and important though that may be in many areas. It is an entity reflecting normative societal values. At bottom it encompasses, for example, neonatal technology; we could use it to save a premature baby at a cost of a million dollars which could also be used for *X*, *Y*, or *Z*. Is any one of those something not as wise to do? Should we spend *N* dollars on *X*? If *X* is saving 50 persons with severe heart damage by means of heart transplants which will prolong their lives by ten years each? This is not a question where the economist's cost-benefit calculus is going to help a lot.

A crowding out argument of a different sort which has been proffered in connection with the true burden of the debt suggests that if government borrowing causes funds to be utilized for current consumption which otherwise might have been devoted to building more infrastructure, future generations suffer a burden in the form of a smaller real capital stock to inherit. Certainly this argument is a good deal more sophisticated than the 'burden on our grandchildren' argument considered earlier in this chapter. How serious this possibility has been historically or is at the present time, is difficult to determine. In conventional Keynesian theory the inducement to invest is a critical variable. My reading of Keynes suggests that inasmuch as investment for him requires entrepreneurs to compare the prospective yield on a newly produced capital asset with the known cost, which is to say the interest rate, for such investment to be 'crowded out' would have to mean that the government would borrow money to pay for consumption rather than investment goods. Customarily this argument is used to convey the thought that government expenditures for other than additions to infrastructure are not productive and hence 'crowd out' additions to infrastructure which otherwise would be made. This is a little like arguing that household expenditures for medical expenses crowd out additions to household possessions which might otherwise be purchased with household income. To argue that the medical expenditures provided benefits that were 'not investment' whereas household 'investment' adds to the value of the household assets 'later' is a pretty short-sighted view. A larger estate with a dead household head is worth remarkably little certainly to the head and very possibly even to his or her heirs!

Determining the Appropriate Size of the Public Sector

Another way to reduce the significance of the public sector, if not to trivialize it, is to argue in favor of reducing or limiting its size. Martin Feldstein, one of the best known mainstream economists, has asked the useful question, 'How big should government be?' We need to examine his answer critically.

His answer:

> The appropriate size and role of government depends on the deadweight burden caused by incremental transfers of funds from the private sector. The magnitude of that burden depends on the increases in tax rates required to raise incremental revenue and on the deadweight loss that results from higher taxes. Both components depend on the full range of behavioral responses of taxpayers to increase in tax rates. (Feldstein 1996, p. 1)

As Feldstein says, the answer reflects criteria through which to decide whether the level of taxes and spending is justified. 'The appropriate comparison, as public finance economists have known at least since the time of Pigou (1928), is between the benefits that would flow from increased spending and the cost of financing that spending, including the deadweight losses associated with raising that revenue and with the particular form of spending' (Feldstein 1996, p. 3).

Feldstein makes it sound easy. Even if we restrict our consideration to the variables which conventional theory includes, the Feldstein formulation is still deceptively over-simplified. Consumer surplus is one notion to which he turns to capture 'the benefits that would flow from increased spending.'

On the other side, the cost of the benefits from increased spending involve what Feldsein terms 'the deadweight loss of raising the revenue' (Feldstein 1996, p. 26). Suffice it to say that estimating the part of it that does not go to the recipient of increased spending but instead is simply lost is even more difficult to estimate than consumer surplus. Deadweight loss is frequently ascribed to economic inefficiency. It referred originally to the real income lost when monopolists push up prices to increase profits or governments increase prices by imposing taxes. These and other similar price increases reduce consumer surplus by more than the amount gained by the agency raising the price. The consumer surplus is simply replaced by inefficiency.

We may judge the monopolist's profit increase harshly. But what of the pain of increased taxes in comparison to the gain from the expenditure to which the taxes are devoted? This is the question posed by Feldstein. Clearly the deadweight loss at least on paper is a possible downer, although all pains and gains can't be compared so mechanically. But if the pain of lost consumer surplus is hard to quantify, calculating the benefit to a given individual of, say, a specified increase in national defense is infinitely more difficult. This suggests that judging the benefit of public goods in the same way as private goods (e.g., by notions like 'deadweight loss') may be inappropriate. Price theory can formulate the problem, perhaps. Given the primitive assumptions and limitations with which it is presented, calculating a realistic answer is impossible. (Recall our earlier discussion of George Katona, and behavioral economics in general.)

The heart of Feldstein's notion is that in assessing the cost of a government program one should calculate the amount of increased tax required to fund the program and estimate the deadweight loss of the increase in spending required to fund the program. We have already suggested that deadweight loss may not be an appropriate perspective to take toward public goods. We need to ask, is there a 'consumer surplus' which can be applied to the demand curve for national defense? This must mean that tax-payers can calculate precisely the impact on deadweight loss of not being taxed a given amount. Deadweight losses were originally calculated in connection with items for which a demand curve could be precisely calculated. Calculating deadweight loss is derived from the consumer surplus and so is ultimately based on the individual's utility functions which determine precisely how much the individual would be willing to pay for every unit of the item in question, beginning with the first. (This is, of course, presumably captured in any consumer demand curve.) Are consumers really capable of knowing and stating precisely how much they would be willing to pay for every possible number of units, particularly for a public good or service? Imposing or canceling taxes which alter the market price of the item in question, we repeat, increases or decreases the consumer surplus and so affects the deadweight loss.

In sum, raising the price per unit of a 'normal' item will cause the consumer to buy less and get less consumer surplus but the price raiser – for example, a monopolist – does not get all that the consumer loses. He does not get the deadweight loss. Feldstein argues similarly in the case of public goods. If consumers lose consumer surplus via tax increases, it presumes that they have a demand curve for public goods – otherwise the consumer surplus cannot even be calculated. The difference is the deadweight loss. National defense is a 'public good' precisely because it is *not* possible to derive a market demand curve for national defense. (We say it is something we must have 'regardless of cost'!) Therefore, in effect, because deadweight loss is dependent upon an accurate assessment of consumer surplus, deadweight loss has little meaning for public goods.

Deadweight loss is a useful abstraction to point to the waste produced by monopoly. It is far more difficult to apply to the factors that need to be included in assessing the benefit from government spending financed via tax revenue versus attempting to achieve the same good thorough the private sector. In the public sector, instead of the monopolist gaining, we have 'all of us' gaining from, for example, more national defense. This is what Feldstein attempts and, of course, his effort involves all the assumptions involved in constructing a demand curve, calculating consumer surplus, and setting the size of the deadweight loss. (Feldstein says it is 'a trapezoid, not a triangle,' but either way it is based on a number of assumptions, quite a few of which are arbitrary and/or unrealistic.) Professor Feldstein professes to be able to measure these differences in deadweight loss sufficiently precisely to conclude that, 'Past experience suggests that financing additional government spending by across-the-board tax rate changes would involve a total cost of more than two dollars for every additional dollar of government spending' (Feldstein 1996, p. 27).

In other words the pain of raising the tax revenue for spending is double the increased benefits that the government can create with the proceeds! At least this is Feldstein's contention. He does grant that more research is necessary. There are clearly a number of hidden assumptions which must have preceded this conclusion. What he still doesn't tell us, of course, is what losses in utility were involved in the two. Feldstein is a known and self-acknowledged conservative and, in light of our discussion in Chapter 2, it is not surprising that his two dollar to one dollar conclusion tilts toward smaller government. (He is getting the theory he wants.)

Be that as it may, at the end of the day one basic conclusion that Feldstein reaches which seems unassailable is that in determining the appropriate size of government we face the question of what is the appropriate size of taxes. 'Although economics alone cannot provide an answer to that question, economists can help politicians and the public to analyze the question in the right way and can provide estimates of key parameter values that they need to reach informed decisions. Unfortunately, we are not doing a very good job of that important task' (Feldstein 1996, p. 1). Feldstein's assertion is a major theme of this book.

In effect we have suggested that the assumptions Feldstein has implicitly accepted are rather formidable in themselves. The assumptions that behavioral economists question, considered in Chapter 3, are even larger. Econometrics may make quantitative manipulations easier; it does not improve the accuracy or realism of the results. In its current state economists approach virtually all questions through econometric models. It seems doubtful that psychologists would use 'psychometrics' to calculate the personality disadvantage of a bad temper against the advantage of a love of dogs and small children in deciding about the prospective attractiveness of a potential wife or husband. (In our earlier discussion of Jane Smith's problems, would any emulation of econometric modeling have helped her?)

In the end we must still ask, 'How helpful has Feldstein been to policy makers?' We would argue that in devising his answer to this question,

Feldstein illustrates the difficulty in formulating economic theory as currently construed in a way in which it can be useful as well as internally logical.

Compare Feldstein's approach to assessing the public sector with the view of Richard Musgrave, articulated more than 40 years ago:

> Intelligent conduct of government requires an understanding of the economic relations involved; and the economist, by aiding in this understanding, may hope to contribute to a better society. This is why the field of . . . public finance has seemed of particular interest to me; and this is why my interest in the field has been motivated by a search for the good society . . . The form of this good society involves value judgement, and value judgement may enter into the issues that the economist chooses to examine. (Musgrave 1959, pp. v–vi)

To grant the importance of value judgements is to grant that economic analysis in the service of a better society is a normative undertaking. (It may be quantitatively imprecise.) There is in Musgrave explicitly an ideological perspective from which he begins. If I have read Musgrave correctly he surely has a place for positive analysis, but only after economic analysis has been ideologically moored.

Arguably, value judgements may enter consideration of the size of the public sector as importantly or more importantly than considerations of the changing size of deadweight loss. The latter is seemingly more precise but may in fact be a more palpable will-o-the-whisp in empirical analysis than the direct confrontation of value judgement with which Musgrave begins his consideration of the role of the public sector.

Finally, in sharp contrast to the presumed precision in calculation of gains and losses as in the approach of Feldstein, we may consider the approach of (for example) John F. Walker and Harold G. Vatter, who viewed the public sector much as did Musgrave. Consider, to begin with, the difference suggested by the quotation below. It should be compared with Feldstein's careful suggestion that it is possible to calculate with some precision the deadweight loss entailed in raising taxes to pay for new governmental spending.

> Public managerial and even entrepreneurial functions can be expanded with but little addition to government outlays or employment. The important aspect is the enlargement of direction, control, regulation, resource allocation, and supervised privatization. These activities are almost impossible to measure. (Walker and Vatter 1997, p. 241)

In more specific terms Walker and Vatter argue that big government will continue to grow, not only in the United States but in market economies generally for several reasons. They write:

1. Market participants . . . feel continually impelled to involve government to intervene on their behalf, even as they rail against the costs or potential dangers of public support for other such intervention. (1997, p. 238)

This is, of course, essentially the 'too big to fail' approach we examined earlier.

2. . . . the growth of technologically advanced market economies bring with them two developments . . .

   The first is the increase in socioeconomic requirements of an ever larger and more diversified market economy. The second development is the increasing amount of damage to both the physical environment and the well-being of the human population that accompanies modern economic development. (1997, pp. 238–9)

In connection with the first point the authors have in mind expenditures for things like education, water, electricity, highways, etc. In connection with the second they note that overcoming environmental damage is almost invariably a matter requiring public expenditures.

3. A third cause of governmental growth is what they call an increase in 'administrative management . . . the proliferation of interest-group pressures accompanying socioeconomic development ensures the continued proliferation of public managerial activity' (1997, p. 241).
4. Finally, a fourth reason for governmental growth is the requirements of defense (particularly in an era of super power global involvement of the US), and education.

Clearly political scientists have not contributed any cost as precise as 'deadweight loss' but we may nonetheless ask whether or not they have framed the larger question in a useful, not to say meaningful way.

'Public Choice'?

By now the reader will have observed that these avenues for downgrading the impact of the public sector have become successively broader. From the relatively narrow concerns of the Ricardian Equivalence Theorem we come now to a possible route to reducing the impact of the public sector which is based fundamentally in the way one approaches the task of economics as a discipline. The leading figure to be examined, already introduced earlier in the chapter, is James Buchanan. Despite winning a Nobel Prize he, nevertheless, is an economist who has been described as an outsider as much as an insider in the discipline during his lifetime (Boettke 1998, pp. 21–4). Even many of those who regard the field of economics as excessively narrow currently would, from that viewpoint, regard Buchanan as a dissenter. As one economist has put it:

> A dissenter in economics is . . . one who resists the dominant economic religion. They can do this by (1) eschewing mathematical modeling and econometric testing, and thus the basic *language* and *toolkit* of contemporary scientific economics; (2) articulating a philosophical case against modern economics; and (3) rejecting the professional strictures against normative theorizing and see policy relevance as a virtue. Any one of these positions would constitute a dissent from the current orthodoxy; holding all three is surely grounds for expulsion. It is all three, however, which characterize the work of James Buchanan. (Boettke 1998, pp. 23–4)

It does not take a careful reading of what has come here before to realize that the three positions noted would constitute a reasonably accurate summary of the essential position taken in this book. Having said that, the essential public choice position is, nonetheless, in many ways antithetical to the view taken here. It is the particular attitude of the movement called public choice toward government which is the sticking point. Its basic premise is that one cannot distinguish between the motivation of the public servant and that of the businessman. The businessman is typically regarded as one who might on occasion sacrifice his own interest for the good of society, but in general pursues his own self-interest. For Buchannan et al., the political servant is regarded as constituted in exactly the same way. As Gordon Tullock has put it, '. . . by using a model in which voters, politicians, and bureaucrats are assumed to be mainly self-interested it became possible to employ tools of analysis that are derived from economic methodology' (Tullock 1977). In essence, then, public choice views the public sector with greater doubt and suspicion than any group whose views we have thus far considered. Why? Because public choice adherents view bureaucrats as narrow and self-serving, perhaps more so than those who serve anywhere else in the economy. As one public choice enthusiast put it,

> Men and women elected as politicians or appointed as 'public' officials are not

> transformed into public benefactors. They have access to vastly more resources but, compared with people in the market, they are more likely to use them ill rather than well since they largely lack the guidance of pricing, they can avoid retribution for their harmful decisions, they are using other people's money, and they are inherently unaccountable for their errors because costs of their decisions are usually distant and incalculable. (Seldon 1991, pp. ix–x)

Not surprisingly public choice advocates are most particularly infuriated by Keynesians of any stripe – the most explicitly interventionist group of all economists. Buchanan wrote a book on Keynesians, *Democracy in Deficit*, and later wrote of this book:

> The book was an attempt to examine the political consequences of Mr. Keynes, and the central theme was to the effect that an important element of the American fiscal constitution, namely the balanced budget rule, had been destroyed by the political acceptance of Keynesianism. Economists blindly ignored the asymmetry in application of Keynesian policy precepts, an asymmetry that the most elementary public-choice theorist would have spotted. They naively presumed that politicians would create budget surpluses as willingly as they create deficits. They forgot the elementary rule that politicians enjoy spending and do not like to tax. (Buchanan 1991, p. 42)

We saw in Chapter 1 that Adam Smith, at least in the eyes of mainstream economists, had the invisible hand to protect society – therefore the economy – from the narrow vision and self-centeredness of its individual inhabitants. He seldom, it may be recalled, spoke of the 'guidance of pricing.' In less than competitive markets this may indeed be a slender reed. It points toward the heart of the welfare problems involved in reliance on the unfettered market. Buchanan and his fellow advocates of public choice theory we see have neither invisible hand nor any alternative to protect the economy from the impact of self-centeredness and greed in bureaucrats or indeed from any other participant in the economic process.

What appears to be an even-handed perspective attributing similar motivations to businessman and bureaucrats is actually a severe tilt against the public sector as a factor in economic life. Buchanan does not hide this: he has written,

> One direction for constructive reform seems clear. Much of the moral rot that we observe, in both private and public behavior, is traceable to the exaggerated size of the public sector relative to the total economy. If this sector could be reduced to a proportionate share roughly equivalent to that which described the state at

> mid century, much good would be done. We must acknowledge that the bloated welfare-transfer state that we now live with was allowed to grow in the shadow of the Cold War over the half-century and without attention to its own diseconomies. (Buchanan and Musgrave 1999, p. 217)

What shall we make of this? It surely confirms the previous characterization of Buchanan as passionate about a normative evaluation of the economy rather than the conventional economist's congenital devotion to relentlessly positive assessments of the modern economy. That said, his description of the public sector as 'bloated' needs to be considered against the information with which this chapter began. The public sector at the end of World War II was just under 20 per cent of GDP and had grown to 29 per cent in 1999. In both years Japan was the only major economy with a smaller public sector (see Table 6.1 above). Are we to conclude, therefore, with Buchanan that a sober assessment is that virtually every industrial market economy in the world is characterized by a public sector of 'exaggerated size'? If virtually *all* market economies have 'bloated' public sectors the appropriate judgmental standard must remain within Buchanan and, so far as is known, he has not shared with any country the judgmental equipment with which to determine when the public sector is of 'correct size.'

So how does Buchanan view the role of economic theory? Some years ago he answered this question by writing:

> Economic theory offers an explanation of the relationships between the interactive behavior of persons and patterns of social outcomes on the presupposition that individual action is motivated by economically meaningful and conceptually measurable self-interest . . .
>
> I suggest that [the] woeful record of economists' performance stems from a set of scientific errors that must be put right before economic theory can begin to exert a productive influence on the hard problems of transition from socialism to alternative structures. (Buchanan 1994, pp. 47–8)

For Buchanan the triumph of the market lies in the collapse of socialism in previously planned economies. The 'woeful record of economists' lies in their failure to predict 'socialism's death.' For Buchanan 'economic policy,' therefore, ought to consist (only) in freeing the market of any restraints.

He rejects utterly the idea of the public sector as a necessary adjunct to the market. He therefore rejects the implicit view taken here that at bottom the role of economic theory involves acting as a guide for monitoring policy in carrying out that part of total resource deployment that cannot be done by the market. One presumes Buchanan would join in granting that the market cannot produce national defense. How far he would go beyond that in confronting public goods as distinctive because they are as we have noted 'non-rivalrous' and 'non-excludable' is, as was just suggested, not clear in what Buchanan has written. His central thrust, we reiterate, is on the inability of bureaucrats to concentrate on the public interest and to ignore self-interest.

That Buchanan's position is colored by ideology more than by fact – statistical or otherwise – is supported by contrasting his position with that of Richard Musgrave (whose overall position has been previously suggested):

> Confronted with what Professor Buchanan considers to be the collapse of moral society, he finds that 'much of the rot is to be attributed to the rise of the public sector;' and, based on that diagnosis, his cure is to cut it back. I find both diagnosis and cure unconvincing.
>
> His vision of moral collapse (including not only the United States but the whole Western world!) is overly pessimistic, as suggested before, and his assessment of public sector growth as the causal factor is surely overdrawn. Just what damage is it that we are asked to consider? Is it that availability of a social safety net has weakened work effort, that social insurance has reduced saving, and that taxation has depressed work incentives? While there is a bit of truth in each of these, the effects have been spotty and need to be balanced against the gains to civilized and productive living that the public sector has rendered, including improved education and health. (Buchanan and Musgrave 1999, p. 230)

In contrast to the Buchanan vision, Musgrave describes his own position as follows: 'One of my themes has been that the market, efficient and helpful as it is, does not by itself constitute a moral order. The vision of a moral order, based on self-interest only, is incongruous. The very concept of a moral and good society involves individuals in their relation to others, and that relation to be moral cannot be based only on self-interest or expediency. Respect for others is basic but self-interest, while useful in its place, is not enough' (Buchanan and Musgrave 1999, p. 233).

Between the two they stake out the differences clearly. At the end of the day interventionists leave it to the public sector to referee and monitor the results of what the self-interest-motivated private sector accomplishes. Just as Freud included a super-ego along with his ego and id, Musgrave would insist that the economist must have a public sector in applying his discipline to the task of organizing the deployment of resources in pursuit of the diversity of objectives we currently wish to further. He must recognize that in the absence of the invisible hand in at least moderately concentrated modern industries and in the face of enormous power differences in the modern world as they impinge on macroeconomic activity, 'leaving it to the market' – marvelously efficient and sensitive as that institution is in very much of the processing of resources in the modern world – it is simply not enough.

In 2002 we had ample examples in the United States of the truth of the assertion that self-interest is not enough. If self-interest can organize and channel much economic activity in efficient and productive directions, the Enron, Arthur Andersen, World Com, Mitsubishi, Merrill Lynch, etc. scandals which convulsed the business world in 2002 showed acutely that when even the most self-interested businessmen conduct their activities without retaining a measure of concern for the public interest and their obligations to it, the market system cannot work satisfactorily. This was the raison d'etre for the Sherman Anti-Trust Act, passed by our Congress more than one hundred years ago. One wonders whether these evidences of greed and self-interest in the private sector might cause those who express the public choice perspective most baldly to reconsider. Consider this view, for example: 'No one spends someone else's money as wisely as he spends his own. A key reason the market system works: When people spend their own money, they care much more deeply about its efficient and productive use than any politicians who seek to tax it away and spend it themselves' (Armey 1995, p. 316). Unhappily, this cannot be passed off as the ignorant view of a politician appealing to a backward constituency, someone we might have expected the professional economists to straighten out. The author of this statement is himself a trained economist. It was one more voice adding to the 'we-they' attitude towards government in developing economic policy. As such it exemplifies the demonization of the public sector previously mentioned. Those who take this view make an exception only for national defense where suddenly and rarely the 'public spenders' are transformed for the moment into prudent super-patriots.

The difference between Musgrave and Buchanan is, of course, the difference between public choice economists and what we have called interventionists. The most explicit interventionists would be Keynesians who might counter Buchanan et al. by arguing roughly as follows. The modern economy has no natural tendency to adjust to any particular level of income, output, and employment. Expectations (and uncertainty) play a large role in determining the investment decisions of entrepreneurs. We have learned enough about the operation of the modern-market oriented economy in the past 60 years so that judicious use of monetary and fiscal policy to stabilize the economy and encourage growth can improve on the performance we would otherwise get. Market-determined prices can do very much to deploy resources to their best use but they cannot be relied upon to do so completely, and market results need always to be societally monitored.

Therefore, judicious deployment of some resources though the public sector can provide necessary public goods as well as supplement and channel the activity of the private sector so as to optimize the overall use of resources in the directions which democratic societies choose. This would seem a reasonable and prudent perspective from which to operate.

More generally, interventionists do not despair that human nature is so fatally flawed that a responsible and useful public sector cannot be included as an integral part of the economic system with which we deploy resources. Public malfeasance by some bureaucrat need not signify the hopelessness of operating a responsible efficient public sector any more than the business scandals of 2002, alluded to above, mean that self-interest run amok dooms the market to hopeless failure. There is no reason to assume, therefore, that finding bureaucrats to function responsibly and effectively in the public sector is a hopelessly doomed enterprise. Were that the case, we should also have to tell our fellow social scientists that they should all forget about ever successfully producing a functioning political democracy – the self-interest and greed of congressmen, judges, and the people in the executive branch will invariably conspire every time to sell the public interest down the river. Sociologists and psychologists would presumably have equally grim reports.

Buchanan, we hold, gets himself in a very unfortunate cul de sac by arguing that public servants are invariably and fatally affected by self-interest and greed, just like businessmen. He really can't stop there. He is presumably asserting a fatal flaw in human character. He concludes that, therefore, the assumptions and conclusions of conventional economics will come into their own. But he forgets that in economics the results of the operation of the market are tolerable only because of the assumptions under which conventional economics assumes the market operates – including most particularly the assumption of an invisible hand which converts personal greed into optimal societal behavior. Without that 'moral thermostat' (as we have seen in Chapter 1) the market is no more reliable than a water tank without a thermostat – it will freeze or boil depending on the exogenous environment.

The attractiveness of the conventional model to public choice devotees seems clear. But they are not unanimous in their view of the ideal economy. Specifically, the public choice literature is voluminous but diverse in its view of the dependency of a viable economic structure on competition. On the one hand, one can read in a discussion on 'Public Choice and the Politics of Government Failure' that '. . . for the market process to work effectively does not require the "perfect competition" depicted in neo-classical text-books' (Pennington 2000, p. 9). On the other hand, for example, in a discussion of 'The Politics of Public Choice,' one can read '. . . the economic model used by mainstream public choice is the neoclassical one of perfectly competitive markets' (Self 1993, p. 3). How it might operate in the absence of perfect competition is not clear. Most particularly what *compels* behavior in the public interest in the absence of the invisible hand is not clear. In this connection, recall our previous discussion of the rebuttable presumption against bigness in Chapter 4.

Public choice economists, like many non-interventionists, are fond of commending the work of Anthony Downs to economists (Downs 1957). Downs, a political scientist, advocated taking the economist's methodology and applying it to political science questions, especially to how government decisions get made in the public sector (approach your problem by simplifying it by making the necessary assumptions, so that questions from the real world are confronted only indirectly by asking how they might be answered in a simple ideal world). It has always seemed to me that the reverse might be equally or even more promising; take the political science approach and apply it to economic problems (ask important questions directly and marshal evidence with which to confront the real economy 'warts and all').

The public choice view of human nature makes the participants in the economy so flawed that no viable economy can emerge at their hands in either the public sector or the private sector. As Musgrave points out, there is no credible reason why the private sector should be regarded as uniquely capable of bringing out the best work in human beings. In Buchanan's world there is nothing left to check human greed and deceit except (presumably) the invisible hand. This in fact has been the role assigned to the invisible hand by the entire tradition of classical thought including Hume, Malthus, Knight, and Hayek. The invisible hand never was assumed to operate anywhere but in the market and practically from the beginning, as we have seen, severe doubts were cast on its ability to operate even there. In the end there is nothing left to guarantee that the equilibria which emerge in markets will be consonant with the Panglossian ideal any more than is true of whatever emerges in the public sector.

CONCLUSIONS

What is the role of the public sector? In this chapter we have asserted a number of propositions which, we have argued, bear on that question:

1. Efficiency is not the monopoly of either the public or the private sector.
2. The moral character of participants in economic activity can break down

in either sector because neither sector can claim exclusive dominion of mechanisms guaranteed to compel morality or honest behavior from those who participate in the economy. One often hears about 'the discipline of the market.' If dishonest or dishonorable behavior can arise in the process of operating in the public sector, the US corporate scandals of 2002, whatever else they may have done, should have served to remind all that there are no market pressures whatsoever that can invariably be relied upon to protect us from dishonesty and dishonor. The 'discipline of the market,' like 'the obligations of public trust' is, alas, a fallible guarantee that participation in economic activity will be honest and principled.

3. It may well be that one hears more in the United States than elsewhere about the 'unbearable burden of big government on the backs of the people.' But the truth of the matter is that by most measures the public sector in general, and the federal government most particularly, is smaller in the United States, relative – among other measures – to GDP, than in virtually all industrial market economies, with the exception of Japan.
4. Consideration of the public sector brings out with special vividness the character of the 'we-they' distinction which, unhappily, some economists are willing to join in, instead of contributing to the factually correct assertion that in a political democracy all economic activity can be monitored by a public sector that represents ideally all the people – that is, there is no 'they' – only a 'we' participating in economic activity from different perspectives.
5. All this contributes to the conviction that contemplation of the public sector is more wrapped up in ideology than virtually any other debate in contemporary economics.
6. As we have seen in both microeconomics and macroeconomics modern mainstream economists have been adept at developing avenues down which public sector intervention can be trivialized. That is, the literature is replete with ways one can conclude that public intervention in economic activity is either futile or pernicious or both. Such improvisations would include the Ricardian Equivalence Theorem; the crowding out argument; the 'burden' of the public debt assertion; applying cost-benefit-type reasoning to the assessment of public sector activity (complete with assessments of the increased burden of taxes versus reduced consumer surplus (deadweight loss); and 'public choice economics' which can occasionally appear as a rational investigation of the area of economics concerned with non-market choice, but is in fact the branch of economics customarily dedicated to tell us that if we contemplate the 'economics of politics' we will be rewarded with the reminder that politics is dirty business. (Thus, Buchanan writes of

Keynesian theory that 'they forgot the elementary rule that politicians prefer spending and do not like to tax' (Buchanan 1991, p. 42.) One could as well say that households like to consume but don't like to save, that firms like to make profits but don't much care how, etc.

In sum, and not surprisingly, many of the themes we have heretofore developed in this book come home to roost when we contemplate the public sector and the different views which contemporary economists take toward it. The fundamental task of economic theory, we argue, is to offer guidance to the policy makers in both sectors. Most especially, continuous guidance is needed in determining what can best (including most efficiently) be done in the private sector and what in the public sector. In this manner (and only in this manner!) can economic theory make its optimal contribution to the overall and never ending deploying of resources, in light of prevailing values and the constantly changing state of prevailing technology, so as to further societal objectives at any time in what – for that time – is judged an optimal manner.

REFERENCES

Abel, Andrew B. (1987), 'Ricardian Equivalence Theorem', in John Eatwell, Murray Milgate and Peter Newman (eds), *The New Palgrave, A Dictionary of Economics*, London: Macmillan, pp. 174–8.

Armey, Dick (1995), *The Freedom Revolution, Vol. 4*, Washington, DC: Regnery Publishing Company.

Barro, Robert J. (1973), 'Are government bonds new wealth?' *Journal of Political Economy*, **82** (6), p. 1095, pp. 1116–7.

Barro, Robert J. (1997), *Macroeconomics, Fifth Edition*, Cambridge, MA: MIT Press.

Black, John H. (1997), *A Dictionary of Economics*, Oxford: Oxford University Press.

Blanchard, Olivier (1987), 'Crowding Out', in John Eatwell, Murray Milgate and Peter Newman (eds), *The New Palgrave, A Dictionary of Economics, Vol.1*, London: Macmillan, p. 728.

Boettke, Peter J. (1998), 'James M. Buchanan and the rebirth of political economy', in Richard P.F. Holt and Steven Pressman (eds), *Economics and its Discontents*, Cheltenham, UK and Lyme, USA: Edward Elgar.

Buchanan, James M. (1986), 'Barro on the Ricardian equivalence theorem', *Journal of Political Economy*, **84** (2), 337–42.

Buchanan, James M. (1987), 'Public Receipts of Public Debt', in John Eatwell, Murray Milgate and Peter Newman (eds), *The New Palgrave, A Dictionary of Economics, Vol. 3*, London: Macmillan, p. 1045.

Buchanan, James M. (1991), 'From private preferences to public philosophy: the development of public choice', in James M. Buchanan (ed.), *Constitutional Economics*, Oxford: Basil Blackwell.

Buchanan, James M. (1994), 'Economic theory in the post revolutionary moment of the 1990s', in Philip A. Klein (ed.), *The Role of Economic Theory*, Boston, MA: Kluwer Academic Publishers.

Buchanan, James M. and Richard Musgrave (1999), 'Morals, politics, and institutional reforms: diagnosis and prescription', in James M. Buchanan and Richard A. Musgrave (eds), *Public Finance and Public Choice: Two Countries, Visions of the State*, Cambridge, MA: MIT.

Butlin, N.G. (1984), *Select Comparative Economic Statistics 1900–1940: Australia and Britain, Canada, Japan, New Zealand and USA,* Canberra: Australian National University.

Downs, Anthony (1957), *An Economic Theory of Democracy*, New York: Harper and Row.

Economic Report of the President (1982), Washington, DC: US Government Printing Office.

Economic Report of the President (2002), Washington, DC: US Government Printing Office.

Eisenhower, Dwight D. (1960), *Public Papers of the Presidents*, Washington, DC: Government Printing Office, p. 763

Eisenhower, Dwight D. (1963), ' Spending into trouble', *Saturday Evening Post*, vol. 236, # 19, May 18, 15–19.

Farmer, Roger E.A. (2002), *Macroeconomics, Second Edition,* Cincinnati, OH: South-Western.

Feldstein, Martin (1996), *How Big Should Government Be?* NBER, Working Paper Series, Working Paper 5868. Cambridge, MA: National Bureau of Economic Research.

Fernandez Acha, Valentin (1976), *Datos basicos para la historia financiera de Espana* (1950–1975), Madrid: Ministerio de Hacienda, Instituto de Estudios Fiscales.

Flora, Peter, Franz Kraus and Winfried Pfennig (1983 and 1987), *State, Economy and Society in Western Europe, 1815–1975*, *Vol. I*, 1983, *Vol. II*, 1987, Chicago: St. James Press.

Friedman, Milton (1962), *Capitalism and Freedom*, Chicago: University of Chicago Press.

Geanakoplos, John (1987), 'Overlapping generations model of general equilibrium', in John Eatwell, Murray Milgate and Peter Newman (eds), *The New Palgrave, A Dictionary of Economics, Vol. 3*, London: Macmillan, p. 767.

Geanakaplos, John (1987), 'Arrow-Debreu model of general equilbrium', in John Eatwell, Murray Milgate and Peter Newman (eds), *The New Palgrave, A Dictionary of Economics,* London: Macmillan, p. 116.

Gordon, Robert J. (2000), *Macroeconomics*, *Eighth Edition*, New York: Addison-Wesley.

Kahn, Jonathan (1997), *Budgeting Democracy*, *State Building and Citizenship in America*, *1890–1928*, Ithaca, NY: Cornell University Press.

Keynes, John Maynard (1936), *General Theory of Employment, Interest, and Money,* New York: Harcourt, Brace and Company.

Koven, Steven G. (1988), *Ideological Budgeting, The Influence of Political Philosophy on Public Policy*. New York: Praeger.

Mankiw, N. Gregory (2004), *Principles of Economics, Third Edition*, New York: Dryden Press.

Mitchell, B.R. (1998), *International Historical Statistics: Africa, Asia and Oceania, 1750–1988*, Second revised edition, New York: Stockton Press.

Musgrave, Richard A. (1959), *A Theory of Public Finance*, New York; McGraw-Hill.

Neck, Reinhard and Friedrich Schneider (1988), 'The growth of the public sector in Austria: an exploratory analysis', in J.A. Lybeck and M. Henrekson (eds), *Explaining the Growth of Government*, Amsterdam: North-Holland.

Pennington, Mark (2000), *Planning and the Political Market*, London: Athlone Press.

Pigou, A.D. (1928), *Public Finance*, London: Macmillan.

Public Papers of the Presidents, *Ronald Reagan* (1982), 'Message to the Congress Transmitting the Proposed Package on the Program for Economic Recovery', Washington, DC: Government Printing Office, p. 121. Actual outlay percentages are from *Economic Report of the President* (2002), p. 414.

Public Papers of the Presidents, *Ronald Reagan, 1988–1989* (1991), *Vol. II.*, Washington, DC, Government Printing Office, p. 1077.

Romer, David (1996), *Advanced Macroeconomics*, New York: McGraw-Hill.

Samuelson, Paul A. (1948), *Economics,* New York: McGraw-Hill.

Samuelson, Paul A. (1958), 'An exact consumption-loan model of interest with or without the social contrivance of money', *Journal of Political Economy*, **LVXI** (6).

Samuelson, Paul A. and William Nordhaus (2001), *Economics*, *Seventeenth Edition*, New York: McGraw-Hill.

Seldon, Arthur (1991), 'Introduction', in James M. Buchanan (ed.) *Constitutional Economics*, Oxford: Basil Blackwell, pp. ix–x.

Self, Peter (1993), *Government by the Market?* Boulder, CO: Westview Press.

Stiglitz, Joseph E. (1988), *Economics of the Public Sector*, *Second Edition*, New York: W.W. Norton & Company.

Tanzi, Vito and Ludger Schuknecht (2000), *Public Spending in the 20th Century*, Cambridge: Cambridge University Press.

Tullock, Gordon (1977), 'Public Choice', in John Eatwell, Murray Milgate and Peter Newman (eds), *The New Palgrave, A Dictionary of Economics*, London: Macmillan, p. 1041.

Walker, John F. and Harold G. Vatter (1997), *The Rise of Big Government in the United States*, Armonk, NY: M.E. Sharpe.

7. Focus on 'mainstream economics': obstacles to the competition for new ideas

The market metaphor implies competition in ideas, and mainstream economists – insofar as they consider the matter at all – tend to assume that the spread of ideas works rather well, according to an invisible hand species of argument. So long as there is perfect or effective competition, all will be well: true or sound ideas will tend to prevail over ignorance, error, and vested interest. Would that this were so! But unfortunately, in the market for ideas perfect competition is no more likely there than elsewhere. (Coats and Colander 1989, p. 13)

The relative impact of economics journals focused on mathematics and statistics increased markedly between 1970 and 1990. In this regard our behavior as academic researchers stands in stark contrast to the fact that faculty, current graduate students, and recent graduates all decry the emphasis on mathematics in the graduate economics curriculum of the late 1980s. (Hansen 1991, pp. 1054–87)

We cannot help but wonder whether the strong market showing (popularity) of the *Journal of Economic Perspectives*, with its emphasis on presentation of arguments and findings in essay form, reflects a widespread reaction within the profession to the mathematical/statistical emphasis of the 1970s and 1980s. If so, we should expect some fraction of new entrants as well as current editors, in the 1990s, to follow the *JEP*'s example with respect to style. (Laband and Piette 1994, pp. 640–66, 657–8)

The fact that graduate education in economics emphasizes technical puzzle-solving abilities at the expense of imparting substantial knowledge of the economic system is simply a reflection of the empty formalism that has come increasingly to characterize the whole of modern economics. (Blaug 1992, p xxii)

NOTHING SUCCEEDS LIKE SUCCESS: GUARANTEEING THAT PROPHESIES WILL BE SELF-FULFILLING

This chapter is devoted to examining the structure and functioning of 'the economics business' in the United States.[1] The guts of any business presumably consists in determining what to produce, how to produce it, how to package it, how to distribute it, and how to judge its success. This last question, one could assume, involves asking how successful the product is in accomplishing what it was designed to do. A goal of this chapter is to add specificity to the questions, 'What is mainstream economics?' 'Who produces it?'

Having surveyed (we hope critically but fairly) the state of economics in several crucial areas, we come now to confronting the questions just posed. Answering them necessarily involves examining the various facets of the economics education process (we focus primarily on graduate education); assessing the teaching of the young including what the objectives are; and evaluating the role of publishing ongoing research. This will involve examining the results of the publication process in both instructing the young and judging the teachers of the young as they confront the ladder of academic success. We have touched on this earlier and briefly in Chapter 3 in considering what areas of economics are and are not stressed in mainstream graduate education.

More generally, one could perhaps take the 'economist qua economist's' view – that economics education is a major industry involving the use of enormous resources. How does it run and with what consequences? Can it survive cost-benefit analysis? Even if it can, are there ways that it could be amended or revised so as to be even more useful in smoothing, understanding, and enriching human life?

THE PRODUCTION OF ECONOMIC THEORISTS

American graduate programs in economics are flourishing. They do not lack for students (true, many are not American); they attract many of the brightest and most promising students entering postgraduate work; they have prestigious faculties including Nobel prize winning professors. Faculty in no other social science are awarded Nobel prizes! They produce a long list of

---

1. Because there is considerable respect among American economists for the Royal Economic Society and the *Economic Journal*, which it publishes, there are some references to these manifestations of the British economics business.

economics journals, many of which are considered highly prestigious – among the best produced by social scientists. Economics faculty receive impressive grants for research. They consult widely in Washington and in state capitals and in the inner circles of American business and high finance. There is a Council of Economic Advisors to the President! Political scientists and sociologists and psychologists and anthropologists and historians can only look on with envy! Presidents are forced onto their own resources to glean what useful insights they can acquire from our sister fields. Advice from economists is mandated by federal law! Economists have never blushed at their discipline being referred to as the Queen of the Social Sciences. Why should this be so?

As a first approximation, we can begin with the simple assertion that combining resources with technology to produce goods and services is surely one of the preeminent and essential activities of human beings, critical to human survival on this earth. But we can go further. The field of economics exists because the economies of the world encounter difficulties and obstacles to their efficient and productive operation. Some of these can be laid at the feet of nature – but some must be laid at the feet of the human beings on whose behalf economic activity is carried out! The field, therefore, exists to expose and analyze the problems and to develop techniques for coping with them successfully. Successful coping, one might assume, involves eliminating the problems or over-coming the obstacles. Were this actually what the field is all about it might well look quite different than it really does. In point of fact, modern economists wrestle with an enormous conflict which goes to the very 'core' that the core courses presumably confront. There are those who think the problems mostly take care of themselves (if 'left to the market') and there are those who think we can and should do what we can to confront them and eliminate their impact on the operation of the economy.

In previous chapters we have been at pains to make the case that there is now a severe disjunction between basic or core economic theory and the world of applied economics. As a crude generalization we can surely say that economic theory is (or was originally) designed to offer a base for applied economics. In other social sciences there is a fairly straightforward line from theory to applied work to modifications of public policy.

One way of identifying the basic conflict is only slightly exaggerated when it is characterized by saying it is between those who attempt to make the case for intervention as clear, effective, and simple as possible and those who would like to explain why doing nothing is best. The latter – mainstream economists – all too often, perhaps implicitly but all too vigorously, end up saying said explanation should be as complicated as possible so that only highly trained economists will understand it. This effectively requires that conventional economic theorists say to the public, 'Doing nothing is best, but you will have to take our word for it.'

How theory evolves, it is fair to say, is typically determined initially in academia where the graduate theory courses are designed and implemented by curriculum committees. So it is natural, I suppose, to ask, 'What do our graduate programs in economics in American universities see as their chief objective? What is proposed? Who is benefitted?'

In this chapter, then, we explore the signals and substance of two diverse instrumentalities involved in the contemplation of the inherited knowledge base we call 'economics.' These instrumentalities are (1) graduate programs in economics, (2) research and publication in journals. We will urge modifications of teaching to make an instrumentality as useful as possible in confronting continuing problems in the economies of the modern world. First the graduate programs are charged with absorbing the discipline as we receive it and refashioning it in light of modern insights so as to confront the substance and significance of the current economic scene. So we need to ask, what are the objectives of a modern program of study in the field of economics?

Second, and closely related to the graduate teaching program, of course, is the written record of current research efforts. This involves the world of journals devoted to economics. Reflecting that record is one of their functions. But the other function is to provide the crucial publication record without which young economists do not get tenured or promoted. Without publications in academia, as we like to say, you perish. In the profession one hears mention of the top three or the top ten or the top twenty-five, or the top one hundred journals. What are the standards which lie behind these 'consensus rankings'? Presumably the judgments of the profession are related somehow to the perceived judgements of the journals themselves. How do the journals set standards? What influences the journals? What are their objectives and how are they determined? How do they judge their impact on the academic world and on the 'real' world? Are the same influences at work on both? This, of course, is where one faces a question which has been raised periodically in the preceding pages – what kind of assistance are the theorists in academia providing to the policy makers? Who cares? Presumably in some sense the public, but do the journals care, and if so, which ones?

What influences the journals is not unrelated to how the graduate programs get set. The theorists are doing the work which provides the major grist for the graduate economic theory sequences which in turn form the core of graduate programs in the discipline. We examined these programs earlier.

One of the thought provoking aspects of this line of questioning is that many of the core graduate courses are currently taught in our most prestigious universities by new assistant professors who, of course, teach what they have just learned in their own PhD programs. This means that in the absence of assiduous efforts to avoid it, these programs can become avenues for passing along highly abstruse bodies of thinking, often unrelated (or only distantly related) to the world of policy, and having as their major justification that they interest the people who are contributing to the various lines of thought involved.

There is nothing wrong with some of this. 'Basic research' including speculative research can enrich insights and encourage genuine maturation in the approaches to many aspects of any discipline including economics. We would assert that, ideally, young scholars including young economists ought to be encouraged to study any aspect of their field that interests them and methodologically they should be encouraged to explore widely and deeply. Economics is not different from other fields in that both areas of study and techniques of study tend to come and go. There is a faddish aspect to academic research. The previous chapters have suggested some of this. But one can scarcely label quantification as the principal avenue of research in economic inquiry a fad – it has lasted too long and by now has swept virtually the entire field, as we were at pains to lay out in Chapter 3. Moreover, it shows no signs of abating. More significantly, in economics there has developed a tendency to treat these waves of interest in areas and methodologies as if they were engraved in stone and were mandated for all those who toil in the discipline, most especially the aspiring young. We have seen earlier what has happened to economic history. It would be difficult to avoid trying to dissuade an aspiring young graduate student from pursuing some corner of the history of economic thought for a PhD. Faddish lines of work come to dominate what is thought about and what is taught. It is not unfair to say that all too often economists care how students think about what problems they choose to investigate (and the how goes well beyond paying attention to the scientific method). But economics is not a religion and what our theorists teach cannot be regarded in the same light as what practitioners of various religions do in their seminaries devoted to passing on the tenets of a given religion more or less intact to the next generation. (Even religions have periodic councils in which articles of faith are 'updated'!)

We need to ask whether the possibility of change to new perspectives is currently considered in graduate education in economics. And we need to ask what if anything is done to keep even part of the perspective in the graduate presentation of economic theory focused on its role as an explanatory adjunct to better policy making and on its contribution to basic analysis generally.

Accordingly we ask a number of difficult but important and inter-related questions. What is the fundamental objective in the teaching of economics, especially at the graduate level? What are 'the most prestigious' journals attempting to publish? And why are they the most prestigious journals? What do those in the profession who are widely regarded as the leaders see as the ideal relation (if any) between the theorists and what they do and the applied economists and what they do? Along the way we shall ask how the acquisition of grants to fund research enters the picture in light of the current importance being placed on obtaining such grants in part to demonstrate readiness for both tenure and promotion at major graduate schools in economics. Finally we need to consider how 'citation counts' as a measure of impact on current thinking reflect factors of relative importance of this overall evaluation process to which young economists-in-the-making are now subjected. No one can say that we have not evolved an elaborate and complicated process, complete with an equally complex set of criteria by which to judge success in becoming a newly minted economist ready for our most prestigious programs in economics. A final and complicated question – how are we to judge the judging process itself and its criteria for success?

GRADUATE EDUCATION IN ECONOMICS – THE STATED OBJECTIVES

Pick up any university catalogue and look at the announced program at the graduate level leading to the PhD in economics. It will probably tell you that it is designed to prepare the student for a career in teaching, research, or the civil service. What it probably will not tell you is what should be the objective of the research, or to what end the budding teacher should be prepared to teach. That is, what should the student expect to learn to teach? If one plans to enter the civil service what sort of preparation ideally would our young economist undertake? We need to recognize that economics is not alone here. Graduate catalogues rarely begin their description of any discipline by announcing what it is about the discipline that is important or how it fits into the overall picture of the current state of knowledge.

Still one often gets a clue or two. Thus if one reads that psychology has a field in clinical psychology or industrial psychology one can imagine that the field explores problems that children face in learning or the cognitive problems that arise in the work place. There is, of course, a specific if unstated reason for this obscurity. Among the economists recognized as being the most brilliant and the most influential, what economists ought to do and what their students ought to learn, and what, therefore they should teach, and (finally) what any of their students who should chance to end up in the civil service ought to be attempting to accomplish – all these are implicitly understood. The implicit rules here are to be gleaned from the preceding pages. The over-riding message in economics today has been confronted in Chapter 3. 'Saying it with numbers' is the bottom line. 'Mathematical economics' is a recognized field of specialization today. Other social sciences have followed suit in part in applying mathematical techniques to the study of these disciplines – but there is no such thing as a field in 'mathematical psychology,' or 'mathematical political science' etc. It is entirely possible to hear presentations in, say, advanced seminars in economics which are couched entirely in the vocabulary of mathematics – no word dealing with economic areas or problems need ever get uttered.

Beyond this generality, what can we say? Perusal of the stated objectives of the 16 graduate programs in economics considered in Table 3.1 of Chapter 3 reflects a good deal of agreement on what a rigorous exposure to economics at the graduate level ought to include. If one peruses the catalogues of the 16 universities we examined in Chapter 3, one is struck initially by the fact that very few of them have anything to say about their overall objectives. Relatively few graduate programs make any attempt at a statement of what they are about. They begin by listing required fields, or they begin by stating the prerequisites for the program that will be assumed. Sometimes they include a general statement to the effect that the program will provide training in techniques of analysis or in applications of these techniques.

Most of the time it is simply assumed that everyone knows what economics is, why it is important, and what will be the mainstream view of what the responsibility of a graduate program in economics involves.

Surely the catalogues never suggest that the role of graduate education is what some of the economists we have considered in previous chapters have charged: no one says that one should pursue advanced economics because it is 'an intellectual attraction: . . . a good game' (Hicks 1979, p. viii). Nor would one ever say that advanced degrees in economics are designed to instill in the student 'a crusading faith . . . that makes students prone . . . to fanaticism and intolerance' (McCloskey 1985, p. 4).

Often catalogues simply plunge in and begin by announcing what the first year program looks like, the second, etc. They tell the students what fields are required and what choices they have and how long they have to complete their work and what the various formalized steps along the way will be which they will be expected to complete successfully if they are to receive a degree.

In those cases when there is an attempt to formulate a verbal description of the objective of the economics program it tends to be very general. Thus the Stanford University catalogue, one of the few which pays attention explicitly to the purpose of the program in economics, asserts:

> The department's purposes are to acquaint students with the economic aspects of modern society, to familiarize them with techniques for the analysis of contemporary economic problems, and to develop in them an ability to exercise judgement in evaluating public policy. There is training for the general student as well as for those who plan careers as economists in civil service, private enterprise, teaching, or research. (Stanford University *Graduate Student Handbook* 1999, p. 344)

This statement, general though it is, looks quite promising. However, when one gets to the specifics of the program, the first thing one reads under requirements for the Doctor of Philosophy, 'Admitted students must be adequately prepared in calculus, linear algebra, and statistics' (Stanford University 1999, p. 345). It is true that there is a reference to acquiring a 'broad understanding of institutional structures' (1999, p. 345). But the point we under-score is that there is no explicit mention in these preliminaries about the necessity of understanding any economics. We need not dwell on this again; we have adequately stressed the singular obsession with math in Chapter 3.

What does one need to know in order to be well acquainted with 'the economic aspects of modern society?' Whatever these aspects may be they are not mathematical, or even necessarily quantitative (which is not to say that mathematics as a tool might not be useful in analyzing certain of these aspects). In university catalogues in general the 'economic aspects of modern society' do not seem to be spelled out very explicitly or clearly (and frequently not at all!). What might a reasonable and straightforward description of the economic aspect of modern societies look like? Our modest effort to answer this question follows.

The basic function of a modern market economy is to get resources deployed by firms, bent on maximizing their profits, or by the public sector directly, so as to enable all the participants in the economy to live as well as they can, given the current state of technology and the impact of the wider current culture on their tastes and preferences. Technology determines the range of uses of resources in this process. A whole host of public policy problems arise because the size required for firms to be efficient frequently gives them sufficient market power so that their drive to maximize profits comes into conflict with the resource deployment consumers would deem to be ideal. These problems, considered in some detail in Chapter 4, arise in varying degree and in various ways in both the manufacturing and agricultural sectors of virtually any modern economy. Such an economy must also encompass the inevitable but critical relationships which are developed among nations, as well as those which arise within the government sector. (Often the latter present themselves as problems among different levels of government.)

Beyond all this, any economy must always confront the problems raised by those who cannot or do not derive a sufficient level of income from their participation in the system to enable them to attain the societally determined minimum standard of living. Confronting the problems of those who cannot or do not survive on their own is a constant challenge to a modern economy. How the economy confronts these challenges, of course, is dependent upon the values emanating from the wider culture in which the economy is set. The challenges posed by the less fortunate can, therefore, be paid attention to in some degree varying from scarcely at all to a very great deal indeed. Hence in the final analysis all economies need to monitor their operation with a view to confronting questions of efficiency, but also questions of equity as they arise in the monitoring. We will consider the full range of criteria required to monitor modern economies in Chapter 8.

We make no special plea for this particular formulation. But we do say that, insofar as we can ascertain, no economics department in the United States formulates its objectives to be assisting in confronting the kinds of questions this formulation poses. The University of Michigan, for example, is quite typical: 'The graduate programs in economics at The University of Michigan offers preparation for the wide range of careers now open to professional economists in academic, business, and government sectors . . . Designed primarily to train professional economists, its emphasis is on the theoretical core of the discipline, and its applications together with the essential research skills.' In light of what was just said, the reader will not be surprised that an italicized sentence tells the prospective student: 'Because modern economics is highly quantitative, students without sufficient mathematical preparation often have great difficulty completing the program.' Once again, presumably you need also to master a good deal of economics, although this is not explicitly added.

What is the problem? The tendency of American graduate schools of economics to say simply that the purpose of the graduate program is to prepare for a career in teaching, research, or government service does not distinguish our discipline from other social sciences. (They too presumably prepare students for one of these three ways to be a practicing social scientist.) The problem lies in what mainstream economists say (and do not say!) about their focus. If all social sciences tend to assume that the problems on which each focuses are too well known to require elaborate restatement in graduate catalogues, one can fill in the blanks explicitly far more easily in the case of the other fields. The reason goes well beyond what has been said about the emphasis in economics on the quantitative skills. If one reads that political science is designed to prepare one to teach, do research or have a career in the public service, one knows what each entails principally because political scientists generally devote themselves to the flaws which they observe in the operation of the democratic process. Thus in recent years, rather than describing the operation of an ideal representative democracy they might well have been focusing on the obstacle to the functioning of such a system exemplified by, say, the voting procedures in Florida, or the impact of fairly unlimited contributions by wealthy individuals or corporations to political campaigns. The latter has, of course, led to introduction and passage of campaign finance reform legislation. It is not difficult to envisage a research program dealing with the issues involved in campaign finance reform, the advisability of various legislative measures to ameliorate the situation, etc. Nor is it difficult to imagine what this area would offer in the way of a sensible unit in a class in democracy in action. The link between theory and policy is strong and explicit. The same is true in other social sciences and, indeed, in a number of other areas of human study. In economics it would be surprising if, for example, the Enron or Worldcom scandals in the United States in 2002 have made much of an impact on, say graduate industrial organization courses or microeconomic theory courses.

Economists have a problem because they are the only social science in which the mainstream or trend-setting group places primary emphasis on the general inadvisability of interventionist policy. The theory courses, as we have seen, make simplifying assumptions, with the result that they have the great advantage of examining the operation of ideal units. This approach leads all too facilely to admiration of the implications for the system of the operation of ideal firms. They begin with the assumption they generally end with – that economic operations are mostly 'best left to the market.'[2] If that is literally true then most of the time presumably the end result for policy

---

2. The macroeconomic equivalent, as we have seen in Chapter 5, consists of formulations typified by 'real business cycle theories,' which have the effect of ridding us of the vexations' surrounding Keynes's 'underemployment equilibrium' and smoothing the way to the macro-equivalent of the 'leave it to the market' policy guide we see above in the micro-economy. We might go further. If the Great Depression, as has often been argued, was so huge a flaw in a presumably well functioning 'natural' system, that it gave the Keynesian perspective a chance to be heard, one might think Enron or Worldcom, would do the same for an interventionist microeconomic perspective. No doubt the 'too big to die' sentiment, considered in Chapter 4, is partially to blame for this not happening.

implications of research in the field of economics would be that no intervention is necessary, and this presumably is the primary message to be delivered in teaching, as well.

It is probably true in most fields of human endeavor that intervention by central authorities is advisable only when operation without higher authority intervention is clearly not feasible or would clearly worsen the situation. (That is, either way, when intervention would not lead demonstrably to a worse situation.) But still no one would suggest, for example, that traffic in a large city should be left to 'natural forces.'[3] There was a time when the anti-trust laws in economics were regarded as indispensable much as traffic light systems are still regarded. In their attitude toward intervention, economists have moved more or less in tandem. If monetarists argued against interventionist monetary policy and rational expectations adherents argued that all stabilization policy was futile, they were moved by the same ideological and related forces which led to the declining emphasis on anti-trust from, say, its once influential place in Thurman Arnold's time. (We saw in Chapter 4 that today in some quarters anti-trust laws are regarded as passe.)[4] These changes in attitudes toward interventionism reflect changes in the prevailing ideology. The differences reflect the increasingly sacrosanct character of 'leave it to the market' in economics compared to the far less dominant role of 'letting natural forces do what they can' in most other social sciences. Clinical psychologists would not approach their discipline with the similar assumption that most aberrations, dysfunctional behaviors, evidences of instability or psycho-pathologies are 'best left to exposure to life.' 'Don't come to a therapist or let the therapist prescribe drugs. Go out and live!' A likely scenario? It would be hard to believe. Like Keynesians in macroeconomics, they confront flaws in human operation.

All these conditions will be studied with the explicit (though perhaps not verbalized) assumption that the conditions are studied in order to reduce the symptoms and/or somehow improve the quality of life of the individuals. One can say pretty much the same thing about 'why study sociology?'; 'why study medicine?'; 'why study nutrition?'; 'why study agronomy?'; etc. In most fields involving aspects of human life the primary assumption is that if the field is studied the problems that it presents to human beings in the process of living their lives can be reduced, if not eliminated, by adopting the policies which emerge as a result of applying what one can learn from the

3. Instead city officials, guided by traffic control experts determine where and how traffic signals should be installed.

4. We refer the reader to the comments on William Bork's attitude toward anti-trust in Chapter 4.

study.

We have seen where this leads economists. The destruction – widely but not universally regarded as successful – of the theory-policy link as the natural focus of economics is part of the change in the past half century that we have focused on in earlier chapters. It is reflected in the difference in the central focus of modern mainstream economics and the central focus in most other social sciences. It provides the opening for the charge that modern economics is a highly stylized game. No doubt many economists agree with Robert Lucas that one studies business cycles in order to understand them so as to realize that they are best left to their own devices. But were that literally true why do we need so many economists in government service? Some might simply ask, do we need so many economists? Do we really need so many economists in the public sector if we already know enough to see that intervention is futile or wrongheaded or both? Is economics unrelated to policy as an area of concentration in research less critical in a time of limited resources? Do we economists really want to look down this road very far?

We suggest that in point of fact improved understanding, while always useful, is by no means the raison d'etre for much research and teaching, and surely for much public service. Government departments at all levels scarcely hire as many economists as they do in order to facilitate better understanding of why most of the time government should not intervene in the operation of whatever field of economic activity a given unit is charged with monitoring!

Moreover, a closer look at the operations that actually go on in graduate economics programs suggests that practitioners in graduate education may not invariably practice what they preach. Consider the list of PhD thesis titles included in Table 7.1, the *Harvard Graduate Catalogue* listing of the dissertation titles for 1998–1999. Harvard is surely a prestigious economics program, and we suggest it is also in many ways representative of what these programs in the United States strive for. It is probably a fairly representative list of what American PhD students were producing at that time. The format is surely very popular currently. Instead of a single topic students write two or three essays – shorter papers summarizing the research carried out. The titles suggest frequently that the papers were not mere descriptions of what was going on in, say, banking and corporate finance, or corporate ownership. In a number of cases a more active approach is clearly suggested as in 'Public Policies and Private Behavior.' If private behavior, with or without an invisible hand, can be more or less relied upon to lead to socially acceptable resource deployment, clearly no public policy, other than laissez faire, would be required. It is difficult to imagine that a piece of research on public policy pointing relentlessly to the conclusion that public neglect, whether benign or malignant, is invariably the best policy would make for a very interesting research project.

Similarly, 'Taxation, Appropriation and the State' sounds a bit activist if the conclusion is to be that spending be left entirely to the market. And 'Examining the Effect of Federal Financial Aid on Higher Education: A Study of Pell Grants' conjures up an example of applied normative economics, rather than a dispassionate confirmation of the futility of interventionist economic policy. 'Medical Innovation and Managed Care' does not sound too market-oriented, nor does 'Taxation, Appropriation, and the State.' The reader gets the idea.

In fairness to Harvard, we might add that their discussion of the purposes of their particular graduate program in economics is somewhat atypical. True, it begins by announcing that 'The graduate program of the Department of Economics is addressed to students of high promise who wish to prepare themselves in teaching and research or for responsible positions in government, research organizations, or business enterprises.' But then it continues:

> Several kinds of knowledge are required of a professional or academic economist. An economist must understand the nature of long-term changes in the economy (economic history); the best thinking about the ways in which economic units interact with each other and with their environment, respond to change, and develop over time (economic theory and its intellectual development); and the techniques by which economic data are assembled, evaluated, and analyzed (statistical method and its application). (Harvard Graduate Programs, p. 1)

One must exercise considerable care in inferring what might be entailed in all this, but except for 'understanding the nature of long term changes' the rest suggests more involvement than simply careful observation so as to understand what in fact is occurring. 'The best thinking about the ways in which economic units interact' would especially be required if thinking were to lead to action!

More generally it is clear that graduate schools of economics are highly aware that many economists work for the various levels of government and, if they think about it at all, they must surely realize that these public sector economists are not hired merely to observe how the private economy goes about its business. This would be as ludicrous as training medical doctors and hiring them to observe the aging process so as to understand the rate and nature of natural deterioration of bodily functioning. Take away the aspect of medicine charged with improving bodily functioning at all stages of life and

Table 7.1 Harvard University Economics PhD thesis titles, 1998–1999

Essays in International Economics and Finance
The Economics of Participation
Essays in Banking and Corporate Finance
Family, Schooling, and Earnings: An Empirical Investigation for Malaysia
Essays on Rational Growth, Capital Flows and Technological Differences across States
National Borders and International Trade
Essays on the Economics of Location Price
Public Policies and Private Behavior
Essays on International Changes in Industrial Structure of Production and Trade
Essays on Corporate Ownership
Essays in the Economics of Organization
Pirates and Planters: Trade and Development in the Caribbean, 1492–1680
Essays on Internal Organization and Industrial Organization
Essays on Consolidation in Medical Care
Essays on Institutional Economics and Finance
Local Economic Growth
Taxation, Appropriation and the State
Three Essays in Applied Microeconomic Theory
Essays on International Asset Pricing
Three Essays in Economics
Essays on Portfolio Choice over the Life Cycle
Essays on Arbitrage
An Econometric Implementation to the Theory of Mirrless Taxation
Essays on the p-Core and Multilateral Bargaining
Urban Life Cycles
The Political Economy of Public Deficits
Essays on Pension Systems, Uncertainty and Economic Growth
Examining the Effect of Federal Financial Aid on Higher Education: A Study of Pell Grants
Essays in Applied Behavioral Microeconomics

Source: Harvard University Graduate School of Arts & Sciences, Catalogue, 2001.

it becomes a vastly less critical focus of both interest and activity. Is the role of economist any different?

In short, it is difficult not to conclude that economists are hired in applied positions to improve the operation of the economy. An economist who turned in an annual report stating that he or she now understood better why people were unemployed, or why prices were contributing to high inflation, or why there was excess capacity, or shortages of X or Y could scarcely expect more than a 'good first step' reaction from superiors evaluating the reports turned in. It is not too believable that only rarely if ever would somebody say, 'what do you suggest we can do about this?' And surely replying 'leave it to the market and wait' might in all too many cases for comfort lead to short term employment as economist in any agency on which we chose to focus.

Does anyone doubt that somewhere in their hearts, those who plan and organize and run American graduate programs in economics would recognize the truth of what has been said? In fact we may go further: it probably is not often forgotten anyplace in an economics program with the exception of the 'core theory' courses in America's premier graduate economics programs.

In the end the argument we have been making is not that economics programs pay no attention to applied fields where better operations are sought. It is that the economic theorists have so little to contribute to what the applied economists are doing. It is the theory which gives initial status and prestige to an economics program – which crowns economics the 'Queen of the Social Sciences.' But this queen has virtually nothing to do with the daily lives of her subjects! The queen instead is heavily preoccupied with her own abstruse pastimes. And these pastimes have an elegance and a precision, and a brilliance that outshine any crown jewels she may own.

IF IT'S WRITTEN IT MUST BE TRUE

The upshot of what has just been said is that relatively few graduate programs in economics make any attempt to include empirical content on the statement of objectives of a graduate program or to explain what it will attempt to accomplish. If asked no doubt one would be told that 'everyone knows' why you should get a PhD in economics and what you can do with it.

We turn now to a different aspect of the 'education business' as it pertains to economics: namely, the professional journals. We need to characterize the quite diverse roles they play. It will be our thesis that while, once more, 'everyone knows' what they try to do and why they are important, we shall argue that at critical places the manner in which many important journals play these roles may not be as clear as is customarily assumed.

What is clear to everyone in the profession is that professional journals play several critical roles. They are, first of all, the major points of display for what is going on as we like to say 'at the cutting edge' of economic research. One of the first things a graduate student will learn is that in economics, unlike, say English or a foreign language, books are not considered critical to success, but articles are! Thus if one looks back at the previous chapters one will be struck by how often the critical issues raised in the various debates we have looked at are raised in journal articles as opposed to books. The glaring twentieth-century exception, of course, is Keynes's *General Theory*. On the other hand while Milton Friedman has written a number of books, his major well known jousts with heterodox or Keynesian economics have mostly come in journal articles and, similarly, virtually all of Robert Lucas's attacks have appeared originally in journal articles.

If the reader is still unconvinced of what has been said, exposure to many other graduate programs will find the students intimately involved with the great books of the field. English graduate students read Shakespeare, or Chaucer, or Victorian novels, etc. Anthropologists read Meade and William Grant Sumner, etc. Philosophers read Plato and other Greeks, as well as other books up through John Dewey, etc. The reader should ask when was the last time a graduate student was seen in economics in a major program displaying within reach on the desk or book shelf, let alone actually consulting, Adam Smith's *Wealth of Nations*, Ricardo's *Principles*, John Stuart Mill's *Principles of Political Economy*, or (from the twentieth century) Schumpeter's *History of Economic Analysis* or Clark's *Social Control of Business*. But they are all assigned and read and discuss intensely the lead article from last month's *Journal of X*. Being *au courant* is the name of one important economics game. *Au courant* does not mean – what is the latest thinking about one of the classics mentioned above? It refers to the latest hypothesis proffered in the most recent issue of prestigious *Journal X*. Being steeped in the history of thought, we have already seen in Chapter 3, is – at best – a very old-fashioned goal.

The first point to note then is that as grist for the graduate school mill, economics journal articles (mostly recent journal articles) provide the major fodder for seminars and classes. (There are, of course, some major text book exceptions to this.) They also provide, therefore, the major material for the all-important 'review of the literature' section of many PhD dissertations!

The second role they play is the critical one for the next step when the budding economist obtains the degree and is hired at a major university – one which 'plays the game.' To succeed, as is well known, the fledgling economist must prove to be adept at jumping through rigidly prescribed hoops. Said hoops, when successfully negotiated, provide a critical record for successful tenure and promotion. One of the most important of these hoops is 'the publication record.' One can, therefore, presumably get information from one's own department chair about what is expected before one can be tenured, and before one can be recommended for each promotion through to full professor. Little appears to be written to provide a basis for comparing expectations concerning publication achievements at different universities which aspire to comparable degrees of excellence (to the extent these things can be measured with any accuracy). Thus presenting a table, 'Publication Requirements for Promotion to Associate Professor at Twenty-five Leading American Economics Departments,' must remain an idle subject for daydreams or perhaps speculation about what it might show. (The requirement will stress publishing articles, while many other fields require books for promotion.) However, generally (and obviously in economics, which is the field with expertise in the operation of the market) if vast discrepancies existed between expectations in University A and other universities in the 'same class,' raiding of promising faculty from the highest expectation schools would be carried out to the benefit of the lower expectation school or schools (especially if expectations and budgets were negatively correlated!). If all presumably wish to be known as high expectation schools, holding on to one's faculty would presumably guarantee some degree of rough similarity in expectations among departments considered (or wishing to be considered) 'comparable.' Here presumably is a case where 'the unregulated market' may work! As we have said, if one's standards are too high recruiting is difficult if not impossible and if too low, retaining the desired faculty would be impossible.

What this all calls for is first, recognition that for graduate students what is written and published in our major professional journals provides the basis for much of their own reading and learning and class discussion. Second, therefore, mastery of what is in journal articles is critical to the successful completion of advanced degrees. But it is equally important for aspiring scholars in producing the written record of publication on which successful advancement up the academic ladder depends.

Finally, the major journals presumably provide a written expression of the growth of the knowledge base which undergirds the discipline. We are surely all led to assume that the published output of 'the major journals' by the very fact of its being and growth is a critical aspect of the existential evidence testifying to the rate and degree to which the field is advancing. It is thereby also a critical 'Exhibit A' – living proof of what we mean exactly by 'advances in the field of economics.' That such advances are occurring is more or less assumed virtually all the time by the overwhelming majority of those of us who call ourselves economists. But how to tell if they are occurring is rarely if ever contemplated and how to affect that rate of progress is a subject on which economists are mainly mute. Why? Because it is so much assumed that, like the weather, it is regarded as an important topic which is beyond being a necessary topic for consideration. Among the aspects left undiscussed, therefore, are how one tells if progress is occurring and whether its rate is increasing or decreasing and even whether it bears contemplation.[5]

A principal reason judging progress is difficult is because of the insistence of so many that interventionist policy is a misplaced activity for economists. Economic theory, therefore, must be judged by some non-empirical test, not by whether the economy functions better (less inflation, more rapid growth, less unemployment, etc.) as a result of carrying out via policy the implications of this or that theory. Instead, though it is rarely if ever stated explicitly, many conventional economic theorists would insist that it can be judged only by more complex standards – like 'do we now better understand why the economy has functioned better (or worse) with respect to X or Y than heretofore?'

'Understanding' is a murky standard of measurement.[6] A given explanation may make things 'clear' to one person, but not another. Moreover, as the methodology for investigation has gotten more complex, as we discussed in Chapter 3, the number of individuals who can follow any given explanation in very many instances has surely shrunk. The result is that in very many areas the coterie who are capable of understanding a given explanation is small and the result is that they, in effect, tell everyone else, 'Take our word. This explanation really explains what previous efforts only attempted to explain.' It is like asserting, 'Take my word for it, Chekhov's *The Cherry Orchard* is much better in Russian.' If you don't know Russian, you take this on faith, or on some other basis, one which will doubtless be dismissed as 'spurious.' (In Chapter 3 we discussed 'proof' and 'truth' for various theories all in terms of logic, or as the result of empirical testing. The evidence was presumably comprehensible and thus persuasive to many economists.) Recall that for what we have termed the 'non-interventionists' virtually all aspects of the economy function better if 'left to the market.' How a given theory provides greater understanding than other proffered

5. The relationship between the acceptance policies of the major journals and actual progress in confronting the major problems in the various fields is not a subject that, so far as we know, has received a lot of attention.

6. The reader will recall that this was the objective suggested (Chapter 2 above) by Robert Lucas.

explanations is often left unstated or for the reader to figure out. No doubt 'better understanding' could be considered part of 'progress' although better understanding that cannot be applied to better performance would be viewed by many as, at the very least, a frustrating state.

For those economists who accept the view that an appropriate justification for improved economic theory is interventionist policy of some sort which in turns leads to 'better' performance, one can presumably judge progress by the extent to which the established objectives of the various interventionist policies are being fulfilled. But for those who regard themselves as non-interventionists the criteria for judging progress, we reiterate, are less clear. We have no clear and explicit standards for defining 'better understanding.' An explanation that becomes more logical, for example, may or may not be reflecting better real understanding. Logic requires that assumptions be consistent (not contradictory or based on antithetical assumptions) and lead without breaks in reasoning to some conclusions. But these logical chains may or may not be reflective of real world processes. We would argue that using the results of this process to develop and test policy in the real world is the only sure way to test whether real progress has been made or not.

All this is relevant to evaluating journals because it seems fundamental to answering the question how one can tell if any given journal is getting 'better'. That they rise and fall in popularity is, we shall see, assuredly true. Change in the popularity of journals has long been a part of the economics journal scene. It is arguably true that some of this rise and fall in popularity of economics journals can reflect changing fads in subject matter or methodologies or interests. We shall argue that changing fads merely complicate the task of judging 'real progress' in what is published in journals. It also complicates the task of evaluating the impact of new young faculty on journals and symbiotically the impact of journals and their 'standards' or policies, to the extent these can be ascertained, on the evaluation of young faculty members' progress.[7]

---

7. For example, it is doubtful that very many faculty members would be judged today to have made meaningful progress toward tenure by demonstrating that they have increased their understanding of the Corn Law controversy or the Physiocrats' distinction between productive and sterile labor.

These may constitute an accretion of knowledge, but it would be a rare graduate program that would view an increase in understanding in the examples just given as exemplifying 'progress.' Partly, this involves the changing views of what subjects in economics are 'esoteric.'

What Each Journal Looks for – What Is Vendible?

What sort of guidance do the major journals give prospective authors? This turns out to be a deceptively simple question which in the end is not simple at all. We can begin by considering what have sometimes been called the 'flagship' journals – the journals of the American Economic Association, the Royal Economic Society, the Econometric Society, plus two journals long considered highly prestigious – the *Journal of Political Economy* from the University of Chicago and the *Quarterly Journal of Economics*, the major journal of Harvard University.[8]

It will surprise no one to hear that techniques for judging the importance and prestige of journals have evolved into a highly complicated business. Today such judgements are part science, part art, and some might add part intellectual chutzpah. Before turning to all these difficulties, it seems useful, therefore, to begin very simply with these five journals which all living economists were raised to regard as important and significant journals. What guidance do they give potential contributors?

The *American Economic Review* gives scarcely a word of assistance for the fledgling author seeking to know what sort of articles they might look on with favor. He or she can learn that the journal is concerned that research reported should include data so that others can replicate the study in hand and presumably come to the same conclusion. He or she will learn that merely having one considered for publication will cost $75 ($150 if not a member of the American Economic Association). The prospective author can learn that whatever he or she submits better not be more than 50 pages long. That is as close as substantive help comes in selecting a topic and method for pursuing it. Elsewhere in the ivied halls where work by young scholars is done, he or she will learn that modeling will improve the chances of success materially, particularly if the models assume overlapping generations, or rational expectations, or Nash equilibrium, or that business cycles if they exist must be real, or if they assume away most of the identifying characteristics of the real world, or other similar restrictive perspectives that appear to be *au courant*. But the struggling young economist will not learn any of these highly useful tricks from anything published in the journal itself. He or she will also learn that specifying assumptions involving the culture surrounding an economy or the behavior of the agents under scrutiny are not 'in' things to do. (Passion, heart, or strong emotional reactions are all

---

8. These five journals were termed 'flagship journals' by Erkin I. Bairam who ranked some thirty departments of economics by the number of pages each department published in these five journals during the years 1985–1990 (Bairam 1994).

frowned upon.) But what subjects are especially appropriate one can learn only by examining a number of issues in any given era for oneself very carefully. By so doing one can observe the changing fashion in what sort of work is considered prestigious at any particular time. In this not very scientific way one can learn to recognize appropriateness by intuition.

We chose a relatively recent issue at random: it happens to be the *American Economic Review* for June 2002. It includes essays by the three 2001 recipients of the Nobel Prize in Economics. Of these three, George Akerlof and Joseph Stiglitz both write essays in words, old-fashioned as this approach may be. Akerlof writes on 'behavioral macroeconomics' which is old-fashioned to begin with and Stiglitz writes on information and change in the paradigm in economics. Only Michael Spence is hip enough to employ the tools of mathematics explicitly – he is writing on signaling and the information structure of markets (Spence 2002, pp. 411–501). Arguably, the Nobel Committee has always been less bound by current tradition than would be the case were prizes awarded by 'the market.' For the rest of the June 2002 issue of the journal, some ten essays are included and every one of them is quantitative – that is, the author or authors employ a mathematical approach to what they wish to convey. The fledgling contributor would have to be very dense not to realize that saying it with symbols is the current name of the game.

What has been said about the *American Economic Review* pretty much applies to the other flagship journals as well. The *Economic Journal* is perhaps slightly more helpful than the *American Economic Review*. It informs the reader, 'The policy of the editors is to publish the best papers in economics from any field, be they theoretical, applied or empirical. To be acceptable for publication they should make a substantial contribution to the subject, be technically well-crafted and be of broad interest to economists at large. No paper will be rejected solely on the grounds of being too technical, or too applied.'[9] One could clearly debate what is a 'substantial contribution' and what is of 'broad interest' but at least a bit of information is supplied. (Submissions are free to members of the Royal Economic Society and non-members have to join the Society in order to submit a paper.) The general state of the process is implicit in the comments that no papers can be too technical. This is in line with the situation decried earlier in Chapter 3. Obviously that a paper can be rejected on grounds of not being technical enough is clearly well within the bounds of what is possible. We have noted previously that in the old battle between rigor and relevance rigor was long ago pronounced the unquestioned victor as the presumed preeminent quality

9. *The Economic Journal*, any issue, in 'Notes to Contributors.'

prized above all else in economic research. That relevance was the vanquished quality appears to have caused few if any tears to be shed.

In the *Economic Journal*, official journal of the United Kingdom's Royal Economic Society, the instructions for authors are entirely procedural and the reader is left with the clear impression that a high standard for technicality is simply implicit because of the perspective which it is assumed all submissions to such a journal would reflect. 'When setting out mathematical equations, contributors are asked to conform to the conventions adopted in recent articles published in the *Economic Journal*. The full mathematical workings necessary for justifying each step of the argument should accompany all articles of a mathematical character, in order to assist the referee.'[10] Once again, presumably a parallel injunction about writing clearly and/or logically would not be explicitly demanded in an essay of 'a non-mathematical character.'

In the case of the third flagship journal, *Econometrica*, ambiguity as to method clearly cannot exist. The name itself was devised to cover the new approach. (Perhaps today a case could be made for a journal devoted to – what – perhaps it could be called *Verbalized Economics*! 'The submissions will be expected to conform to the highest standards of literary writing'.) However, there is not a clue in *Econometrica* as to what subjects or approaches would enhance the chances of successful submission.

As for the other two 'flagship' journals, the *Journal of Political Economy* is the major journal published by the University of Chicago, a university whose credentials in the rigor and technicality arena are unquestioned. The editors say absolutely nothing about the kind of essays they seek. Presumably, again, 'everyone knows' the orientation of the *JPE*, what kind of standards this journal has, and what approach in a submitted paper is most likely to lead to a successful endorsement by the journal.

Finally, the major journal of Harvard University is, of course, the *Quarterly Journal of Economics*. Like the *Journal of Political Economy* it offers not a clue as to the subject, orientation, perspective or methodology they encourage. Presumably, they, too, simply assume that 'everyone knows' what sort of papers they are apt to look on with favor.

In short, for all five of these 'flagship journals', whatever the story to be told in a submission, it is mostly left to the author to intuit requirements which a successful submission will need to meet. The general approach which mainstream economics has increasingly insisted on is today considered so well known and widely accepted that little need be said about what is required about either subject or methodology for successful

10. *The Economic Journal*,' Notes to Contributors', any issue.

submission to these, the generally recognized top journals. This was, of course, the message we conveyed in Chapter 3.

'Top 30' Journals – Guidance for Prospective Authors

What we have said about the degree to which the top five journals give prospective authors any specific guidance as to how they might enhance the probability of success in seeking publication is in general equally true of other journals. We will restrict our comments to the 'top 30' journals as measured by 'impact-adjusted citations,' a widely accepted current measure of journal prestige, discussed in more detail below.

We begin by considering the 'top 30' journals as shown in the first column of Table 7.2. Let us begin simply by asking whether the tendency of the 'flagship journals' to tell the prospective author little if anything by way of what would be expected of a successfully submitted paper is true as well of a larger and possibly more representative group of journals. The answer is that the flagship journals are all too representative. We focus initially, as we said we would, on the top 30 journals listed in column 1 (the other journals in the column, as we shall see, were in the top 30 either in earlier years or as measured by a different way). Of these journals, 19 give absolutely no substantive clues as to what they seek in the way of subject matter, methodology, perspective, presumed implications for policy or any other area of intellectual concern. However, 11 make some effort, however peremptory, to delineate an area or an approach for the guidance of the contributors. We will characterize these comments briefly.

The *Journal of Financial Economics*, the most influential journal, measured by number of 'impact-adjusted citations,' has what turns out to be one of the more explicit statements of what it seeks. This journal tells its readers that it '. . . provides a specialized forum for the publication of research in the area of financial economics and the theory of the firm placing primary emphasis on the highest quality analytical, empirical, and clinical contributions in the following major areas: capital markets, financial institutions, corporate finance, corporate governance, and the economics of organizations.' This is very helpful one would say only relative to what others of these journals say (any issue first page under 'Aims and Scope').

One of the more useful statements appears in the *Journal of Monetary Economics*. Under 'Aims and Scope' each issue informs the reader,

> The profession witnessed over the past twenty years a remarkable expansion of research activities bearing on problems in the broader field of monetary economics. The strong interest in monetary analysis has been increasingly

> matched in recent years by the growing attention to the working and structure of financial institutions. The role of various institutional arrangements, the consequences of specific changes in banking structure and the welfare aspects of structural policies have attracted an increasing interest in the profession. We also note lastly the growing attention devoted to the operation of credit markets and to various aspects in the behavior of rates of return on assets. The *Journal of Monetary Economics* provides a specialized forum for the publication of this research. (*Journal of Monetary Economics,* 'Aims and Scope,' any issue)

One can actually imagine a young scholar reading this and finding it helpful in determining whether the research he or she has been pursuing would fall within the expressed field of interest of this journal. This journal is relatively rare even among the group of journals regarded as at all helpful in establishing a productive record.

At the other extreme, helpful but to the least degree possible, is the comment of the *Review of Economic Studies*. Their sole presumably helpful comment to the potential contributor is to note that the *Review of Economic Studies* is published '. . . to encourage research in theoretical and applied economics, especially by young economists, and to publish the results . . .' (first page, any issue). They do not even suggest what they mean by 'young.' Would the same paper be regarded as brilliant if written by a 30 year old but dreary if submitted by a 40 or 50 year old?

Helpful in the manner that the *Journal of Monetary Economics* is helpful is the statement of the *Rand Journal of Economics*. This journal states its purpose to be '. . . to support and encourage research in the behavior of regulated industries, the economic analysis of organizations and more generally, applied microeconomics. Both theoretical and empirical manuscripts in economics and law are encouraged. *The Rand Journal of Economics* welcomes unsolicited manuscripts' (initial page, any issue).

We may perhaps wish to dispute the thoughts expressed but one cannot dispute the clarity with which the perspective is expressed. Whatever else, such clarity, ceteris paribus (the author, do not forget, is a trained economist!) should help in enabling a young scholar to determine whether the work done is appropriately submitted to this journal.

Another journal which offers guidance to the prospective author is the *Journal of Mathematical Economics*. It is also somewhat unusual because it offers a substantive position to the reader up front. The journal begins by saying, 'In the editors' view, the formal mathematical expression of economic ideas is of vital importance to economics. Such an expression can determine whether a loose economic intuition has a coherent, logical meaning. Also full formal development of economic ideas can itself suggest new economic concepts and intuitions.'

> The primary objective of the journal is to offer a forum for work in economic theory which expresses economic ideas using formal mathematical reasoning. To this primary objective, it is not sufficient that the mathematical reasoning be new and correct. The work should have real economic content. The economic ideas should be interesting and important. These ideas may pertain to any field of economics or any school of economic thought. The ideas may be well known, provided they are expressed and developed in a novel way. ('Aims and Scope' *Journal of Mathematical Economics*, any issue)

This formulation has a number of admirable qualities. It is clear and 'up front.' While the reader will not be surprised to learn that we would question whether all worthwhile ideas in economics that are 'coherent' and have 'logical' meaning can be expressed mathematically, there are some undoubtedly which can. Moreover, this journal would presumably explicitly reject the sort of piece clothed entirely in mathematics we used in an earlier chapter to illustrate the approach currently so much in vogue, which is utterly devoid of economic content and deals entirely with what we might call mathematical mechanics. The reader may recall we compared such a piece to an essay from the old days written entirely in words but devoted entirely to syntax and grammar. We suggested that no one would have written or published such an essay then because editors then would have insisted that the economic content must be the significant focus even were attention paid to good writing. Good writing like correct mathematics is the means to the end in clarifying economic problems and policies.[11] In any case, this journal is rare, because it offers more guidance as to what the path to successful acceptance of a paper might involve than most of the journals in the top 30 manage to include.

Another journal offering guidance, perhaps not quite as clearly as the *Journal of Mathematical Economics*, but far above what most of the top 30 manage, is the *Journal of Econometrics*. By way of guidance to prospective contributors the editors offer their Editorial Policy:

> *The Journal of Econometrics* is designed to serve as an outlet for important new research in both theoretical and applied econometrics. Papers dealing with estimation and other methodological aspects of the application of statistical

11. Parenthetically, we might add that economists – even great economists – have rarely been known for their writing style. But good mathematical mechanics is nowadays central in the work of virtually any mainstream economist.

> inference to economic data as well as papers dealing with the application of econometric techniques to substantive areas of economics fall within the scope of the journal. Econometric research in the traditional divisions of the discipline or in the newly developing area of social experimentation are decidedly within the range of the journal's interests. ('Editorial Policy,' on the first page of any issue)

It is refreshing to read of a journal devoted to econometrics still referring to the traditional divisions of economics. The point to underscore, however, is that this statement gives the potential contributor a good idea as to the subject matter and approach that are likely to be viewed favorably by the editors. This is considerably more than most of the journals under review here do.

Another journal which lays out with reasonable clarity the area of interest which it espouses is *Brookings Papers on Economic Activity*. It is perhaps not quite fair to include this publication, as much of what they publish is by invitation. Still there are many journals of which the same thing could undoubtedly be said which are far less clear about what they seek (for example the *Papers and Proceedings* of the American Economic Association). Brookings makes the following statement: 'The Brookings Institution is an independent organization devoted to nonpartisan research, education, and publication in economics, government, foreign policy, and the social sciences generally. Its principal purposes are to aid in the development of sound public policies and to promote public understanding of issues of national importance' (*Brookings Papers on Economic Activity*, in Statement 'The Brookings Institution' at the beginning of each issue of the *Papers*).

'Non-partisan' is an interesting adjective to use, from the perspective of economic analysis, to describe research, education, and publication. Is belief that allocation should be left to the market a partisan or a non-partisan approach? Is the assertion that there is an active role for the public sector a partisan or a non-partisan statement? Does the sponsor of research affect whether or not it is non-partisan? Is it possible for a government agency to sponsor research which concludes that there is no place for government in resolving whatever problem it is investigating? ('We wish to thank the Federal Government's Agency X without whose sponsorship this study could not have been undertaken. It reaches the conclusion that government has no place in solving the problem under review'.)

We have in previous chapters considered whether monetarism, supply side economics, Keynesian economics, rational expectations, etc. are normative or positive economics. Is 'non-partisan' synonymous with 'non-normative,' with 'positive,' or does it deal with a different set of issues? We think that consensus among current economists would not easily be obtained

Table 7.2 Rankings of 'Top 30' economics journals, 1965–1990

1990 Citations to articles published, 1985–1989			Rankings based on citations to articles published			Rankings based on all articles EVER published by journals
Rankings based on impact-adjusted citations per article		Rank	1985–1989	1975–1979	1965–1969	
	1	2	3	4	5	6
Journal Fin Econ	100.0	1	2	15		
Econometricia	78.4	2	6	3	6	
Journal Pol Econ	63.0	3	4	2	4	4
Journal Mon Econ	41.9	4	12	13		3
Quart J Econ	41.6	5	16	20	4	9
Rev Econ Studies	40.7	6	21	10	1	8
Amer Econ Rev	40.2	7	11	1	2	1
Bell Journal Econ (Rand Journal Econ)	40.2	8	15	9		14
Journal Econ Theory	34.9	9		11		13
Journal Fin	34.1	10	18	6	12	7
Journal Econ Lit	28.8	11	1	19		27
Journal Acc Econ	25.8	12	7			
Journal Econ Per	23.3	13	14			
Journal Bus	21.2	14	13		8	21
Journal Math Econ	20.6	15				
Journal Econometrics	18.6	16	28	12		
Brookings Pap Econ Act	15.9	17	27	17		23
Journal Labor Econ	15.4	18				
Journal Finan Quant Anal	14.3	19				29
Int Econ Rev	12.3	20		16	14	16
J Law Econ	11.7	21	20	26	10	18
Journal Money Cred Banking	9.0	22				30
Amer Econ Rev Pap & Proc	8.8	23			16	
Journal Public Econ	8.6	24		24		
Journal Amer Statist Assoc	8.0	25	9	4	13	2
Journal Bus Econ Statist	7.9	26				
Journal Int Econ	7.6	27				
Econ Journal	7.5	28	29	14	11	11
Rev Econ Statist	6.5	29		7	3	6
Ind Econ	6.1	30				
Yale Law Rev			3	5		5

Table 7.2 cont.

Mich Law Rev	4	12		12
J Cons Res	5	21		
J Legal Stud	10			
J Roy Statist Ser A	17	25	29	25
Demography	19	18		17
J Roy Statist Ser B	23	23		10
Pop Devel Rev	23			22
J Health Econ	24			
J Int Bus Stud	25			
Oxf Bul Econ Statist	26			
Ind Lab Relat Rev	30			
Am J Agric Econ		8		15
Reg Stud		27		
World Dev		28		
Econ Inquiry		29		
J Human Res		30		
J Reg Science			5	
Economica			9	20
Econ Plan			15	
Ind Rel			17	
Oxford Econ Pap			18	
J Econ Hist			19	26
Lloyd's Bnk Rev			20	
Yale Essays Econ			21	
Econ/Dev Cult Chng			22	
So Econ J			23	24
Econ Hist Rev			24	28
Kyklos			25	
Int Mon Fund Staff Pap			26	
Pub Finance			27	
Nat Tx J			28	
Expl Econ Hist			30	
Mo Lab Rev				19

[1] Values . . . 'which range from 0 to 100, represent citations per article reviewed by each journal in the reference year as a percentage of the citations per article received by the leading journal that year' (Laband and Piette 1994, 642).

Source: Table constructed from Laband and Piette (1994), 640–66. Column 6 constructed from Liebowitz and Palmer (1984), 77–88.

on these questions. The Brookings Institution has a different reputation from, say, the American Enterprise Institute, and both have a different reputation from the Heritage Foundation. They are all different from the National Institute of Health or the National Science Foundation. We leave it to the reader which if any of these research organizations are 'non-partisan.' But we do seriously raise the question what 'non-partisan' in research means.

From a heuristic perspective we would assert that the Brookings statement is educationally more useful than many of the statements one finds staking out the road to be traversed by a particular economics journal. That alone would appear to be an encouraging sign to be held up against much of what is currently being said by way of advice for prospective contributors to the journals under review.

A statement of very little help, but still better than the nothing found in many top 30 journals, appears in the *Journal of Public Economics*. Under 'Editorial Policy' they inform the reader, 'The aim of the *Journal of Public Economics* is to encourage original scientific contributions on the problems of public economics, with particular emphasis on the application of modern economic theory and methods of quantitative analysis. It provides a forum for discussion of issues of public policy of interest to an international readership' ('Editorial Policy', on first page of any issue). With the emphasis in mainstream economics mainly on seeking market solutions to all economic problems, it is refreshing to find a journal which has as its implicit premise the idea that a public sector is essential and needs, therefore, to be planned for rationally.

One of the most detailed and explicit statements to guide authors is provided by the *Journal of Business & Economic Statistics*. Their 'Editorial Policy' statement reads:

> *The Journal of Business and Economic Statistics* publishes articles dealing with a broad range of applied problems in business and economic statistics. Appropriate topics include applied forecasting, seasonal adjustment, applied demand and cost analysis, applied econometric modeling, empirical finance, analysis of survey and longitudinal data related to business and economic problems, impact of discrimination on wages and productivity, returns to education and training, effects of unionization, and applications of stochastic control theory to business and economic problems. Many of the articles published in the *Journal of Business and Economic Statistics* contain empirical applications, though submissions of papers in the areas of computation, simulation, networking and graphics are encouraged as long as the intended applications are very closely related to the general topics of interest of the journal. Papers are expected to have significant results, high quality methodological content, and excellent exposition.

(*Journal of Business and Economic Statistics*, first page, any issue)

It's interesting to speculate about the impact on the profession were the major journals to include a statement as explicit and detailed as this journal. But that is just the point. The major journals (the 'flagship journals', we earlier called them) have the great advantage that their readers simply assume that what they publish is consonant with what, they have been taught, is the only methodologically acceptable way to do economic research. A detailed statement about the objectives or methods is unnecessary because the mainstream consensus is so detailed and so well known. We return to this below.

Another field journal which offers some guidance to its prospective authors is the *Journal of International Economics*. Under 'Aims and Scope' it offers this:

> The *Journal of International Economics* is intended to serve as the primary outlet for theoretical and empirical research in all areas of international economics. These include, but are not limited to the following: trade patterns; commercial policy; international institutions; exchange rates; open economy macroeconomics; international finance; international factor mobility. The journal especially encourages the submission of articles which are empirical in nature, or deal with issues of open economy macroeconomics and international finance. Theoretical work submitted to the journal should be original in its motivation or modeling structure. (*Journal of International Economics*, first page, any issue)

It is difficult to imagine a major journal listing a series of topics they would like to see chosen by prospective contributors. The meaning of 'original motivation' for a piece of research is ambiguous. On the other hand the reference to 'modeling structure' tells the prospective author that submissions looked on approvingly will need to conform to the limits imposed by modern quantitative analysis. (We assert only that, useful as this approach might be, there must surely be room for alternative approaches which could also be useful.) This suggests that it conforms most to the implicit limits and regulations which methodologically the model building approach requires. It belongs in the 'mainstream paradigm.' (We confront this head on in the next chapter.)

An interesting side-light from this review of the top journals is that it is the quantitatively oriented journals which do the most detailed and specific job of guiding their potential authors. The 'flagship' journals say nothing, but seemingly assume that since theory in a modern journal would perforce be squarely in the methodological mainstream, 'everyone knows' what is required. If indeed, it is true, as heterodox economists never tire of pointing out, that all economies exist in a wider culture which is ignored to the peril of those who do so, it is also true that the discipline itself exists in a wider intellectual venue to which it has itself contributed very much. That contribution we have earlier been at pains to suggest is the cause of much pride among modern economists. It is the object of much envy by many other social scientists and at the same time, we have argued, it is also a major obstacle to facing economic activity as in fact it is carried out in many of the world's countries. The requirements for elegance are, in short, among the principal roadblocks to tackling real problems.

We have already suggested that the education of economists in many American graduate programs is designed to teach them the joys of the non-interventionist cocoon as they have been adumbrated for the discipline in the past half century or so. In this, the graduate courses, often taught by the newest PhDs in the department (teaching what they just learned!), play their part. The journals also play their part – they report the latest rounds in the ongoing debate – mainly among non-interventionists, discussing the fine points. Truly big truths between interventionists and non-interventionists rarely need discussion. (Thus, the Bible does not discuss whether God exists; the US constitution does not debate the virtues of freedom.) The 'flagship' American economics journals do not debate whether the prevailing methodology in contemplating economic theory is too narrow or too restrictive or too anything. It is simply assumed to be, by universal agreement among economists of weight, the appropriate approach to all research which comes within its purview. (This was certainly a critical part of the story told in Chapter 3.) So viewed it would be very surprising if the 'flagship journals' bothered to tell the reader what kind of essays they sought. 'We' should all know.

In summary we have looked at the top 30 journals as most recently ranked. Of these journals 19 tell the reader absolutely nothing about the kind of papers they will be most likely to find publishable. The other 11 tell the reader something, although often it is so general and so prone to being a string of near-cliches that its ability to be of substantive help to prospective authors is of dubious value. The field journals seem to be a bit more helpful to potential contributors than the general journals. If writing essays for publication is ideally a learning experience, the journals generally do very little to contribute to helping young economists learn what the journals are seeking.

Possible Non-Substantive Influences in Successful Journal Submissions

There is some evidence to suggest that trying to second guess the journals as to what they seek may be the wrong approach, or at least perhaps not the most promising path to publication. Were this in fact the case then, of course, this whole discussion would at the very least, be misguided. Some insight into this possibility was shed by Erkin I. Bairam (1994), who made an initial inquiry into where the successful submissions to major journals came from. This is a necessary first step in confronting the questions we have been considering. We concentrate on the same five journals we considered above in looking at what Bairam found, as shown in Table 7.3.

The overwhelming impression one gets from this table is that an author has an advantage from the outset if he or she is considered 'one of their own' by the journal. This is most clear, of course, in the case of the *Economic Journal* – the only foreign journal in this list. Not surprisingly, perhaps, it published more pages by English economists than from anyplace else. (Of course, the fact that American journals publish mostly American authors goes relatively unnoticed and is certainly not discussed.) The same sort of networking shows up among the American journals – that is, the *Journal of Political Economy* published more pages written by 'its own' – University of Chicago authors – than from anyplace else. *The Quarterly Journal* similarly favors authors from MIT and Harvard (plus Princeton, which we comment on below).

Along with a tilting toward authors from home as opposed to from other places the other tendency that is strong is that all the American journals tend to publish the largest number of pages from the same small group of departments. Looked at this way we can say that MIT is the only department that shows up on all five lists of the top five. Harvard and Princeton show up on four; Stanford shows up on three; Chicago on two; and Michigan, Yale, and Northwestern on one each. To the extent that publication activity in top journals is the source of departmental clout, the departments just mentioned may be regarded as the premier departments in the United States.

The Role of Journals in Contributing to Departmental Prestige

The professional journals are important not only for assisting the young faculty to avoid perishing by publishing. They play an integral role in the education of graduate students. We have previously alluded to the preference of economists for assigning students articles rather than books and this shows up, as we have seen, in the tendency of economists, unlike some other disciplines, to place higher value on indications of successful publication in professional journals than they do on the successful publication of book length studies.

In all of these roles, 'playing the game' is critical and so the factors we have seen earlier that mainstream economists admire – elegant modeling, precision, sophisticated use of quantitative analysis, etc. – all play a part in determining the role played by professional journals. A 'well played game' here means the graduate students are more apt to pass doctoral exams; the young professors are more likely to get their efforts published – and, they hope, get tenured and/or promoted; and departments whose members are successful in these ways, will in turn contribute the most by common agreement to the prestigious rankings of their own departments.

We reiterate an important point made above – there is much circularity in

Table 7.3 Top five universities, by number of pages published in the five 'flagship' economics journals, 1985–1990

American Economic	*Econometrica*	*Economic*	*J Pol*	*Quart J Econ*
MIT	MIT	LSE	Chicago	MIT
Harvard	Princeton	Cambridge	Stanford	Princeton
Princeton	Yale	Oxford	Harvard	Harvard
Chicago	Harvard	Warwick	MIT	Northwestern
Michigan	Stanford	MIT	Princeton	Stanford

Source: Bairam (1994), 674–79).

all this, vicious or virtuous, depending on one's viewpoint. The prestige of the journals is directly influenced by the percentage of their authors who are regarded as top economists. And who are regarded as the top economists? Well, the reputation as being a top economist is heavily influenced by the extent to which an economist is published in the top journals. Thus, the authors help the journals achieve higher standing even as the journals help the economists achieve higher status. In both cases the ranking may well be strengthened by the fact that top economists 'know' what are the top journals just as the journals 'know' who are the top economists. All of this is helped along considerably by 'citations' and their impact, to which we now turn.

Changing Views of Journal Prestige

We have just seen that publishing in the 'best' journals adds to the luster of the authors as well as to that of the scholars with whom they are associated. There is one more critical variable involved in determining the clout derived from publishing in the 'best' journals. As Table 7.2 makes very clear – what are considered the best journals changes from time to time. That is, there are trends in what are considered trend setting journals. (This is clearer in the case of work in macroeconomics than in microeconomics. In the latter case, the quantification revolution has been the main factor which has changed how one should 'do' microeconomics.) In any case, before we can go much further in understanding the complicated and interactive system that American graduate education in economics has become, we need to pause long enough to clarify the use of the term 'top journal.' We assert, again, that the standings of the journals are by no means immutably fixed. Table 7.2 makes it abundantly clear how much the consensus view of economists as to what constitutes the 'top 30' journals has changed in the past half century or so. Thus the concept of 'top' journal is a dynamic rather than a static concept.

The reader will not be surprised to learn that modern economists, consistent perhaps to a fault, have found a quantitative way (but a complicated way) – to avoid the otherwise subjective task of ranking journals. The favored technique consists in counting 'citations' as a way of judging the importance of a journal. As it was put in one widely noted paper,

> Our position is that citations are the scientific community's version of dollar voting by consumers for goods and services . . . Economists who study industrial organization do not make any distinctions between 'good' sales and 'bad' sales. Sales are sales, period. All sales count toward determining each producer's market share. We do not treat the consumption of scientific literature any differently. (Laband and Piette 1994, 640–66)

The Social Science Citation Index first appeared in 1956. It shows for all listed economists (among others) the total number of citations to each published article that appeared in a given year, and where the citations appeared. In view of what we have already said it will surprise no one that counting citations is a way, perhaps a fairly crude way, of measuring the 'impact' which a given economist, or a given article by an economist had in a given time period. If one takes Laband and Piette literally, counting citations is merely how scholars roughly measure 'popularity.' Getting the most citations is viewed as reflecting the economist, the article, or the journal with the greatest impact. The Social Science Citation Index, therefore, has provided an enormous amount of grist for the quantitative mill which is, of course, the modern economist's favored means of making value judgments.

It is not the only way such judgments can be made. It is doubtful whether theologians would count the number of times God gets mentioned in a given body of published material as pertinent to judging His influence. The analogy leaves a good deal to be desired but perhaps can serve to introduce a point that needs to be made. The impact of ideas in general and scholarly contributions in particular can probably not be appropriately reduced to anything so mechanical and relatively simple as a count of the number of mentions received in a given body of commentary. But economists have seized on it with a vengeance and today probably most junior faculty in major economics departments are required to report their 'citation counts' to their superiors each year as part of the process of evaluating their progress toward tenure and promotion.

In this regard the appropriateness of the comparison to sales as a measure of a product's impact with which we began this discussion needs to be considered carefully. A basic and fairly early article on the use of citation counts ended with a caution which has, to our knowledge, never been repeated. The authors wrote, 'One final caution: if these results should ever play an important role in promotions, salary or tenure, we should expect the practices of scholarship to change in a manner which would lead to citation-inflation. Such endogenous behavior could alter the significance and meaning of future studies of this kind' (Liebowitz and Palmer 1984, p. 84). (The use of out of context phrases from reviews of motion pictures, plays, and books in advertising blurbs comes to mind by way of illustration here.) That the role of these counts has grown is undeniable. Whether 'citation inflation' has become a problem has never to our knowledge been investigated. Clearly it was not a worry for Laband and Piette, and their 'a sale is a sale' view.

Citations can, as we shall see, be used variously. Here they are used very simply by noting the number of times authors publishing in a selected list of journals cite articles published in *Journal X* or *Journal Y*. This is a rough and ready standard. The authors of the quoted article have admitted as much. A statement that 'Professor Jones used incredibly sloppy scientific standards in reaching his conclusions' produces a citation for both Professor Jones and the journal where he made this statement just as surely as a quotation that reads, 'Professor Jones made a major contribution to our understanding of X by introducing a variety of new statistical tools to assess the true impact of the problem.' This is what the authors mean by their reference to 'good' and 'bad' sales.

In Table 7.2, column 3 shows the journal ranking for the top 30 journals based on their citation counts. (The calculation of the percentages (column 1) is explained in footnote 1 to the table.) In column 2 the ranking of the journals is given based on 'impact-adjusted citations per article.' Comparison of columns 2 and 3 shows, therefore, what differences in ranking occur when an effort is made to include the 'standing' of the journals in which the citations appear. (Presumably, the higher the standing the greater the impact which a citation will have.) Because this is a matter of highly subjective judgment and could, therefore, vary greatly from one evaluator to another we have stuck to the unweighted citation counts for the rest of the table. This adds citation counts for 1980 and 1970 so that we can trace the changing composition of the 'top 30' journals based on citation counts over a fairly long period of time.

In short, columns 3, 4 and 5 show the changing popularity of journals, glossing over the difficulties with the measurement technique already considered. In each column the numbers as we have said reflect the percentage of all citations in the Social Science Citation Index received by each of the listed journals. Thus the most recent reflection of journal impact (column 3) is based on the per cent of all citations received during the year 1990 to work published between 1985 and 1989.[12] We begin with a comment or two concerning the 'flagship journals.' Perhaps most striking is the fall off in ranking of the *American Economic Review* in 1990. It is important to note that the decline is slightly less severe for the impact-adjusted ranking (column 2). The decline also corresponds to a rise (to number 1) for the *Journal of Economic Literature*, another journal of the American Economic Association. In sum there would seem to be continued high attention to the American Economic Association's journals viewed collectively.

The most recent ranking of the *Journal of Political Economy*, considerably ahead of the *Quarterly Journal of Economics*, reflects no doubt the attention received in this period by the work of University of Chicago economists (rational expectations, etc.). The standing of the *Journal of Political Economy* reflects some of the currents discussed in earlier chapters, particularly Chapter 5. Finally the drop for the *Economic Journal* reflects the tendency, arguably, of American economists to pay less attention to work outside the US even than was heretofore their practice.

More generally, what one sees is that six journals got replaced between 1990 and the earlier count in 1980. If one goes back ten years earlier to 1980 one finds that more than nine journals dropped out of the top 30 between

12. Counting citations in this way prevents the older journals with more issues and, therefore, more articles and citations from having an advantage over newer journals.

1980 and 1990. In 1970 these journals were ranked as high as fifth, but most were in the bottom of the top 30. Other more detailed trends are reflected as well: the declining importance of agriculture as a per cent of GDP shows up in the declining importance of the *American Journal of Agricultural Economics*. The methodological changes previously noted are visible in the declining importance of a journal like *Economic Development and Cultural Change*.[13] All in all, despite the title of the table as presenting the 'top 30' journals it takes twice that number of journals to track the top 30 over the past 40 years.

Finally we may note that column 6 shows the 'top 30' journals if we base the citation count on all the citations each journal has gotten since its inception. Obviously older journals get an advantage here even if the counts are based on the per cent of all citations in the index. The other columns adjust for this, we reiterate, by measuring citations for five year periods and concentrating on journals in existence for the entire five years.

In any case, the information in Table 7.2 as conventionally interpreted by economists means that every citation to an article adds to the standing of the author(s) of the article as well as to that of the journal in which it is published. And an economist's standing goes up every time a given article is cited. Therefore, a comparison of columns 3, 4, and 5 of Table 7.2 reflects, as we began by pointing out, the changing views of journal popularity as measured by citation counts. But changes in popularity in turn reflect changing interests, changing tastes, changing methodological preferences, along with changes in the economy itself as reflected in this picture of changing relative importance attached to various journals in the recent past. All of these factors play a role in the success or failure which young scholars will have in getting their work published in different eras. If citation counts, therefore, do in fact reflect impact, the potential putatively successful scholars in setting a research agenda for themselves need to be conscious of a great many factors other than where their natural interests may lead them.

A Closer Look at Citation Counts

There are problems, however, with simple counts which sophisticated interpretations of citation counts try to take into consideration. We consider some of them here. We have previously noted that journals play a role in the advancement and standing of scholars in the field of economics which is hard

13. This despite, as we saw earlier, the case that can be made, many would argue quite convincingly, that the field of economics itself is well immersed in a culture of its own. The truth of this has never depended on its recognition by practicing economists.

to exaggerate. One virtue attached to the top five journals is that scarcely anyone doubts the worth of the journals, however measured. (They do vary somewhat in ranking over time.) They can, therefore, be used to measure the relative prestige that attaches to various characteristics of economics journals – elegant modeling, precision, sophisticated use of qualitative analysis, clarity of exposition, the subdiscipline of the field to which the journal is devoted, and the current intensity of faddish interest in that area, etc. Thus, for example, in the article previously referred to as labeling the five journals we have considered the 'flagship journals' they are used to measure the number of published pages in these journals within a chosen period of time to indicate the rank appropriate to that department. (We earlier noted the circularity in all this.)

The consequences of this process have profound importance to all the other questions discussed in this chapter – where to publish, what topics are likely to be accepted, how strong is the likelihood that a given line of research will lead to a successful PhD or tenure for a young scholar or promotion for young professor, etc. A by-product of these factors, of course, is that what is faddish is involved in a self-reinforcing process which lasts until it is superseded by an even newer fad. More generally, 'mainstream' approaches, even while they are constantly threatened with becoming more or less instant anachronisms are, until overcome with such a fate, self-reinforced through this process while heterodox or alterative approaches are kept safely out of 'influential' avenues of discourse.

Table 7.2 traces the changing perceptions of importance of economics journals in several ways. The simplest approach is shown in column 6 which ranks the importance of a journal simply by the number of citations ever made anywhere to an article published in a given journal. Economists, however, discount citations to non-economic journals so that is the first adjustment made. (A citation in, say, a law journal, is weighted zero.) So, as we have seen, they compute what is called the 'impact-adjusted value' for a given journal. Secondly they regard citations in 'influential' journals as worth more than a citation in journals not considered influential. But how do we measure influence? Naturally, influence is measured by the number of citations to all its articles that a given journal gets in a given period compared to all the citations which occurred in this period.[14]

More generally, the relationship between citations and journal importance

14. By now there have been a number of efforts to rank the importance of economic journals. A partial listing would include: Leibowitz and Palmer (1984), Laband and Piette (1994). As the reader might suspect calculating impact-adjusted values has become as complicated as most other reasonably similar measurement efforts in economics.

affects the citation practices of economists at any given time. They, in turn, were carefully considered by George J. Stigler and Claire Friedman (Stigler and Friedman 1975). They examined the citations of doctorates from six major universities in the period 1950–1965. 'The hypothesis we propose is that numerous citations, unless they are heavily unfavorable, reveal allies, especially if they are reciprocated' (1975, p. 500). They give examples of 'allies' – that is Professor X cites Professor Y favorably *N* times and Professor Y cites Professor X *N* + times. The same numbers increase the importance of both the professors and the journal. The professors thus contribute to increasing the importance of the journal – that is its 'impact-adjusted value' goes up as does the impact of the professors. In this way 'significant' authors play a major role in enhancing their own significance, the significance of like-minded economists ('allies') and the ranking in impact-adjusted terms of the journals through which they do their cross-citing (Stigler and Friedman 1975, p. 500).

Finally it is clear that citations and publications figure prominently in the relative prestige of various departments. Citations and pages published frequently point to the same universities. This is further attested to by several studies of departmental ranking (cf., especially, Conroy, Dusansky, Drukker, and Kildegaard 1995, and Dusansky and Vernon 1998).

CITATIONS, PUBLICATIONS, AND DEPARTMENTAL PRESTIGE: THRIVING SYMBIOSES

Citations to a journal sponsored by a given university are surely one way that departmental prestige is built. What about the composition of the boards which run the organizations which sponsor these journals? We again concentrate on the 'flagship' journals considered in connection with Table 7.2 above. To begin with both the *Journal of Political Economy* and the *Quarterly Journal of Economics* are produced entirely by faculties of Chicago and Harvard respectively. Therefore, it might not be surprising if a journal produced entirely by a given department tended to publish papers from its own faculty or graduate students. Similarly along with the influence of having a 'house journal' so to speak, geographic factors can affect acceptance. Thus, the *Economic Journal* has English faculty from a number of English schools on its Board of Editors, and this no doubt accounts, at least partially, for the high number of acceptances of papers from economists affiliated with English universities.

Only in the case of the *American Economic Review* and *Econometrica*, therefore, can one meaningfully ask whether the same schools which dominate journals in pages published are similarly top heavy in representation on the executive boards which control the organizations publishing the *American Economic Review* and *Econometrica*. We shall focus on the *American Economic Review* and the American Economic Association, the latter being the recognized basic organization in the United States representing consensus thinking about priorities, trends, current research methods, perspectives on policy, interests, and approaches to the multi-faceted concerns of the profession. We again focus attention on the period 1985–1990, but this time we ask, who was running the American Economics Association during this period? We see the answer in column 3 of Table 7.4. The first observation is that universities whose faculty ran the American Economic Association between 1985 and 1990 are (with one exception) the same universities leading the ranking of universities whose affiliated faculty published the most pages in the *American Economic Review*. The top ranking universities for pages published in all 'flagship' American journals are shown in column 2 of Table 7.4.

Second, the concentrations of schools represented on the Executive Committee of the American Economic Association during these years bears a strong similarity to the concentration of universities called 'home' by the most successful of the published authors in the four American flagship journals. Trend setting journals are apt to attract authors from trend setting graduate programs.

Grants, Grantsmanship, and Departmental Prestige

There is one final factor contributing to the prestige of a modern economics program which we can include in this discussion. This concerns the matter of obtaining research grants, preferably from a large and prestigious foundation or a similar well known sponsor of economic research. It is highly probable that prestige would devolve upon a research program which succeeded in obtaining a research grant from a little known source provided the sum was sufficiently large. Who better than an economist to be impressed with a high price?

So far as we can discern, there are no explicit statements in place for the relevant American economics departments specifying formally the requirement that economics faculty obtain grants as one of the requirements for either tenure, or more certainly, promotion. But there seems to be a general understanding that one of the major changes in recent years in the requirements for advancement in mainstream economics departments has been that the candidate for promotion (most often to full professor) demonstrate that he or she has added to his or her 'impact and significance' by obtaining fairly hefty dollar amounts of research grants. This is frequently expressed as an obligation that all faculty 'contribute to the funding of departmental research.' There are, of course, myriad sources of such research funds and major departments have access to specialists prepared to assist junior faculty (and often senior faculty) in preparing grant applications and pursuing them through the application process, often pretty convoluted.

Without further belaboring the point, we assert simply that getting a line on who is getting research grants and which universities do well in these activities is a final dimension by which modern economics departments can add to their reputation at the same time that the individual economists who are successful in getting such grants are able to add to their own luster. It is obviously impossible to examine the full panoply of sources of research grants. We have here contented ourselves with examining the records of a major source of funding for economic research in much of the last half century – the National Science Foundation. They have awarded some three thousand grants for economic research in the years 1980–2000, and during the same period they have denied requests for funding to some five thousand projects.[15] The results of our examination of the grants awarded in economics for this period are shown in Table 7.4 columns 4A and 4B which are limited to the same years for which the other measures of significance in the table were available.[16]

If we examine the evidence concerning which universities were among the top five in getting grants in the same way roughly as is covered in the rest of Table 7.4 we find the same handful of universities which figure prominently in the rest of the table are prominent in NSF award grants. The only addition to our list might be UCLA.

In the relevant column, column 4, the reader may see that we have ranked the awarding of grants in two ways. The simplest way is to ask, in how many of the six years did a given university appear as one of the top five recipients of NSF grants? So viewed Northwestern and Stanford dominate the results.

A more discriminating measure is once again to rank the leading universities (any that got in the top five at least twice during the six years) by the dollar value of the grants they received. This produces a clear ranking of the top seven universities. Northwestern University was the top grant

15. We are grateful to Dan Newlon, director of the economics program at the National Science Foundation (NSF) for making these data available to us.

16. We follow the traditional practice of citing awards to individual universities by year. There are exceptions – awards made for multi-years or joint awards made to more than one university which are difficult to show in this simple scheme. Our claim is mainly that the presentation we give follows the usual precedent and gives a roughly accurate picture of how awards have been distributed.

receiver in this period but did at least show up in other measures earlier in the table as well. Stanford, MIT, Yale, and Chicago should surprise no one by their appearance in column 4. The only newcomer to the top group is UCLA.

More generally, if in considering the role of grants we broaden the focus and ask which universities dominated the NSF economics awards during the entire period 1980–2000 we get the results shown in Table 7.5. Virtually all the universities which appeared in one of the 'top five' by other measures show up prominently in Table 7.5. Chicago is somewhat less prominent, and California Institute of Technology and Minnesota are slightly more prominent. But the top seven in Table 7.5 are the same universities that dominated all the other measures in Table 7.4.

One final factor should be mentioned in connection with the grants. We have concentrated on the awarding of grants to universities, and this is indeed the traditional type of award made since the National Science Fund was established. In the past quarter century the granting of awards to research organizations has become increasingly prominent. Chief among these has been the awarding of grants to the National Bureau of Economic Research (and to a lesser extent the Brookings Institution, the National Opinion Research Center, and a few others). Table 7.6 shows that over the period shown the awards to the NBER were around a million dollars a year in the beginning and have more than trebled over the 20 years shown in the table. If we look just at the years 1985–90, for which we have already shown the top university grants, it is clear that the total amount going to the NBER is as large or larger than the amount going to the most heavily supported universities in many of these years. Because most of the economists affiliated with the NBER are also affiliated with a university it is clear that were the NBER awards reallocated according to these NBER staff members' university affiliations it would alter the pattern significantly. It is well, therefore, to keep the NBER relationship in mind when looking at the grants to universities alone.

In the end, the point to under-score is that the awarding of grants by the NSF is, first, probably, no different in overall pattern than other major awards for economic research. (We may say that, broadly speaking.) All the measures we have examined reflect prevailing mainstream views of what constitutes 'excellence in economic research.' The awarding of grants for research has become increasingly important in determining success in academia for economists. While, therefore, it has become an important contributory factor in judging academic achievement and potential, it has reinforced other measures rather than driven them in a different direction.

It is unclear what the implications of this trend are for the larger theme

Table 7.4 Four measures of prestige – American economics departments

Top five universities by number of pages published in *Am Econ Review*, 1985–90 (a)	Top five universities by number of pages published in four American 'flagship' journals, 1985–90 Number of universities (b)			Top five universities by number of faculty in AEA exec. positions 1985–90 Number of positions (c)			Top five universities by national science grants measured and ranked two ways, 1985–90 (d)				
								A Number of years university was one of top five in dollar amounts	Rank	B Total dollar value of grants NSF to university ($mil)	Rank
(1)	(2)			(3)					(4)		
1. MIT	1. MIT	4	(Tie)	1. MIT	7		Northwestern	6	1	3.52	1
2. Harvard	2. Harvard	4	(Tie)	2. Harvard	6	(Tie)	Stanford	5	2	3.22	2
3. Princeton	2. Princeton	4	(Tie)	2. Princeton	6	(Tie)	U. of PA	2		1.22	3
4. Chicago	4. Stanford	3		2. Chicago	6	(Tie)	MIT	2	3	1.08	4
5. Michigan	5. Chicago	2		5. UC Berkeley	5		Yale	2		1.04	5
							Chicago	2		0.94	6
	Other:			Other:			UCLA	2		0.91	7
	Northwestern	1		Brookings	4		Universities appearing once (1) – 9 universities	-9	8		
	Yale	1		Minnesota	3						
	Michigan	1		Univ. Washington	3						
				Urban Inst.	3						
				Stanford	2						
				Northwestern	2						
				Yale	2						
				Carnegie Mellon	2						
				BLS	2						
				World Bank	2						
				Other	5						
Totals		20			60			30			

Table 7.4 cont.

Notes:

(a) For the *American Economic Review*, the pages published ranking for Stanford is 6th and for UC Berkeley the rank is 8th.

(b) Column 2 summarizes the number of appearances among the top five for universities for all four of the American journals. There are thus 20 appearances in all (top five universities times four journals).

(c) For executive positions we have included for each year the President of the American Economic Association, the President-Elect, the two Vice-Presidents, and the six elected members of the Executive Committee. This gives ten positions for each of six years. Hence the number of positions shown for each university in the last column is out of a total of 60.

(d) Column 4 attempts to indicate the relative ability to obtain grants, using the National Science Foundation awards to typify this ability. The first column shows the number of years out of the six covered in the table in which the university was one of the top five universities in terms of dollar volume of National Science Foundation economics awards for research granted to its faculty. This means that there are 30 possible positions available. In terms of the number of years in which a university can appear the maximum is six and only one appears in all six years (Northwestern). Stanford appears in five years. The other universities shown in the table all appeared twice. Universities appearing in one year among the six included Rochester, Princeton, Cornell, Illinois-Urbana, Harvard, UC-Berkeley, and UC-San Diego. The other way to measure the success of universities in obtaining NSF grants is to look at the total value of all awards to each university over the six years. These totals are shown in the other column, along with the rank obtained by indicating the total amount each university obtained.

We have left the University of Michigan off. The books of the NSF indicated that they received a grant of 9,844,525 in 1987 to conduct a Panel Study of Income Dynamics. In actual fact this was a five year commitment of which 41,500,0000 was paid in 1987 and was shared between the Economics program and the Sociology program. Part of the total award came not from NSF funds but from other agencies. All in all, clearly this award was a special award. In total amount it dwarfed other NSF grants, and therefore, we have not included it in either Table 7.4 or 7.5. The reader should be aware that, however measured in this single case, this university received substantial help from the NSF over a period of time. Despite its size the award does not significantly change the pattern of 'most prominent economics programs' revealed generally.

In the table it is the tendency of many universities to recur in all these categories which is of primary note.

Sources:

Column 1 Bairam (1994), 675.

Column 2 Bairam (1994), 675, 676, 678, 679.

Column 3 Calculated by author from front pages of *American Economic Review*, 1985–1990.

Column 4 Calculated by author from data provided by National Science Foundation on 'Economics Program Awards, 1980–Present.' Grateful acknowledgment to the National Science Foundation is made for their assistance in providing the data.

under consideration. As noted earlier it may be becoming increasingly necessary, if one wishes to present a complete picture of which universities are the most prominent, to trace the university affiliation of all the economists who receive awards through these research organizations. But it may well be that the complete affiliations of recipients of awards would not cause the list of their university affiliations to deviate substantially from the distribution we have seen repeatedly in this chapter.[17]

We conclude that ranking of American economics departments in terms of research grants received by their faculty merely confirms the findings of the other measures utilized. All measures of prominence considered here point generally to the same small group of universities as 'top ranking.' It is clear that however one measures 'impact,' the universities prominent in shaping the discipline during the years in question were MIT, Princeton, Harvard, Chicago, and Stanford, with Michigan, the University of California at Berkeley, Northwestern, the University of Pennsylvania, and Yale not much if any distance behind. These universities, then, may be thought of as the nub of what is meant by 'mainstream economics' certainly for the years in question. We have in this chapter used a variety of criteria to identify mainstream economics. Some time ago Philip Mirowski wrote, 'we . . . provisionally define the orthodox in economic theory . . . as the composite of standard curriculum prevalent in American or American-influenced graduate programs.' He argues that after World War II that curriculum became much more homogeneous, a view we have earlier in this chapter corroborated. He concludes that 'there are now only two schools of thought to chose from: the predominant neo-classical economic theory, and a European variant of an attenuated form of Marxian economic theory. Although other schools of thought have flourished in the past and still claim adherents, in a surprisingly short interval German historicism, American Institutionalism, Austrian subjectivism, and yes, even Keynesian macroeconomics have been displaced

---

17. In connection with the broad themes of this book, it is worth noting the views of Dan Newlon, director of the economics program at the NSF:

> . . . we at the National Science Foundation's Economics Program are proud of our version of the peer review process and its results. We think we've done a good job. Contrary to the beliefs of some economists, it is inappropriate to blame 'close-minded' reviewers for the relative lack of success experienced by researchers outside the mainstream of economics in publishing influential articles or obtaining research grants. In fact, peer review provides a reasonably open forum for new ideas. A wide variety of innovative alternative avenues of research have received NSF funding and have been thoroughly debated in articles in the leading economics journals. If these alternatives have not met standards of rigor and explanatory power and, as a consequence, are no longer pursued, then we need more and better ideas. We want to know about promising new researchers and original ideas not currently funded by NSF so we can avoid future mistakes. (Newlon 1989, pp. 221–228)

and superceded as active research programs in the schools that train the majority of the next generation of economists' (Mirowski 1986, p. 3). This was written 20 years ago, and arguably – as we shall see in the next chapter – a number of varieties of heterodox economics (including several mentioned by Mirowski) have gained ground in both the United States and Europe in the intervening years.

But Mirowski is certainly right in his basic characterization of US economic orthodoxy and this book gives considerable evidence in support of his view. Mirowski also points to the essential conflict between the current organization of the mainstream discipline and the problems faced by the economy.

A recent essay published by the Levy Institute on economic policy asserts,

> Not long ago, official circles insisted that monetary policy was the most effecive tool, and that fiscal deficits were not only unnecessary but also harmful . . .
>
> Yet fiscal policy has made a swift and major comeback, not simply as tax cuts and military expenditures, but also as huge budget deficits. (Papadimitriou et al., 2004, p. 1)

This illustrates almost perfectly our theme that modern orthodox economics is not confronting the economy. The decline in Keynesian macroeconomics in graduate theory curriculums suggests that its contribution to any 'swift and major comeback' in fiscal policy has probably been minimal. If the economics programs considered in this chapter are worried about this they give little evidence of it. As such it suggests that the role of graduate economics programs in producing economic theorists continues to go its own way with little regard for its putative role in contributing to the intellectual equipment of the next generation of economic policy makers. Other universities and also unaffiliated economists who were like-minded have certainly contributed to the work that falls under this rubric. But the impetus for new trends and new areas of research in mainstream economics was heavily influenced by this small group of universities. We return to this state of affairs at the end of the chapter.

The group is, as we say, quite small. Therefore, no one should be surprised at the results of a recent *US News* ranking. This magazine did a survey of department chairs and the heads of graduate programs and calculated, on the basis of information they provided, something they called the 'average reputation score' for 25 American universities and found that MIT, Princeton, Chicago, Harvard, and Stanford were tied for first place. UC Berkeley and Yale came in tied for sixth (*US News and World Report*, 2000).

Table 7.5 Number of appearances in the top five universities getting NSF awards, by dollar volume of awards in economics, major overall award receiving universities, 1980–2000

University	Number of appearances in top five major award receiving universities
	Appearances
1. Stanford	14
2. Northwestern	13
3. Yale	10
4. Princeton	8
5. MIT	7
6. Univ. of Pennsylvania	6
7. Harvard	5
8. Cal. Inst. of Technology	4
9. Minnesota	4
Appearing 3 times:	
Chicago, Illinois-Urbana, Carnegie-Mellon, Rochester, UC-Berkeley, UC-San Diego, Michigan	
Appearing 2 times:	
Columbia, UCLA, Cornell, Pittsburgh, Wisconsin-Madison, New York	
Appearing 1 time:	
Iowa	1
Total appearances	105

Note: For the 21 years there are 105 (21 x 5) positions for 'top five grant receiving universities.'

Source: As Table 7.4, col. 4.

A ranking based on a more restrictive basis (total pages in journals per economics department) in 1996 ranked Harvard, Chicago, Penn, MIT, Northwestern, Stanford, and Princeton as the top seven (in that order) (Scott and Mitias 1996, 378). Without undertaking any sort of quasi-scientific survey, our impression is that the economists we have referred to the most in the previous chapters are largely to be found concentrated in the relatively small list of universities mentioned here also. How should these findings be interpreted? We begin by underscoring that we do not suggest anything sinister here. The journals all have systems of blind reviewing and the process is as honest as human beings can make it. And certainly no aspersions are being cast on the reviewing system at any of the journals or at the election procedures followed by the American Economic Association. As for the NSF and its system for awarding grants it is not surprising that it mirrors the rankings found by other criteria for making these judgments. They rely on committees of prominent economists and 'prominence' will undoubtedly follow the other ranking systems reported here.

Identifying the prominent economics programs, and by diverse criteria which nonetheless give similar results, has major implications for the discipline.

DIFFERENTIATING THE MAINSTREAM AND HETERODOX APPROACHES TO ECONOMICS

We turn finally in some greater detail to the implications of all this for our view of mainstream economics. Its definition comes up periodically, and has been the subject of some dispute among heterodox economists, and perhaps among mainstream economists as well (though the latter are most apt simply to assume that, in the manner of 'l'etat c'est moi!' they *are* the mainstream, because what else could the term mean?). So a result of our efforts in this chapter, we argue, is to help in the definition of 'mainstream.'

We have here been engaged in an effort to clarify the criteria by which 'prominence' or 'impact' is determined today in the discipline of economics. From time to time heterodox economists become discouraged or depressed by current terminology and insist that the heterodox approach is really the mainstream and the mainstream is correctly classified elsewhere. (After all, they argue, the least one should expect of a mainstream theory is useful public policy!) Tempting as it is to declare the war won and go home, it seems to us to do too much violence to the customary meaning of the vocabulary used in discussing all this to make this case. We have instead come to the conclusion that 'mainstream' in any area is determined ultimately by a consensus commonly reached by those in a position to exert influence. Thus to be a mainstream economist is not necessarily to be an economist who is always or even frequently right, or who has his ear to the pulse of the public, or 'really' understands the fundamental relationships which produce the field today. 'Mainstream' would seem to mean exactly what it says – it is the principal current with which a consensus of us economists identify, for better or worse.

We may even remind the reader, harking back to the original meaning, that more than once in civilized history a community has concluded that a river bed needs to be altered and so have set about deliberately to redirect a mainstream into a new direction. In short, to be in the mainstream, therefore, has no normative implications. To be mainstream is not unlike 'popular belief' which no one has ever suggested is necessarily correct, efficient, equitable, or even useful. It simply is. It has sometimes been argued that 'mainstream economics' cannot truly be mainstream because sound and useful public policy cannot even be derived from it. To argue that laissez faire is effective interventionist policy would surely be classified as an oxymoron! In this book we have certainly argued that economics needs to undergo considerable alteration in perspective, approach and methodology if it is successfully to confront modern economies. In our sister social science, the Jeffersonian dictum that 'that government is best which governs least ' is scarcely taken to mean that the ideal government, therefore, does not govern at all! The last chapter is devoted to spelling out a possible heterodox perspective. For now we say only that by successful economics, of course, we mean concentrating on developing economic theory that is useful in assisting in the creation of sound public policy which can materially assist in achieving a number of goals that, by its own logic, economics ought to cherish. Such goals as the utilization of resources and technology in ways which are efficient seem clear. Efficiency here means that standards of living, including minimal standards of living, are commensurate with what is technologically and allocatively achievable and possible.

Suffice it here to say that the core of economics, its theory, needs to be directed at solving critical economic problems. Entirely too much of the time at present, the purposes of economic theory are to be found in other directions. We refer, of course, to the old charge attributed earlier to John Hicks, that economics is a game, a grand game perhaps, but a game. Why does no mainstream economic theorist ever ask, from his classical, mainstream, hard-nosed, positive point of origin whether, things being how they are in the modern world, modern societies can really afford to divert so important a discipline from problem solving to game playing, no matter how elegant, precise, logical, and grand the game may be? We shall return to these questions in the final chapter.

Table 7.6 NSF awards to NBER, 1980–2000

Year	Number of awards	Total awards for year ALL	Amount	Per cent awarded to NBER
1980	11	$10,245,939	$1,408,743	13.7
1981	9	$ 5,800,652	$ 562,933	9.7
1982	17	$ 6,019,001	$1,456,045	24.2
1983	18	$ 7,606,605	$1,173,452	15.4
1984	24	$ 8,506,533	$1,610,961	18.9
1985	16	$10,398,352	$1,508,273	14.5
1986	24	$ 9,843,640	$1,858,949	18.9
1987	20	$17,935,527	$1,571,244	8.8
1988	21	$11,783,946	$2,232,511	18.9
1989	29	$10,157,770	$2,802,222	27.6
1990	18	$10,643,574	$1,973,826	18.5
1991	29	$13,538,940	$3,179,112	23.5
1992	30	$31,633,241	$4,083,441	12.9
1993	22	$16,360,955	$3,258,250	19.9
1994	34	$15,324,663	$5,827,881	38.0
1995	21	$14,841,630	$4,078,593	27.5
1996	20	$13,469,600	$3,775,004	28.0
1997	19	$27,888,431	$4,220,544	15.1
1998	35	$20,729,268	$7,613,142	36.7
1999	21	$16,217,901	$3,272,882	20.2
2000	24	$16,652,158	$3,469,528	20.8
	462	$295,598,326	$60,937,536	20.6

REFERENCES

Bairam, Erkin I. (1994), 'Institutional affiliation of contributors to top journals, 1985–1990', *Journal of Economic Literature*, **32** (2), 674–9.

Blaug, Mark (1992), *The Methodology of Economics or How Economists Explain*, Cambridge: Cambridge University Press.

Coats, A.W. and David C. Colander (1989), 'Introduction', in *The Spread of Economic Ideas*, Cambridge: Cambridge University Press.

Conroy, Michael E., Richard Dusansky, David Drukker and Arne Kildegaard (1995), 'The productivity of economics departments in the US – publications in the core journals', *Journal of Economic Literature*, **33** (4), 1966–71.

Dusansky, Richard and Clayton J. Vernon (1998), 'Rankings of US economics departments', *Journal of Economic Perspectives*, **12** (1), 257–70.

Hansen, W. Lee (1991), 'The education and training of economics doctorates', *Journal of Economic Literature*, **29** (3), 1054–87.

Hicks, John R. (1979), *Causality in Economics*, Oxford: Blackwell.

Laband, David N. and Michael J. Piette (1994), 'The relative impacts of economics journals: 1970–1990', *Journal of Economic Literature*, **32** (21), 640–66.

Liebowitz, S.J. and J.P. Palmer (1984), 'Assessing the relative impacts of economics journals', *Journal of Economic Literature*, **22** (1), 77–88.

McCloskey, D. (1985), *The Rhetoric of Economics*, Madison, WI: University of Wisconsin Press.

Mirowski, Philip (1986), 'Introduction: paradigms, hard cores, and fugelmen in modern economic theory', in Philip Mirowski (ed.), *The Reconstruction of Economic Theory*, Boston/Dordrecht/Lancaster: Kluwer, Nijhoff Publishing, pp. 1-11.

Newlon, Dan (1989), 'The role of the NSF in the spread of economic ideas' in David V. Colander and A.W. Coats (eds), *The Spread of Economic Ideas*, Cambridge: Cambridge University Press, pp. 195–228.

Papadimitriou, Dmitri, Anwar M. Sharikh, Claudio H. Dos Santos and Geraaro Ongenn Zezzizamaro (2004), 'Is deficit finance growth limited? Policy prospects in an election year', *Levy Institute Policy Notes*, April.

Scott, Loren C. and Peter M. Mitias (1996), 'Trends in rankings of economics departments in the U.S.: an update', *Economic Inquiry*, 378–400.

Spence, Michael (2002), 'Signaling in retrospect and the informational structure of markets', *American Economic Review*, **92** (3), 411–501.

Stanford University (1999), *Graduate Student Handbook*.

Stigler, George J. and Claire Friedman (1975), 'The citation practices of doctorates in economics', *Journal of Political Economy*, **83** (3), 477–508.

US News and World Report (2000).

8. Economics confronts the economy: an alternative view – don't cry for me, economics

The time will come when we shall see that the root of all economic confusion and the cause of intellectual impotency which has brought economics into general disrepute is the obsession of our science with price theory – the virtual identification of economics with price analysis to the almost total exclusion of what Veblen called the 'life process' of mankind. (Ayres 1944, p. v)

Economists tend to be scientific optimists. They believe in their discipline, in its methods or tools, and in their ability to deal with major questions. Among themselves they may speak in disparaging terms about psychologists and sociologists, asserting, they never agree on anything, use imprecise methods, and have no measurements. They then crown economics the queen of social sciences . . . economists insist that empirical tests will determine who is right. Their intent is to reach agreement . . . in principle economists are detached scientists who suppress their normative ideas (on what ought to be) in favor of positive insights (on what is). They depict the acquisition of economic knowledge as the outcome of a rational process little influenced by external factors, such as political alliances or personal inclinations. This picture of what happens within the world of economists is both incomplete and misleading. (Klamer 1983, p. vii)

Institutional economics is dying out at a fantastic rate – though still not fast enough to suit me. (Stigler 1993, 788)

Practicing economists may be proud and confident about the way they study the economy, but they should not be too arrogant to assume that their success negates the value of other practices . . . It is difficult to imagine what this discourse would look like without 'human capital,' 'demand elasticity,' 'transaction costs,' 'agency costs,' 'moral hazard,' 'Nash equilibrium,' 'rent seeking behavior,' 'price leadership,' 'adverse selection,' 'free riders,' and many other concepts that have been added by economists in the last half of the century. But the victory of mathematical economics in the institutional level and their manifold achievements do not prove that they have found the best theory and that older approaches had nothing worthwhile pursuing and remembering.

(Tonay 1998, p. 221)

> We do not believe that scholars can continue the posture of 'eschewing value judgements' in their analyses of social, political, and economic problems. Whether or not we succeed in formulating an analysis of social value which is . . . largely devoid of ism-ideology . . . we do address directly and continuously the task of choosing a criterion (or criteria) of judgment to employ in deciding 'which direction is forward' . . . . (Tonay 1998, p. 221)

> As always before, economic change will have to make its peace with social and political realities, and in this continuing mutual adjustment, the role of economic forces is far from a "mechanical one". (Heilbroner 1962, p. 231)

As we have earlier seen, there is no discipline which proclaims more loudly or consistently the virtues of being a positive science than economics. Most economists, in fact, speak and write as though it were a foregone conclusion that economics is a positive science. But paradoxically, there is also no discipline in which, we argue, normative values are more constantly lurking in the arguments put forth. There is a reason for this. If one harks back to the old distinction between 'what is' and 'what ought to be' one can say that in the natural sciences the 'what is' is existentially present without any action on the part of human beings. There is a body of material, therefore, for the physicist, the mathematician, the chemist, or the biologist, for example, to study absent any activity by people. The social sciences are different. The 'what is' to be studied is the work of human beings, deliberately constructed to fulfill a purpose. This distinction is clearer in some social sciences than others – it is least clear perhaps in psychology, which in some areas is tangent to natural sciences (anatomy, physiology, etc.). It is clearest in the case of political science (all government is the work of the people who constitute the polity). In the case of economics all societies need to solve economic problems somehow; how they do so is in their hands, but subject to some exogenous factors mainly (but not entirely) luck – the weather, available technology, resources. The latter, after all, is a matter of the piece of real estate on which a given people try to construct an economy. The US is very lucky (good climate, lots of resources, a low person/land ratio, etc.). The Russians are a bit less lucky (lots of resources, a good person/land ratio, but a hostile climate). Third world countries are often merely unlucky . . . (few resources, ungrateful climate, etc . . .). Without affecting in the slightest the fundamental importance of applying the scientific method in studying all fields (and studying economic problems requires this as consistently as any other field of human study), it is nonetheless true that the process of constructing the basic 'what is' which constitutes an economy involves making decisions which are suffused with value judgements of one sort or another. (For example, the mainstream core assertion that decisions should be 'left to the market' is quite as much a value statement as that they should be 'left to the plan!')

If indeed we were correct earlier in asserting that economics, like other disciplines (most especially including the social sciences), exists in a culture, the culture of American economics is compatible with the *weltanschauung* from which it comes and that culture is orthodox (as opposed to heterodox) economics. The culture produces or influences consensus thinking as to trends in methodology, important topics, initial assumptions etc.). The same culture produced the change from a verbal to a numeric approach to economic theory and the shift from an institutional to a game theoretic approach to industrial organization, etc. We have earlier characterized the rigidities and the inflexibilities in how economic problems are viewed, as well as the currently acceptable techniques for studying these problems. Today mainstream economics is consonant with the theory presently designed to explain economic problems. It is, therefore, no coincidence that among the economists included in column C of Table 7.4 as officers or board members of the American Economic Association during the five years included in the count, the only heterodox economist to be included was Mancur Olson of the University of Maryland. Economists, like other social scientists, do not work in a values vacuum. The values environment in which they work is a manifestation of the larger culture.[1]

The view of problems, the techniques for studying them, and the theory which emerges all conform to these characteristics. This book has attempted a critical examination of mainstream economics; in this chapter we sketch an alternative approach. It is crucial, therefore, that we be as precise as possible about what we mean by 'mainstream' economics. The term has meaning only if it can be specified. That was the task undertaken in Chapter 7. The prominent universities enumerated in the tables in that chapter are, as we tried to show, all among the leaders in fleshing out the perspective we have characterized as mainstream. By calling this perspective an outgrowth of 'culture' we mean to suggest that attitudinal and/or value changes are reflected in changes in many aspects of society which in turn both reflect that dynamic culture and contribute to ongoing changes in it. These universities are, of course, affected in similar fashion by the impact of that common culture. One way to pose the underlying question is to ask, how shall we

1. The same is undoubtedly true of natural scientists as well. But the relationship is more immediately obvious in the case of the social sciences.

explain the fact that the end result of a mainstream economist's 'positive economic analysis' all too often leads to policy implications which are consonant with the culture from which they emanate? That is to say, the results of mainstream economic analyses all too often advance findings which support the assertion that non-intervention is the best policy. In the case of the heterodox analysis, considered in this chapter, the analysis begins with the acknowledgement that it is normative economics. It, too, reflects underlying normative positions.[2]

What is involved in all this, of course, is what Thomas Kuhn would call a paradigmatic shift, and such shifts do not occur in a vacuum – they rather reflect the point we have just made – that is, they reflect shifts in the underlying culture (Kuhn 1962, 1970, 1996). Why they occur requires extensive study. All we are saying is that the changes we have been contemplating in earlier chapters do indeed reflect such a shift. A major aspect of this shift, as earlier considered in detail, has been a downplaying of institutional factors so as to make possible the use of the simplifying assumptions required to make mathematical model building feasible. This shift is reflected in the recent history of virtually every field in economics. The universities on which we focused in the last chapter would, we suggest, be rather universally regarded by economists of all persuasions as chief among the major contributors of agents who played a major role in promulgating the changes in economics we have focused on in earlier chapters. But it is important to be clear that what we attempted was a look at what is meant by the mainstream and how the mainstream paradigm has developed in the past half century. The earlier chapters dealt with the changes in the recent past; pinning down what is meant by the mainstream was the ultimate objective of Chapter 7. We trust it is now clear that by mainstream economics we mean the view espoused, taught, and researched in the handful of universities considered in Chapter 7. Even more, the term subsumes the vast majority of graduate programs in economics whose organizing principles take the same viewpoint, make the same assumptions, reach the same curricular as well as substantive conclusions, and present both the challenges economics faces and the proposed presumed ideal ways of confronting them in the same fashion as is generally espoused by those universities we identified in the previous chapter as 'top' or leading universities. The mainstream view includes the thinking about economic issues evolving in these places as well as at all the lesser venues where thinking about economic issues derives from efforts to emulate the approach evolving from the 'top.'

2. This is, of course, what was the underlying basis for our earlier discussion of proof and truth in economic theory.

An example may clarify the point. Clearly the rational expectations approach was part of evolving mainstream thinking. It originated at the University of Chicago and a few other places. It became well established in fairly short order at a number of lesser places. Its conclusions support the non-interventionist viewpoint long connected with mainstream thinking. It was regarded as an advance in positive economics and is an important development in 'the new classical economics.' In this case, as we saw earlier, the advance was a retreat back to pre-Keynesian thinking.

Here attention focuses on the heterodox view of the discipline and the cultural (or counter-cultural) milieu from which it emanates. In previous chapters, in the process of criticizing the mainstream view, its *weltanschauung* has been implicitly exposed. Now it is time to attempt to clarify similarly the heterodox view and the *weltanschauung* from which its criticism has been derived.

HETERODOXY, ORTHODOXY, AND PARADIGMATIC INSIGHTS

One fundamentally significant way to begin considering an alternative approach to economics is to recognize that in a very real sense modern mainstream economics all too often fails to confront the real economy at all. It is not inaccurate to say that often conventional economics treats the real economy with what can only be described charitably as benign neglect. The origin of this view, as we have previously seen, is the invisible hand and the mantra with which it has been larded over by generations of economists. Our sister social science, political science, has at least as rigid a dictum with which to anchor itself as economics. In political science, the practitioners have the stance of Thomas Jefferson as basic: 'That government is best which governs least.' This is as proscriptive as the invisible hand; even in its conventional interpretation self-interest leads greedy and selfish participants in economic activity to undertake that 'which is no part of their original intention' so that they act in the public interest in the bulk of their economic dealings.

The difference, of course, as we shall try to show in this chapter, is that Jeffersonian views never kept political scientists from focusing on the flaws in the way the polity functions. The difference is crucial. The invisible hand as we tried to show in Chapter 1 became a miraculous kind of moral thermostat that automatically converted personal greed into that which was optimal for the community – no wonder all allocation could be 'left to the market'! So it was, as we earlier detailed, that economists took Adam Smith's casual comment (the invisible hand) and converted it into a cardinal principle of economic life to which they have pledged fealty ever since. In contrast political scientists, even with Jefferson's dictum in front of them, had no moral thermostat, and so always recognized that government might strive to be as small as possible but still had to be big enough and powerful enough to rein in any selfish personal behavior that was destructive of community interests.

The economists' reliance on their automatic moral thermostat is, among other things, the explanation, at bottom, for the benign neglect which orthodox economists believe to this day is the appropriate response to any effort to rely on the public sector for any significant part of the provisioning process for getting resources devoted to solving economic problems. These words are written in early 2003 just as President Bush is unveiling his proposed budget for Fiscal 2003. It features a budget of well over two trillion dollars and projects the biggest budget deficit in our history. This is an idiosyncratic view of 'benign neglect' to say the least. It illustrates yet again the severe disjunction between orthodox theorists, on the one hand, and the world of applied economics, on the other hand.

Another way to pose this basic problem is to recognize that mainstream economists have a tendency to confuse means and ends. Methods of analysis and tools of analysis as means are, in the final analysis, not the justification (ends) for any discipline. Such methods are tested by their efficacy in identifying genuine problems and obstacles which interfere with the resolution of real problems. With their solution the real economy can accomplish its provisioning purposes more effectively.

In '*Le Bourgeois Gentilhomme*' Molière has the gentleman totally shocked to learn that he has been speaking prose all his life. Somewhat similarly many economists are so preoccupied with developing and refining their communication system that they are in danger of forgetting that the function of that system in economics (whether numeric or verbal) has always been and still is to solve real economic problems. This view was vigorously underscored earlier.

For heterodox economists the discipline is then at bottom as empirical as, say, Wesley Clair Mitchell always argued it was. Mitchell was a founder of the version of heterodoxy known as American Institutionalism. How much impact heterodoxy in general or institutionalism in particular has is a matter of some contemporary dispute, even among its adherents. For starters we can refute the view of Paul Samuelson, who some time ago wrote of institutionalism '. . . 40 years ago institutionalism withered away as an effective counter force in economics. Who can explain it when a movement turns sterile?' (Samuelson 1976, p. 847). As a forecaster Samuelson's record is not unblemished. He also thought some time ago that business cycles were passé (Samuelson 1972, p. 172). The consideration of American Institutionalism today in this chapter will show that it has clearly not withered away as Samuelson predicted.

A Tale of Three Approaches to Social Science Research

As was alluded to earlier Thomas Kuhn's *Structure of Scientific Revolutions* had a tremendous impact on the world of science, including social science, when it was introduced in the 1960s. In economics, heterodox economists took up the challenge almost immediately. Mainstream economics espoused one paradigm; heterodox economics had another. Institutional economists, with their approach to heterodoxy, addressed this challenge directly. Allan Gruchy, a well known institutionalist, wrote:

> The cultural approach of the institutionalists has led to a paradigmatic shift from the scientific paradigm of the orthodox economists, oriented to the concept of static equilibrium, to a new scientific paradigm oriented to the concept of a dynamic process. Both . . . are primarily concerned with explaining individual and group behavior . . . The difference between the two paradigms is that the orthodox paradigm addresses itself to an explanation of human behavior in a static, culturally neutral economic system, whereas the institutionalist processual paradigm addresses itself to an explanation of human behavior in economic systems embedded in actual cultural circumstances. (Gruchy 1987, p. 4)

Gruchy referred to the difference between these two approaches as involving a 'paradigmatic shift.' There is some evidence that neither mainstream nor institutionalist economists think in terms of paradigms as much as once they did.[3] It is useful to compare the paradigm of mainstream economics with that of heterodoxy by comparing both to what, in my presumption, I called the paradigm of political science. I still find that

3. The term rarely appears in either modern institutionalists' writings or modern mainstream texts. Deborah Redford recently has written, 'Mark Blaug has argued that the term paradigm should be banished from economic literature, unless surrounded by inverted commas.' It is a view which, she makes clear, she shares most vigorously. She argues (with Blaug) that rather than illuminating thought paradigms often obscure and clutter thought. She does however agree with 'paradigms and research programs are essentially the same thing,' and that it is in the effort to clarify contemporary approaches to thinking in two social sciences that the paradigms below are offered (Redford 1991, pp. 144–5).

Table 8.1 Three theoretical frameworks or paradigms

	Economics		Political science
	Mainstream economics	Institutionalism	
Basic outlook	1. Invisible hand (with imperfections) 2. Harmony	1. Cultural conditioning with technological dynamic 2. Conflict	1. Cultural conditioning 2. Conflict
Basic function of system	Allocate scarce resources	Express emergent values of participants through resource deploying decisions	Deploy values authoritatively
Basic mechanism	Market prices	Interactive value system	Interactive value system
Assumptions:	1. Primarily competitive interaction 2. Automaticity	1. Concentrated power distorts value system 2. Value result from interaction of system and participants	1. Concentrated power distorts value system 2. Values result from interaction of system and participants
Motivation	Self-interest	Perceived self-interest	Perceived self-interest
Assumed distribution of decision making authority	One dollar = one vote	Control over constellations of dollar votes, reflecting concentrated wealth and power	Control over constellations of one man, one vote reflecting con-centrated wealth and power
Objective of system	End-in-view: static market equilibrium, i.e., all markets cleared. Efficiency, narrowly defined, also called allocative efficiency.	End-in-view: progress of economy consonant with emergent community values. Achieving the 'higher efficiency'	End-in-view: progress of polity constant with emergent community values

Table 8.1 cont.

'Ideal' system	Pure competition	Decision making process sensitive to changing views of all participants in economic process. Full relevant information available to all	Decision making process sensitive to changing views of all participants in the political process. Full relevant information available to all
Ultimate arbiter of actual system	Invisible hand shaped by sovereign consumers (demand) and technological state (supply)	Technological progress – shaped by big producer sovereignty, concentrated power, and managed information flows	Decision making process – (voting, etc.) shaped by big unit power
Result	Optimal efficiency and progress through producer acquiescence	Manipulated consumer	Manipulated voters
Basic units in system	Households, firms	Individuals and groups of individuals	Individuals and groups of individuals
Corollary	Households and firms express demands (wants) and supplies (costs) through prices with optimal technological productivity	Both households' and firms' decisions are the result of power deployment by individuals and groups (trade unions, corporations, trade associations, etc.)	All political units' decisions are result of power deployment by individuals and groups (parties, lobbyists, interest groups, media conglomerates, big businesses)
Result	Socially ideal resource allocation (implication: higher efficiency same as efficiency narrowly defined)	x-inefficiency; x-disutility. Corrupt results of ideal systems (above)	Actual allocation of values deviates from ideal system (above)

Table 8.1 cont.

Obstacle	Imperfect knowledge of households and firms	Power blocs deliberately distort information flows	Power blocs deliberately distort information flows
Solution	Assume it away	Improve information flows to individuals and groups	Improve information flows to individuals and groups
Welfare assumption	Competitive market equilibria define community welfare (subject to Pareto optimality constraint)	Achieving community welfare is an ongoing process. It is not definable as an absolute end. The means for moving in the direction of greater community welfare are discernable in the process itself	Fulfilling the public interest is an ongoing process. It is not definable as an absolute end. The means for moving in the direction of greater public interest are discernable in the process
		There is a means-end continuum that enables the polity or the economy to progress along the continuum despite the absence of a definable absolute end.	

Note: This is a revised version of an earlier table in Klein (1980).

I thank Deborah Redman for helpful advice in improvements to this presentation.

comparison helpful. Unfortunately (from my viewpoint) the intervening years have merely driven the two paradigms in economics further apart. In the process of deepening that division, as was the subject of Chapter 3, the conversion of mainstream economic theory from largely verbal to mostly numeric expression has made it more difficult than ever to engage in dialogue with its proponents both for non-mathematical economists (that dying breed!) as well as with many other social scientists.

In a recent issue of the *American Political Science Review*, the official journal of the American Political Science Association, a book review begins with a sentence which would cause any economist to sit bolt upright: 'The connection between morality and politics is the core of political theory' (Federici 2001, 983). An economist cannot avoid looking about furtively to see where we shall find the discussion about whether political science is a normative or a positive science. It is nowhere in sight.

Perhaps, then, 20 years have not diminished the potential gains in insight from attempting a paradigmatic comparison of the fields of economics and political science. Let us, therefore, consider Table 8.1.

When Thomas Kuhn first published his *Structure of Scientific Revolutions* (1962) it caused quite a stir. Many scholars paid attention to whether Kuhn spoke to their discipline, and debates and symposia about how it applied to any given field and what its implications were for specific disciplines were very common. Economics was certainly not immune to this wave of interest and we have already noted the Allan Gruchy view that much could be understood about what was going on in economics by characterizing the debate between heterodox and mainstream economics as a debate about the character of the paradigmatic shift involved. From the institutionalists' point of view the transformation involved in moving from the mainstream perspective to the institutionalist perspective was clearly an example of a viable and significant paradigmatic shift.

The economic mainstream has been the focus of attention thus far in this book. It is, essentially, the world with which orthodox economists are comfortable. The change from classical to neoclassical economics has been suggested as an example in economics of a paradigmatic shift.[4] We would disagree with this view. While the introduction of marginal analysis represented a refinement in thinking, it scarcely involved a fundamental change in perspective of the sort involved, say, in the switch from regarding the earth as flat to the modern view that the earth is global, or the switch from the view of Ptolemy (the earth is the center and all heavenly bodies move around the earth) to that of Copernicus (all bodies move around the sun). These switches radically changed virtually every assumption and conclusion that the disciplines involved had previously formulated. The switch to marginalism in economics did not involve much of a fundamental change in the role of the invisible hand, competition, consumer sovereignty, the welfare implications of the system, etc. – all the matters with which we have

4. 'Perhaps the most significant development in economics that resembles a paradigm is that of marginalism, in particular, the subjective theory of value and the associated methods of marginal analysis' (Urbach 1987, p. 796).

previously been concerned. I have previously argued the institutionalist view, without so labeling it, that the switch from classical and neoclassical economics to Keynesian economics did indeed represent a paradigmatic shift. We shall here argue that the institutionalist paradigm did involve a major, therefore paradigmatic, shift. The line of thought pursued by economics from Adam Smith's *Wealth of Nations* to John Maynard Keynes's *General Theory of Employment, Interest, and Money* was fairly consistent in many of the crucial assumptions made. Paradigmatic shifts, we reiterate, represent a total reordering of the common perspective taken in a given discipline. They are not easily accepted, but once they have been, it becomes incumbent on all the scientists in that field to rethink virtually all aspects of the area in which they are considered experts.

As we have seen, mainstream economists have been very busy in the past 50 years attempting to reshift the paradigm back to its classical beginning. We remind the reader that the prevailing view in economic theory today goes by the all too appropriate name of the New Classical Economics. Bearing in mind what has earlier been said, we may suggest that were geography to launch a new organization self-proclaimed to be the New Flat Earth Society its paradigmatic basis would be clear for all to see, but it is doubtful that modern geographers would gravitate to it. The origins of New Classical Economics are no less clear, but the paradigm, new or old, holds great appeal to many modern economists. (It is not clear Kuhn ever contemplated an area where a new *weltanschauung*, having proclaimed itself – even convincingly for a time – as the new Promised Land, could then be rejected and retreated from so that the field could return to an old paradigm. The Promised Land, they would claim, was founded on false promises!)

The plain truth today, it seems, is that whatever interest economists may have had in relating the implications of scientific paradigms to their own field 40 years ago when Kuhn first popularized the notion, they clearly have no such interest in the opening years of the twenty-first century. A perusal of the major reasonably new books in micro and macroeconomic theory suggests that none of them even mention paradigms. The lone exception is William Greene in the fourth edition of his econometrics text (Greene 2000). He begins by listing the prerequisites for the course based on his text as including 'an introduction to the paradigm of econometrics.' It is unclear to me what this may mean. We may add that all of the economists who figured prominently in earlier chapters have one thing at least in common: none of them mention paradigms or paradigmatic shifts.

But this does not mean that Kuhn is irrelevant or that paradigms are unimportant. It is somewhat more ominous than that. The underlying paradigm to their work, like the language in which they write, is fundamental, but so widely agreed upon as to be simply and implicitly assumed. Their shared paradigm, like the English in which they write, needs no comment or discussion because for them it is not in the least controversial or even noteworthy.

For those who do not share the paradigm, this conclusion could not be further from the truth. In any case, institutionalists as noted earlier were for many years charged with having nothing new to contribute. They were further charged with being entirely negative. They insisted, so it was said, that mainstream theory was off the mark, but had nothing to offer in its stead. I developed the paradigm shown earlier. Most particularly, they were told that they had no paradigm of their own and, therefore, had no right to criticize the prevailing paradigm. 'If you don't like the mainstream paradigm, produce one of your own.' Being the sort who likes a challenge, I made an initial stab at a provisional paradigm.

At the time I presented the original paradigm, I wrote:

> Its essential message is clear and the conclusions obvious. First, if one compares the structures of mainstream microeconomic theory, institutionalism, and mainstream political science, one finds very many striking parallels between the assumptions, perspective attitudes, and presumed results emerging from the latter two. Second, whatever bows to reality conventional economists may have made, they have never rid themselves of the theory-as-benchmark psychology that prevents economic theory from confronting the critical reality of economic power. Third, whatever the faults and flaws of both institutionalism and modern political science, both attempt to confront the world as it is. This means preeminently, that they begin by seeing the deployment of power in the economy and the polity as it is – not as one might wish it to be. (Klein 1980, reprinted 1994, pp. 133, 136)

Several additional comments are in order. The economics paradigm, particularly the mainstream paradigm, is clearly based on microeconomics. What, then, is the status of macroeconomics? Whether the implications of mainstream microeconomics depend on the macroeconomy behaving well or the performance of the macroeconomy depends on the microeconomy functioning well may well be like the old question of the chicken and the egg. For many editions Paul Samuelson used to report in his *Economics* on what he called 'a grand neoclassical synthesis.' This was at the height of the feeling that we had learned enough about macroeconomic policy so that we could 'fine tune the economy.' So Samuelson wrote of the 'grand neoclassical synthesis:'

> By means of appropriately reinforcing monetary and fiscal policies, our mixed

> enterprise system can avoid the excesses of boom and slump and can look forward to healthy progressive growth. This fundamental being understood, the paradoxes that robbed the older classical principles dealing with small-scale 'microeconomics' of much of their relevance and validity will now lose their sting. In short, mastery of the modern analysis of income determination genuinely validates the basic classical pricing principles; and the economist is now justified in saying that the broad cleavage between microeconomics and macroeconomics has been closed. (Samuelson 1964, p. 361)

In short the grand neoclassical synthesis really pointed to the assertion that the flaws in the macroeconomic system identified by Keynes had been answered by monetary and fiscal policy so successfully that the economy could indeed function as the neoclassical economist had thought. Putting this another way, successful macroeconomic policy would enable the microeconomy to function as is implicit in the mainstream paradigm.

In an earlier time economists had in effect argued the reverse of the neoclassical synthesis which produced a synthesis, also neoclassical, but different. If the microeconomy truly performed according to the implications of the mainstream paradigm, the result would be microeconomic equilibria. This was the way in which Leon Walras, for example, related microeconomic equilibria to the macroeconomy. Equilibrium is achieved in competitive markets by arriving at a price at which supply is equal to demand. Economic agents found these prices in competitive markets through a process he called tatonnement (strictly translated as groping). As Eric Roll summarizes it, 'once we have these equations of supply and demand at equilibrium prices for each good we can proceed . . . to the problem of general exchange equilibrium' (Roll 1942, p. 433). By relying on some standard which was an accounting unit for determining the value of everything else (Walras called it the numeraire), Walras was able to conclude, as Samuelson says,

> The use of this device enables us to say that if there are n goods, we have n-1 equations of supply and demand (the one for the numeraire is derived from the others) and n-1 prices to determine. This Walras said, means there is a determinate solution for the problem of general equilibrium. (Samuelson 1964, p. 433)

In other words Walras reasoned backwards from the grand neoclassical synthesis. Walras tried to show that if the microeconomy behaves as it should, then the macroeconomy will function well.

One problem, of course, is that Walrasian general equilibrium is based on very many microeconomic equilibria. (Walras did not worry about the fallacy of composition!) It is not, therefore, the same thing as modern macroeconomic equilibrium. The fallacy of composition was factored in by Keynes as a key factor differentiating macroeconomic analysis from microeconomic analysis. Because of this fallacy one could not simply add individual microeconomic markets, even in equilibrium, and get macroeconomic equilibrium.

Where does all this leave us? It leaves us still to confront the major obstacle to regarding any equilibria as ipso facto 'ideal.' The problem, we assert, is not that it is macroeconomic failures derived from microeconomic disequilibria which prevent the mainstream paradigm from accurately reflecting reality. Perusal of the two economics paradigms suggests that it is not necessarily even macroeconomic failures which are at the root of the problems. The impact of concentrated economic power is much more to the point. Our mainstream paradigm is derived from microeconomics because all three paradigms begin with the basic units, which for economics are firms and households (i.e., individuals and groups of individuals). This means ultimately firms, households and the organizations into which firms and individuals form themselves for the purpose of carrying out economic transactions (e.g., corporations, trade associations, trade unions, etc.). The political science paradigm can deal with voters and groups of voters, but it does not confront political parties explicitly. In this sense it is 'micro-unit' oriented just as are the economics paradigms. (Whether or not there is a fallacy of composition at work in political science is not clear. There is a comparable phenomenon in other areas of social science. For example, a mob in sociology is clearly more than and different from a mere collection of individuals.)

The fascination with the grand neoclassical synthesis eventually disappeared. (Samuelson has not included discussion of it for a number of editions now.) No one presumes that macroeconomic policy can operate so successfully that even the more important problems associated with stability and growth in aggregate economic activity can be mostly eliminated. Beyond this, what examination of the mainstream paradigm under-scores is that the serious problems which arise when one assumes the paradigm is a correct reading of reality in economic analysis are not related to the relation of the paradigm to macroeconomic performance. It is to these problems that we need to turn our attention.

The Paradigms, Concentrated Power, and Economic Performance

The overwhelming message of the three approaches being compared is that the institutionalist and the political science approach have very much in common, in contrast to the mainstream economics approach. This commonality, on closer inspection, revolves around a similar view of what concentrated power does to the operation of the system, whether one looks at the economy or the polity. Political science has never had a construct even for analytical purposes which regarded the voter as an independent entity unrelated to any other entity intent on pursing its own interests exclusively through the political system. Political science is shot through with all the concerns which earlier we referred to in quoting Ruth Mack's iconoclastic views about the myriad influences on consumer behavior. The point underscored was that economic decisions are influenced by all sorts of interpersonal relations. (The assumption that 'tastes are given' reduces all this to irrelevancy.) The same is true of political decisions, and so political scientists care about lobbies, parties, interest groups, voter profiles, how campaigns are conducted, etc. They are concerned with the extent to which political decisions are influenced by factually correct information but also about the role and impact of misinformation, particularly information which is deliberately incorrect.

Political campaigns are from the start recognized as being significantly affected by how they are financed. Concentrations of wealth mean concentrations of power to influence the outcome. (Where would political science be were it to begin by assuming that voter views are given!)[5] The initial assumption in political science is that concentrations of power in the system have significant impact on the way it operates. The process of its operation is recognized as a process which distorts the results, in the sense that they are often profoundly different than they would be had the voters received alternative information packets. The way the system actually works governs, therefore, the way in which the discipline studies its operation.[6]

We have been at pains to suggest that this is not the way economists study the operation of the economic system. The impact of economic power concentrations on the operation of the economy clearly affects the operation of the microeconomy. This was, as we saw, the focus of what is now regarded as 'old-fashioned' industrial organization – case studies, the problem of monopoly, oligopoly, anti-trust, regulatory agencies, etc. were the curricular grist for this approach. It has largely been replaced by game theory, as we saw, and while there are undoubtedly many logically fascinating puzzles to be considered by the new approach, the attention to the manner in which economic power affects the way in which the economy deploys resources has, at the very least, been considerably dissipated.

---

5. Parenthetically, we add that another social science, psychology, could get rid of the entire field of abnormal psychology, a major area of concentration for psychologists, by simply assuming that all human beings could be assumed to behave 'normally,' or 'rationally.'
6. I have always thought that political science theory frequently asks better questions than economics. The only problem is that all too often they do not have better answers.

Table 8.1 under-scores the insistence in institutional economics of recognizing, as does political science, that economic activity is based on conflict and that, therefore, power involves seeking leverage so that one economic unit can prevail against one or more rival economic units. The paradigm is shot through with how concentrated economic power (for which one can read 'disproportionate influence in economic interactions') affects diverse aspects of the way the institutionalist paradigm structures the discipline.[7] This illustrates how much farther away the mainstream is from recognizing the problems and obstacles raised by reliance on competition and how much more the mainstream now stresses leaving it to the market. In contrast institutionalists have always and continue still to worry about concentrated power and its impact on economic operations. Here the gap between the mainstream and heterodox economists has widened yet again because of the movement of the mainstream.

The distinction between efficiency, narrowly defined, and what I call 'the higher efficiency' is fundamental and is mostly fleshed out by the impact of concentrated economic power. The way in which the market and the public sector together end up deploying resources clearly deviates significantly from how participants in any economy would deploy resources, were they given all the information pertinent (correct information, we repeat) to the decisions to be made. The welfare implications, so cherished by mainstream microtheorists, are clearly different if the system involves manipulated consumers. Obviously what manipulated voters do may not be ideal from the point of view of the model of representative democracy in action. So similarly what manipulated consumers do could well have different welfare implications than are found in a perfectly competitive model.

We may add that if the paradigms are essentially based on micro-units as we saw, they clearly have implications for the macro-units as well. It isn't that

---

7. One of the major developments in mainstream economics of the past 50 years has been finding ways to ignore or minimize the effect of concentrated power on the operation of the economy. It is reflected in the changes made in industrial organization, already commented on. We may illustrate this change by noting that George Stigler, a conservative mainstream University of Chicago economist, in his widely used price theory textbook asserts, in terms reminiscent of the treatment accorded the Robber Barons of an even earlier era, that the behavior of the 'captains of industry' cannot be understood without factoring in 'power and prestige.' In this context he quotes Taussig from 1915:

> The instinct for domination plays a considerable part, I believe, in the movement for combination . . . They [the industrialists] will talk of the economies from large scale operation and consolidation, of the wastes of competition, of better service, lowered prices, and what not. But in truth the schemes for overpowering combinations are to a great degree mere manifestations of megalomania. (Taussig 1915, pp. 92, 93. Quoted in Stigler 1947, p. 201)

the results emanating from manipulated voters in local elections operate significantly differently than when the same sort of manipulation is carried out in national elections. The fallacy of composition may not loom as large in the polity as it does in the economy.

We have seen that in microeconomic theory one can ask what the impact will be of concentrated economic power on the operation of the system. The same question is murky in macroeconomics. Consider the following. A recent macroeconomics textbook in the glossary defined macroeconomics in a perfectly straightforward and unambiguous way – 'The study of issues that affect the economy as a whole, especially unemployment, inflation, and economic growth.' In the very next entry they define a macroeconomic question this way: 'Do current institutions coordinate the decisions of individuals sufficiently well, or should we modify the institutions and adjust the market in some way?' (Colander and Gamber 2002, p. G–4). What is the problem? By focusing on 'the decisions of individuals,' they gloss over the distinction between micro and macroeconomics. The decisions of individuals have a different impact on 'employment, inflation, and economic growth' than they do on the price of individual goods and services, for example, because of the fallacy of composition. Macroeconomic problems often emerge primarily because the macroeconomy (the whole) is indeed greater than the sum of its parts (individual units). We know reasonably well how the economic power of individual units affects prices in individual markets. But we know less about the way in which the size of individual units and their power affects employment, inflation, and growth. But one insight from microeconomics is clearly valuable. From microeconomics we know that with economic power goes the possibility that self-interest and community interest can conflict. (We are back to the economist's clever moral thermostat!). There is no reason to think, therefore, that concentrated economic power will not cause complications at both levels of the economy.

In short, if concentrated power distorts the results of the interaction of individual firms and households, as undoubtedly it does, it is highly likely that their interaction could easily carry over to affect as well the growth and stability of the entire system. The divergence between self-interest and community interest is very likely a major impediment to ideal economic performance, however and wherever one looks at the economy.

What Is Mainstream Economics? Once More, with Feeling

A final question which the three paradigms pose is, what is mainstream economics? Marc Tool gives the usual answer to this question. In his index under 'mainstream economics' he says, 'See classical and neoclassical economics.' 'Classical economics,' he tells us, refers to 'a self-adjusting economy, organized with natural capitalist institutions . . . Neoclassical economics narrows the focus to the examination of the allocation of scarce means among unlimited ends; the price system in competitive markets is the efficient allocator' (Tool 1979, p. 27). Geoffrey Hodgson reminds us that in 1992, 44 leading economists contributed 'A Plea for a Pluralistic and Rigorous Economics' to the *American Economic Review* that noted 'Economists today enforce a monopoly of method or core assumptions, often defined on no better ground than that it constitutes the mainstream' (Hodgson 1999, p. 263). Similarly Allan Gruchy writes 'the mainstream or conventional position among mainstream economists . . . see no basic evil in "bigness" in industry' (Gruchy 1987, p. 90). We have already seen that this is more true today than a generation ago.

What these definitions have in common, of course, is that they all point to the group of economists settled on in Chapter 7 as the mainstream. More particularly what we there identified as the trend setters, the change producers, and the judges for changes which do or do not pass muster when it comes to being 'generally acceptable' are the economists institutional economists have in mind when they speak today of the mainstream. There are the very many more economists who constitute the mainstream, in that they accept the verdicts handed down by the influential economists as constituting alterations in what it is acceptable for economists to think. One recent example would be Francis X. Diebold's comment: 'Structural forecasting, which aligns itself with economic theory and hence rises and falls with theory, receded following the decline of Keynesian theory.'[8] Diebold makes it sound as though, like the view that the earth is flat, or that coal could be converted into gold, the central thrust of Keynesian analysis has now simply been declared to be in error. He continues, 'in recent years powerful new dynamic stochastic general equilibrium theory has developed' (Diebold 1997). Our effort in the previous chapter to define 'the mainstream' was also an effort to identify who becomes and how they become trend seters in economics and by whose authority these seismic changes in attitude in the discipline are adjudicated to be genuine rather than either fallacious or ephemeral revisions in 'correct thinking.'

Thus, for example, the reader will recall that earlier in discussing rational expectations and the rational expectations hypothesis we quoted Holden, Peel, and Thompson to the effect that 'Perhaps the single most important

8. We have seen that there are economists who dispute Keynesian findings. Note that there are no qualifiers in this statement. The attack on Keynes which we contemplated in an earlier chapter has presumably led to a new era in which this new view of Keynes is no longer even controversial.

hypothesis to have been "discovered" in macroeconomics in the past few decades is that of rational expectations' (Holden, Peel and Thompson 1985, p. 174). Why is this true? Most especially, why is it true when on the same page, the authors add, '. . . the rational expectations hypothesis cannot be taken as literally true' (p. 174). It is because the actors are part of the mainstream in the sense that they accept the judgements handed down by the economists generally conceded to have sufficient brilliance . . . brilliance as well as persuasive powers . . . to be, by common concurrence, leaders of professional thinking. Clearly Robert Lucas qualifies, by these criteria, as a leading mainstream economist.[9] The example serves to clarify, we hope, the difference between leading mainstream economists and the rest of the mainstream.

In the end, it is clear that the mainstream paradigm presents the gravest problems and faces the most severe obstacles when the real world deviates most from the assumed world of that theory. Thus the have nots on the household side and the firms with concentrated power, particularly when it is technological in origin, offer the most difficult policy challenges when we stick to a world of 'real facts.' Obviously, therefore, either an assumption of pure competition or a limitation to Pareto optimality for welfare considerations will suffice to cope with the challenge (convert 'real facts' into 'stylized facts').

RETHINKING ECONOMICS

Taking a leaf from the secret life of Walter Mitty, let us consider how the discipline of economics might look if its current structure were altered dramatically by powerful forces so as to confront some of the problems we have raised in the previous pages. (Economists are experts in the art of assumption, so I simply ask the reader to indulge me – assume the problems have been correctly isolated. How should we confront them?) Mirowski[10] is right – efforts at suggesting a new approach are ripe for efforts to shoot them down. Successful efforts may be rare, but they are tempting and hope springs

---

9. If rational expectations are no longer riding quite so high as this hypothesis was in 1985, Lucas is nonetheless firmly established as a leading mainstream economic theorist. He was awarded the Nobel Prize in Economics in 1995. He was President of the American Economic Association in 2002, as clear a proof of confirmed leadership recognition as the profession has to offer.

10. Some years ago Philip Mirowski began a book entitled *The Reconstruction of Economic Theory* with the observation that books with titles promising to reconstruct a field are most often a big disappointment – they are not as novel as they assert they are, they are long on criticism but short on originality etc. (Mirowski 1986, pp. 1–2).

eternal.

A recurring theme of this book has been that whatever else economics is, it needs never to forget that at the end of the day it is justified by its usefulness. If economics did not exist it would undoubtedly have had to be invented because it concerns itself with a fundamental and indispensable area of human life. Adam Smith, the subject of our attention in the first chapter, understood this simple point. He began with this assertion:

> The annual labour of every nation is the fund which originally supplies it with all the necessaries and conveniences of life which it annually consumes . . .
>
> According, therefore, as this produce, or what is purchased with it, bears a greater or smaller proportion to the number of those who consume it, the nation will be better or worse supplied with all the necessaries and conveniences for which it has occasion. (Smith 1776/1985, p. 3)

This simple statement still encompasses the intellectual territory which is distinctively the field of economics. If one allows for the advances of technology, the ever increasing division of labor, and the complexities of modern life, it is still a good place to begin because it points toward the critical link between the field of economics and the public policy to which it is inextricably linked. This link was under-scored 20 years ago by the title Marc Tool chose for a collection of essays '. . . addressed to the American economy, and to the economic problems with which it is beset – instability, unemployment, monetary management, income maldistribution, poverty, non-accountable economic power, resource misuse, environmental pollution, misguided development aid, and the like . . .' (Tool 1984). The title of the book is an *Institutionalist Guide to Economics and Public Policy*, and what are these enumerated areas requiring public policy but the logical implications of 'how well supplied with all the necessaries and conveniences for which it has occasion' people in the modern world are?

Stripped to its barest fundamentals, if 'the mainstream' truly believes that economic problems should be left to the market, there is little need for economists, except perhaps as monitors and facilitators . . . I write these words in the United States in the first decade of the twenty-first century where the stark truth of this is driven home everyday. If the Federal government's major raison d'etre really revolved only or even largely around defense, the policies being pursued make no sense. These policies involve constant effort to reduce (eliminate?) taxes so that 'the people' have 'their own money' to spend as they see fit. Downsizing government would merely be an alternative way of referring to reduced defense spending. Instead, as these efforts to 'downsize government' continue, the real results are increasingly clear. They lead to anguish at the state and local levels in the United States, where economic crises, aggravated by less funding from the federal government, are exacerbated. The anguish is not merely fiscal – it reflects people deprived of services they desperately need and want. This is not a personal assertion. Ask them (by ballot, by survey, etc.). The results of such inquiry reflect what may accurately be called emergent social value. These ideas I developed originally as long ago as 1974 (Klein 1974, especially pp. 10–18).

It is still true, perhaps more true than it was in Smith's day, that it cannot be automatically assumed that all people will be well supplied with the necessaries and conveniences on which daily life depends. ('Necessaries' are surely dynamic in their conception.) Reducing taxes federally merely forces state and local government to cope with public services, a significant per cent of which can in all probability be more efficiently offered at the federal level. In the case of defense no one argues otherwise. Here is one area where also no one argues that people 'should be allowed to spend their own money'! Money which is 'their own' when any other use is detailed is, miraculously, not 'their own' when it is to be directed to defense![11] In the preceding pages we have tried to suggest that the world, including the United States, is replete with applied economists working to contribute to making this process of supplying the necessaries and conveniences on which economic health depends flow more satisfactorily to all the peoples of the world's economy. But economic theory has increasingly concerned itself with other more esoteric and less basic questions.

Economic theorists quite literally frequently choose to play games. That is why we earlier highlighted John R. Hicks's painfully prescient observation, 'There is much in economic theory which is pursued for no better reason than its intellectual attraction: it is a good game' (Hicks 1979, p. viii). In the years since he wrote that it has merely become an appropriate comment on a larger and larger part of what mainstream economists are turning out. It could be justified perhaps if economic problems had truly been mostly resolved, or if they could indeed resolve themselves in the market or anyplace else! We are back where we were in Chapter 1 where we noticed that in spite of 'inventing' the invisible hand Smith also formulated the modern discipline of economics! Do we need to ask why? We take the position that neither of the possibilities just mentioned can be supported by reference to real economies in the real world coping with the real situations in which all too often they find

11. Some years ago I suggested that, in addition to a narrowly viewed 'efficiency', 'security' is the only judgmental criterion that is explicitly recognized by mainstream economists for judging economic performance. In point of fact, any economy also reflects judgement (of one sort or another) with respect to freedom, equity, and compassion (Klein 1974, p. 195).

themselves.

Diversity in Pain Thresholds

We have surely seen that a major difference among modern economists is derived from a rarely mentioned factor. I call it the pain threshold differential. Economists, for example, react differently in their attitude toward unemployment. For some, 2 or 3 per cent is tolerable, for others these percentages would be far too high. The famous 'trade off' between unemployment and inflation, discussed earlier and at some length in connection with the Phillips curve, is similarly affected by the differential pain threshold notion. Moreover, it is interesting to note that while some economists insist that the only acceptable inflation rate is zero per cent, no one argues that unemployment rates – even allowing for frictional and seasonal unemployment, would, could, or should ever be pushed to zero. Moreover, in contemplating attitudes and pain thresholds, the time period and the place matter also (recall Samuelson's relatively benign view of low inflation rates, quoted in Chapter 5). In the middle of the twentieth century 2 or 3 per cent unemployment was considered high in the US, but not in Europe. Overseas, the willingness to endure higher unemployment rates on some occasions than would be accepted in the US can be discerned. In most places most of the time in the market-oriented world people have to be persuaded that higher unemployment is an unavoidable cost of keeping inflation rates down. It is entirely possible that economists can differ about the unfortunate consequences of say, a 5 per cent per year inflation rate. But more than that, they might agree that the result of a given inflation rate decline will perforce result in changing the unemployment rate from *X* per cent to *Y* per cent. For some economists *Y* per cent unemployment might not be 'too high a price to pay' for a promised gain in lower inflation rates, but for another economist it might be too high a price to pay. (One could argue that if the Milton Friedmans of this world really believed what they said, they should voluntarily be first in the unemployment line, fighting thereby to keep inflation down.)

In the over-arching difference between what I have called interventionists and non-interventionists, the differential pain threshold notion crops up repeatedly in all sorts of ways. For example, it is all well and good to argue that single parents on welfare must substitute work for welfare to a significant extent, but how many hours of work on top of family responsibilities can one reasonably expect? Economic policy and one's attitudes toward the pain threshold are difficult to separate totally.

In another area one's attitude toward the acceptability of union strikes in areas affected with the public interest involves, in the final analysis, careful offsetting of different kinds of pain that can be inflicted on participants in the economy.

All the health and safety issues constantly adjudicated by regulatory agencies are yet another example. While there may be an all too human tendency to assume that others can appropriately absorb more pain than oneself, the economists' job is, of course, if they are to engage in the cost-benefit analysis so dear to their hearts, to assume a genuinely social rather than a personal attitude toward both pains and gains. In this endeavor economists, like other mere mortals, can expect to succeed only partially.

Voices of Dissent

The dominance of the mainstream, as we have identified it in Chapter 7, is particularly pronounced if, as we have done here, one focuses on the prevailing stance of graduate education in economics, particularly at the universities which are generally conceded as having the most acknowledged prestige. We would surely not wish to leave any reader with the impression that ours is the first or the only voice raised in dissent from that approach. Here we think it appropriate, therefore, to sketch in some of the more prominent voices raised in dissent in the recent past. Our survey is meant to be neither complete nor definitive. It is offered in support of the assertion that there are economists worthy of some attention who question the current stance of one or more aspects of the organized economics profession.

Dissent from the mainstream perspective is, of course, nothing new. In the 19th century there were a whole host of dissenters – many of those Robert Heilbroner once labeled 'the underworld of economics' (Heilbroner 1953, 1967, Chapter 7, pp. 154–91). In the underworld (by which Heilbroner means economists who dissented from mainstream assumptions and assertions, and in consequence found themselves not quite respectable, Heilbroner, of course, includes Marx and Engels, but also the Utopian socialists (Mandevilla, Bastiat, Henry George, Under-consumptionists, John Hobson, etc.)

Not only have there always been dissenting voices from mainstream economics (in the 19th century it was classical and then neoclassical economic theory) but the mainstream did not entirely ignore what those dissenting voices were saying. Thus, it is generally ignored today that, for example, Alfred Marshall in his *Principles* comments not only on what Marx and Engels were saying but on Darwin, Hobson, Fourier, St Simon, Roberts, Proudhon, etc. In fact, of the French Utopians he writes, ' . . . Fourier, St Simon, Proudhon, and Louis Blanc have made many of the most valuable, as well as many of the wildest suggestions of socialism' (Marshall 1890, 1949,

p. 633).

This is by way of introducing modern dissenters, of whom the first comment that needs to be made is that I do not think one will find a reference to any of these people, nor their organization, in any of the mainstream theory books referred to in earlier chapters. If any field can benefit from discussion of diverse points of view it is fair to say that modern economics exhibits remarkably little interaction between what we have called the mainstream and the voices we discuss here.

Institutionalist Economics – Old and New

Before we go further with a consideration of the attitude of mainstream economics toward heterodoxy in general in the past half century, we need to consider briefly the place of what has come to be known as 'New Institutional Economics.' If one considers the use of the phrase 'institutional economics' in the mainstream journals during this period the chances are high that what is being referred to is 'New Institutional Economics' rather than the heterodoxy we wish to focus on – that is, the view of the economy taken in the United States by Thorstein Veblen, Wesley Mitchell, John R. Commons and their followers. We shall return to this perspective. Here we ask only, are the 'new institutional economists' appropriately included in this group?

We have already made the first point to be noted – without question, they have received more attention from the mainstream economists in recent years than have the 'Old Institutional Economists.'

Ronald Coase asserts that the group now known as 'New Institutional Economics' was started by a 1937 article of his.[12] Writes Coase,

> . . . it is commonly said, and may be true, that the new institutional economics started with my article, 'The Nature of the Firm' (1937).
>
> The phrase, 'the new institutional economics,' was coined by Oliver Williamson. It was intended to differentiate the subject from the 'old institutional economics.' John R. Commons, Wesley Mitchell, and those associated with them were men of great intellectual stature, but they were anti-theoretical, and without a theory to bind together their collection of facts; they had very little that they were about to pass on. Certain it is that mainstream economics proceeded on its way without any significant change. And it continues to do so. (Coase 1998, p. 72)

We may add that Oliver Williamson (the above-mentioned phrase coiner) clearly agreed with this assessment. Says Williamson, 'The proposition that

---

12. Coase (1937).

institutions matter is embraced by institutional economists of all kinds, old and new. What distinguishes the NIE from earlier (and some contemporary) work on institutions is that institutions are susceptible to analysis. Older-style institutional economics was content to critique orthodoxy and collapsed for failure to advance a positive research agenda . . .' (Williamson 1998, pp. 75–9). Clearly new institutional economists share a certain air of self-congratulation with mainstream economists. Whether old institutionalism has indeed 'collapsed' we leave to the reader to decide after perusing this chapter. Coase adds that by 'mainstream economics' he is speaking of microeconomics only.

My first comment on all this is that 'new institutionalists' clearly agree with mainstream economists that (old) institutionalists had no theory. A theory that grounds the discipline in a dynamic cultural setting is surely trying harder to be realistic. The price of greater realism, of course, is that it is also not as neat and simple as mainstream microeconomic theory, encased as that unrealistic world is in all its well known simplifying assumptions. But this does not mean that institutionalist theory is not theory or that those who espouse it are anti-theoretical.[13]

The second comment is to under-score the implication of the other assertion that Coase makes '. . . when I speak of mainstream economics I am referring to microeconomics. Whether my strictures apply also to macroeconomics I leave to others' (Coase 1998, p. 72). Modern macroeconomics, as we saw in Chapter 5, at least as Keynes put it together, is compatible with old institutionalism, as the discussion above suggests. Furthermore, Mitchell, a founder of old institutionalism, made significant contributions to macroeconomic theory, embraced by many old institutionalists and an increasing number of mainstream economists concerned with business cycles and stabilization policy. It is, of course, true that modern mainstream microtheory emerged from the efforts to adumbrate the implications growing out of assuming that Smith's invisible hand could flower fully in the 'free' market so as to account for all resource deployment. In earlier pages we have assessed the futility of sticking to that simplified world. It is also true, as was considered in earlier discussion, that the 'new classical economics' has attempted simply to read macroeconomics out of the discipline as irrelevant. Nor can we forget that the world of Keynes, which gives theoretical legitimacy to macroeconomics is still with us, as our ongoing

13. Some years ago, I attempted to show that Mitchell, at least, was not only obsessed with 'getting the facts,' but ultimately searched the facts for 'pattern.' His search for patterns in the data produced what ultimately many economists now realize is a highly useful theory, in this case, explaining business cycles. Mitchell's research process was in a real sense a contribution to theory based on the real world (Mitchell 1983).

problems with both unemployment and inflation can attest. We have tried earlier to suggest that those who insist these are merely manifestations of micro markets in disequilibrium base their conclusions on assumptions difficult to swallow for those wishing to focus on the real world. Here we add only that Mitchell's work was a clear contribution to macroeconomic theory, suggesting that in the real world there is indeed both a micro and a macro system; both real, clearly inter-related, but considered individually with benefit and improved insight for both. Out of the study of both emerges the critical conclusion that 'natural equilibrating processes,' though making valuable contributions to the functioning of both, operate neither perfectly, nor ideally, to the process of applying continuously improving technology to resource deployment so as optimally to 'enhance the lives' of all the participants in economic life. It is clear that 'new institutionalists,' like 'old institutionalists,' insist that the proper study of the way resources are deployed in the modern world must go farther than mainstream economists are willing to go. In the terminology of a bygone era both would sacrifice some 'rigor' for some 'relevance.' The mainstream, in contrast, insists on ever greater rigor.

It is not surprising, therefore, that Coase continues with a devastating description of 'mainstream economics.' Here there is little difference between old and new institutionalism. Mainstream economics, says Coase, takes '. . . a view disdainful of what happens in the real world.' It is '. . . long on theory if weak on facts.' It is, therefore, a '. . . tribute to the staying power of a theoretical underpinning.' In the end, he is even more devastating. He suggests that mainstream '. . . economists think of themselves as having a box of tools but no subject matter' (Coase 1998, p. 72).

None of this serves to distinguish old from new institutional economics. Bush and Tool recently suggested that the 'New Institutionalist Economics' '. . . attempts to take into account the role of institutions and institutional change while remaining true to most of the methodological presuppositions of neoclassical economics' (Bush and Tool 2003, p. 10).

What new institutional economics concentrates on is the idea that the difficulty with conventional price theory is that it focuses on essentially sterile transactions between buyers and sellers that have been over-simplified. They are rational; they focus on maximizing profits or utility, etc. The difference between the two has recently been put as follows. 'A frequently silent presupposition on the orthodox analysis is that transactions are frictionless and costless, or that institutions do not matter. In the heterodox framework, arranging transactions always necessitates social negotiations, requires time, uses resources, conduces individually and collectively borne risks, and incurs potential enforcement burdens' (Adams 1999). What, they add, therefore, is the insight is that the modern economy is composed of a complex set of transactions with the transactors influenced by the complex of institutions which color human behavior acting within various cultures to deploy resources.

This is all well and good as far as it goes. Substituting transactions culturally determined for transactions between transactors so cleaned up and prettified as to be little more than abstract stereotypes of human beings is surely a step in the right direction. It differs little if at all from the long standing insistence of institutional economists that we need to ask what lies back of demand curves and supply curves. The critical social and value questions have always lurked in the ceteris paribus world of mainstream theory.

So there is no disagreement that modern economies cannot be examined critically without considering what lies back of the transactions by which actual economic activity overtly manifests itself. 'Old institutional economists' focused on resource deployment as a process reflecting emergent valuation in contrast to the mainstream emphasis on a relatively sterile process of allocation of resources by prices. This, of course, is a mechanical process which reflects the value system – never examined – which underlies it. This point has been made in various places in the previous pages and distinguishes economic activity in the mainstream mechanical view from economic activity in the (old) institutional view as being engaged in 'enhancing human life' to use Veblen's telling phrase. More than 30 years ago I distinguished the two views of the economy in an essay entitled, 'Economics: Allocation or Valuation?' (Klein 1974). Clarence E. Ayres put the matter this way: 'Whether or not it continues to be a science of price, economics must be a science of value' (Ayres 1944, p. 3). (When I showed this quotation to Lionel Robbins many years ago, his comment was 'I don't know what that means'.)

In the end the difference between old and new institutional economics may revolve around the latter's insistence that old institutionalists have no theory. If ruminating about the factors which color and shape transactions constitutes 'theory,' so too can concern with the factors which lie back of demand or supply as well as relevant determinants of resource deployment outside demand and supply. Consideration of both approaches under-scores that the necessary concern with the impact of culture on economic behavior may ineluctably make economic theory more complex, more nuanced and textured, but the alternative is to leave economic theory fatally at odds with the world in which, for better or worse, it has to occur. Old institutionalists might agree that new institutional economics surely considers factors which need our attention. But the new group do not go far enough in confronting the fundamental factors which both determine the choices made, and provide the basis for judging the degree to which those choices have contributed optimally to economic progress, as it can meaningfully be defined at any given time.

A Cornucopia of Heterodox Organizations that Actually Exist

Few movements have been proclaimed dead as often as has heterodox economics. In his monumental *History of Economic Analysis*, Joseph Schumpeter in a discussion of the various strains of the German Historical School (the School commonly said to be a precursor of American Institutionalism) says, ' . . . with the possible exception of American Institutionalism, none of them was strong enough to cause a break in traditions and to redirect research . . .' (Schumpeter 1954, p. 820). That is quite a strong – if tentative – positive evaluation of the American movement. Schumpeter's book was in the works for a very long time, so it's not clear when exactly Schumpeter took this position. However, as early as 1942 Eric Roll in his *History of Economic Thought* wrote,

> An 'institutionalist' school did make its appearance on the American theoretical scene, and until comparatively recently its tenets formed one of the most popular subjects of debate in the field of economic methodology. It is not necessary to re-examine this debate and the voluminous literature in which it is embodied; for one of the most striking things about it is the fact that it is now almost completely dead, and that intermittent attempts to revive it have invariably failed to arouse much interest. (Roll 1942, pp. 498–9)

From there it has been pretty much downhill. Paul Samuelson puts the death in about 1936. He wrote of institutional economics, '40 years ago institutionalism withered away as an effective counter force in economics. Who can explain it when a movement turns sterile?' (Samuelson 1976, p. 847). Earlier in this chapter we have already seen that Oliver Williamson recently asserted that institutionalism had 'collapsed.' Coase stated that it 'had very little to pass on.' And according to Thomas Sowell, George Stigler around 1959 had said that it was 'dying out at a fantastic rate' (Sowell 1993, 788).

These comments cover the past 60 years, which encompasses the working life of all those institutionalists we shall be considering in the remainder of this chapter. The earlier comments were made before Ayres published either of his two books on the subject. The later comments were made in spite of the work not only of the founders of American institutionalism but after the work of all those, including Ayres, whom Allan Gruchy labeled 'the Second Generation.' Let us grant that the 'institutionalism is dead' view can point to some evidence in support of that position. A casual perusal of a group of the most popular current basic economics texts will produce nary a mention of heterodox economics, institutional economics, or even (with one exception) a mention of Thorstein Veblen.[14]

Another piece of evidence lies in the attention paid to institutionalism by the mainstream journals. If again we restrict our attention to the five 'flagship journals' considered in Chapter 7, a computer search of mentions of institutionalism in these journals in the years since 1980 produces the results shown in Table 8.2.

Table 8.2 Number of citations to 'institutional economics' in flagship journals, 1980–2000

Journal	Total number of citations to institutional economics	Of these, the number to 'new institutional economics'
American Economic Review	10	5
The Economic Journal	9	0
Journal of Political Economics	3	0
Quarterly Journal of Economics	2	0
Econometrica	0	0

The results are not surprising. None of the journals has dwelt particularly on heterodox topics or points of view. The *American Economic Review* appears to lead except that half the citations were to 'new institutionalism.' Moreover, the articles were devoted to new institutionalism, and were not mere references in passing. Beyond this American journals have not considered old institutionalism very much. On the other hand none of the journals have devoted much attention to new institutionalism except for the cases noted.

It is difficult not to conclude that were a funeral held today for American institutionalism there would be very many happy mourners present. They would be distinctive only because by their very presence they distinguished

14. The textbooks examined included the following recent texts: McConnell and Brue (1990); Miller (2004); Gwartney and Stroup (1997); Mankiw (2001); Samuelson and Nordhaus (2001). (The Samuelson book is the one with the only mention of Veblen. There is a brief reference to 'conspicuous consumption,' p. 180).

themselves from the huge sea of indifference which characterizes the general attitude toward institutionalism arising among today's run-of-the-mill economists. That the current crop of widely used basic texts does not even bother to disavow heterodoxy in any form is, as we have just seen, not hard to show. It is not surprising in view of the current prevailing ideology and general stance of the discipline as was sketched in Chapter 7. Like most academic disciplines the prevailing perspective is set at the graduate level and the introductory work follows along because successful texts have to present the field in a manner that the trend setters and leaders of the prevailing school or schools of thought will find congenial. This is not said pejoratively but simply as a description of what would be expected.

Before we leave the stage to these mourners we might recall from previous chapters that – along with the non-existence of institutional economics – mainstream economists insist on the non-existence of (among other things) business cycles, uncleared markets, involuntary unemployment, economic behavior not motivated by self-interest, impulse buying, macroeconomics, fiscal policy, and a whole host of related notions that spoil the magical world of 'stylized facts' the explaining of which is the announced objective of a great many practitioners of mainstream economic theory. So viewed, one might argue that institutional economics is in very good company.

If in the eyes of mainstream economists institutional economics is dead, the remainder of this chapter is devoted to demonstrating that there are movements on both sides of the Atlantic which attest to the fact that in very many places institutional economics is very much alive. These are the people who, finding themselves at the funeral just mentioned, would sit up in the coffin and say, 'Hold on! Not yet!' We now turn, therefore, to a consideration of what a colleague of mine used to call 'rivulet economists' (in contrast to mainstream economists), among whom institutional theory and the discussion to which it gives rise are lively topics indeed.

In 1993 a group of heterodox economists from a number of countries formed the International Confederation for the Reform of Economics (ICARE). More recently it changed its name to the International Confederation of Associations for Pluralism in Economics (ICAPE). They describe their organization as '. . . a consortium of groups in economics that are working cooperatively to maintain diversity and innovation in methodologies, approaches, policy analysis, and higher education in the profession' (ICARE 1999, p. 3). This group has put together what is undoubtedly the most comprehensive list of organizations which take a non-traditional approach to the discipline of economics. In their tentative directory (the list is almost always under revision) the current list names over 40 organizations which regard themselves as non-traditional in their approach to the discipline of economics. The organizations which they list are: Agent-Based Computational Economics (ACE), Association for Evolutionary Economics (AFEE), Association for Heterodox Economics (AHE), Association for Institutional Thought (AFIT), Association for Social Economics (ASE), Association for Social and Political Economy (ASPE), Belgian-Dutch Association for Institutional and Political Economy (AIPE), Conference on Problems of Economic Change (COPEC), Congress of Political Economists International (COPE), Cambridge Social Ontology Group (CSOG), Dollars and Sense (D&S), Eastern Economic Association (EEA), Economists Allied for Arms Reduction (ECAAR), European Association for Bioeconomic Studies (EABS), European Association for Evolutionary Political Economy (EAEPE), European Society for the History of Economic Thought (ESHET), German Association for Political Economy (GAPE), The Gide Society (GIDE), Global Development and Environment Institute (GDAE), Institute for Institutional and Social Economics (IISO), International Atlantic Economic Society (IAES), International Association for Feminist Economics (IAFFE), International Economics and Philosophy Society (IEPS), International Joseph A. Schumpeter Society (ISS), International Network for Economic Method (INEM), International Papers in Political Economy (IPPE), International Review of Applied Economics (IRAE), International Society for Ecological Economics (ISEE), International Society for the Intercommunication of New Ideas (ISINI), International Society for New Institutional Economics (ISNIE), International Thorstein Veblen Association (ITVA), International Working Group on Value Theory (IWGVT), Japan Association for Evolutionary Economics (JAFEE), Japan Society of Political Economy (JSPE), Journal of Post Keynesian Economics (JPKE), Karl Polanyi Institute of Political Economy (KPIPE), Post-Keynesian Economic Study (PKESG), Regional Economic and Social Development (RESD), Rethinking Marxism (RM), Society for the Advancement of Behavioral Economics (SABE), Society for the Advancement of Socio-Economics (SASE), Society for the Development of Austrian Economics (SDAE), Society of Political Economy (SEP), System Dynamics Society (SDS), Union for Radical Political Economics (URPE), and United States Society for Ecological Economics (USSEE).

We cannot comment here on all these organizations individually but we do comment briefly on a few that are either of long standing or are representative of new or different trends.

Perhaps the oldest of the modern organizations of non-traditional economists is the Association For Social Economics, founded in 1941. It was founded '. . . to advance scholarly research and writing about great questions of economics, human dignity, ethics, and philosophy.'[15] It has a journal, the *Review of Social Economy*.

Another early organization devoted to heterodoxy is the Union for Radical Political Economics, founded in 1968. It today publishes the *Review of Radical Political Economics* which ' . . . promotes critical inquiry into all areas of economic, social, and political reality . . .'. The *Review* publishes innovative research in political economy broadly defined as including, but not confined to, Marxian economics, post-Keynesian economics, Sraffian economics, feminist economics, and radical institutional economics.[16] From the outset URPE adopted an explicitly inter-disciplinary approach and based its work on 'a new value premise.' It was concerned with 'the economics of the ghetto, poverty, imperialism, interest groups, and the military-industrial complex' (Fleck 1998, p.1). Though they grant that 'The period of greatest prominence ranged from its inception through the 1970s', (Fleck 1998, p. 2) it nevertheless continues as one of the best known non-traditional organizations in economics. As of the summer of 2003 it had some 270 members.

Two US organizations are devoted to institutional economics: the Association for Evolutionary Economics (AFEE) carries on in the tradition of Veblen, Commons and Mitchell and is devoted to investigating the implications and consequences of adhering to the perspective that economies are dynamic entities always and everywhere that are a manifestation of a larger culture. They are charged with deploying resources with the aid of current technology so as to enhance the lives of the participants in an optimal manner. They publish the *Journal of Economic Issues*.

The second institutionalist organization, the Association for Institutional Thought (AFIT), is an offshoot of AFEE and was originally designed as a focus for institutionalists in the western part of the United States. It grew out of a feeling that there were schools of thought within institutionalism. So while there are some who still adhere to this view and while there are undoubtedly differences in focus, methodology, and emphasis from one institutionalist to another, today many members of the institutionalist school belong with apparent comfort to both organizations, attend both meetings, and if pushed would argue that currently in the mainstream-dominated world there is basically only one alternative, termed institutionalist economics. Members of this school have far more in common than they have differences among themselves. (For discussion of this issue cf. Ramstad 1989). There have been times in the past when all institutionalists would not agree with this assessment. There have been historically those who thought Veblen followers

15. Association for Social Economics, Homepage, p. 1.
16. First page of any issue, *Review of Radical Political Economics*.

and Commons followers needed to be classified separately (Klein 1990). Both groups have long been committed to the dissemination of the principles of institutional economics and to an exploration of alternative approaches to public policy questions (ICARE 1999, p. 119). This is a characterization with which it is doubtful any AFEE member would disagree.[17]

The European Association for Evolutionary Political Economy (EAEPE) is an outgrowth of a meeting held in London in 1988 to explore the best way to organize European institutionalists. It was attended by a number of European heterodox scholars as well as members of the US organizations who agreed that it would be better to have a separate organization for Europeans in which Americans could become members rather than making the new group a branch of an American organization. American scholars now work closely with institutionalists in Europe. Clearly American institutionalism has spread to Europe and to other parts of the world. Their aim has been to 'promote evolutionary, dynamic, and realistic approaches to economic theory and policy' (EAEPE 1988, p. 28). Readers of the previous pages of this book will immediately see that these are clearly major areas which differentiate heterodox from mainstream thinking.

The International Atlantic Economic Society (IAES) is somewhat different. It is more than 25 years old and is devoted to trying to bring economists of all persuasions – mainstream and heterodox – together. Their position is that 'all are welcome.' When the alternative is to be ignored, this is progress.

A number of the heterodox organizations are devoted to particular points of view or causes – the history of economic thought, feminist economics, post-Keynesian economics, an economic analysis of ecological questions, etc. We shall return to the question raised by this aspect of heterodoxy. There is a place for such organizations even though they may not all fall under the umbrella defined here as institutional economics.

We cannot here consider all these organizations in detail. Suffice it to say that they give evidence that heterodoxy has not withered away, and that indeed there are a variety of ways in which non-mainstream economic issues are being explored currently. Diverse organizations of economists are clearly part of the contemporary scene. Before attempting to assess the implications of these efforts, we need to consider other ways in which the push for diversity in economics is making itself manifest.

---

17. A question which the reader may well raise is the relationship between institutionalist economics and other forms of heterodoxy. We shall return to this rather complicated question below.

Recent Evidence of Ferment in the Discipline

Examination will show that most of the non-traditional organizations are or aspire to be global in approach, are global in terms of membership, and that there are now heterodox organizations headquartered in virtually every major area of the world (except perhaps Africa). Needless to say, these organizations do all the things mainstream organizations do – they have conventions, they publish journals, etc. They just are not tied into the prestigious network we described in Chapter 7.

We need to recognize that all the important threads in the story of recent dissent from mainstream economics cannot be encompassed in a consideration of formal organizations. An important part of the recent story involves the dissent which has arisen among students, initially primarily in Europe, and the subsequent response of the mainstream economics establishments. No discussion of current waves of dissent with conventional economics would be complete without reference to the student movement which has come to be known as Post Autistic Economics. This movement began in France (Autism-Economie). These students began with their unhappiness with what they were being offered in economics classrooms; it was their initial and clever assertion that mainstream economics of the sort we have been discussing in earlier chapters was economics expressed autistically. We can here with profit recall the dictionary definition of autism: 'A psychiatric disorder of childhood characterized by marked deficits in communication and social interaction, preoccupation with fantasy, and abnormal behavior patterns' (*American Heritage College Dictionary* 2002). The use of the term autism was, in short, deliberately designed from the outset to assert that modern mainstream economics, with all the characteristics we described in Chapter 3, is designed to make difficult if not impossible, communication between the economists so expressing themselves and everyone else, uninitiated economist or the general public. To insist on some communicating, argued 'Les jeunes francais' meant that the people so affected suffered from a psychiatric disorder, behaved abnormally, and communicated only in a childlike way with the uninitiated.

And what was it that the young French advanced students were so upset about? They put out a petition in June 2000 in which they protested against:

> the lack of realism in economics teaching; economics' 'uncontrolled use' and treatment of mathematics as 'an end in itself,' with the result that economics has become an 'autistic science', lost in 'imaginary worlds;' the repressive domination of neoclassical theory, and approaches derivative from it in the university curriculum, and the dogmatic style in economics, which leaves no place for

critical and reflective thought. (Fullbrook 2003, p. 7)

A major difference between the post-autistic economics movement as it developed in France and other student protests is that in due course the mainstream economists in France answered the charges of the PAE. In due course *Le Monde* published a reply by Robert Solow and another by Oliver Blanchard, Chairman of the Economics Department at MIT.

In June 2001 the French students' protests made themselves manifest in the UK as well, when 27 Cambridge University students organized themselves into a protest group fighting for the same things. They published a petition entitled 'Opening Up Economics' which referred to their feeling that economics should become '. . . mindful of the limitations of the competing approaches to understanding economic phenomena', of 'learning their domain of applicability,' and of using 'the best methods for the question at hand' rather than 'restricting research done in economics to that based on one approach only' (Fulbrook 2003, p. 7).

At about the same time the discontent surged across the Atlantic to the University of Missouri at Kansas City where 75 students and professors from 22 countries called for various changes. In particular, they expressed their support for the general position taken by the students both in France and in Cambridge. Their support took the form of an open letter to all Economics Departments.

The group wrote:

> The undersigned participants, all committed to the reform of our discipline, have developed the following open letter. This letter follows statements from other groups who have similar concerns. Both in agreement with and in support of the Post-Autistic Economics Movement and the Cambridge Proposal, we believe that economic theory, inhibited by its ahistorical approach and abstract formalist methodology, has provided only a limited understanding of the challenging complexity of economic behavior. The narrow methodological approach of economics hinders its ability to generate truly pragmatic and realistic policy prescriptions or to engage in productive dialogue with other social sciences.
>
> All economics departments should reform economics education to include reflection on the methodological assumptions that underpin our discipline . . . Most immediately, the field of economic analysis must be expanded to encompass the following:
>
> 1. A broader conception of human behavior. The definition of economic man as an autonomous rational optimizer is too narrow.
> 2. Recognition of culture . . . economic activities . . . are embedded in culture, which

includes all kinds of social, political, and moral value-systems and institutions . . .

3. Consideration of history. Economic reality is dynamic rather than static . . .
4. A new theory of knowledge . . . The positive–normative dichotomy . . . is problematic . . . the investigator's values are inescapably involved in scientific inquiry and in making scientific statements . . .
5. Empirical grounding. More effort must be made to substantiate theoretical claims with empirical evidence . . .
6. Expanded methods. Procedures such as participant observation, case studies and discourse analysis should be recognized as legitimate means of acquiring and analyzing data alongside econometrics and formal modeling . . .
7. Interdisciplinary dialogue. Economists should be aware of diverse schools of thought within economics, and should be aware of developments in other disciplines, particularly the social sciences.

Although strong in developing analytic thinking skills, the professional training of economists has tended to discourage economists from even debating – let alone accepting – the validity of these wider dimensions . . . Critically-minded students of economics seem to face an unhappy choice between abandoning their speculative interests in order to make professional progress, or abandoning economics altogether for disciplines more hospitable to reflection and innovation.[18]

All in all, this would seem to be a reasonable statement of the perspective taken by many institutional economists. It is probably a fairly accurate overall portrayal of the complaints of many heterodox economists. We discussed their perspective earlier. What is the response of the mainstream to this view? For answers we refer the reader to the later discussion of the cow and the fly. In the three years of their existence this student group has established the *Post Autistic Economics Review*, which is published periodically on the internet and currently has over 6000 subscribers in something like 140 countries.[19] They debate many of the issues they feel the mainstream journals ignore. It can be argued some of their internal discussions are over details which will fail to help them in their overall goal of attracting the attention and interest of more mainstream economists. But they are also involved in some internal debates which are difficult to avoid in the modern world. For example, it is clear that 'heterodox economics' can include a variety of views of which institutional economics and the concerns of its adherents is but one group. But

18. This letter was written by David Pringle and Aine Ni Leime on behalf of the AFEE Summer School Students gathered at the Second Biennial Summer School of the Association of Evolutionary Economics at the University of Missouri-Kansas City, June 23–28, 2001, Post-Autistic Economics newsletter, www.btinternet.com/~pae_news/issue8.htm.

19. pae_news@btinternet.com.

beyond that there are 'good causes' which may or may not be legitimately folded in with the concerns of Veblen, Commons, and Mitchell around whose concerns institutional economics was launched. That the PAE, as launched by the French students had largely similar concerns is not hard to establish. But the list of heterodox or pluralistic organizations previously presented included some devoted to issues of conservation or ecology, some to feminist issues, some to special fields (history of thought, economic history) etc. Whether all these organizations, heterodox or pluralistic though they legitimately may be, can also all be considered part of institutional economics is a highly dubious proposition if the term is to retain any recognizable intellectual focus[20] (Ayres 1944, p. v). Institutionalism is the group with which the author is most familiar. Thus Allan Gruchy wrote 'In the first three decades of the current century the American movement to revamp economic science came to be known as "institutionalism"'. Gruchy meant the work of Veblen and the 'considerable modification' of that work by Commons, Mitchell, Clark, Tugwell, and Means (cf. Gruchy 1947, p. vii). From the outset there was some confusion as Gruchy also used the term 'institutional economics' to refer specifically to Veblen, and used 'collective economics' for Commons' work, 'quantitative economics' for Mitchell (wouldn't that confuse a modern reader!), and similar more explicit names for other founders mentioned above. On the other hand, Schumpeter refers simply to the institutionalist controversy, meaning all these people (Schumpeter 1954, p. 431n). Clearly they were both commenting on institutional economics explicitly but in a way that was probably appropriate to virtually all heterodox thinking of the period. It also avoids the complications which set in when selecting a name for the non-traditional economists. 'Heterodox' is probably the most generic term available. But diverse groups of heterodox economists give themselves diverse names. Thus, among a number of other appellations we have today one encounters: Conservative Institutionalists, Dogmatic Marxists, Critical Marxists, Old and New Institutionalists, etc. In the text we have attempted to describe the position contrary to the mainstream which would appeal to the widest group of non-traditional economists. The problem as we have suggested is complicated today by the addition of groups devoted to one or another aspect regarded as being overlooked or minimized by mainstream economists (e.g., the environment, history, feminism etc.). It is more than doubtful that any organization which aspires to professional recognition can include all the 'good' causes currently before us without losing the focus

---

20. In this book we have mostly used the term 'institutional economics' to delineate a position which is contrary to the mainstream economists. (Terminology is not simple – we devoted Chapter 7 to identifying 'mainstream economists.' Ayres's original called them 'orthodox economists'.)

which both distinguishes it from other organizations and gives it meaning. The post-autistic economist movement, it was argued, would mean that finally alternatives to mainstream neoclassical economic theory would be presented as legitimate alternative approaches and made the subject for debate. We have suggested that the focus of traditional institutional economics and that of the PAE seem compatible insofar as we can trace and compare the expressed objectives of each. We have noted that institutional economics is rarely mentioned in mainstream media so far as we can tell. The post-autistic economist movement has begun to get discussed in the public media. Thus, the *New Statesman*, for example, wrote, 'Paris has become the birthplace of a revolt against the preeminence of theory over practice, of economic abstraction over reality, and statistics over real life' (Boyle 2002, pp. 23–4). It has not yet, to our knowledge, received any attention from the mainstream economics world (as described in Chapter 7). Arguably the young people in their newsletter are debating small points which threaten to lose the interest of many potentially sympathetic economists whose support is necessary to mount a genuine alternative to the orthodoxy currently prevailing. They are debating also whether institutional economics is distinctive and has a paradigm and methodology of its own or can instead can be regarded as an umbrella group of diverse 'good' causes – feminist economics, environmental concerns, radical viewpoints, etc. In due course these issues will presumably be resolved and institutional economics will emerge as a clear voice dissenting from mainstream orthodoxy.[21] Whether a movement involving this many young economists can be ignored by the world of economics only the future can reveal. However, at the very least we can say that to describe the institutionalist movement as having 'withered away' seems less accurate than was perhaps the case only a few years ago.

We need add only that we have not attempted a definitive or a complete listing of current heterodox or institutional economic efforts. There are many organizations devoted to doing research on what are often called 'social indicators.' (We come back to some of these considerations later). All of these groups in one way or another are considering evidence – statistical and other kinds – which suggests that even economies viewed in the abstract as essentially units in 'equilibrium' derived from market clearing activity need not necessarily reflect the results of resource deployment which any society, including our own, will invariably regard as acceptable. We earlier considered differing degrees of pain threshold on the part of economic investigators as one explanation for differing attitudes toward the resource deploying results

21. I am grateful to Geoffrey E. Schneider for extended discussion about these issues.

of these efforts. How much intervention is 'required' to make economic performance 'acceptable' can vary, partly depending on how much pain is regarded as 'too much.' All kinds of economies from basically market clearing to those with a good deal of intervention can at any given time be regarded as needing more or less intervention, depending on the degree of perceived pain. Marginal adjustments in the degree of intervention are the stuff of most legislative sessions. What at any given time a 'civilized society' regards as the minimum owed each participant in that economy is a critical aspect of any dynamic economy. (This social minimum is really a minimal social pain threshold.)

We have throughout this book stressed in various ways the difference between growth and progress, between value and price, etc. The normative variants of these words point toward a variety of unfortunate conditions: infant mortality, child abuse, children and the elderly in poverty (anyone in poverty perhaps), suicide rates, drug abuse, school drop-outs, alcoholism, homicides, income inequality, etc. These and sundry other misfortunes are all unhappy conditions which diverse societies can tolerate in very different degrees. The new classical economists never tire of suggesting that equilibria say nothing about human happiness. Pain thresholds are themselves culturally influenced. One can expect that the same economic performance from the market will not prove equally acceptable in different cultures. How much (unemployment, inflation, income inequality, people in poverty, etc.) is 'too much'? The answer(s) to such question(s) is (are) a major determinant of the extent of interventionism one finds in a given economy and the extent, therefore, to which a given economy is prepared to augment market activity with resource deployment in the public sector.

The only other thing to add here is that these questions are obfuscated in discussions of the economy and its functioning by declaring that all the unfortunate conditions enumerated are 'non-economic.' If the markets all clear, thereby making Walras happy at the results of the allocation of resources, no observable human misery falls within the province of the economist. Such a world makes Pareto's contribution to a tranquil life for an economist seem modest indeed.

Orthodoxy and Heterodoxy in the Twenty-First Century

In general, as we have tried to show, it is fair to say that the mainstream network presented in Chapter 7 has no explicit policy with respect to all the heterodox organizations. De facto the solution is simply to ignore them. Put in the most graphic terms, the mainstream approach to heterodoxy is not unlike the attitude of cows to flies. Cows have no 'policy' with respect to the flies that light on their hides. They have a de facto habit of generalized but random swatting with their tails. That is not conscious policy of how to cope with flies. Consciously, cows have no specific attitude toward flies. At best, their attitude is indifference.

From the point of view of heterodox economists and their efforts at recognition, the practical problem is how to get the explicit attention directed at them which is required to convert a splinter group into a genuine alternative perspective toward the discipline. Mainstream economists have no policy toward heterodox economists – they simply ignore them. In Arthur Miller's play *Death of a Salesman*, Linda Loman says of her husband, Willy Loman, 'He was a human being and attention must be paid.' Willy was a failure and he was ignored. The world was treating him as a cow would treat a fly. Her point was that if Willy ended up a discarded failure it mattered because human life – any human life – to civilized human beings has to matter (hence the importance of adhering to the sanctity of human life as a fundamental value).

The heterodox economists have somewhat the same problem as Willy Loman except that it is inaccurate to call them a failure. They make arguments which would need to be effectively shown to be inaccurate in order to term them a failure. (For example, when Samuelson said institutional economics had 'withered away' he clearly was in error. It had not withered away, although it may have dwindled below Samuelson's level of consciousness.) The world could turn Willy into a failure simply by ignoring him because he had no quarrel with the standards of evaluation. How he played the game was – by the prevailing standards – not very efficient or effective and so it can be argued he deserved being ignored. That cannot be said of heterodox economists unless and until mainstream economists explicitly pay attention to what heterodox economists are saying. They begin by questioning the standards of evaluation. To ignore the alternative standards without addressing the questions raised is, therefore, merely arrogance. (And no one can accuse the aforementioned cows of being arrogant with respect to the flies – they are merely too dumb to notice.) I, therefore, echo Linda Loman by saying of the economists that make up the memberships of all the heterodox organizations just enumerated, 'They are made up of real economists with a point of view that is distinctive and before they are ignored or dismissed attention must be paid to what they are saying. Their arguments deserve to be addressed. Market clearing and enhancing the life process are not the same standard of evaluation. Once again, I reiterate a point I first made 30 years ago – allocation and valuation are fundamentally different. There is nothing wrong with market clearing, efficiency, or profit maximization – they have their place – provided attention is also paid to equity, security, freedom, and compassion. Economic activity cannot be judged by narrow allocative efficiency alone – it must ultimately be judged by what long ago I called 'the higher efficiency.'[22] Conventional microeconomic theory texts traditionally assert that what is being sought through interplay in markets is 'equilibrium.' Achieving equality of supply and demand via price in each market is what conventional theory is all about.

Keynesian macroeconomics at least in the pre 'AS-AD' days broadened this somewhat to suggest that other outcomes are sought such as a satisfactory level of employment etc. So in striving for the 'higher efficiency' real economies are judged on their own performance by the extent to which they measure up to a number of criteria. Along with allocative efficiency they may also be judged by how they reflect concern for equity, security, freedom, and compassion. The critical point is that they do not all place the same degree of concern on each of these – but whether they like it or not they will perforce exhibit some degree of concern (from zero to a great deal) toward equity, security, etc. Thus a very equal income distribution, a highly unequal income distribution, or any of the infinite variety of distributions in between contribute to the unique characterization of a particular economy in terms of – in this case – equity. One can, of course, similarly characterize for any given economy its degree of concern with each of the other criteria mentioned. In the end each economy can be characterized not alone in terms of GDP. The resultant profile of each economy – in terms of all these criteria – is what is meant by the 'higher efficiency.' Allocative efficiency we saw even Adam Smith found an inadequate standard. One need only read the daily papers to realize how critically the US public, for example, regards the quality of health care provided, and the per cent of the public it covers, but it is not included in judging allocative efficiency.

So in the real world we judge 'lower efficiency' (allocative efficiency) but also 'higher efficiency.' There is another difference. The commercial world, in which Willy Loman tried to function, could scarcely be said to have malfunctioned in a significant way, at least not given what it set out to do. Willy did not question it – he was merely poor at playing the role which he espoused. The malfunctioning which heterodox economists point to can't be dismissed quite so easily because as we have just seen again they question some of the standards by which it is judged. The core *weltanschauung* of most of the organizations we have enumerated falls somewhere within the point of

---

22. In 1973 I said, '. . . it does no disservice to the notion so fondly advanced by mainstream economists – that the price system does much allocation in a remarkably efficient way – to suggest that the whole system as in fact it operates is a far from perfect method of converting emergent values into allocative decisions' (Klein 1994, p. 196).

view we have just expressed. That is why it was worth considering with some specificity the raison d'etre for some of the major heterodox organizations we have denoted.

In short, heterodoxy in economics points to some failures in orthodoxy which deserve being addressed. Why? Because there is a large cost in human misery which must be paid as the price of ignoring what people's lot is. In the end, flies we repeat are merely an annoyance for cows. But civilized societies cannot ignore the misery they now evade because it is concentrated in pockets of society often kept relatively hidden. In the past 50 years group after group has begun to be rescued from their 'have not' prison. Those who are there by reason of race or gender or religion or physical and mental disadvantage or sexual orientation are often increasingly regarded as in an intolerable place. This leaves a large group who are still in an intolerable place because of the flawed way in which the economic system in virtually all market-oriented societies continues to enable some to prosper while a significant segment suffers. This group suffers inadequacies generated by, e.g., age, race, gender, or discrimination based on other factors which lead to generalized failure to train and employ all in the labor force to their capacity and in ways consonant with their talents and abilities. Correcting this, say heterodox economists, will require a combination of self-help and societal help. Ensuring that all people flourish will pay cold hard economic dividends in the form of greater productivity, higher outputs, and more adequate living standards everywhere. That is why heterodox economists with justifiable conviction insist, 'Attention must be paid to the reality of invidious denial of adequate economic participation for major segments of the community'!

Some Basic Postulates of Heterodoxy

In the interests of clarity we may summarize our discussion of heterodox economics by setting forth some of its basic principles as we see them. They have mostly been made explicitly or implicitly in the earlier critique of mainstream economics.

1. If as we insist the economy is everywhere and always embedded in a wider culture, it is essential to state up front that we need constantly to assess, so as to further, the vitality of the economy. This is true because an essential part of that wider culture constitutes a democratic polity. Thus issues of equity are present at the outset of the deliberations of a political economist.
2. If equity is extant as a criterion for judgement at the outset of analysis the inquiry must perforce be normative as well as positive. Even for purposes

of analysis it is untenable to accept without comment 'what is' because all such states are flawed to begin with. In other areas this simple fact is clear, but not in economics. The medical profession may think its first obligation is 'to do no harm' but they also would say their task is not to 'accept what is' but to improve on what is. 'Perfect health' for individuals and 'ideal public health conditions' cannot be assumed. This does not mean that debate cannot be about what 'improving' on it involves. But defining 'progress' in medicine is no different from defining progress in economics. The debate needs to be intense, but debate there must surely be. 'Prolonging human life' is a normative question to which much positive analysis can contribute in meaningful and significant ways. In precisely the same way prolonging an economic expansion is not just a matter of positive debate about unemployment versus inflation, but a normative matter about who bears the costs of avoiding various unpleasant consequences of a failure to prolong expansion. In addition the dangers attendant upon prolonged expansions (inflation, excess capacity, etc.) and what society should strive for when it faces these questions must be addressed.

3. Tool put this question of progress at center stage years ago when he challenged economists to state precisely what and how they choose which way is 'forward' – that is, how do we define progress? Tool's contribution to an answer was the 'social value principle' which has become undoubtedly the most widely quoted statement of the bedrock principle of modern institutionalism. Said Tool in defining this social value principle, 'We now affirm that that direction is forward which provides for the continuity of human life and the non-invidious recreation of community through the instrumental use of knowledge' (Tool 1979, p. 293). This formulation is a model of succinctness. The essence of modern institutionalism is found in its emphasis on the importance of all individuals, of democracy, of caring for each other, and basing a modern economy on the latest and best technology which dynamic technical processes can provide. It is all implicitly there in the 'continuity of human life,' the notion of community, the insistence that human organization based on genuine community had to be 'non-invidious' in all matters involving choice, and had, finally, throughout to use all knowledge (the knowledge base is essentially dynamic) incrementally.

It is odd that mainstream economists regard statements such as Tool's as 'mushy' and difficult to understand. The same economists have no problem with a statement such as the following sentence selected at random: 'If the technology is not convex, perhaps because of the presence of some underlying invisibility, then satisfaction of the first-order necessary condition . . . no longer implies that q is profit maximizing' (Mas-Colell, Whinston, and Green 1995, pp. 143–44).

We make this comparison not because there is anything inappropriate about the latter quotation but only to under-score a point we have made previously: Seemingly a young economist who is 'with it' needs to be able to think precisely with numbers, but no such standard can or should be held up for verbal comprehension.

4. Mainstream economists have had no problem seeing the advantages that accompany the use of econometrics – indeed they have embraced it – because they see that time and dynamics generally can be included only in a world where variables can be dated. However, they have not been willing to follow the implications of the dynamic perspective to its logical conclusions. In a static world they have consistently equated price and value, when as heterodox economists have long noted they have profoundly different meanings and implications. Courses in microeconomics are consistently labeled either price theory or value theory as though the terms were quite interchangeable. In truth (as I noted at least 30 years ago), price is to value precisely as growth is to progress. Using econometric techniques to measure growth rates has a high appeal to mainstream economists. Using any techniques at all to measure progress has little interest. (Those who follow William Nordhaus in his concern for measuring 'net economic welfare' have never been embraced by conventional economic analysts).[23]

   Specifically, Samuelson and Nordhaus in their basic text made something of the discussion of net economic welfare. The term is defined as ' . . . an adjusted measure of total national output that includes only consumption and investment items that contribute directly to economic well-being' (Samuelson and Nordhaus 1995, p. 417). In some earlier editions they even included a chart designed to make the major point that over time net economic welfare grows more slowly than GDP because producing more output is not without costs – environmental pollution, rapid growth in the underground economy, etc. By the seventeenth edition (2001) the term, net economic welfare, still appears in the glossary, but it has been banished from the text discussion. The authors content themselves with a brief discussion of 'non-market activities' as well as correcting for harmful activities that are included as part of national output (Samuelson and Norhaus 1998, pp. 448–49).

23. The term has been used in *Economics* by Samuelson and Nordhaus for a number of editions, culminating in the fifteenth edition (1995, p. 405). The term was introduced by Nordhaus and Tobin (1972) at the Fiftieth Anniversary Colloquium.

5. The implications of the above are that enhancing human life and achieving market equilibria are not necessarily congruent. Thorstein Veblen's assertion was that the task of economic theory is 'to enhance human life.' An important way to do this is to follow Wesley Clair Mitchell's example and imbue the studying and development of economic theory with a thoroughgoing empiricism. Conventional model builders begin with simplifying assumptions which create an 'ideal world' for study. In contrast, Mitchell's empirical approach, exemplified by his focus on business cycles, takes the world as empirically given and searches for pattern or theory in the real world. Institutional theory focuses on the flaws in the system and seeks ways to mitigate or eliminate the effects of the flaws. Conventional theory begins by defining flaws away. The one focuses, therefore, on 'real facts' while the other is, therefore, more comfortable in a world of 'stylized facts.'
6. The most critical link for the economist is the link between theory and policy. Human life can never be enhanced if explanations of economic phenomena are directed at a world which has never existed. 'Understanding' the real world is given meaning only when it is applied to improving the real world. The old debate between rigor and relevance has not lost its importance with time. It has indeed become more and more critical as mainstream theorizing has shifted ever more in the direction of rigor and its attractions and away from relevance and its attractions.
7. To recover its relevance economic theory needs to shift its principal focus from endless preoccupation with its logic and precision and direct focus on the real world challenges.
8. Theorists in economics should at long last come completely to terms with the implications of being part of the social sciences rather than the physical sciences. The principles of, for example, physics are universal. The law of gravity we saw earlier is not influenced by the particular arrangements under which human beings in a given community choose to live. This is not true of economics. Beyond some rudimentary truths ('We all have to eat') economies are profoundly affected by the culture in which they function. It is commonly said that all economies must determine: What to Produce? How to Produce? and For Whom to Produce? Institutional economics affirms that how these three basic functions are carried out by the wider culture in which they operate varies hugely from culture to culture. That being the case, economists err in regarding their science as governed by universal principles as witness textbooks which like to confront the world with titles like 'The Principles of Economics'rather than, say, 'The Functioning of the US Economy' or 'The Functioning of the Economy of Country X.'

9. Heterodox economists have never argued with the proposition that the discipline needs to be deeply concerned with market allocation. The essential importance of market allocation has never been denied. Rather its importance is recognized and its functioning is in many ways admired. What has always been insisted is that however marvelous market allocation may be, and no matter how high a percentage of resource deployment can be accomplished successfully in this manner, all societies have a continuing obligation to monitor market allocation and to measure its consequences against the underlying values that determine a given economy's notions of equity etc. at any given time. Emergent social value is always the ongoing valuational parameter against which the consequences of resource deployment, whether through the market or through another mechanism, need to be evaluated. It is the monitoring process that defines the essential role of the economist and the underlying justification for the field.
10. An implication of the points enumerated above is that economic man, customarily presented as a very convenient summarization of the essential message of orthodox microeconomic theory is, in fact, something of a caricature. It is because of the implications customarily drawn from economic man that 'the principles of economics' are regarded as universal. The role of economic man is little more than that of a pleasure-pain robot. The principles of economics are regarded as universal because the robot is imbued with universal attributes. But if economies are set in diverse cultures and we recognize that cultural variation is attributable to psychology, sociology, political science, history, aesthetics, and a whole host of other influences on human character and personality, we realize that the robot called economic man accurately describes human behavior about as well as – say do our nursery rhymes. It follows that in order to assess the implications for how a given set of participants will interact over matters of economic activity it is critical to contemplate the impact which the diverse cultural stimuli will have on the manner in which any given group of economic participants will carry out their economic activities.

Were economic man in fact the set of entirely predictable stimuli it is convenient for orthodox theory to assume he is, business firms would not have as much difficulty forecasting their sales as in fact they do now. By the same token, consumers would not be influenced by the efforts of firms to sell them on their products in so large but varied degree as in fact they are. Both of these result in surrounding market interactions with uncertainty which conventional maximizing assumptions simply gloss over more or less completely. Were these interactions at the microeconomic level as invariant as it is customarily assumed by letting them revolve around economic man, the consequences of group interactions, the domain of macroeconomics, would not be so difficult to predict or to monitor or to control as in fact they are.

11. In view of what has just been said, all economies will perforce require a public sector, and the operation of that sector, no less than the market, requires constant monitoring with a view to determining what activities should be continued and which eliminated. Moreover, for those which are kept, modernizing will be required more or less constantly so as to reflect changing underlying societal values and the growth of knowledge – the dynamic base for all economic activity.
12. The foregoing considerations, especially points numbers 2 and 5, lead us to see that economists need to focus on confronting the real economy and attempting to analyze its problems. The ultimate objective must be improving economic performance. So far as is known, economics is the only field which has always been most comfortable – and continues so to this day – in assuming away all imperfections. The perfectly competitive market and its macroeconomic equivalent (the self-stabilizing economy) is the preferred focus of attention. Psychologists do not assume human interactions invariably without friction; physicians do not assume that perfect health is the norm; political scientists do not assume that ideal representative democracy is the governmental norm; meteorologists do not assume the weather is always ideal. Economists are, as has frequently been said, in a class apart in the fundamental perspective with which they regard their field. We have noted that where efforts to change this have been attempted the mainstream finds ways to thwart these efforts. My own field of business cycles is a unique instance in which the 'warts' became the central focus of attention. Not surprisingly, as we saw earlier, the field of cycles is under attack by the 'real business cycle' group. We saw that they are but the latest in the recurring effort to declare business cycles to be dead. If successful they will have succeeded in defining cycles away (again!) thus eliminating business cycles as a subject of serious inquiry. In their view – cycles are just the growing pains of a normal well-adjusted viable economy! Recall our earlier discussion to the effect that just for good measure there is a strong move to restore the good old days and so, just for good measure, the same groups urge us to scrap the whole field of macroeconomics (just a figment of the mistaken or misplaced imagination of Keynes!).

Alas, economies like most human efforts show the influence of human fallibility. Economies work imperfectly. We need to face this, as economists, and – at long last – accept our true responsibility, which, it turns out, is the logical counterpart to scientists' responsibility in every other field we can contemplate! And what is that? It is simply to accept the flawed system we have and try to make it work more efficiently and sensitively so as to a do a better job of enhancing human life (yes, Veblen was right!).

13. The result of all these points is to insist on recognition of the dynamic nature of any social science, including economics. The theory needs to be kept up to date just as the task of confronting any actual economy is a dynamic task, confronting as it must changing techniques in a continuous need to adapt to changing technology, changing resources, changing tastes, changing culture, and changing global conditions.

CONCLUDING THOUGHTS

Sixty years ago Clarence Ayres began his *The Theory of Economic Progress* by writing, 'The purpose of this book is to set forth a new way of thinking about economic problems' (Ayres 1944, p. v). In a real sense the purpose of this book has been to set forth the same way of thinking about economic problems, except, of course, it is no longer new. Ayres was attempting to contrast the kind of economics which is 'obsessed with price theory' with the view of the discipline taken by Veblen – that economics is essentially concerned with 'enhancing the life process' of mankind.

The problem with price theory as the exclusive focus of economics is that it concentrates on the mechanics of allocation and virtually ignores the far more fundamental question of how we should harness resources and technology to improve the way all human beings live on this earth. The emphasis on the second way of viewing the discipline draws attention to two fundamental aspects of Ayres' 'new way of thinking.' The first concern is the whole question of how we tell when things are getting better for us; how do we know when we are making progress? (We considered this earlier in this chapter in connection with Tool's social value principle.) In this valuation process, price has a very modest role to play.[24]

The second concern is the basic justification for all our efforts to understand the economy, i.e., why struggle at all with economic theory? Economic theory obviously is concerned with explaining how the economy

24. Indeed there is a whole approach which argues that measuring GDP is but the first crude step to charting progress. Cf. for example Miringoff and Miringoff (1999) and also Cobb, Halstead, and Rowe (1995), pp. 2–15.

functions. Relevant theory equips us to improve the instrumental functioning of the economy. This in turn requires institutional change in the form of public policy. In short, the bedrock role of the discipline is to enable us always to do the best job of assuring that, given our resources and the state of technology, we are deploying both to make economic aspects of the life process for all people as adequate and rewarding as they can possibly be. This, of course, means that we do not just leave resource deployment to the market, we monitor it. We leave it to the market but only when our best judgment tells us, through deliberate monitoring of market allocation, that a particular resource deployment through the market will most efficiently enhance, equity, freedom, security, and compassion. Deployment overall may require market allocation, regulated market allocation, deployment by federal, state, or local government agencies, or it may require deployment through still other channel(s) where special kinds of expertise are concentrated. We note in passing that the categories praised and pilloried in the past, e.g., a pure market system, a centrally planned system, are far too simplistic for the complex and sophisticated goals of a modern technologically up to date economic system. All such are driven by complex, overlapping – but on occasion conflicting – criteria for measuring success. Viewed in the light of this broader perspective, we may say that prices, their determination, and their role in allocation are but a part of the larger process of determining how to deploy resources, in light of current technology, to make economic life for all people as close to instrumentally ideal as we at any given time can achieve. Defining and redefining 'what ought to be' and then striving always to achieve it is the never ending and essential challenge to our discipline.

Reducing this set of objectives to the shibboleths of the day – 'Get the government off our backs!' 'Turn it over to a public agency,' 'Give the people back their money' etc. – will infuriate diverse groups, confuse the voters (and for the economy, therefore, the resource deployers) and delay genuine progress for long periods of time. One thing is certain: the foregoing will not contribute to the solution of real economic problems – not any of it!

Ayres saw these alternatives clearly long ago. His focus was on contrasting his new approach with its emphasis on value, welfare, and progress with what he called 'the classical tradition.' In his later book, *Toward A Reasonable Society*, he elaborated on the aspects of the value problem which he regarded as critical. While he emphasized what he called 'the unity of value,' he stressed that the judging progress in bettering the life process was a multi-faceted challenge. His formulation of the criterion of value included freedom, equality, security, abundance, excellence and the 'moral values' (being truthful, etc.) (Ayres 1961). My particular list, mentioned above, goes back to 1982. How the economy fulfills its value-oriented role I called 'the higher efficiency' and we have considered it earlier (Klein 1994, pp. 194–6). Tool carried all this one step further by relating the operation of the economy to the polity, which involves the way in which the polity is involved in making the economy operational. Tool, too, ended with concern for basing the operation of the economy on social value not just price. In Tool's formulation this meant stressing freedom, equality and justice (Tool 1979).

Other heterodox economists have used different words, but the focus is always on suggesting that growth and progress are not the same and that in the end what we are concerned with is the role the economy is playing in enriching and bettering the lives of all the participants in the community. So viewed the logical implication of downplaying the role of the discipline in contributing to progress in bettering the lives of human beings can only mean that many mainstream economists have concluded that their discipline cannot contribute much to improving life or that it is irrelevant to that goal. The other explanation is that they have lost interest in this goal. A good example of this is David Colander's characterization of the impact Lucas had on macroeconomic theory. Recall that he suggested that macroeconomic theory in Lucas's hands had been recast away from concern with 'business cycles, unemployment, inflation, and low growth.' (Cf. Chapter 5, p. 57 above for Lucas's full statement.) We have attempted to explain in this book that so to argue is really to remove the justification for the discipline and to enshrine Hicks's view that for some 'economics is just a game.' The choice is clear – either it is just a game or it is engaged in a critical and perhaps deadly business of making life bearable for many for whom now it is not, and for improving it for many more people.

This is not a new thought. It has appeared periodically and from a number of sources. One which received world-wide attention was that of E.F. Shumacher in 1973. He wrote,

> If [economy thinking] cannot get beyond its vast abstractions, the national income, the rate of growth, capital/output ratio, input-output analysis, labor mobility, capital accumulation; if it cannot get beyond all this and make contact with the human realities of poverty, frustration, alienation, despair, breakdown, crime, escapism, stress, congestion, ugliness, and spiritual death, then let us scrap economics and start afresh. (Schumacher 1973 republished 1999, p. 56)

Back of Schumacher's distinction is the fundamental institutionalist distinction between, on the one hand, counting the stuff produced with resources by adding up their prices and, on the other hand, contemplating what the economy has contributed to making life better for all its people. The latter, of course, is, yet again, the Veblenian emphasis on the use of resources in pursuit of the life process. It is what as long ago as 1973 I called economics as valuation rather than allocation (Klein 1994). It is as simple as distinctions get, and is increasingly lost rather than rediscovered in the modern world.

In the years since Schumacher wrote, the standard economics has moved much farther in the direction of being a mathematical discipline whose function is to comment on a mechanical process of doling out resources and converting them into things – the more the better. As we have tried to suggest in earlier chapters, the major change has been to enable economists to address this process elaborately but quantitatively through large numbers of simultaneous equations rather than only (or even mainly!) with verbal explanations of institutional change.

On an individual basis we have progressed sufficiently to understand what is being said when we note that a single man getting richer and richer is not necessarily getting happier or more fulfilled. At the societal level we have seemingly lost the ability to focus on this same process, and we seem deliberately to turn our backs on the implications of our distribution system which fails to focus on the have nots. We know at one level that the economy is not a zero sum game, that there is no reason for some to stay or become poor so that others can get or increase their wealth. We know this, but clearly neither economic theory nor the polity which it reflects has wished to focus on the kinds of problems to which Schumacher calls attention.

As I have made my way through this book the essential message has become more and more clear to me. In economics as in every field there is surely room for 'basic research,' by which I mean exploring new ideas; investigating new possibilities; wrestling with fundamental and interesting questions about basic assumptions; testing new techniques of development, finding alternative research paths, and exploring myriad other logistical, and heuristic, implications.

But in order to maintain some semblance of rational balance every field has periodically to ask itself – what is the essential reason for the field's existence and how can one tell if progress is being made? The major fields into which knowledge is conventionally divided do not exist without reason. They are not created in a vacuum. For example, each of the social sciences is considered a science in its own right, though inter-related to all other social sciences to be sure, because it has an inquiry function to fill. Each of the social sciences is addressed to an area of human life where things do not invariably operate smoothly – where, in short, public policy is called upon to play a critical role. In each case that role requires that the field of inquiry rest on a set of fundamental positions which undergird the current explanations for how inquiry and conduct relate. Theory then is the necessary prerequisite for good and ever relevant public policy.

The basic challenge to modern economics is to reestablish, at its core, the theory–policy connection. So even an 'in house group', charged to recommend improvements in how the discipline is passed on to graduate students, saw this problem. In a commissioned note written in 1999 Anne Krueger reiterated the point. She said, '. . . our major concern with graduate education [in Krueger 1991 – ed.] was the "disconnect" between training in tools of economics taught in the first year . . . and ways in which economics graduate students learned – or more accurately, did not learn – how to apply those tools to the economic problems they confronted' (Krueger 1999, 154). But her final remark was, 'Yet there is little evidence that the profession has addressed these issues of linkages any more successfully in the 1990s that it did in the period covered by COGEE' (her Commission on Graduate Education in Economics (Krueger 1999, 156). In short, the profession did not take the views of its own commission any more seriously than it took the views of heterodox economists. If the discipline would like a theme song to guide it on its way to the immediate future, may I suggest an old torch song, 'Why Was I Born?'. I submit in all humility, that economics was not born to play games, to adumbrate ever more complex mathematical methods, or to spin out ever more sophisticated, elegant, esoteric, abstract, webs of doubtful relevance.

Imagine for example, a language devoted to ever more complicated laws of grammar in which practitioners devoted themselves to new and more complicated but elegant ways of expressing these laws of grammar. Imagine that the occasional voice asked 'What is language for? Why are we doing this? Should it not have something to do with the current problem, namely that human communication is far from perfect? Language should be devoted to enabling human communication to be more accurate, to express more subtle shades of meaning, etc.' Finally, imagine that those who took this latter position were laughed out of the discipline on grounds that they wore hopelessly anachronistic blinders rendering all their efforts puerile, simplistic, crude, useless and futile.

The basic researchers and the theorists who think of theory creation as a way to improve policy have increasingly become a shrinking minority of economists. By the beginning of the twenty-first century very few members of the club would be caught dead taking the position just expressed, that applying theory to policy making is the core inquiry and the source of its significance.

The triumph of orthodoxy has not so much been to kill off Keynes in analysis, although many modern young economists talk in those terms. It has been primarily the triumph of conformity, of methodological uniformity, of a one dimensional perspective on how economists are allowed to pursue their discipline. While this appraisal of the current state of the discipline is far from the mainstream view there are, as we have seen, increasing numbers of heterodox voices heard.

Let us be absolutely clear. There is nothing wrong with having some economists dickering with the niceties of allocation – far from it. The role of prices in the allocation process, one presumes, does not work perfectly by anyone's standards, and therefore, devoting attention to it would have a place in anyone's list of areas to which attention should be paid. It is a question of balance.

The assumption that price determination of allocative patterns is all there is to resource deployment is a monumental oversimplification. It is by now a cliche to point out that a discipline conforming to the stricture just suggested could never get resources devoted to national defense. Cliches are cliches often because they contain enormous truths. Things we want 'regardless of cost' are not non-economic. They involve deployment rather than allocation. Our discipline is seemingly quite comfortable seeing itself as a positive discipline in which it makes enormous normative exception for the process by which resources get deployed to military purposes. Hence it will appear that resources devoted to the military are viewed by mainstream economists as based on a positive discipline which finds nothing uncomfortable about the failure of that deployment system to conform in any way whatsoever to the basic gut level premises of extant mainstream theory. However, any discussion of resources devoted to civilian constructive purposes is definitionally out of order because it is a flagrant attempt to circumvent 'the market.'

As we have seen, cost-benefit analysis, one way to defang these inconsistencies, is never really applied to defense, and flounders on any question of usefulness with questions where, to put it as clearly as possible, price cannot convey value.

The failure of price to convey all societal value is the root reason why concentration on allocation cannot actually deal with the economic problem. That problem is not how to allocate resources with prices, but how to deploy resources so as to enhance human life. These are *NOT* one and the same. The issues involved are not resolved by insisting that one deals with important economic problems and the other tries to focus on some pie-in-the-sky mushy confusion. George Soros expressed this thought some years ago: 'Laissez-faire capitalism holds that the common good is best served by the uninhibited pursuit of self-interest. Unless it is tempered by the recognition of a common interest that ought to take precedence over particular interests, our present system is liable to break down' (Soros 1997, p. 47).

What, therefore, the discipline desperately needs is better economic theory that guides resource deployment along paths of greater enhancement of human life. Such theory explains better, provides relevant policy options, and enables economists to say that the discipline is, at any given time, doing all it can to improve the lives of all inhabitants. Smooth and efficient allocation has its place, but efficient creation and equitable distribution are also essential!

What we plead for, to underscore the point, is some balance. Let young economists pursue their own interests. Let graduate programs in economics be broadened. Let there be some curricular options, even in 'theory.' Let all kinds of research projects get funds. Let students be respected who choose kinds of research that don't require big grants! Let the meaning of economic progress be a topic of serious discussion in graduate education. Let economic history and the history of economic thought receive the same attention in economics that the parallel fields do in other social sciences. Let those for whom increasing our understanding of recognized real world problems is totally satisfying pursue that goal. But let those who wish to improve public policy so the economy can work more efficiently and equitably prepare themselves for that task.

More broadly, it would be useful if the profession worried more about making what it does comprehensible to intelligent but concerned non-economists. It is not inaccurate to say that over the past 50 years economists have cared less and less about how many people could follow and benefit from what they were doing. Economists are now often so specialized that they cannot effectively follow each other's work. Too many implicitly reason the other way. If what they are doing is too complicated to be appreciated except by the handful of appropriately trained and appropriately narrow specialists, that is the indispensable but exquisite final proof required of the elegance and sophistication of the work being pursued. After all, elegance and sophistication is the real name of the game!

AFTERWORD

Perhaps the reader is as surprised as I am to find that I end where I began. Invisible hand notwithstanding, the attention Adam Smith paid to the public sector, along with the profoundly normative prose he often uses in dealing with the world around him, suggest that he probably thought that the economic theory he laid out was meant to be a guide to public policy. He doubtless would have concurred that the market does great service in letting the price system deploy resources, but said public policy was what he thought could be done additionally to make for a better life for the people in his economy.

The notion which lurks below the surface (but sometimes is more prominently displayed than that) in the discipline today is that there can be a real disconnect between economic theory and the real economy because the latter runs as well as it can if only we 'give the free market a chance.' Adam Smith knew better than he probably could ever have dreamed for his world. And his insight was quite apart from the fact that he undoubtedly could not have imagined what the technological changes of the next 230 years would do to the shape and size of the efficient producing unit. Economists used the invisible hand to remove the obstacles (technological and other) to an ideally functioning economy encompassed in pure competition. They relied on a short list of ceteris paribus assumptions to remove the remaining obstacles to installing in the real economy not only a purely competitive system, but a perfectly functioning competitive system. It was but a short skip from there to recognition that economic theory coped perfectly with a static world of 'stylized facts.'

This 'undoing process' was completed by ignoring the implications of the fallacy of composition for the functioning of the macroeconomy. In this fashion all the 'improvements' (more accurately perhaps efforts to keep theory modernized as one would expect would be required in a dynamic world) of the years since Smith in economic theory could be undone and we could be returned to the halcyon world before Ricardo, Malthus, Marshall, Walras, Robinson, Chamberlin, Fellner, and Keynes (among others) had so complicated and muddied the positive waters of our original pure micro and macrotheory.

In no other field, certainly no other social science, do its current practitioners feel (1) that their world untouched by human intervention is the best of all possible worlds, and (2) that most of what the great names in their past became famous doing was moving their disciplines in the wrong direction. Finally no other field puts policy makers in the position of ring masters at a perpetual motion machine. For them economic theory is like spending time writing out directions and regulations to guide the ring master in the operation of that perpetual motion machine.

The majority of heterodox economists in general, and certainly the institutionalist economists with whom I am most familiar, insist that we reconnect economic theory to economic policy. We need to relearn that the unfettered market does not produce the ideal world or even the best world which human beings are capable of achieving. Economics is a wonderful discipline. Its practitioners have made incredible progress in developing technical tools. But it has all but forgotten what the tools are for. Economics is not a game, it is not an exercise in logic. It is not an elaborate and elegant system for outlining why virtually nothing can or should be done to improve the operation of the system. Conventional economists must view themselves as peculiarly well equipped to see how well the system operates and why no criteria except allocative efficiency and security need be contemplated to augment the quite incredible way in which market forces can deploy resources efficiently. These traditional economists are presumably entirely comfortable ignoring the other criteria we have mentioned – freedom, equity, and compassion. To ignore the criteria other than allocative efficiency and perhaps security, which we hold a modern economy needs to include, means that we can assert that any economy which we can admire and respect makes resource deploying judgements via the market based in efficiency which invariably conform to what a compassion criterion could require. Otherwise we should need to assert that the deploying of resources is guided by a complex set of criteria rather than a simple, let alone mechanical, criterion. This complex set of criteria would need to operate automatically. Does anyone believe this to be the case? If not then our economy needs some policies which are derived from these complex criteria. If this is true, developing economic policy is a complicated business after all.

As is now apparent, this book on economics has not been about ridding the discipline of mathematics, getting rid of precision, ignoring logic, forgetting about models, extolling inefficiency, or a whole host of similar bad ideas. Instead of regarding all these things as ends in themselves, or as minor adjustments to a precise and elegant intellectual bauble, consider that, far from that interpretation – all these need to be harnessed to the real goal of economics as a social science in the twenty-first century.

That is to say, economics is a social science devoted to making life better for the human beings who populate each extant economy. How can economists help generate and assess the performance of public and private institutions in creating and deploying resources so as to enhance human life? Let that be the question we pose to students at the beginning of basic economics and let that be the question which guides our students in their graduate studies, and in the professions for which these studies prepare them. Let that be the question acknowledged by those holding positions of political discretion as they participate in the creation and implementation of public economic policies that provide remedial and humane adjustments of institutions seeking policy solutions for impaired and discriminatory economic performance. So perceived, economic inquiry and its employment can make a substantive and continuing contribution to the efficiency and continuity of the life process.

REFERENCES

Adams, John Q. (1999), 'Transaction costs', in Phillip Anthony O'Hara (ed.), *Encyclopedia of Political Economy*, London: Routledge.

American Heritage College Dictionary, Fourth Edition (2002), Boston, MA: Houghton Mifflin.

Ayres, Clarence E. (1944), *The Theory of Economic Progress*, Chapel Hill, NC: University of North Carolina Press.

Ayres, Clarence E. (1961), *Toward a Reasonable Society,* Austin, TX: University of Texas Press.

Boyle, David (2002), 'The storming of the accountants', *New Statesman*, London, **15** (690), pp. 23–24.

Bush, Paul D. and Marc R. Tool (2003), 'Foundational concepts for institutionalist policy making', in Marc R. Tool and Paul D. Bush (eds), *Institutional Analysis and Economic Policy*, Boston, MA: Kluwer Academic Publishers.

Coase, Ronald (1937), 'The nature of the firm', *Economica*, New Series **4** (16), 386–405.

Coase, Ronald (1998), 'The new institutional economics', *American Economic Review, Proceedings*, **88** (2), 72–4.

Cobb, Clifford, Ted Halstead and Jonathan Rowe (1995), 'If the economy is up, why is America down?', *The Atlantic Monthly*.

Colander, David C. and Edward N. Gamber (2002), *Macroeconomics*, Upper Saddle River, NJ: Prentice-Hall.

Diebold, Francis X. (1997), *The Past, Present, and Future of Macroeconomic Forecasting*, NBER, Working Paper no. 6290, Cambridge, MA: NBER.

European Association for Evolutionary Political Economy (EAEPE) (1988), home page for URPE is at http://www.urpe.org. The article itself is at http:www.urpe.org/history.html. It was there as of June 16, 2005.

Federici, Michael P. (2001), Review of *The Values Connection*, *American Political Science Review*, **95** (4), 983–44.

Fleck, Susan (1998), 'Union of radical political economics: history and nature of URPE', http://www.urpe.org. Article itself is at http:/www.urpe.org/history.html, as of June 16, 2005. ICARE Homepage www.ICARE, p. 1.

Fullbrook, Edward (2003), *The Crisis in Economics: The Post-Autistic Economics Movement: The First 600 Days,* London: Routledge.

Greene, William H. (2000), *Economic Analysis*, Englewood Cliffs, NJ: Prentice Hall.

Gruchy, Allan (1947), *Modern Economic Thought*, New York: Prentice-Hall.

Gruchy, Allan G. (1987), *The Reconstruction of Economics*, New York: Greenwood Press.

Gwartney, James D. and Richard L. Stroup (1997), *Microeconomics, Eighth Edition*, Fort Worth: Dryden Press.

Heilbroner, Robert (1953), *The Worldly Philosophers*, New York: Simon & Schuster, 1967, Chapter 7.

Heilbroner, Robert L. (1962), *The Making of Economic Society*, Englewood Cliffs, NJ: Prentice-Hall.

Hicks, John R. (1979), *Causality in Economics*, Oxford: Blackwell.

Hodgson, Geoffrey M. (1999), *Economics and Utopia*, London and New York: Routledge.

Holden, K., D.A. Peel and J.L. Thompson (1985), *Expectations: Theory and Evidence*, New York: St Martin's Press.

ICARE (1999), *Directory of Heterodox and Pluralistic Economics*, John Adams (ed.), web page address in text.

Klamer, Arjo (1983), *Conversations With Economists*, Totowa, NJ: Rowan and Allanheld.

Klein, P.A. (1974), 'Economics: allocation or valuation?', *Journal of Economic Issues*, **8** (4). Reprinted in Klein (1994).

Klein, P.A. (1980), 'Institutionalism and concentrated power', *Journal of Economic Issues*, **14** (4), 871–96. Reprinted in Klein (1994).

Klein, P.A. (1990), 'Institutionalism as a school – a reconsideration', *Journal of Economic Issues*, **24** (2), 381–8. Reprinted in Klein (1994).

Klein, P.A. (1994), 'Institutionalist reflections on the role of the public sector'. Reprinted in Klein (1994).

Klein, Philip A. (1994), *Beyond Dissent*, Armonk, NY: M.E. Sharpe.

Krueger, Anne O. (1991), 'Report of the Commission on Graduate Education in Economics', *Journal of Economic Literature*, **29** (3), 1035–53.

Krueger, Anne O. (1999), 'Applications of the labor market for graduate education in economics', *Journal of Economic Perspectives*, **13** (3), 153–56.

Kuhn, Thomas (1962, 1970, 1996), *The Structure of Scientific Revolutions*, Chicago: University of Chicago Press.

McConnell, Campbell R. and Stanley L. Brue (1990), *Economics, Eleventh Edition,* New York: McGraw-Hill.

Mankiw, N. Gregory (2001), *Principles of Economics, Second Edition*, Fort Worth, TX: Dryden Press.

Marshall, Alfred (1890, 1949), *Principles of Economics, Eighth Edition*, London: Macmillan.

Mas-Colell, Andreu, Michael Whinston and Jerry R. Green (1995), *Microeconomic Theory*, New York: Oxford University Press.

Miller, Roger Leroy (2004), *Economics Today, Twelfth Edition*, Boston, MA: Addison-Wesley.

Miringoff, Marc and Marque-Luisa Miringoff (1999), *The Social Health of the Nation*, New York: Oxford University Press.

Mirowski, Philip (1986), *The Reconstruction of Economic Theory*, Boston, MA: Kluwer-Nihoff Publishing.

Mitchell, Wesley Clair (1983), 'The theoretical basis for business cycle indicators', *Journal of Economic Issues*, **17** (4). Reprinted in Klein (1994).

Nordhaus, William and James Tobin (1972), 'Is growth obsolete?', in *The Business Cycle Today, Fiftieth Anniversary Colloquium, Vol. V*, New York: Columbia University Press for the National Bureau of Economic Research.

Parked, Michael (2000), *Economics, Fifth Edition*, Reading, MA: Addison-Wesley Longman, Inc.

Ramstad, Ingve (1989), '"Reasonable value" vs. "Instrumental value": competing paradigms in institutional economics', *Journal of Economic Issues,* **23** (2).

Redford, Deborah A. (1991), *Economics and the Philosophy of Science*, New York: Oxford University Press.

Roll, Eric (1942), *A History of Economic Thought*, New York, Prentice-Hall.

Samuelson, Paul A. (1964), *Economics, Sixth Edition*, New York: McGraw-Hill.

Samuelson, Paul A. (1972), 'Discussion', in Victor Zarnowitz (ed.), *The Business Cycle Today, Fiftieth Anniversary Colloquium*, Vol. **1**, New York: Columbia University Press for National Bureau of Economic Research.

Samuelson, Paul A. *Economics* (1976), *Tenth Edition*, New York: McGraw-Hill.

Samuelson, Paul A. and William Nordhaus (1995), *Economics, Fifteenth Edition,* McGraw-Hill.

Samuelson, Paul A. and William Nordhaus (1998), *Economics, Sixteenth Edition*, New York: McGraw-Hill.

Samuelson, Paul A. and William Nordhaus (2001), *Economics, Seventeenth Edition*, New York: McGraw-Hill.

Schumacher, E.F. (1973), *Small Is Beautiful; Economics as if People Mattered*, London: Blond and Briggs. Republished 1999, Point Roberts, WV: Hartley and Marks.

Schumpeter, Joseph (1954), *A History of Economic Analysis*, New York: Oxford University Press.

Smith, Adam (1776/1985), *The Wealth of Nations*, New York: Modern Library College Edition.

Soros, George (1997), 'The capitalist threat', *Atlantic Monthly*, **279** (2), 45–58.

Sowell, Thomas (1993), 'A student's eye view of George Stigler', *Journal of Political Economy*, **101** (5).

Stigler, George (1947), *The Theory of Price*, New York: Macmillan.

Stigler, George (1993), Quoted in Thomas Sowell, 'A student's eye view of George Stigler', *Journal of Political Economy*, **101** (5), 784–92.

Taussig, F.W. (1915), *Inventors and Money Makers*, New York: Macmillan.

Tonay, Youval P. (1998), *The Struggle for the Soul of Economics*, Princeton, NJ: Princeton University Press.

Tool, Marc R. (1979), *The Discretionary Economy*, Santa Monica, CA: Goodyear.

Tool, Marc R. (ed.) (1984), *An Institutionalist Guide to Economics and Public Policy*, Armonk, NY: M.E. Sharpe.

Urbach, Peter (1987), 'Marginalism', in John Eatwell, Murray Milgate and Peter Newman (eds), *The New Palgrave, A Dictionary of Economics*, London: Macmillan.

Williamson, Oliver E. (1998), 'The institutions of governance', *American Economic Review*, **88** (2), 75–9.

Index